just JAVA™ 1.1

and Beyond — THIRD EDITION

THE SUNSOFT PRESS
JAVA SERIES

▼ **_Core Java 1.1_** _Volume 1: Fundamentals_
Cay S. Horstmann & Gary Cornell

▼ **_Graphic Java 1.1,_** _Second Edition_
David M. Geary

▼ **_Inside Java WorkShop_**
Lynn Weaver & Bob Jervis

▼ **_Instant Java,_** _Second Edition_
John A. Pew

▼ **_Java by Example,_** _Second Edition_
Jerry R. Jackson & Alan L. McClellan

▼ **_Just Java,_** _Second Edition_
Peter van der Linden

▼ **_Not Just Java_**
Peter van der Linden

▼ **_Jumping JavaScript_**
Janice Winsor & Brian Freeman

just
JAVA ™ 1.1
and Beyond   THIRD EDITION

PETER van der LINDEN

Sun Microsystems Press
A Prentice Hall Title

The publisher offers discounts on this book when ordered in bulk quantities. For more information, contact Corporate Sales Department, Prentice Hall PTR, One Lake Street, Upper Saddle River, NJ 07458.
Phone: 800-382-3419; FAX: 201-236-7141.
E-mail: corpsales@prenhall.com

Editorial/production supervision: *Eileen Clark*
Cover designer: *Anthony Gemmellaro*
Cover design director: *Jerry Votta*
Manufacturing manufacturer: *Alexis R. Heydt*
Marketing manager: *Stephen Solomon*
Acquisitions editor: *Gregory G. Doench*
Sun Microsystems Press publisher: *Rachel Borden*

10 9 8 7 6 5 4 3 2 1

ISBN 0-13-784174-4

Sun Microsystems Press
A Prentice Hall Title

I would like to dedicate this book to George McPartlin, who taught gym classes and math classes at my old high school, Wimbledon College, London, England. George infused his math classes with the towel-snapping vigor of a session in the gym, grabbing the attention of many students, including me. His approach has inspired me to explain things in clear, simple terms and to enliven dull topics with interesting information. And occasionally to snap towels. Thank you, Mr McPartlin. How to solve quadratic equations wasn't the only thing I learned from you.

Contents

Chapter 2

The Story of O: Object-Oriented Programming, 29

Chapter 4

Java
Building Blocks, 99

Chapter 6
Practical Examples Explained, 219

Chapter 7
All About Applets, 261

Chapter 8

Utilities and Libraries,   301

Chapter 10

Graphics Programming, 441

Chapter 11

Java Foundation Classes (JFC) Preview (Swingset),   497

Introduction

"In a five year period we can get one superb programming language. Only we can't control when the five year period will begin."

—*Alan Perlis, uncle of Algol-60*

Why I Wrote This Book

Just imagine that you have been given the opportunity to design the ultimate programming language! What would you put in it?

Well, first of all, objects. And plenty of 'em. Object-oriented programming is moving to general acceptance as a superior implementation technique. Perhaps like me, you would want support for multi-threading. Better reliability and error handling are important, so let's find room for exceptions. Programmers need help with tiresome details, so let the compiler take care of making sure that all source files are up-to-date in a link.

And so on, and so on. I think you can see where this starts to lead. In the 1995 Pebble Beach Concours car show in California, one of the exhibits was a Rolls-Royce which had been similarly pieced together out of bits and pieces of the best. The Rolls featured a body from a 1931 Phantom II, modern racing carburetors, a custom-built chassis, and the engine from a Spitfire aeroplane. The 12 cylinder 28-liter Merlin engine used in the Spitfire was also built by Rolls-Royce. All of these

Bounty paid for corrections!

Every book on a technical subject has errors when it goes to press. That's even more true when the technical subject is as new as Java is. The goal of this author is to ruthlessly search out inaccuracies in this text, and eliminate them in future printings.

The general website for this book, containing reader feedback, sample programs, and the current errata sheet is http://www.best.com/~pvdl

There's a bounty of $1 per error to the first person who brings a programming correction to the attention of the author, so it can be corrected in future printings. The policy is that all errors will be corrected, but the bounty is reserved for programming related things in the English version (because that's the only one I can change directly).

Please send your corrections and feedback by e-mail to pvdl@best.com.

components are the best of their type, but put together the whole is an ill-matched over-complex mess that doesn't seem much fun to drive. Just as a duck is adapted to fly, walk, and swim, but does all three poorly, this aero-engined car can't fly, and is almost impossible to drive with finesse. It has covered an average of just 50 miles per year since it was completed a decade ago. Apart from anything else, you can't stray far from a gas station when you only get 2 m.p.g. A careless stamp on the throttle could twist the chassis. The engine is mounted backwards so the prop. shaft comes out where the propeller used to go.

Too many good things—an airplane-engined car

The vehicle was commissioned by an eccentric and rich used-car dealer, and must be driven gingerly at all times. It develops around 1000 bhp (a Corvette has about 20% of this), but heavy-footedness on the accelerator pedal could set the clutch on fire, or screw the mainshaft right out of the gearbox. The result of this "throw in everything good" design is an impractical and nearly undriveable vehicle. The question then is, "Is Java like this?"

The answer is a resounding "No!" For one thing, Java wasn't commissioned on the whim of an eccentric. Rather it was a considered approach designed by a top engineer, trying to solve practical problems. Aspects of Java have been borrowed from other languages, but they have been carefully integrated into the whole. Practicality is the hallmark throughout. Design decisions have been made with good judgment and thoughtfulness. Java benefited greatly from the C++ experience—seeing what was needed, what worked, and what should be discarded.

Once every generation or so in the computer industry, a new technology arises that is so compelling, and so well-fitted to the issues of the day, that it sweeps everything away before it. This happened in the 1960s with the shift to transistor logic, eventually leading to large scale integrated circuits. It happened again in the early 1980s with the unexpected success of the IBM PC. It was the right product at the right time, given credibility by the right company.

On the software side, a paradigm shift happened in 1982 through 1984 with spreadsheet software. Lotus123, and Visicalc before it, met people's needs so well that Lotus shot to prominence in a wave of profitability that other companies could only dream of.

And it is happening with Java right now. The success of Java represents the convergence of several unstoppable industry trends:

- Popularization of the Internet
- Consumer electronics merging into PC and telephone technologies
- Computer industry drive to interactive multimedia everything
- Rejection of the complexity of C++
- Desire for independence from Microsoft/Intel desktop monopolies

The speed of adoption of Java by programmers everywhere has been truly remarkable. However it is not Java per se that the industry seeks, but a resolution to the challenges raised by the issues above. Java is the only serious contender to address these issues. As a result, it has met with immediate and overwhelming acceptance. Java is not just another language. Because Java addresses these issues it is the beginning of a phenomenon that is changing the nature of computing.

Java is particularly convenient for use in Internet applications, but it is a general purpose language too. Its features will be quickly understood by programmers, if explained in the right way. What programmers need now is a book on Java that combines three elements:

1. An introduction to Java, relating it to more familiar languages,

2. Clear explanations, describing the significance of new features with their common pitfalls, and

3. Short practical examples that can be tried by readers using the compiler supplied.

This is an introductory book on Java, intended for people who are already programmers. You can use this book if you have knowledge of any language: Pascal, or Visual Basic, Fortran, or Ada. Knowledge of C or Lisp or their descendants will give you a head start. The central theme is to help you learn Java easily, quickly, and well.

As you learn Java, you will see that it is much more than a language; Java programs, including the window system and all the numerous libraries, work on all systems, so Java is really a complete environment for running programs. This text is a tutorial for the language and some key libraries. We include a roadmap of every part of Java, but we don't attempt exhaustive coverage of everything Java. That would take multiple volumes, and a lot of your time. We don't cover JavaBeans topics here or native libraries that let you produce nonportable code. This book is a convenient one-book introduction to Java programming. When you have mastered the fundamentals from this text, you can easily study more, using one of the exhaustive (but dry) reference encyclopedias. I like the Chan and Lee *Java Class Libraries* book.

I have taught Java to many programmers inside Sun Microsystems, using the same text you are holding in your hands. You can learn Java in your spare time reading a chapter a week, or you can you devote more time and pick up the language in just a few days. Either way, it's important to do the programming exercises.

Prior knowledge of programming and web browsing is assumed. But if you haven't worked much with the Internet or web browsers, please take a look at my book *Not Just Java*. That is not another book on programming: rather, it is an executive briefing explaining the advances in distributed processing and all the new Java-related terms you may hear.

In this book, I start by setting the context: what Java is and how it compares to other languages. Next comes an introduction to object-oriented programming before we launch into a bottom-up appraisal of Java. The accompanying CD has a Java compiler system for Windows 95, Windows NT, the Apple Macintosh, and Solaris 2 on SPARC, which includes everything you need to try Java.

What You'll Need

As everyone knows, the only real way to learn a programming language is to write some programs in it. For that you need the Java system and a Java-capable browser. This book comes with a CD that contains the Java compiler system. However, you may want to to download a Web browser or later release of Java as explained in Chapter 12 .

In theory, you could forgo the Web browser and Internet access, and just learn Java application programming on your local system. In practice, however, this would be a mistake. You would be missing a key part—seamless client-server programming on the network—which is responsible for the vast interest in Java.

How To Use This Book

Sometimes we do things in an order that looks funny from the table of contents. Sometimes we mention a topic only to say we're deferring discussion to a later section. This is because learning a subject isn't usually done in a depth-first manner. When you learn a foreign language you don't learn all the adjectives, followed by all the nouns finishing with all the verbs. If you did it that way you wouldn't be able to utter a whole sentence until you had completed all the lessons! It's the same with learning a programming language: it's best to cover enough to get you going, then look at the next thing by building on that, and eventually revisit anything that needs further attention. It gives a funny look to the table of contents though.

I tried to map out this book in three stages: first by covering the roots of Java and the resurgence of Object-Oriented Programming up front; then providing practical examples with clear explanations; and finally preparing advanced elements, such as window and network programming. Each chapter will cover a specific topic and most will end with the following sections:

- Some Light Relief (intended to amuse you, beginning at the end of this Introduction)

- Exercises (a little something to pick your brain, beginning in Chapter 1)

- Further Readings (provides a source of additional information, beginning in Chapter 1)

Icons in the Text

The following icons are used to call special attention to particularly important information in this book:

The "Software Dogma" icon is used whenever there is some background information to convey. Often these items are articles of faith in the industry. Things that are done that way because they've always been done that way. The "Pitfall" icon points out places where it's easy to make a mistake or develop a misunderstanding. Save yourself needless grief and read the pitfall paragraphs carefully. The "Programmer Tip" icon is used to indicate code idioms, shortcuts, sources of other information, and generally useful things to know. The "Important!" icon highlights particularly crucial bits of information.

"Programming Challenge" marks a Java programming exercise in the text. Some of these come with solutions later in the text, and are marked with the "Programming Solution" icon.

"FAQ" (Frequently Asked Question) answers a query that programmers often have.

As I wrote this book, I also wanted to convey a sense of the enjoyment that lies in computer programming. Programming is challenging, exciting, enjoyable and satisfying. A book on computer programming should be exciting and educational, factual and fun. It should occasionally delight as well as inform. The major goal is to pass on the skill of a new programming language, but I'd also like to show a little of the fun of programming too. I hope that by the end of the book you'll agree that both goals have been met.

Software Dogma

Pitfall

Programmer Tip

FAQ

Programming
Challenge

Programming
Solution

Important!

Some Light Relief

We end each chapter with a section of light relief to amuse readers and reward them for completing another milestone.

All I really need to know I learned on Internet

Peter van der Linden

All I really need to know about how to live, and what to do, and how to be, I learned on Internet. Wisdom was not at the top of the graduate school mountain, nor in the sandpile at Sunday school, but right there at the active endpoint of a TCP/IP session. These are the things I learned:

1. *Always* log your terminal off when you leave, even if you're only going to the bathroom for 5 minutes.

2. The only people who MAKE MONEY FAST on the Internet are those who manufacture routers and disk drives.

3. The net's memory is no longer than its attention span, so if you wait a little while you're sure to see the same thing go round again.

4. Some net-kooks are noisy, some net-kooks are stupid, and some net-kooks are rude. But the net-kooks whose attention you will attract are the net-kooks who are noisy, stupid AND rude.

5. Not all Usenet moderators and FAQ-compilers eventually become power-mad and insane. Some of them started out that way.

6. The net's memory is no longer than its attention span, so if you wait a little while you're sure to see the same thing go round again.

7. If you're not sure about the facts when posting something, be louder and more insistent to compensate. Asserting something stridently enough can make it so. When someone points out your mistakes, first sulk, then laugh them off as deliberate sarcasm, irony or cynicism which went over the heads of the audience.

8. There was something about the net's memory, but the details are a little hazy right now.

9. Remember that early release of "rn" that prevented a posting unless it contained more new lines than included lines? That was actually a pretty good idea.

10. How to have the last word in real life: "You're right!" How to have the last word on Usenet: "You're in my killfile!"

Using the Just Java CD-ROM

About the CD-ROM

Welcome to the *Just Java* CD-ROM—a disk packed with all the Java tools and source code discussed in the book, and more.

Since this CD-ROM has been designed for use by Windows 95, Windows NT, Macintosh and Solaris users, you'll notice a directory for each of these operating systems. The *Just Java* CD directory structure is as follows:

goodies	About the author (see index.html) plus sample Java programs and image and sound files
book	Programs from *book* (one directory for each chapter, plus justjava.tar)
linux	The JDK for Linux
mac	The JDK for the Apple Macintosh
sgi	The JDK for Silicon Graphics systems
solaris.sparc	The JDK for Solaris (Sparc)
solaris.x86	The JDK for Solaris (Intel)
win95nt	The JDK for Windows 95 and Windows NT

You can explore the CD-ROM quite effectively using a browser.

Using the CD-ROM on Windows 95 and Windows NT

This CD-ROM does not have a Java compiler for Windows 3.1. However, a windows 3.1 version of Java can be downloaded from http://www.alphaworks.ibm.com/formula.

NOTE: Some of the files on this CD use long file names, which is one of the features of Windows 95. If you are unable to see the long file names on the CD, your Windows 95/NT system may not be configured correctly. Windows 95/NT 4.0 users can check by double-clicking on the "System" icon in the Control Panel and then clicking on the "Performance" tab. If the "Performance" section does not indicate that "Your system is configured for optimal performance" then you have a configuration issue which needs to be resolved. Consult Windows "Help" or contact Microsoft Technical Support for further assistance.

To install the JDK on Windows 95 or NT:

1. Put the CD in the CD drive, and go to the directory win95nt.

   ```
   d:\win95nt
   ```

   Your CD drive may be called d: or e: or something else.

   The release takes up about 9 Mb.

2. Execute the self-extracting archive jdk113.exe file

   ```
   jdk113
   ```

   This will ask you a couple of questions and install the Java compiler and tools. A good place to install the compiler is in c:\jdk1.1.3

3. Once the JDK files have been unpacked onto your hard drive, you will need to add (or modify) one variable in your autoexec.bat file with a text editor.

   Add the "java\bin" directory to your path:

   ```
   SET PATH=c:\jdk1.1.3\bin; (...the rest of your path)
   ```

4. Save the change to your autoexec.bat and restart your computer so the new variables take effect. Earlier versions of the JDK required you to set an additional variable, CLASSPATH. From JDK 1.1 on this is no longer required. If you have a line in your autoexec.bat that sets CLASSPATH, remove it.

5. There is a file called "INSTALL.TXT" on the CD in the same directory as the JDK. It contains a much longer explanation of installation, along with a troubleshooting guide. Please refer to it as necessary.

Using the CD-ROM on Macintosh (System 7.5 or later)

To install the JDK on a Macintosh:

Because this is an ISO-9660 CD-ROM, the JDK is stored on the disk as a self-extracting archive. Copy the archive (JDK-1_0_2-MacOS.sea) to your hard drive and double-click to open. The same archive is supplied in .hqx and .bin form; use whichever is more convenient for you.

Updated copies of the JDK for the Mac can be downloaded from Apple's site at http://applejava.apple.com.

NOTE: You should note that Macintosh, Windows, and UNIX text files have slightly different conventions for end-of-line. Macintosh expects a carriage return, Windows expects a carriage return and a linefeed, and UNIX expects a newline character (linefeed).

Most Macintosh editors are able to cope with UNIX and Windows conventions. Be aware, however, that some Macintosh editors will not display line breaks properly if you try to read text files that were created on a Windows or UNIX system. Even though some text files may not appear to be properly formatted, however, the Java compiler handles source files created under either convention.

You should also note that file names longer than 31 characters will be truncated. Therefore, some of the sample Java files on this CD will have to be renamed to execute properly on a Macintosh.

Using the CD-ROM on Solaris 2.x

NOTE: Because this is a cross-platform CD-ROM, Solaris users may encounter a warning message when loading the CD indicating the presence of files that do not conform to the ISO-9660 specification. These warning messages should be ignored.

To install the JDK (Solaris 2.3 or later):

The solaris.sparc directory contains the JDK for Sparc. The solaris.x86 directory contains the Intel version. Updated versions of the JDK for Solaris can be downloaded from http://java.sun.com. Installation instructions are the same for Solaris 2.x for SPARC and Solaris 2.x for x86. On Intel systems, use "x86" instead of "sparc" in the filenames below. Insert the Just Java CD into your CD-ROM drive

1. If Volume Manager is running on your machine, the CD is automatically mounted to the /cdrom/just_java directory when you insert it.

    If the Volume Manager is not running on your machine, create a directory called /cdrom/just_java and mount the CD manually by becoming root and typing:

    ```
    # mkdir -p /cdrom/just_java
    # mount -rF hsfs /dev/dsk/c0t6d0s0 /cdrom/just_java
    ```

2. Copy the file from the CD to your hard disk. Assume you're putting it in /home/linden

    ```
    cd /cdrom/just_java/solaris.sparc
    cp jdk1.1.3-solaris2-sparc.bin /home/linden
    ```

    This is about a 10Mb file, so it will take a few seconds to pull off the CD.

3. Change directory to /home/linden and execute the file you just copied off the CD.

    ```
    cd /home/linden
    jdk1.1.3-solaris2-sparc.bin
    ```

    This will create /home/linden/jdk1.1.3 containing the JDK.

4. Once the JDK files have been unpacked onto your hard drive, you will need to add (or modify) the PATH environment variable in your shell initialization file. The file may be called .cshrc or .login or something else.

    Add the java "bin" directory to your path:

    ```
    setenv JAVAHOME   /home/linden/jdk1.1.3
    set path=( $JAVAHOME/bin  ... rest of path ... )
    ```

5. Save the changes to the file, and log out then log in so the new variables take effect. Earlier versions of the JDK required you to set an additional variable, CLASSPATH. From JDK 1.1 on this is no longer required. If you have a line in your shell initialization file that sets CLASSPATH, remove it.

6. There is a file called "INSTALL.TXT" on the CD in the same directory as the JDK. It contains a much longer explanation of installation, along with a troubleshooting guide. Please refer to it as necessary.

To install the Just Java programs (all systems):

The "book" directory contains sample programs that are mentioned in the book. There is one subdirectory for each chapter. These files can be copied to your hard drive or browsed on the CD.

Acknowledgments

I would like to express my heartfelt thanks to Tom Cargill, Tom Cikoski, and Brian Scearce, who read the whole book in draft form, and made many suggestions for improvements. I take responsibility for all remaining errors. If you notice one that isn't in the errata sheet (obtainable from the website), report it to me.

The layout and design of this book was greatly improved by the hard work of Eileen Clark, Mary Lou Nohr, and previous editors who have earned my warmest appreciation.

Thanks to the people who encouraged me to write this book: Simon Alexander, Rachel Borden, John Bortner, Greg Doench, Zahir Ebrahim, Karin Ellison, and Jim Marks.

I'm grateful to these people who suggested several improvements to the second edition:

Jim Bernstein

George Reese

Pratik Patel

Greg Turner

I would also like to thank the following people who provided significant help:

Steven Abbott

Sandy Anderson

Deepak Bhagat

Keith Bierman

Dan Berg

Matthew Burtch

Teresa Chinn

Phil Gustafson

Mark Scott Johnson

Login Jones

Tim Kirby

Henry Lai

Bil Lewis

Robert Lynch

David Mikkelson

Ahmed Mohamed

Nicholas J. Morrell (what a taste he has in expensive Scotch!)

Mike Morton

Tom O'Donnell

The Old Hats of AFU (Cayman Islands) Inc.

Bill Petro (Henry Ford never said "History is bunk"—he said it was bunk to him!)

Craig Shergold (who's feeling a lot better thanks, and doesn't need any more cards)

Peter Soderquist

Kathy Stark

Panagiotis Tsirigotis

Tom van der Linden (who instilled in me his love for reading, writing, and consolidated statements of stockholder equity)

Wendy van der Linden (who pointed out that Citrus was a subclass of Fruit)

Terry Whatley

Ron Winacott

My team of colleagues at Sun Microsystems also deserves my gratitude for helping me in numerous ways while I worked on this text:

Oscar Arreola

Hui-Mei Chen

Sudershan Goyal

Stephen Littrell

Jim Marks

Saeed Nowshadi

Terry Whatley.

CHAPTER 1

What Is Java?

"Come into my parlor," said the spider to the fly.

J ava is a new programming language from Sun Microsystems, but Java is much more than just a programming language. Java is really a computing platform, just as the Mac and Windows 3.1 are platforms. Because it is an entire execution environment, Java is able to provide the long-sought benefits of software portability, network awareness, and security. As Java grows in popularity and capability, it presents a robust way for organizations with lots of incompatible computer systems to streamline and integrate everything.

Java offers convenient libraries for GUI (Graphical User Interface) programming, I/O, and Internet access that are easy to use and independent of the underlying operating systems. Best of all, Java has the great virtue of simplicity.

What Is Java?

Briefly,

Java is a new programming language from Sun Microsystems, with elements from C, C++, and other languages, and with libraries highly tuned for the Internet environment.

Java is also a complete execution environment that allows programs to be run from a web browser.

The single best feature of Java is its portability: a compiled Java program runs on all computer systems. Software portability greatly benefits users by providing choice, competition, and lower costs. Software portability is feared by OS vendors; if software runs on any system, then the underlying OS is less important, and users can easily switch to another.

Java was developed in the early 1990s for a research project at Sun. The researchers started out using C++ but quickly decided they needed something better. They were all world-class systems programmers, so they just went ahead and designed a new programming language, reusing good ideas from other programming languages. The designer of Java was long-time Sun employee James Gosling, and the programmer who implemented the first public version of the compiler was Arthur van Hoff. Kim Polese was the marketing person who dreamed up the name "Java" for its exotic, exciting, adrenaline-pumping connotations.

Since this was a research project rather than a for-profit product, Sun agreed to make the Java Development Kit (the compiler and runtime system) available for free via the Internet. In 1994, there were perhaps a dozen people, of whom I was one, who had heard of Java (at that time still known by the insipid original name of "Oak"). The free publication of Java in mid-1995 coincided with the enormous, continuing surge of interest in the Internet. Within six months, Java was in use by more than 100,000 programmers. Two years later, Java has more than 400,000 developers. Since Java runs anywhere, the total potential market for all these developers is the 250+ million computer systems in the world.

> **Will Java Replace C++?**
>
> People always want to know whether Java will replace C++. My opinion is that Java has already replaced C++ as the first language to consider when writing new application software. The financial community is already writing much of its front-end software in Java. Venture capital funding has dried up for projects using C++ as a cornerstone. Over 160 schools and universities have switched to Java for their courses in beginning programming. Most compiler and software tools companies have shifted their resources to Java development, in some cases, totally.
>
> However, high-level programming languages never really die. My local technical bookstore still has a little shelf space devoted to C++ books (about one-third as much as it devotes to Java). C++ will be around for a long time for legacy applications. There are three reasons to continue coding in C++: compatibility with existing code, deferment of employee retraining, and better (faster) tools. Only the first of these reasons has any relevance beyond the short term, and it applies only to code maintenance. C++ has probably reached its high-water mark, and it now will hold steady or decline. The combination of C and Java leaves no long-term niche for C++.
>
> If you have not yet learned C++, you can now leapfrog it entirely. The dynamics of the industry have already switched to Java. IBM, the world's largest computer company, is backing Java publicly and with great commitment. Java has united almost all players in the software industry behind it.

No programming language in the past has ever gathered so many adherents in such a short space of time. Because of the speed of acceptance, you sometimes hear people complain about "Java hype." It is easy to overlook that sometimes a new development gets attention because it really is better than all that has gone before. Now is an excellent time to learn how to program in Java. You have the opportunity to get in near the start of one of the most exciting developments ever in the software industry.

The Java system has several pieces:

- Java programming language
- Java Virtual Machine (interpreter)
- Software libraries accompanying the system
- HotJava™ web browser or other Java-enabled web browser

In this chapter, we will summarize each of these pieces in turn and review how they fit together. We will also provide a roadmap to the chapters later in the book that cover the language and libraries in detail.

While mentioning the pieces that make up Java, I should also note some software that includes the Java name but is only marginally related to Java. I am talking about JavaScript, the scripting language developed by Netscape Communications Corporation. JavaScript is used in the Netscape browser to prompt the user for input and then to read it, open and close additional windows, and so on. JavaScript supports an elementary browser programming capability, but is not a general-purpose applications language as Java is.

By building Java support into Netscape Navigator 2.0, Netscape helped popularize Java. In return, Sun Microsystems allowed them to use the Java name on their scripting language. Netscape's stock is notoriously volatile, but on the day that Netscape renamed LiveScript to "JavaScript," its stock rose by 20 points. JavaScript is unrelated to Java, and you don't need to learn JavaScript to be a Java programmer. If you already know JavaScript, it neither helps nor hurts.

As you read through the following sections describing the features of Java, you may recognize various good ideas that were pioneered by earlier systems. Java does not introduce many things that are wholly new; the innovation is in the blending of established good ideas from several sources.

The Java Language

Java is an object-oriented, imperative programming language in the same family as C++, Pascal, or Algol-60. Java programs have data declarations, and statements grouped into functions (since Java is an object-oriented language, we call the functions "methods"). Methods can call other methods. Program execution begins in a method with the special name: `main()`.

Java is quickly recognizable to many programmers. The statements and expressions are similar to those in many languages and, in most cases, identical to those of C or C++. Although Java adds some new things, it is most distinctive for what is left out. Compared with C, Java does not have

- Memory address (pointer) arithmetic

- Preprocessor

- The goto statement

- Automatic type conversion,

- Global functions and variables

- Type definition aliases (typedefs)

Compared with C++, Java does not have

- Templates (yet—people are talking about adding them)

- Operator overloading

- Multiple inheritance

- Multiple ABIs

If you are not a C++ programmer and don't know what some of these things are, don't worry. Even if you are a C++ programmer, you might not be fully conversant with all these features. With Java, you don't need to know.

Java Virtual Machine

Java source code is compiled to produce object code, known as *bytecode*. So far, this is just like any other language. The critical difference is that bytecode is not the binary code of any existing computer. It is an architecture-neutral machine code that can quickly be interpreted to run on any specific computer. You execute a Java program by running another program called the Java Virtual Machine, or JVM. The JVM is in most cases invoked by running the program called java. The JVM reads the bytecode program and interprets or translates it into the native instruction set.

This feature is highly significant! Running bytecode on a JVM is the reason that Java software is "Write Once Run Everywhere," as shown in Figure 1-1. Java executables provide a single binary that runs on every processor.

Figure 1-1: Total Platform Independence: Your application just runs on every system that supports Java. No more "123 for DOS, 123 for Windows 3.1, 123 for Windows 95"

Software Portability

Software portability is the Holy Grail of the software industry. It has long been sought but never really attained. Java brings the industry closer to true software portability than any previous system does. At present, if you walk into a computer store, you can see walls of software for Windows, perhaps an end of a shelf of Mac software, and nothing for Unix. When Java is the dominant language, you can choose from all the software in the store, and it will all run on all your computer systems no matter what you have. Choice will be increased for everyone, and costs will come down because software vendors can spread their development expenses over a potential market of 250 million computers, instead of the 91 million Windows 3.1 systems, or the 20 million Macintosh systems, or the 8 million Unix systems.

The only people who will not benefit from software portability are those who have an interest in locking users in to the current high-volume platforms, namely, Microsoft and Intel. Microsoft is energetically trying to undermine the portability of Java by supplying Java libraries that link to the underlying Windows libraries, by implementing a different Java to C interface than the rest of the world uses, and by threatening to change or not support some of the APIs, among other things. Microsoft derailed Sun's attempt to make Java an ISO standard in Spring 1997. I recommend that readers use a Java compiler that has "Java" in the product name and that adheres strictly to the Java standard. If you are a Microsoft user, the Sun Java Development Kit for Windows 95 and NT is ideal, and it is on the CD accompanying this book.

The Java Virtual Machine (a fancy name for the interpreter) needs to be implemented once for each computer system; then all bytecode will run on that system. There are several alternative JVMs available for the PC and the Mac, and they differ in speed, cost, and quality. Java has not been available all that long, and there are still a few bugs causing differences between JVMs. These bugs place a current limit on software portability. The critical point is that the bytecode is universally portable. As quality test suites mature and the JVMs are fixed, the incompatibilities will vanish over time in exactly the same way that all PCs took a year or two to become 100 percent DOS-compatible 15 years ago.

Report incompatibility differences to your JVM vendor, demand that they pass the relevant test suites, and reject any vendor who tries to deliberately introduce nonportable features. If companies started to diverge on what was in bytecode or what operations a JVM supported, then portability would be lost. Software portability is the single most important advantage of Java. The non-Microsoft part of the computer industry is strongly supporting the "100% Pure Java" test suites and certification aimed at keeping code portable.

Bytecode is not just for Java. If you modify a compiler for some other language (such as Ada or Visual Basic) so that it outputs bytecode, you can run it equally happily on the JVM on any computer. A number of companies are retargeting their compilers to do exactly that. Being able to run your code on every computer system on the planet is a powerful inducement to change. Companies launching new kinds of computer systems will be able to count on having a large volume of Java application software available from day one. Java greatly helps innovation, while retaining the investment in software and training.

Performance

Portability initially comes at the cost of some performance. It's a reasonable bargain. Imagine if all the systems that had been built over the years had not tried to shave off the costs of two extra bytes of storage and had stored 4-byte years instead of 2-byte years. We would not now have a year-2000 problem.

If a binary is not compiled down to a specific machine code, extra work is needed at runtime to finish the job. The first Java programs were about 10 to 20 times slower than equivalent C code. People are very interested in making Java as fast as possible, and several clever approaches are being tried. Some JVMs can even compile the bytecode as they run it, a technique known as Just In Time compilation, or JIT. The first time through, the code is run at interpreted speed; subsequent passes through a loop are executed at native binary speed. A JIT compiler knows the exact details of the execution environment (cache sizes, whether floating point is emulated, amount of main memory, etc.) so can conceivably generate higher performance code than a C compiler, targeting a more general environment. The current generation of Java tools runs quickly enough that performance is not an issue for all but the most critical programs.

Software portability perhaps isn't of much interest to students learning a language, but it is of great value to those who must purchase their software or pay to develop it. Portability also helps programmers looking for a job; instead of being typecast as a "Windows MFC programmer" or a "Mac programmer," a Java software developer can work on any hardware and thus can choose from a much larger selection of employment opportunities. Employers have a wider pool of candidates to choose from, too. A little later in this chapter we will show the steps to follow to compile a Java program. When you have compiled it, you can put that same one program on a floppy disk and run it on your PC, your Apple Mac, and any other computer with a JVM. This is heady, exciting stuff for an industry that has been built on the rule of thumb, "Choose your software first, then buy the system that runs it."

Java takes several other steps to ensure portability.

- It offers the same Application Programmer Interface (API) on all platforms.

- Java has the same ABI on all platforms, namely, the Java Virtual Machine.

- The Java Language specification mandates several things that are normally left to the discretion of the compiler writer. By requiring that operands are evaluated in a strict left-to-right order and stipulating the sizes of all the primitive types (ints are 32 bits, doubles are 64 bits, etc.), Java offers not just program portability but identical program behavior on different systems. In other words, not only does the program run everywhere, but it will get the same arithmetic results everywhere, despite different hardware models of arithmetic and overflow.

A Small Explanation of API and ABI

Application Programmer Interface (API)— is what the programmer sees and uses when writing source code. It consists of the names of the library calls, and the number and types of arguments they take. Source standards such as Posix, and XPG4 specify an API. For example, POSIX 1003.1 says every system that complies with the standard will have a function with this prototype:

```
int isascii(int c);
```

that returns nonzero if c is in the range of the 7-bit ASCII codes.

An API is of most value when it exists on a range of different processors because it helps obtain program portability. Solaris 2.5 meets POSIX 1003.1, and Microsoft has announced that Windows NT will also meet the POSIX standard. So a well-behaved program that uses only the features from this API can (in theory) be ported from one of these OSs to the other simply by recompiling it using the correct libraries.

To properly benefit users, an API must not be under the control of just one vendor. An API controlled by a monopoly is as bad as no API at all, or even worse than that.

Application Binary Interface (ABI)—is the environment that the executing program sees at runtime. It is the format of an executable file, the OS specifics such as process address space, and hardware details such as the number, sizes, and reserved uses of registers. Binary standards such as the SPARC Compliance Definition specify an ABI. Every processor architecture (Intel x86, Apple/Motorola Power PC, Sun SPARC, etc.) will usually have its own ABI. Compliance to an ABI allows a hardware clone market to exist. A program that conforms to a system's ABI will run on any processor that complies with the ABI, regardless of who built the system (original manufacturer, clone maker, or OEM).

- Java uses the Unicode character set, which is a 16-bit superset of ASCII. Unicode can represent the symbols in most of the alphabets in the world, including Russian Cyrillic characters, and Asian ideograms. Chapter 3 delves into this topic.

As we have already mentioned, Java is an object-oriented programming language. If you are already familiar with object-oriented programming, great! If not, chapter 2 explains the terminology, the ideas behind it, and how the ideas are expressed in Java. The other key features of Java are threads, exceptions, garbage collection, and applets. We'll summarize these in this chapter, and deal with them at length in chapters 3 to 7. Chapter 6 is a full-length Java program with comments and commentary.

Threads

Most programmers will be familiar with the idea of timesharing. The computer has several jobs to run, and it gives them each a little bit of time (typically a few milliseconds) before moving to the next job. In this way, all the jobs proceed in parallel, and the computer seems to be doing several things at once.

Threads extend this idea from having several different processes running at once, to having several independent pieces of the same one process able to run at once. All these pieces, or threads, share the same address space and get a share of the process's time slice. Threads in the same process have to take steps not to get in each other's way.

The classic example of a use for threads programming is a GUI. It is very convenient to have a thread dedicated to handling the buttons, scrollbars, etc., while other threads do the lengthy calculations, read files, and so on. Without threads, a user must wait for one of these tasks to finish before the GUI responds to new input. With threads, the GUI can respond instantly while still carrying out background tasks. Chapter 5 deals with threads and the idioms of threaded programs.

Java programmers can create, start, suspend, resume, and stop their own threads. On a multiprocessor system, those threads may truly proceed in parallel. Or they may not. This is a quality-of-implementation issue. The first Java compiler for Sun Solaris workstations used a quick-and-dirty implementation called "Green threads." Green was the code name for Sun's research project at that point. Green threads did not use the underlying Solaris threads library and were replaced by Solaris native threads for Solaris 2.6. Sun's implementation of Java for Windows 95 benefited from the Solaris experience and used native threads from the outset. One word of warning: threads programming involves doing things in parallel, and it can be harder to write and debug than unthreaded code.

Exceptions

Exceptions have been described as "software interrupts." They are a way of reporting an error condition by stopping the regular flow of control and picking it up again elsewhere.

There are two aspects to exceptions: generating ("raising") the exception at runtime and writing a handler to catch the exception and deal with it. When an exception is raised, it propagates back up the chain of procedures that have been called and are still active, until a handler is found or the exception reaches the top. If it reaches the top, execution ceases with an error message. If it finds the right handler for that kind of exception, it handles it, and execution can resume from the point after the handler.

Exceptions are a lot more reliable than previous methods of error handling involving flags, switches, special return values, or the like.

Garbage Collection

Garbage collection is the term given to part of dynamic memory management. In particular, garbage collection refers to reclaiming storage that is no longer in use. As programs run, they allocate memory to hold new objects. When those objects reach the end of their lifetimes, their storage space should be reclaimed and reused for other objects.

If memory is not reclaimed, the process will grow larger and larger and will eventually run out of memory completely. Some languages, like COBOL-74, do not feature dynamic memory allocation (so certain programs are hard or impossible to write). Other programs, like Pascal, C, and C++, put the burden of memory management on the programmer. The C++ programmer must keep track of which memory is in use and must explicitly free memory as needed.

It turns out that explicit memory management is very hard to do correctly. Many, perhaps the majority, of C++ programs that do extensive memory allocation have bugs in their storage management. The most common bug is a failure to free memory, leading to "storage leaks" in which memory is never reclaimed. Other bugs are more spectacular and lead to data corruption as memory is freed when it is still in use. Java programs are memory managed at the system level, and the programmer never has to worry about it. The Java runtime library keeps track of data structures. When there are no remaining references to a data structure, it cannot possibly be in use (because the program has no way to read or write it), so it is a candidate for garbage collection.

Automatic garbage collection has an effect on performance, as it involves another thread running in the background to monitor memory use. But experience has shown that it is an acceptable bargain; a little system overhead leads to a huge improvement in system reliability by removing an entire class of bugs from Java programs. C++ programs are responsible for their own heap storage management. They take longer to code, much longer to debug, and big programs frequently retain latent garbage collection bugs. Chapter 5 describes how garbage collection interacts with the programmer.

Summary of New Terms

- Java is a compiled language. The output from the Java compiler is a universally portable machine language called bytecode.

- Bytecode is a little higher level than any existing machine code but can be trivially rewritten into any machine code.

- Bytecode is interpreted by an interpreter called a "Java Virtual Machine" (JVM). Java bytecode is fast moving from an interpreted language into a "deferred compilation" or "runtime compiled" language.

- Any compiler can be modified to output bytecode. Then, programs run through that compiler will have the same universal portability that Java programs have.

Java Libraries

The Java language is nice, but much of the real value of Java is in the set of cross-platform APIs that come with the system. Java has possibly the easiest-to-use networking and windowing (GUI) of any language, which has helped its widespread adoption.

A GUI application written in Java has the same total portability of other Java programs. It just runs on all computer systems. A network program written in Java is much the same as any other kind of I/O. You create an object of the appropriate type and read or write it. The runtime system does all the painful low-level work of making the connections and sending the bytes over the wire for you.

The Java libraries can be divided into two categories:

- Core libraries bundled with the JDK
  These are the class libraries that every JDK must support.

- Optional additions to the JDK
  These are the class libraries that are optional. But if the feature is supported, it must be supported with this API.

Note that subset implementations are not allowed. If an API is in the core set, all JDKs must have it. If an API is in the Standard Extension (optional) set, an implementation can choose whether to include all of it or omit all of it.

There are so many additional libraries and packages announced for Java at this point, that that aspect alone would make a topic for a pretty thick book. What we'll do here to cover the topic is provide an overview of the classes in this chapter; in chapters 8 to 12, we'll cover the use of selected libraries.

In greater detail, the API families that have been announced by July 1, 1997 are as follows.

- "Core APIs"—libraries required to be bundled with the JDK

1. Java Development Kit

2. Java Foundation Classes

3. Java Enterprise (mostly core)

4. Java Commerce

5. Java Security

6. JavaBeans

7. Java Media—2D graphics and audio

- Standard Extension APIs—optional additional libraries

8. Java Media—3D, video, and telephony.

9. JavaServer™

10. Java Management

11. Java Automation

12. EmbeddedJava™

13. PersonalJava

Note that some of the Java Media libraries are in the Core API and some of them are Standard Extensions. The Java Media libraries that make heavy demands on the hardware (like video streaming) or require special peripherals (like the telephony library) are optional standard extensions.

Each API family generally contains several related APIs, and each API (termed a *package* in Java) may be composed of several classes. So, there is a hierarchy, as shown in Figure 1-2.

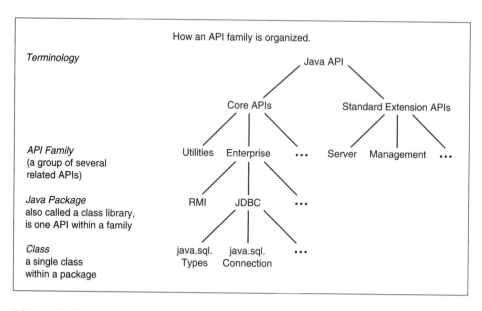

Figure 1-2: The hierarchy of an API family.

Java windowing (the "Abstract Window Toolkit" or AWT) currently uses the underlying window system on a computer. In other words, on Windows 95, the AWT uses the Windows software. On the Mac, the AWT uses the MacOS™ window system, and on Solaris, the AWT is built on top of the X Window System™. There is more about this in chapter 9. Bill Gates (CEO of Microsoft) has criticized Java by saying that it is a "least common denominator" API, meaning that you can only do in Java the things that can be done on all window systems. Although Java supports, say, threads on Windows 3.1 when Windows 3.1 does not itself support threads, there is a little truth to the criticism. If Windows 95 offers some unique feature that simply cannot be programmed on any other window system, then that lack of portability would keep it out of the AWT.

It is true that a feature unique to one window system probably doesn't belong in the Java API, but that is hardly a bad thing. Since the rest of the world manages without the nonportable feature, it cannot be that critical. It may even have been put there to seduce programmers into writing nonportable OS lock-ins. Probably the most successful data access API ever, Microsoft's ODBC, is a lowest common denominator API, and you don't hear developers complaining that it prevents them doing their job. HTML is a highly successful "lowest common denominator" standard.

The World Wide Web and Java

Applets

There are two kinds of Java programs: stand-alone programs, known as *applications*, and programs that run in web browsers, known as *applets*. An applet is simply an application program that runs inside a browser. There are very few differences between programming an applet versus programming an application, in fact, a single binary can even be both. Everything you learn about Java application programming carries over to applet programming, and vice versa.

You can put a web page with hypertext on a server, and clients such as browsers can download the page on demand to see the formatted text. Applets work in the same way. You write and compile a Java applet program, then place a URL or HTML reference to it in the web page. When a client browses that page, the Java applet binary is downloaded to the client along with the text and graphics files. The browser contains a JVM, and it executes the applet on the client computer.

This sounds simple and perhaps not very interesting. In fact, it is galvanizing the computer industry. Before Java, the World Wide Web (WWW) was a read-only interface. You browsed URLs, it served you pages. Now that web pages can cause programs to be run, the browser is well on the way to becoming the universal computer interface. Originally, an applet was considered a little application, but in fact there is no size restriction on applets. Because the model is useful, applets of all sizes exist. Chapter 7 is devoted to applets.

HotJava is Sun's web browser with a Java applet capability. The world's leading browser comes from Netscape Communications Corporation, and is called Navigator™ (version 3) or Communicator™ (version 4). If you are using a browser other than one of these two, I recommend you use your existing browser to download the Netscape browser from http://www.netscape.com, then junk your existing browser. Netscape offers a 90-day free trial offer.

Java applets fit very neatly into the client/server model of computing. By writing your Java program as an applet, you can put it on a web page and allow anyone, with any kind of computer, anywhere on your intranet or in the world to access and execute it automatically, without installing anything. When you update or change your applet, you simply put the new version on your web page, and on the next access, clients get the updated copy automatically. Software distribution problems, which were a major headache for installations with more than a dozen PCs, become a thing of the past. Again, this feature of Java isn't really for SOHO (small office/home office) users. It is highly useful on a network of systems.

A common question asks of what use are applets? They just do useless stuff like web page animations of steaming coffee cups. Like many other people, I started out hearing that Java applets were all about toy animations in web pages. I sat down with my team of software technologists, and we started to analyze the issue. We quickly realized that movement in web pages was just a tangible and easy-to-program demo.

Instead of a steaming coffee cup, imagine looking at graphs of your stock portfolio being drawn and updated in real time as share prices change. Imagine seeing a route map of a long distance journey with the different flight choices showing costs, times, and durations. Imagine viewing a diagram that shows how to test and repair some electronics component, where you enter the readings from different points on the board, and the applet dynamically figures out the right subassembly to focus on. All of these are other, more practical possibilities than coffee vapors.

A less-visible but more valuable benefit is in system administration. Having one applet that is kept on a server and downloaded on demand by dozens or hundred of clients is a great way of doing zero-install client machines. These clients can just browse your page and go. When you update the software, you just put one new version on the server instead of sending disks to all the clients. The next time they browse the server, they automatically get the new version.

Java applets run on the client CPU, not the server—a true realization of distributed processing. A near-alternative technology, CGI scripts, are run on the server on behalf of the client. In other words, the server does some of the client's work as well as its own. When there are only half a dozen clients, that load might not be noticed; when there are scores or hundreds of clients, they put a significant load on the server.

A third benefit of applets is the automatic multimedia framework that the web browser provides (yes, the animations, sound effects, video, and so on).

Finally, the platform-independence of Java is a boon to software developers and users alike. Applets make it much, much easier to program the "client" side of the client/server architecture. The applet concept provides the framework for free without the developer expending any effort on programming the underlying network transport protocols. These benefits can be realized by industrial-strength applets that do real work, as well as by toy animations.

Applet Security

Applets are the second major benefit of Java, enabled by Java's binary software portability (the first major benefit). But there must be restrictions on applets too.

When any user can cause any program, anywhere in the world, to appear on his system and start executing just by virtue of his browsing a web page, there are security implications. No one wants to see a repeat of the virus problems endemic in the PC world.

Without serious attention paid to the security aspect, Java applets would be too risky to run except in controlled circumstances on private nets. Any method for automatically downloading code into a browser and executing it should have some answers to the questions of computer security, not pose further problems.

Fortunately, the designers of the Java system realized this from the outset and carefully put strong protective measures in place to allow applets to run without compromising a system. Java is the only system in use today which allows for safe, secure downloading of executable content.

Summary of New Terms

- All *modern web browsers* contain a JVM to allow bytecode to be executed with web pages.

- A Java program associated with a web page is called an *applet*.

- A *JVM* can load bytecode from the local file system or from a URL indicating a location anywhere on the Internet or a local network.

- Java takes steps to protect *computer security* of those running downloaded code. Computer security is required for all forms of downloading code and execution.

Releases of the JDK to Date

If you'd rather get straight on with the programming, then just skip this section entirely.

Table 1-1 lists, as a reference, the major releases of the Java Development Kit (JDK) that Sun Microsystems has made. Most of these releases are on the CD that accompanies this book, so it forms a historical archive of Java.

Table 1-1: Java Development Kit Releases

Release	Date	Content
various alpha, beta	mid-end 1995	Proof of concept. Java mania starts.
JDK 1.0	Jan. 23, 1996	The now-historic first FCS release of Java for Solaris 2.3 and Windows 95/NT. Did not include the HotJava browser that had been part of earlier releases.
JDK 1.0.1	Mar. 15, 1996	Some security fixes to 1.0, including a fix for the "DNS spoofing" hole (advertising a false IP address for yourself).
JDK 1.0.2	May 7, 1996	A maintenance release with dozens of bug fixes, including blocking some more security holes. Introduced support for the Mac and for Solaris on Intel.
JDK 1.1	Feb. 18, 1997	The first feature release after 1.0, this introduced a new event model for the window system to enable JavaBeans (component software). I/O was changed to better support internationalization. Offered further security improvements, including signed applets. Included many additions—inner classes, printing from an applet, Java database access, and some performance improvements.
JDK 1.1.1	Mar. 27, 1997	Bug fix follow-up release. The pressure to ship JDK 1.1 with the new event model was intense, and some essential bug fixes just didn't make it. Hence this update after just 5 weeks.
JDK 1.1.2	May 28, 1997	Bug fix follow-up, but no API changes from 1.1. Support for the Mac and for Solaris on Intel.
JDK 1.2	est. Dec. 1997	Estimated date. This release will introduce support for drag & drop (windowing data transfer) and other new APIs, such as 2D graphics.
JDK 1.2.1	est. Mar. 1998	Estimated date. This release will introduce support for the remaining new APIs, such as the Java Embedded API, and the Java Naming and Directory Interface.
JDK 1.3	est. mid-1999	Estimated date.

The only two releases of consequence to date (summer 1997) are JDK 1.0.2, and JDK 1.1. All other releases are minor, compatible, maintenance releases. There have been a few of them because Sun takes applet security holes very seriously and will rerelease, rather than merely issuing a patch.

JDK 1.1 is backward compatible with JDK 1.0.2 (your old programs can be compiled by the new compiler and will still run), but JDK 1.1 introduced a new event-handling model for the window system. Code that uses old interfaces that have now been replaced is deprecated (officially frowned on). The compiler will compile programs that use old interfaces, but it will issue a "deprecated code" warning.

Note that these are the releases from Sun. Other companies have licensed the software from Sun and applied their own version numbers to it. Sometimes these numbers are unaligned with Sun. Microsoft called one of its versions of Java "1.1," even though it was based on JDK 1.0.2. Apple has a free `javac` compiler too. Apple's Java environment is called Macintosh Runtime for Java (MRJ). Apple's Java Kit releases are listed in Table 1-2.

Table 1-2: **Releases of Apple's Java Kit**

MRJ 1.0.2	June 1997	Supports Java 1.0.2
MRJ 1.5b1	June 1997	Beta version of 1.0.2 update
MRJ 2.0	Sept 1997	Supports Java 1.1

More information on Apple Java is at http://applejava.apple.com/

Old browsers cannot (generally) run Java programs that use new features. They can run programs that contain only older features, even when compiled with the new compilers. Although Java licensees are contractually obliged to upgrade their JVMs within a certain period after the release of a new JDK, it takes a while for this to happen.

As Java grew in popularity, it grew in size too. There were 8 java packages in the 1.0.2 release, and 22 in the JDK 1.1. There were 211 classes in those 8 packages in JDK 1.0.2, and the number more than doubled to 539 classes and interfaces in JDK 1.1. Now that Java has won over developers everywhere, we hope that the pace of new releases will moderate.

Compiling and Executing a Sample Program

In the last technical section of this chapter, we will walk through the compilation and execution of a Java program. Just follow these numbered steps.

1. Do not use an Integrated Development Environment at first. As the all-wise Yoda remarked "Once you start down the dark path, forever will it dominate your destiny. Consume you it will."
    IDEs just make one more thing for you to learn, and they introduce unnecessary complications of where to type and where to look for output.
    Your first example should involve an editor, a command shell, a Java compiler and a Java interpreter only. You can switch to an IDE once you have mastered the basics, if you wish.

2. Make sure you have installed the Java system from the CD as described earlier (see "Installing the CD-ROM" earlier in the book).

3. When you write and compile your own programs, follow these rules *very carefully*.

    *   Use an editor to create a file with your source code. You must use an editor that saves in an ASCII format, not a word processor format. On a PC, "edit" works.

    *   The name of your Java class must match the name of the file that it is in. Exactly match! If you call your Java class TrYmE, then it *must* be in a source file called TrYmE.java.
        Be certain that the letter case and spelling match exactly. Letter case matters throughout Java (as in most programming languages). The word "System" is different from the word "system," and you cannot use one in place of the other.
        Most professional programmers prefer a language that is case sensitive, for several reasons, mostly involving not having the compiler try to be more clever than they are.

4. Type this program into a file called yes.java.

```
class yes {
    static public void main(String s[]) {
        for (int i=0; i<3; i++)
            System.out.println("good!");
    }
}
```

Note: I am tempting fate by printing these lines in a book and asking readers to copy them exactly. Such examples are notoriously prone to proofreading and printing errors. Please check the website http://www.best.com/~pvdl for any updates if you have trouble with this step, yet you typed the lines exactly as they are shown here.

5. Check that you followed the rules about the file name matching the class name, even to the letter case! The file name has the suffix of .java, too. If you are using a system that doesn't permit 4-character file extensions (probably Windows 3.1), then read the documentation accompanying its Java compiler on the correct form of names. Open a command-line window (get a DOS prompt on Windows or a command shell on Unix). Compile by typing:

```
javac yes.java
```

There should be no error messages from this compilation. If there are any, you probably typed something wrong in the file or the command. Put it right.

6. A successful compilation will create file `yes.class`. Execute the Java class file by telling the JVM the name of the class (not the name of the file that contains the class).

```
java yes
```

Note: Compilers take files as input, so you need to give the file a file name, such as `yes.java`. A JVM is comfortable dealing with a Java class, so you can just give it the class name `yes`, and it knows which places and files to search to find the right class. Perhaps you feel this is inconsistent. It is, but sometimes programming is like that.

If you have done everything correctly up to now, you will be rewarded with the splendid message:

```
good!
good!
good!
```

Now you are ready for a slightly more substantial program. Type this program in, or copy it off the CD or from my website **[http://www.best.com/~pvdl]**. It is only 30 lines long, and it demonstrates platform-independent windowing. Put it in a file called `myframe.java` (all lowercase letters).

```
// 30 line Java demo, Peter van der Linden
import java.awt.*;
class myframe extends Frame {
    int xy[]= {120,0}, ci=0, mi=0, turn=0;
    Font fb = new Font("TimesRoman", Font.BOLD, 36);
    String m[]={"Easy", "Portable", "Secure", "Java"};
    Color c[]={Color.red, Color.yellow, Color.green, Color.blue};

    public void paint(Graphics g) {
        g.setFont( fb );
        g.setColor( c[mi] );
        g.drawString(m[mi],xy[0],xy[1]);
        if ( (xy[turn]+=3) < 200) return;
        mi=++mi==m.length?mi=0:mi;
        xy[turn]=(turn+1)*60;
        xy[turn=1-turn]=0;
    }
    static public void main(String s[]) throws Exception {
        myframe mf = new myframe();
        for (int i=0;i<4;i++)
            for (int j=0;j<200;j++) {
                mf.repaint();
                Thread.sleep(5);
            }
        System.exit(0);
    }
    myframe() {super("Java is easy"); setSize(200,200); show();}
}
```

Try compiling it with

```
javac myframe.java
```

Figure 1-3 shows the process of compilation. If you try this under a JDK 1.0.2 system, you need to change `setSize` (in the second to last line to `resize`) because the name of this library call changed. Fix up the inevitable typing errors, and run it with

```
java myframe
```

Figure 1-4 shows a screen dump from the program running on a Windows 95 system. It's exciting that such a program can be written in less than 30 lines of code. Go ahead and copy the `myframe.class` file onto a floppy disk. Walk it over to any different architecture system to which you have access. Run it on the Java system you install there. Marvel at the possibilities of universally portable software.

Don't drive yourself mad trying to understand each and every line of this code now. You will be able to read and understand it by the end of the book. Finally, please visit the book website http://www.best.com/~pvdl to pick up the errata sheet and to get the Java Programmers FAQ.

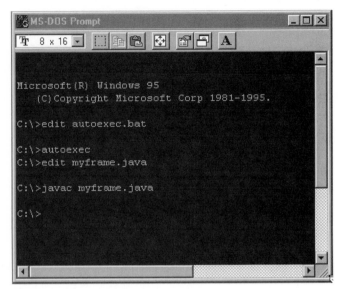

Figure 1-3: The process of compilation.

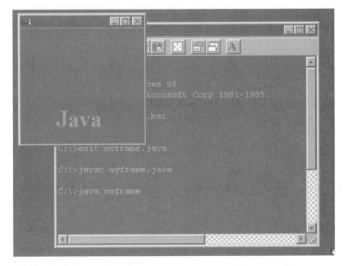

Figure 1-4: Running the program on Windows 95.

Light Relief: The Winchester Mystery Disk

Who remembers the name "Winchester disk"? For a long time, "Winchester" referred to any disk using the floating-head technology pioneered by IBM. Earlier disks had heads that could not be allowed to touch the platter, and when IBM introduced the Winchester disk in 1973, it virtually eliminated disk head crashes, cut costs by 75 percent, and quickly became the dominant disk technology.

Winchester disks were so successful that they quickly replaced all other kinds of disk. Since there were no other kinds of disk, the term "Winchester" then fell out of use in the mid 1980s, in favor of "hard disk," which contrasted with "floppy disks." Few people remember the term Winchester disk, but even fewer remember what it is named for.

One of my hobbies is tracking down interesting but useless information, so naturally I dropped everything and got on this one right away. The Winchester disk was developed in great secrecy at IBM's Almaden, San Jose, research lab, so my first thought was that it was connected with the Winchester Mystery House.

The Winchester Mystery House, also in San Jose, California, is a story in its own right. It was built by Old Lady Winchester in the late 1800s, with the money she inherited from her father who founded the Winchester rifle company. This is California, remember, and Sarah Winchester's psychic adviser told her that she was haunted by the ghosts of people killed with Winchester rifles and that they would get her when her house was completed. Or so the story runs. I think it much more likely that the psychic issued the more traditional warning of "you will not live to see your house completed," but the story is never told this way.

In any event, the gloomy prophecy caused Sarah Winchester to embark on a house-renovating jamboree that lasted the next 38 years! The wealthy but weird widow kept workmen constantly employed building walls, windows, doors, stairs, passages, and ramps, then tearing them up and moving them for nearly four decades. But all she did was prove the psychic correct in the end, for she did indeed die in 1924, as the work continued around her. The house is still standing today, and you can tour it for a modest investment of $20. Some rooms are now closed since the 1989 Loma Prieta earthquake, and where are those never-ending construction crews when you need them, eh?

Well, it turns out that Winchester disks are connected with Winchester rifles, but not through the Winchester Mystery House. The Winn Rosch Hardware Bible says, "The name is a carryover from the original disk drive that used this terminology. Built by IBM, it was once code-named the '3030' because it had two sides, each of which could store 30 megabytes." The designation, of course, mirrors the famous Winchester 3030 repeating rifle. In the case of the "rifle that won the West, or at least took it all away from those who formerly had it," the first 30 referred to caliber and the second to the grain weight of the charge.

Rosch adds, "Another story holds that the name Winchester was derived from disk technology developed in an IBM laboratory in Winchester, England. When queried in 1987, however, IBM officially supported the rifle story."

All that remains is to sing the name of the unsung hero who actually coined the term. Ken Haughton led the IBM 3340 project from the summer of 1969. The IBM 3340 was announced in March 1973, with shipments from November 1973. Referring to the configuration of the 3340 (two spindles, each of 30 megabytes, which his engineers called a "30-30"), he said "If it's a 30-30, then it must be a Winchester." The source for this coda? Some data that I snagged off the net years ago and squirreled away on my trusty Winchester disk.

Exercises

1. What is a browser? Why does it use HTML instead of unmarked-up regular text?

2. What is the difference between an API and an ABI? Give examples of each.

3. What are the two most important breakthroughs that the Java language system offers?

4. Define these terms: applet, HotJava, CGI, WWW, URL.

5. How might software be distributed over the Internet in the future? How might this affect software retail stores?

Further Readings

The Whole Internet

by Ed Krol,

published by O'Reilly & Associates, Sebastapol CA, 1992

ISBN 1-56592-025-2

An excellent and exceptionally able description of all key aspects of the Internet for the intelligent lay reader.

How the Internet Works

by Joshua Eddings

published by those slack-jawed gimps at Ziff-Davis, Emeryville CA, 1994

ISBN 1-56276-192-7

A book for people who like looking at pictures and a lot of blank space. Uses the word "Cyberspace" rather too frequently.

As We May Think

by Vannevar Bush

reprint of an article in Atlantic Monthly, July 1945

URL: http://www.isg.sfu.ca/~duchier/misc/vbush

HTML Visual Quick Reference

Dean Scharf, publ Que Corporation, IN, 1995

ISBN 0-7987-0411-0

This is the book on HTML that most programmers will prefer; it's inexpensive, well-written, not padded with fluff, and it covers everything you need to know to write WWW documents.

Client/Server A Manager's Guide

by Laurence Shafe

published by Addison Wesley, 1994

ISBN 0-201-42790-7

A clear, jargon-free look at the client/server paradigm. It provides the background for understanding many trends in system software, and explains the significance of client/server computing.

Voices From the Net

by Clay Shirky

Ziff-Davis, Emeryville, CA, 1994

ISBN 1-56276-303-2

CHAPTER
2

The Story of O: Object-Oriented Programming

"C makes it easy to shoot yourself in the foot, C++ makes it harder, but when you do, it blows away your whole leg."

—Bjarne "Stumpy" Stroustrup (originator of C++)

I t's a surprising but accurate observation that software development trends seem to be running in the opposite direction to the universe in general. The universe has entropy—it is gradually "winding down," or proceeding to a less and less coherent state. By way of contrast software development methodologies over the past 30 years have become more disciplined and more organized. The prime example of this is Object Oriented Programming (OOP), an old idea enjoying a powerful revival at present.

Java is an object-oriented language, and to understand Java you have to understand OOP concepts. Fortunately, the big, well-kept secret of Object-Oriented Programming works in our favor here: Object-Oriented Programming is based on simple ideas.

The big, well-kept secret of Object-Oriented Programming is that it is simple. It is based on a small number of common-sense fundamentals. Unfortunately OOP has some special terminology, and it suffers from the "surfeit of Zen" problem: to fully understand any one part, you need to understand most of the other parts. Most programmers can understand OOP instinctively if it is explained clearly. However it is not usually explained clearly. Look at the power-babble you can find in the introduction of any book on C++, for example: "Object-oriented programming is characterized by inheritance and dynamic binding. C++ supports inheritance through class derivation. Dynamic binding is provided by virtual class functions. Virtual functions provide a method of encapsulating the implementation details of an inheritance hierarchy."

Completely accurate, but also completely incomprehensible to someone encountering the topic for the first time. Here we describe OOP in simple English, and relate it to familiar programming language features.

> ### Teach Yourself OOP the Hard Way
>
> Alan Kay, an OO expert who is now an Apple distinguished Fellow, began studying the topic in the early 1970s. He was leafing through 80 pages of Simula-67 listing. Simula was the first OO language, but Alan hadn't seen it before and didn't know that. He thought it was Algol or an Algol-variant.
>
> He literally taught himself the principles of OOP from reading 80 pages of code in the first Object-Oriented language. Not everyone will want to duplicate that achievement, so this chapter provides the missing background.

Object-Oriented Programming ("OOP") is not a new idea; Simula-67 pioneered it around thirty years ago. Most experts agree that OOP is based on four key principles: abstraction, encapsulation, inheritance and polymorphism.

We'll take these concepts one at a time, and describe them in terms of real-world examples, and then programming abstractions.

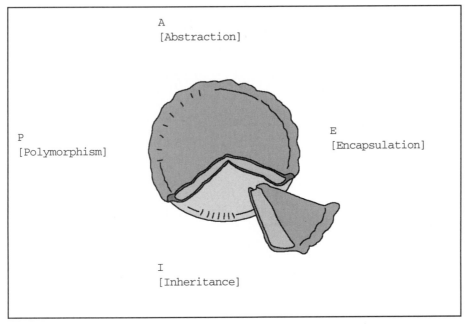

A
[Abstraction]

P
[Polymorphism]

E
[Encapsulation]

I
[Inheritance]

Figure 2-1: OOP has four key concepts which you can remember by thinking A PIE: Abstraction, Polymorphism, Inheritance, and Encapsulation

Abstraction

To process something from the real world on a computer, we have to extract out the essential characteristics. The data representing these characteristics are how we will process that thing in a system.

The characteristics which we choose will depend on what we are trying to do. Take a car for example. A registration authority will record the Vehicle Identification Number (the unique code assigned by the manufacturer), the license plate, the current owner, the tax due, and so on. However when the car checks into a garage for a service, the garage will represent it in their computer system by license plate, work description, billing information, and owner. In the owner's home budgeting system, the abstraction may be the car description, service history, gas mileage records and so on.

These are all examples of data abstractions. Abstraction is the process of refining away the unimportant details of an object, so that only the appropriate characteristics that describe it remain. These, together with the operations on the data, form an abstract data type. We just mentioned three different data abstractions for a car

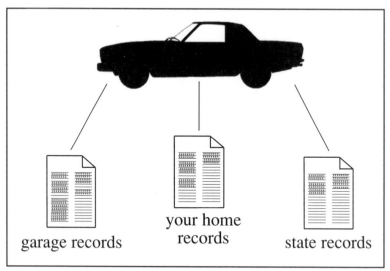

Figure 2-2: Three abstractions of "a car"

above. Abstraction is where program design starts. All mainstream programming languages provide a way to store pieces of related data together. It is usually called something like a structure or record.

Encapsulation

One step beyond abstraction is the recognition that, equally as important as data, are the operations that are performed on it. Encapsulation simply says that there should be a way to associate the two closely together and treat them as a single unit of organization. In language terms, data, and related functions should be bundled together somehow, so you can say "this is how we represent a blurf object, and these are the only operations that can be done on blurfs".

This is actually a subtle principle because non-OOP languages support encapsulation very well for built-in types, and not at all for user-defined types. Take floating point numbers for example. In most languages, the only valid thing you can do with them is arithmetic operations and I/O. Even in C, if you try to shift left the bits of floating point number:

```
float       f = 2.0;              C EXAMPLE
int         i,j = 1;

i = f << j;
        ^^ operand must have integral type
```

the compiler will print out an error message. The valid operations for a float are encapsulated (bundled together) as part of the type information, and shifting isn't one of them. You cannot directly get your hands on the bits that represent the internal fields of the type, such as the significand, the sign bit, or the exponent. The compiler enforces the rule that "the operation must be compatible with the type."

C provides header files that group together variables, types (typedefs) and function declarations, but this is just lexical grouping, not true encapsulation. C header files do not enforce the integrity of a type (i.e. prevent invalid operations, like assigning a float to an int that represents month_number). Nor do they provide any information hiding. Any program that includes the header file has full details of what is in the type, can access individual fields as desired, and can create new functions that operate on the internals of the structs.

OOP-languages extend the support for encapsulation (bundling together types and the functions that operate on those types, and restricting access to the internal representation) to also cover user-defined types. They enforce the integrity of a type, by preventing programmers from accessing individual fields in inappropriate ways. Only a predetermined group of functions can access the data fields. The collective term for "datatype and operations bundled together, with access restrictions" is a "class". The individual elements in a class are "fields" A variable of some class type is called an "instance" or an "object". It's pretty much the same as a variable of an ordinary type, except the valid functions that can be invoked for it are tied to it. In a way, OOP is a misnomer; we should really say "Class-Based Programming."

The One-Minute Object Manager

You have already covered two of the four cornerstones of Object-Oriented Programming. Now is a good time to show what this means with programming examples. We'll use C to start out because it's an enormously popular language, and because if you know any algorithmic language, it's pretty easy to map that to C. Let's begin with an explanation that will take no more than one minute to follow.

We'll build our example around a C struct (a record or structure in other languages) that we'll call "fruit". It is our user-defined data type that stores information abstracted from the qualities of fruit. So we'll declare variables like plum, apple, banana that are instances of fruit type. Fruit isn't usually something that gets data processed, but this example keeps everything focused on the new abstraction, rather than the bits and bytes.

Assume we are primarily concerned with the nutritional value of fruit. As a result the characteristics that we abstract out and store might go into a structure like this:

```
typedef struct {
        int grams;                              C CODE
        int cals_per_gram;
} Fruit;
```

We also have a function that can calculate the total calories, given a pointer to a fruit structure:

```
int total_calories (Fruit *this)
{
        return (this->grams) * (this->cals_per_gram);

}
```

Explanation For Non-native Speakers of C

The definition of the Fruit struct should be self-explanatory. It has two fields that are integers. One records the weight, the other the unit calories. The function "total_calories" has one parameter that is a pointer to a Fruit variable. The parameter is called "this". The body of the function says to get the "grams" field of the structure pointed to by "this" and multiply it by the "cals_per_gram" field. Return the result as the value of the function.

In the next example, the declaration "Fruit pear . . ." creates and initializes a variable of the Fruit type. Finally, the last line creates an integer variable called "total_cals". The variable is initialized with the value returned by calling the function on the pear argument. The function expects a pointer to a Fruit, rather than the Fruit itself, so we pass it "&pear" -- the address of pear, rather than pear itself.

Note: "Pointer to" and "address of" mean exactly the same thing in C, unless you're writing a compiler for a really strange machine.

Here's a C example of calling it:

```
Fruit pear = {5, 45};                           C CODE

int total_cals = total_calories( &pear );
```

So far, so good. But the function and the Fruit type that it operates on, are not closely coupled together. It's too easy to get inside the struct and adjust fields independently. It's possible for anyone to add their own extra functions that operate on the fields of the Fruit type.

We seek the quality of "encapsulation", so let's bundle together the type definition with all the functions that operate on it. In C, we bundle things together by enclosing them in curly braces. Our example would then look like:

```
struct Fruit {
        int grams;                                    PSEUDO C
        int cals_per_gram;

        int total_calories (Fruit *this)
        {
        return (this->grams) * (this->cals_per_gram);
        }
};
```

Note that you cannot actually declare a function inside a struct in C, but let's imagine you could. A simplifying assumption is now made. We impose a Fruit argument convention. All the functions that operate on the Fruit datatype will always be passed a pointer-to-a-fruit as the first parameter. This first parameter will point to the fruit that we are going to do the operation on.

So let's save some writing and have the compiler make that first parameter implicit. We won't mention the fruit pointer either in the parameter list, or before the fields it points to. We'll just assume that it exists implicitly, and its name is always "this" (think of it as saying "this here pointer points to the specific piece of fruit you are working on"). At this point, we have created a class. So replace the word "struct" with the word "class". Our three modifications are:

1. bundle together the functions with the datatypes in a struct,

2. give all the functions an implicit first parameter called "this" that points to the struct with the data,

3. replace the word "struct" with "class".

```
class Fruit {
        int grams;
        int cals_per_gram;                            C++ CODE

        int total_calories ( )
        {
        return grams * cals_per_gram;
        }
};
```

There. That's the elements of C++. All the rest is just details (but there are rather a lot of them). That should have taken about one minute to read, although it may take a little longer to re-read and sink in. We get some other benefits from organizing the namespaces: the data fields are implicitly recognized inside the functions without having to say which struct they come from. They come from the same kind of struct that contains the function. There are keywords to control how visible the fields are to other classes.

There are no structs or typedefs in Java. The most important way to group related things together is to put them in a class. The C++ class definition above is also a Java class definition. Here's how you declare variables and invoke object functions in Java.

```
Fruit  plum, apple, pear;                          Java CODE

        // some more lines omitted

int cals = plum.total_calories();

int fruit_salad_cals =
            plum.total_calories() +
            apple.total_calories() +
            pear.total_calories();
```

The programming language takes care of the housekeeping of sending a pointer to the variable as the implicit first parameter, and of using that pointer to find the object variables. If it helps, you can think of the compiler as translating

```
plum.total_calories()                      /* Java */
```

into

```
total_calories(&plum)                      /* C */
```

It's actually doing quite a bit more than that: making sure the method is only called for objects of the correct type, enforcing encapsulation, supporting inheritance, and so on. The new notation is useful to convey all these overtones. We refer to the functions that are in the class as "methods" because they are the method for processing some data of that type

> ## Where Does the Name "Method" Come From?
>
> You might be wondering where does the name "method" come from? Isn't this just an unnecessary new fancy name for "function" or "procedure"? Shhhhhh! You broke the code! Yes, "method" just means "function that belongs to a class."
>
> *Note: Some compiler theorists insist that methods are different from functions because their runtime prolog may be different. This is just splitting hairs. All calls involve a prolog to set them up, and an epilog to return. It doesn't seem very interesting to draw a distinction based on how the prolog locates what is being called.*
>
> The term seems to have arisen by accident. The origin lies in Smalltalk-72 which was a blend of Lisp and Simula-67. Smalltalk-72 methods began with the keyword 'TO' as in TO CalculateTotal ... because they were just "methods TO do something or other." Over time the term naturally shifted from the preposition to the noun. Methods could just as easily have been called a "way" a "plan" a "scheme" (there actually is a Scheme variant of Lisp) or an "action."

To summarize, we've arrived at C++, and the convention of a struct that contains both the datatype fields, and the function(s) that manipulate them. All this is common to Java, too. There's also a notation to suggest we are invoking a method on an object:

```
plum.total_calories();
```

rather than passing an object as an argument

```
total_calories( &plum );
```

This is because OOP stresses the importance of objects rather than procedural statements. One way that might help you grasp this notation is to consider it analogous to the C statement "i++", indicating "take the object called 'i' and do the ++ operation on it." Here we have "take the object called 'plum' and do the 'total_calories()' method on it."

In the Java code above, Fruit is a class. The variables apple, plum, and pear are instances of the class, or objects. The variables "grams" and "cals_per_gram" are instance variables. The function "total_calories()" is a method. The declarations of grams, cals_per_gram and total_calories() are fields. The class as a whole forms a user-defined type.

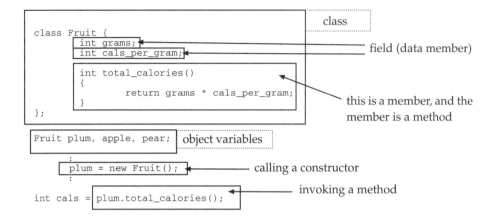

```
class Fruit {
      int grams;
      int cals_per_gram;

      int total_calories()
      {
              return grams * cals_per_gram;
      }
};
```

class

field (data member)

this is a member, and the member is a method

```
Fruit plum, apple, pear;
```
object variables

```
plum = new Fruit();
```
calling a constructor

```
int cals = plum.total_calories();
```
invoking a method

Figure 2-3:   Some class terminology

An Alternative Rationale for OOP

Another way of looking at this class thing is that it's just a way of giving user-defined types the same privileges as types that are built in to the language.

Just as the compiler knows what may and may not be done with a float, classes provide a way to specify the same information and constraints for new types.

The result is software that is more reliable and quicker to debug (because data can only be changed in disciplined ways). A piece of the program that "owns" (declares) an object cannot break it open and fool around with the individual fields.

We come now to a significant and important difference between Java and C++. This change takes a little getting used to when programming, and forms a key divergence in the language philosophies. Java makes significant distinctions between built-in ("primitive") types and user-defined types (i.e classes).

Java treats variables in two different ways, depending on their type:

1.   variables of built-in types: boolean, char, int, etc. (primitive types)

2.   objects

One way to visualize classes and objects is to think of a class as like a rubber stamp. The rubber stamp (class) can create many imprints (objects).

When you declare a class . . .   . . . you are creating a template or stamp that says what fields and methods are in objects that belong to this class.

```
Class Employee  {
   // fields
   String name;
   int salary;
   int employee_number;

   // method
   Employee (string s, int i) {
      // constructor
      this.name = s;
      salary = i;
      employee_number = Global.total;
   }
   void give_raise (int amount) {
            salary + = raise;
   }
}
```

You can use this template or stamp (class) to create actual objects of this kind.

The class defines the "shape" or fields that each object has. On paper, the fields are just areas of paper bordered by ink. You can write different values in those areas. In a programming language, the fields are variables and methods. The methods can calculate and assign new values to the variables.

Figure 2-4: A class is like a rubber stamp. It is a template or mold for creating objects.

The difference is this: when you declare a variable, what you get depends on the type. If it is a primitive type, you actually get the variable and you can read, write and process it immediately. 🍒

```
e.g   int i;
      i =0;  i++;   // all fine.
```

If however, it is a variable of a class type (any class type), you do *not* get an instance of that class immediately, and you cannot read, write or process it immediately! What you get is a reference variable—a location that can hold a pointer to the desired object *when you fill it in*.

Note that this is a big difference from C++, where declaring an object reserves space for the object itself. In C++, if you declare one class inside another, space for the entire size of the nested class is reserved. In Java, declaring one class inside another would simply reserve space for a *pointer to* the nested class. This allows all kinds of implementation magic—object sizes never have to be known on compilation, because they are *all* simply dealt with as two pointers—a pointer to the class information and a pointer to the actual object on the heap.

References, Pointers, Addresses, and Null

You might have heard "Java doesn't have any pointers." Actually, the truth is almost the opposite: all objects in Java are accessed through pointers all the time. However, Java doesn't have arbitrary arithmetic on pointers (the source of so many bugs in C++) and Java automatically dereferences pointers as needed.

Other people say that Java doesn't have pointers, it has references. They mean that references are a refinement of pointers, with restricted semantics. These are the same people who claim that C doesn't have memory addresses, it has pointers. To me, this is splitting hairs. Speaking as a long-time compiler-writer, a reference is another name for a pointer which is another name for a memory address. If C doesn't have memory addresses, why does it have an "addressof" operator? If Java doesn't have pointers, why does it a "NullPointerException"?

In high level languages, pointers can be assigned a special value that says "I don't point to anything." In Java, this is called the null value. When you declare a reference type, it is initialized with the value "null" (usually represented as zero in the underlying system). You can also explicitly assign null or check for it, using the keyword "null" like this:

```
Window MyWindow;  // MyWindow has the value null
MyWindow = new Window(); // MyWindow points to a Window object
if (MyWindow==null) . . .
```

When you declare:

```
Myclass foo;
```

That does not give you an object of Myclass. It gives you a reference variable foo that can reference an object of Myclass—after you have filled in the reference so it points to such an object. You can create a Myclass object for foo. Or you can make it point to an existing object.

Declaring a class does not create any objects. E.g.

```
class Employee {
    . . . // does not create any object
}
```

Declaring a variable of that class type (surprisingly) does not create any objects.

```
Employee you; // does not create an object
```

Declaring a variable of a class type gives you a variable that can point to an object when you fill it in.

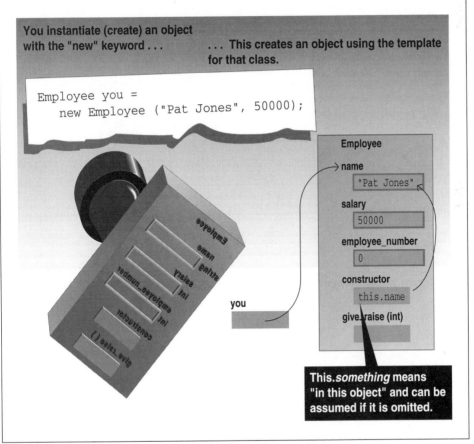

Figure 2-5: An object is created with a "new" keyword.

The assignment:

```
myfruit = apple;
```

does not *copy* the apple object! It makes myfruit and apple have the same reference to it. Changes made through myfruit will be seen by apple!

```
myfruit.grams = 37;
apple.grams is now 37
```

Parameter Passing

The difference between variables of primitive types, and objects (reference types) has implications for parameter passing too. Variables of built-in types are passed by value, objects are passed by reference.

"Passing by value" means that the argument's value is copied, and is passed to the method. Inside the method this copy can be modified at will, and doesn't affect the original argument.

"Passing by reference" means that a reference to (i.e. the address of) the argument is passed to the method. Using the reference, the method is actually directly accessing the argument, not a copy of it. Any changes the method makes to the parameter are made to the actual object used as the argument. So after you return from the method, that object will retain any new values set in the method.

What's really going on here is that a <u>copy</u> of the value that references an object argument is passed to the method. This is why some Java books say "everything is passed by value"—the <u>object reference</u> is passed by <u>value</u> which effectively passes the <u>object itself</u> by <u>reference</u>.

So if all objects are accessed by reference how do you get a copy of an object? It turns out that you hardly ever need to do that (when was the last time you needed a distinct duplicate of the literal "3"?) Think of objects as inherently unique. Replication by copying threatens that uniqueness thus leading to lack of control, chaos, and eventually, a hereditary monarchy based on primogeniture. There is a way to do it if you absolutely must (implement the cloneable interface, as outlined in chapter 4).

Constructors and Finalizers

Whenever you declare an object variable, before you can actually do anything with it, you must make it point to an object instance. One way to do that is to create a new object using a constructor—a process known as "instantiation", like so:

```
foo = new Myclass();
```

or combine the declaration and instantiation into one like this:

```
Myclass foo = new Myclass();
```

A constructor is a special kind of method that initializes a newly-created object. "Create_and_Initialize" would be a good, though long, name instead of "constructor." One reason a constructor (or at least an ordinary method) is needed is because no one outside the class is able to access data whose scope is limited to the class (we call this private data—there is a keyword to label data in this way). Therefore you need a privileged function inside the class to fill in the initial data values of a newly-minted object. This is a bit of a leap from C, where you just initialize a variable with an assignment in its definition, or even leave it uninitialized.

Constructor functions always have the same name as the class, and have this general form

```
classname ( parameterlist ) { . . . }
```

Note that there is no explicit return type, nor the keyword "void." In some senses, the constructor name *is* the return type.

Most classes have at least one explicit constructor. You can define several different constructors, and tell them apart by their parameter types. In the Fruit example:

```
class Fruit {                          Java CODE
        int grams;
        int cals_per_gram;

        Fruit()                    // constructor
          {grams=55; cals_per_gram=0;}
        Fruit(int g, int c) {    //another constructor
          grams=g;
          cals_per_gram=c;
        }
}
        . . .

    Fruit melon=new Fruit(4,5), banana=new Fruit();
```

In this example, a melon is created with grams = 4 and cals_per_gram = 5. Similarly a banana is created with grams = 55 and 0 cals_per_gram. A constructor cannot be invoked explicitly by the programmer other than in object creation, although this might otherwise be quite a useful operation to reset an object to a known initial state, say. The reason is that a constructor is deemed to magically create an object, as well as setting values in its fields.

A class can be used to "stamp out" or create any number of objects.

Each object keeps its own values in its data fields.

The template or class can turn out any number of objects of that kind.

Employee
name
Eugene Desmond

Employee
name
Pat
salary
65
empl
c
con
giv

Each object has the same set of fields. Here the fields are "name", "salary", "employee_number", "Employee" (a constructor) and "give_raise" (a method). Whenever one of these names is used, it refers to the field in this particular object.

Employee
name
"Bill Mudflap"
salary
75000
employee_number
0
constructor
give_raise (int)
name = ...

A constructor is always called to initialize the object. There can be several constructors, and they are distinguished by their arguments. If you didn't provide any constructors, a default one with no arguments is provided for you.

. . means the "name" field of this object, not any of the other objects.

Conceptually, each object has its own copy of the methods in the class. In practice, methods don't change (unlike the values in data fields) so we don't need to keep multiple copies of them. We do need to make sure that when a method references a field, it refers to that field in that object. The compiler takes care of it for you.

Figure 2-6: A class can stamp out any number of objects belonging to that class.

Since almost everything in Java is an object, almost everything is created by a call to a constructor. Constructors have the same name as the class, so it is very common to see something declared and initialized with calls like this:

```
Bicycle schwinn = new Bicycle();
Cheese cheddar = new Cheese(matured);
Beer ESB = new Beer(London, bitter, 1068);
Mammal dalmatian = new Dog("spotty"); // Mammal is the superclass
                                      //of Dog
```

The repeated classname looks quite odd to C programmers at first. 🐛

Every class always has at least one constructor. When you do not provide any explicit constructors (you are allowed to do this), then the default no-arg constructor is assumed for you. Constructors are like the public defender in many legal systems: if you do not have one, a default one will be provided for you, but it won't do very much. The default no-arg (meaning "no arguments") constructor for a class takes no arguments and does nothing, but it does ensure that every class always has at least one constructor.

When an object is instantiated, this is the order in which things happen:

1. The memory for the object is allocated on the heap. The heap is a "scratchpad" area of memory controlled by the runtime system to support dynamic memory allocation.

2. The data fields are filled in with the default values zero, 0.0, null, and so on.

3. Any data fields with explicit initializers have those initial assignments executed.

4. The statements in the constructor are executed.

No Destructors

Java has automatic storage management, including automatic reclamation of unused store. The runtime system does not therefore need to be told when an object has reached the end of its lifetime. Accordingly, there are no destructors in the C++ sense. Just delete, overwrite, or null out the last reference to an object and it becomes available for destruction so the memory can be reused. There is more about this in Chapter 5 on "garbage collection." You can provide a finalizer for a class. It will be invoked on an object right before it is garbage collected.

Inheritance

The last two pieces of OOP are inheritance and polymorphism. You need a solid understanding of these to successfully use the Java library routines. Despite the unusual names, they describe some clear concepts.

Inheritance means building on a class that is already defined, to extend it in some way. Inheritance is what you acquire from past generations. Let us first consider a real world example of "class inheritance" in the Linnaean taxonomy of the animal kingdom, and a similar example using C types.

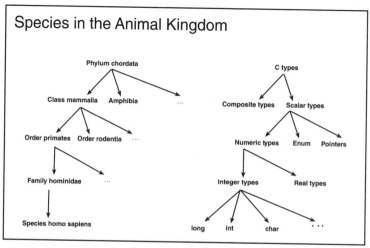

Figure 2-7:   Two real-world examples of an inheritance heirarchy

In the figure above:

- The phylum chordata contains every creature that has a notochord (roughly, a spinal cord), and only those creatures; all told there are some 35 phyla in the animal kingdom.

- All mammals have a spinal cord. They inherit it as a characteristic by being a subclass of the chordata phylum. Mammals also have specialized characteristics: they feed their young milk, they have only one bone in the lower jaw, they have hair, a certain bone configuration in the inner ear, two generations of teeth, and so on.

- Primates inherit all the characteristics of mammals (including the quality of having a spinal cord, that mammals inherited from chordates).

Primates are further distinguished by forward facing eyes, a large braincase, and a particular pattern of incisor teeth.

- The hominidae family inherits all the characteristics from primates and more distant ancestors. It adds to the class the unique specialization of a number of skeletal modifications suitable for walking upright on two feet. The homo sapiens species is now the only species alive within this family. All other species have become extinct.

To be a little more abstract, the hierarchy of types in C can be similarly analyzed:

- All types in C are either composite (types like arrays or structs, that are composed of smaller elements) or scalar. Scalar types have the property that each value is atomic (it is not composed of other types).

- The numeric types inherit all the properties of scalar types, and they have the additional quality that they record arithmetic quantities.

- The integer types inherit all the properties of numeric types, and they have the additional characteristic that they only operate on whole numbers (no fractional quantities).

- The type char is a smaller range within the values in the integer family.

Although we can amuse ourselves by showing how inheritance applies in theory to the familiar C types, note that this model is of no practical use to a C programmer. C doesn't have built-in inheritance, so a programmer cannot use the type hierarchy in real programs. An important part of OOP is figuring out and advantageously using the hierarchies of the abstract data types in your application.

There is a GUI library class in Java called Window that implements the most basic kind of window. A Window object can be moved, resized, iconified, and you can use it in your code. For the sake of this example, let's assume that your program needs a slightly different kind of window: an ImportantWindow. The only difference is that you want ImportantWindows to be colored red to highlight their importance.

There are at least three possible ways to implement ImportantWindow:

1. Change the Window class and add a constructor that creates important windows. This is a bad approach, because you never want to change the standard runtime library.

2. Copy all the code in Window.java into file ImportantWindow.java, making the change you need. This is a bad approach, because it is

impossible to keep duplicated code in synchronization. Whenever the code for class Window changes in future releases, class ImportantWindow is almost guaranteed to stop working.

3. Make ImportantWindow a *subclass* of Window, so it *inherits* all the functionality from Window.

The preferred OOP approach is the third one: make ImportantWindow extend the class Window, so ImportantWindow inherits all the data and methods of Window. This is exactly how the OOP process is supposed to work: find a class that does most of what you want, and then subclass it to provide the exact functionality. There's nothing special about the libraries that come with Java. You can subclass your own classes and system classes as needed.

To summarize, inheritance occurs when a class adapts the data structures and methods of a base (or "parent") class. That creates a hierarchy, similar to a scientific taxonomy. Each level is a specialization of the one above. Type inheritance is a concept that doesn't really exist in C or other non object-oriented languages. Inheritance is one of the concepts people are referring to when they say object-oriented programming requires thinking in a special way. Get ready to spring forward with that "conceptual leap"!

The Key Idea: Inheritance

Inheritance means being able to declare a type which builds on the fields (data and methods) of a previously-declared type. As well as inheriting all the operations and data, you get the chance to declare your own versions and new versions of the methods, to refine, specialize, replace or extend the ones in the parent class.

Terminology:

class = a data type

extend = to make a new class that inherits the contents of an existing class.

superclass = a parent or "base" class. Superclass is a very poor choice of name as it wrongly suggests the parent class has more than the subclass.

subclass = a child class that inherits, or extends, a superclass.

It is called a subclass because it only represents a sub-part of the universe of things that make up the superclass. However, it usually has more fields to represent its specialization.

Note that in Java, almost everything is an object, and in particular, all the classes that you declare are subclasses of the built-in root class Object. So if you have read ahead and written some lines of Java that compile, you are already implicitly using inheritance!

Inheritance usually provides increasing specialization as you go from a general superclass class (e.g. vehicle) to a more specific subclass (e.g. passenger car, fire truck, or delivery van). It could equally subset or extend the available operations though.

Let's invent a class Citrus that has every characteristic of the Fruit class we were playing around with earlier, and a specialized operation of its own: squeeze. Citrus fruits are pretty much the only widely-available fruits that you can hand squeeze to extract the juice from. Our base class is:

Java CODE

```
class Fruit {
        int grams;
        int cals_per_gram;

        int total_calories ( ) { /* ... */ }
}
```

An example of class inheritance is

```
class Citrus extends Fruit {
        void squeeze() {  /* ... */ }
}
```

This makes Citrus a subclass that inherits all the Fruit class operations and adds this squeeze() specialization of its own. You can call the squeeze () method on a Citrus object, and you can also call the total_calories() method.

Most methods return a value. When the return type is "void" as here, it means the method does not return a value. Don't get hung up on how the method might be implemented. Obviously it's removed from usual computing. Remember, we're concentrating on the new concepts, without getting caught up on specific algorithms.

The code says that Citrus is based on ("extends") Fruit. A Citrus is a specialization of Fruit; it has all the fields that Fruit has, and adds a method of its own. In our "rubber stamp" metaphor, inheritance corresponds to overstamping, and changing some of the methods (the analogy isn't that great here).

Here's an example of how various fruits might be declared and inherited. Note, by the way, how everything in Java belongs to a class. There are no global variables or functions outside classes. This example assumes the Fruit and Citrus classes mentioned above.

```
class test2e {
    public static void main(String args[]) {
        Fruit somefruit= new Fruit();
        Citrus lemon = new Citrus();

        lemon.squeeze();

        somefruit = lemon;
    }
}
```

We'll get to the "public static void main" stuff later. For now, that's just there for the adventurous who want to try typing something in and compiling it right now before reading any further. There's a few in every crowd (I'm one of them, in fact). Most methods return a value. Again, the return type "void" just means the method does not return a value.

Notice the assignment of lemon (a Citrus object) into somefruit (a Fruit object). You can always make a more general object hold a more specialized one, but the reverse is not true without an explicit type conversion. All citrus are fruit, but not all fruit are citrus. So you can assign somefruit=lemon, but not lemon=somefruit because somefruit may be a plum.

Casting

Casting is the C term for type conversion, carried over into Java. Just as you can cast (convert) an integer into a double, so too you can cast from a superclass to one of its more specialized subclasses. The previous example explained that you can't assign

```
lemon = somefruit;     // causes compilation error
```

You can, however, cast it. To cast any type, write the typename in parentheses immediately before the object being cast. In this case:

```
lemon = (Citrus) somefruit;     // works fine
```

Type hierarchies are often drawn as tree diagrams with Object (the ultimate superclass) at the top, and all subclasses beneath their superclass as Figure 2-4 exemplifies. Referring to a drawing of this type, you can only cast "downwards" between a superclass and some subclass (or subclass of a subclass, etc). You can never cast "sideways" to force an object to become something it is not.

All objects carry around a little extra information at runtime, saying what type they really are, so casts can be checked. If the somefruit object is actually something that's not a Citrus, the cast will fail at runtime, raising the exceptional condition "ClassCastException". Exceptions are described in Chapter 5. They are a recoverable interruption to the normal flow of control.

Because every class is a subclass of the built-in system class Object, every object can be assigned to something of type Object, and later cast back to the type that it really is. In this way, the type Object is a little like "void *" in C that is used as a general pointer to anything. There are some utility classes that store and manipulate Objects, so you can use them for any object, later casting to get back the same type that you put in.

Inheritance is not confined to a single level. You can have class A extends B, where class B extends C, and so on. If you look at the Java runtimes, you can see several examples of inheritance hierarchies 5 or 6 levels deep. You can cast to several levels down in the hierarchy, not just the immediate subclass.

"Is A" Versus "Has A"

Don't confuse inheritance with having a data field that is another class. It's very common to have a class that only implements a data structure such as a hash table. This is known as a container class, because it "contains" the data structure. You attach that data structure to some other class by declaring an instance of it inside the class as another field. A class is just a datatype remember. Declaring a class inside another just sets up a reference variable to the class with no special privileges or relationship. In contrast, inheritance says the subclass is a variation of the superclass that extends its semantics in some way.

The way to distinguish between these two cases is to ask yourself the "is a" versus "has a" question. Let's assume you have a "car" class and an "engine" class, and you want to decide whether to use inheritance or nesting to associate the two. Would you say "a car has an engine" or "a car is an engine?" If the answer is "has a" use nesting. If the answer is "is a", use inheritance. Similarly, if we have a "mammal" class and a "dog" class, we would tend to say that a "dog is a mammal" so we would use inheritance to extend the mammal class resulting in the dog class.

The rule of thumb is that inheritance is for specialization of a type, and container classes are for code re-use. 🌿

Inheritance and Constructors

At the beginning of this section on inheritance, we suggested the feature could be used to extend Window to support ImportantWindow. Here is the actual code that would do that.

First, review the code that implements Window. It can be seen in file $JAVAHOME/src/java/awt/Window.java. The class Window starts out like this:

```
class Window {

        Window(Frame parent) {        // constructor
                . . .
        }
    . . .
```

All you need to do is give the ImportantWindow class a constructor that just calls the ordinary Window constructor, then adds a line to give it the desired red background color. The ImportantWindow code (in full) looks like this:

```
class ImportantWindow extends Window {

        ImportantWindow(Frame pear) { // constructor
                super(pear);
                setBackground(Color.red);
        }
}
```

(I have used the variable name "pear" to make clear what is a Java keyword, and what is a name the programmer provides).

That's all it takes! This really demonstrates the power of inheritance. Now wherever you were going to use a Window, you could instead use an ImportantWindow that has all the same methods and data, but comes up colored red.

```
// a regular window
Window mywin = new Window(someframe);

// my special window
ImportantWindow alert = new ImportantWindow(myframe);
```

Take another look at the constructor in the ImportantWindow class. That line of code that reads "super(pear)" is a common idiom when one class extends another. The code "super( )" is the way you express "call the constructor of my superclass." That's exactly what we want here: a regular Window to be constructed, and then its color to be changed to red.

As it happens, a superclass constructor is *always* invoked when you create a subclass object. If you don't explicitly call a superclass constructor, then the no-arg constructor of the superclass is called for you. If the superclass doesn't have a no-arg constructor (either an implicit one because you didn't provide any constructors, or an explicit no-arg constructor that you did provide) then you get a compilation error along the lines of "no constructor found in superclass."

Another idiom you may use is "this(...)" to call a different constructor in the same class. Normally "this" in a method means "the object I was invoked on." Here it is re-used to mean "one of my other constructors—pick the one with the matching signature." You would typically call one constructor from another when you have several constructors to allow arguments of several different types. Each constructor will put its arguments in standard form, and then call the main constructor that handles all the rest of the work. When one constructor explicitly invokes another (either super() or this()), that invocation must be the very first statement in the constructor. It's easy to rationalize why, for a couple of reasons. First, something is fully created after a constructor has been completed, and second, something must be fully created before you can start playing around with its fields.

Here is an example of one constructor invoking another with this() (no inheritance is involved here).

```
class FruitPie {
        // data fields
        double weight;
        java.util.Date    whenmade;

        // One constructor
        FruitPie(int i) {
                this( (double) i );    // calls second constructor
        }

        // Second constructor
        FruitPie(double d) {
            weight = d;
            whenmade = new java.util.Date();
        }

        // ... other methods ....

}
```

calls the sibling constructor whose arguments match

Forcing the Method: Abstract and Final

There are two further fine-tuning adjustments to inheritance, available to experts, namely "abstract" and "final". They qualify classes by appearing right at the beginning, before the keyword "class". In some sense, "abstract" and "final" are opposites of each other.

When the keyword "final" appears at the start of a class declaration, it means "No one can extend this class." Similarly, an individual method can be made "final" preventing it being overridden when its class is inherited. It is final in the sense that it is the leaf of an inheritance tree. Typically, you might wish to prevent further inheritance to avoid further specialization: you don't want to permit this type to be adjusted any more. One practical example concerns the thread class. People writing multi-threaded programs will extend the Thread class, but the system implementors must prevent people from accidentally or deliberately redefining the individual methods that do Thread housekeeping, like:

```
public final synchronized void stop(Object o) { ...
public final native boolean isAlive();
public final void suspend() { ...
public final void resume() { ...
public final void setPriority(int newPriority) ...
public final ThreadGroup getThreadGroup() { ...
```

Making the methods "final" accomplishes this neatly. A "final" method is also a clue to the compiler to inline the code. Inlining the code means optimizing out the overhead of a method call by taking the statements in the body of the method and duplicating them inline instead of making the call. This is a classic space versus time trade-off.

When the keyword "abstract" appears at the start of a class declaration, it means that zero or more of its methods are abstract. An abstract method has no body; its purpose is to force a subclass to override it and provide a concrete implementation of it. For example, you may have a class that implements a waterborne vehicle type, expecting it to later be extended to implement a ship, a boat, a canoe class. All of these vehicles can be pointed in a given direction, so it would be reasonable to provide an abstract "Set_Direction()" method in the superclass, forcing this to be provided in the subclass.

```
abstract class WaterBorneTransport {

    abstract void set_direction (int n);
    abstract void set_speed (int n);

}
```

You cannot create ("instantiate") an object of an abstract class. Making a class abstract forces a programmer to extend it and fill in some more details in the subclass before it can be used. You inherit as usual, like so:

```
class Canoe extends WaterBorneTransport {

    void set_direction (int n) { ...
    void set_speed (int n) { ...

}
```

Multiple Inheritance

You may hear references to "multiple inheritance." This means deriving from more than one base class at once. The resulting subclass thus has characteristics from more than one immediate parent type. It turns the tree hierarchy into a directed graph.

Multiple inheritance is much less common than single inheritance. Where it has appeared in languages (like C++) it has been the subject of considerable debate on whether it should be in the language at all. It is a difficult, bug-prone feature in both implementation and use. There are many complicated rules for how the namespaces of the two parent classes interact. Some people say that no convincing examples have been produced where there was no alternative design avoiding multiple inheritance. Java avoids the difficulties by not permitting multiple inheritance. The interface feature described in Chapter 4 helps fill in the gap left by multiple inheritance.

Say there is a class A with some data members, and classes B, and C inherit from A. Now have a class Doofus that multiply-inherits from B and C. Does it have one copy of A's data members, or two identical copies? When you access something in A, do you get B's or C's version of it? All this can be worked out, if you don't mind having a language reference manual the size of the Gutenberg Bible.

Visibility and Other Name Modifiers

You now know most of OOP in Java, and the tone of this chapter changes from conceptual to nitty-gritty details. Let's begin by noting that there are several keywords which control visibility, both of a class, and the individual fieldnames within a class. This section explains these keywords. Turn the corner of the page down—you'll be referring back to this often! Let's start by saying there's a way to group together several classes into a package. We'll talk more about this later, but for now, a package is a group of classes that you want to bundle together.

Class Modifiers

There are modifiers that you can apply to a class. When you declare a class, the general form looks like this:

syntax:

> *modifier* `class` *name* [`extends` *name*] [`implements` *namelist*] *body*

description:

> The modifier can be one or more of "abstract", "final" or "public" ("abstract" and "final" are opposites and are not allowed together).

> `abstract:`   class must be extended (to be useful)
>
> `final:`   class must not be extended
>
> `public:`   class is visible in other packages

examples:

```
abstract public class Fruit { ....
final public class Citrus extends Fruit { ....
```

Data Field Modifiers

The fields in a class body can be variables, or methods. The field can similarly start with a modifier that says how visible it is, and qualifies it in some other way. These are the modifiers that you can apply to a field that is data.

modifiers to data field:	explanation
`public`	field is visible everywhere (class must be public too)
(blank)	what you get by default. field is only visible in this package
`protected`	like default, *and* the field is visible in subclasses in other packages extended from this class, too. So protected is actually *less* protected than the default!
`private`	field is only visible in this class

(above are keywords that modify visibility)

(below are keywords that modify the way the field is used)

`static`	one per class, not one for each object—This is screwy re-use of the confusing C terminology that says static means "not allocated on the stack". It comes from the C keyword that says allocate this in the data segment at compile-time (i.e. statically). Where you see "static" read it as "only one."
`final`	cannot change value (is a constant)
`transient`	a hint used in object serialization. See Chapter 8.
`volatile`	this data may be written to by several threads of control, so the run-time system has to take care to always get the freshest value when reading it.

```
example: protected static final int upper_bound = 2047;
```

upper_bound is visible throughout this package, and in subclasses of this class even ones in other packages. The data is associated with the class, not an individual object, so any change made to it would be seen by all objects. It won't change though, because it has been assigned a final value.

Method Field Modifiers

These are modifiers that you can apply to a field that is a method.

modifiers to a method:	explanation
`public`	field is visible everywhere (the class must be public too)
(blank)	the default—field is visible in this package
`protected`	like the default, and the field is visible in subclasses in other packages too (so protected is *less* protected than the default!)
`private`	field is only visible in this class (and so can never be declared abstract, as it's not visible to be overridden).

(above are keywords that modify visibility)

(below are keywords that modify the way the method is used)

`final`	cannot be overridden
`static`	one per class, not one for each object (and is therefore implicitly final, because overriding is done based on the type of the object, and static methods are attached to a class, not an object.)
`abstract`	must be overridden (to be useful)
`native`	not written in Java (no body, but otherwise normal and can be inherited, static, etc.) The body will be written in another language.
`synchronized`	only one thread may execute in the method for a given object at a time. Entry to the method is protected by a monitor lock around it.

example: `protected abstract int total_calories() { ... }`

Note: several of these modifiers can be chosen together, such as "native protected". We will revisit the semantics of visibility in Chapter 4 when we cover packages. For now, think "package = library". Some combinations of modifier do not make sense, and are not permitted. A method cannot be both abstract *and* final for instance. That would say "you have to override me" *and* "you may not override me." A constructor can only be qualified with public, private and protected.

Don't make any fields public without good reason. In general you should give things the most restricted visibility that still makes it possible for them to work.

Static

There are three varieties of static thing (once-only) in Java. A static thing is something in a class that occurs once only, instead of once for each instance of the class.

Static Data

So far we have explained a class in terms of a template: any object of the class gets its own copy of all the data fields. Usually this is exactly what you want. There is a way to change it though, and label a data field as occurring just once, no matter how many instances of the class there are. This is what the keyword "static" does, as shown below.

```
class Employee {
     String[]  name;
     long      salary;
     short     employee_number;

  static int total_employees;

   ...
}
```

The purpose of the Employee class is to store and process data on an individual employee. However, we also use the class to hold the total number of employees that we have on the payroll. The variable total_employees is a quantity associated with employees in general, so this class might be a good home for it. But it's wasteful and error-prone to duplicate this value in every employee object. total_employees is a value associated with the class as a whole, not each object of it. Applying the storage modifier "static" to a data field makes that happen.

The "static" keyword means that there is just one of these fields, and it is shared by all objects in the class.

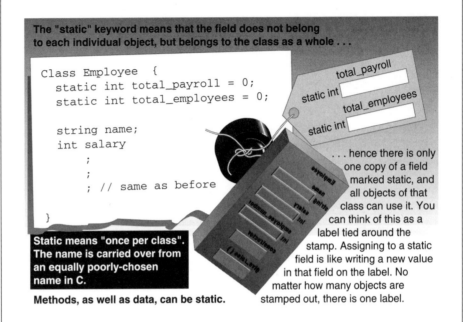

The "static" keyword means that the field does not belong to each individual object, but belongs to the class as a whole . . .

```
Class Employee {
    static int total_payroll = 0;
    static int total_employees = 0;

    string name;
    int salary
       ;
       ;
       ; // same as before

}
```

total_payroll

static int

total_employees

static int

. . . hence there is only one copy of a field marked static, and all objects of that class can use it. You can think of this as a label tied around the stamp. Assigning to a static field is like writing a new value in that field on the label. No matter how many objects are stamped out, there is one label.

Static means "once per class". The name is carried over from an equally poorly-chosen name in C.

Methods, as well as data, can be static.

Static (think "one per class") data is useful for any data that belongs to the class as a whole rather than any instance of it. A version id, and a running total are two examples of this kind of data.

Figure 2-8: "Static" means "only one for the whole class.

Inside the class, static data is accessed by giving its name. Outside the class, static data can be accessed by prefixing it with the name of an object, or the name of the class. Either works, as the following example shows:

```
Employee newhire = new Employee();
newhire.total_employees++; // reference through an instance

Employee.total_employees =0; // reference through the class
```

The second form, referencing static variables through the class name, is preferred because it provides a cue that this is not instance data. Static variables are also called class variables.

Static Methods

Just as there can be static data that belongs to the class as a whole, there can also be static methods (also called "class methods") that do some class-wide operations, and do not apply to an individual object. Again, these are highlighted by using the modifier "static" before the method name. Again, you can call a static method by prefixing it with the name of an object or the name of the class. It is always better to call it using the name of the class so that people don't confuse it with per-instance methods. Here is an example:

```
class Employee {
        String[] name;
        long      salary;
        short     employee_number;

    static int total_employees;

    static void clear() {
        total_employees = 0;
    }

 ...


    newhire.clear();  // reference through an instance

    Employee.clear();  // better: reference through the class
```

Methods, as well as data, can be labeled as "static", meaning "there is only one of these for the class", not "one per object". The "main( )" method, where execution begins in an application is a static method.

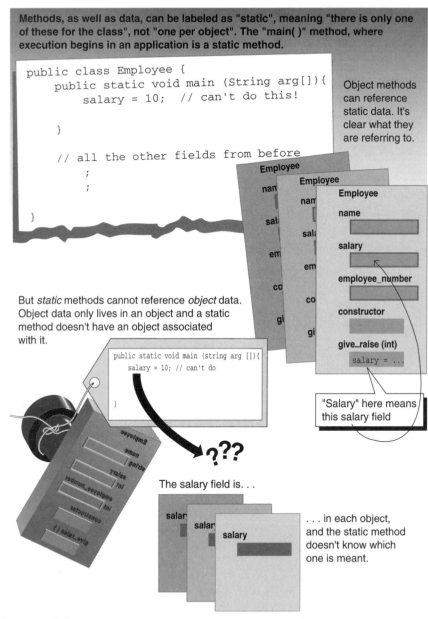

```
public class Employee {
    public static void main (String arg[]){
        salary = 10;   // can't do this!

    }

    // all the other fields from before
        ;
        ;

}
```

Object methods can reference static data. It's clear what they are referring to.

But *static* methods cannot reference *object* data. Object data only lives in an object and a static method doesn't have an object associated with it.

```
public static void main (string arg []){
    salary = 10; // can't do

}
```

Employee

name

salary

employee_number

constructor

give_raise (int)
  salary = ...

"Salary" here means this salary field

?‽?

The salary field is. . .

salary

. . . in each object, and the static method doesn't know which one is meant.

Figure 2-9: Static methods cannot directly reference per-object data.

A common pitfall is to reference <u>per-object</u> data from a <u>static</u> method. This "does not compute," as a static method is associated with a class, not an object. The compiler doesn't know which object you have in mind..

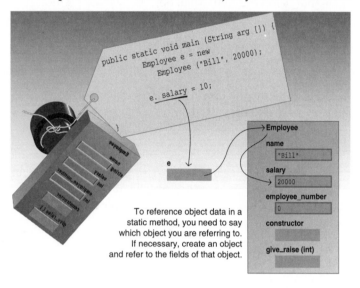

One way to reference instance (per-object) data and methods from a static method is to declare and instantiate an object in the static method. You can then access the data and methods of that instance.

We've already let the cat out of the bag about not really keeping "per instance" copies of instance methods. So what is a static method used for?

You declare a method static when it does something relating to the class as a whole, rather than specific to one instance. The class `java.lang.String` has several `valueOf()` methods that take a primitive type (boolean, int, etc.) argument and return its value as a String. These methods are static, so you can invoke them without needing a string instance. E.g.,

```
String s=String.valueOf(123.45); // OK
```

The `java.lang.Math` package is all static methods: abs(), sin(), cos(), exp(), and so on.

Finally, the main() method where execution starts is static. If it weren't, there would have to be some bogus magic to create an instance before calling it.

Figure 2-10:   Static methods must specify the object containing the per-object data that they want to reference..

Be aware of this "wrinkle"—static methods cannot access any instance data. In other words, the static routine clear() does not have an implicit "this" parameter, is not applied to an individual object, and therefore cannot touch the data fields or call the methods that belong to individual objects. A static method can only directly access other static fields. You will encounter an error message like:

"Can't make static reference to non-static variable"

if you try to access an instance variable from a static method.

One workaround is to declare an object inside the class, and use that instance to touch the fields or (more usually) call the non-static methods you need. 🐌

Static Blocks

The final kind of static thing is a static block. This is a portion of executable code belonging to the class, commonly used for initialization. A static block is executed once only when the class is first loaded. The keyword "static" precedes the curly braces that delimit the static block, as shown here:

```
public class Employee {
        String[] name;
        long      salary;
        short     employee_number;

        static int total_employees;

        static {
    System.out.println("Calculating how many employees");
            if ( some_condition )
                 total_employees =100;
            else total_employees =0;
        }
}
```

Once again, static blocks can only access static data. There can be multiple static blocks in a class, and they are executed in the order in which they occur in the source. They are most useful for sophisticated initialization or guaranteed one-time only initialization.

Of all the many names in Java which are poorly-chosen, "static" is the very worst. It is a legacy from the confusing and confused "static" keyword in C. Static never made much sense in C either—the term originated with data that was allocated statically in the data segment at compile time, but it was re-used with other meanings too. Whenever you see "static" in Java, think "once only".

Polymorphism

Polymorphism is a horrible name for a straightfoward concept. It is Greek for "many shapes", and it means using the same one name to refer to different methods. "Name sharing" would be a better term. There are two types of polymorphism in Java: the trivial kind and the interesting kind.

The trivial kind of polymorphism is called "overloading" in Java and other languages, and it means that in any class you can use the same name for several different (but hopefully related) methods. However, the methods must have different numbers and/or types of parameters so the compiler can tell which of the synonyms is intended. The return type is not looked at when disambiguating polymorphic functions in Java.

The I/O facilities of a language are one canonical place where the overloading kind of polymorphism is used. You don't want to have an I/O class that requires a different method name depending on whether you are trying to print a short, an int, a long, etc. You just want to be able to say "print(foo)". Note that C fails to meet this requirement. Although you use the same routine "printf", it also needs a format specifier (which is a statement in a particularly ugly programming language in its own right) to tell printf what argument types to expect and to output. If you change the type of the C value you are outputting, you usually need to change the format specifier too.

The second, more complicated kind of polymorphism, true polymorphism, is resolved dynamically (at runtime). It occurs when a subclass class has a method with the same name and signature (number, type and order of parameters) as a method in the superclass. When this happens, the method in the derived class overrides the method in the superclass. An example should make this clear.

Let's go back to our base class Fruit, and our subclass Citrus. We will give Citrus a "peel" method of its own, to reflect the fact that citrus fruits are peeled differently to many other kinds of fruit. Let's assume for the purposes of this example, that all citrus fruit are carefully peeled to preserve the zest. We don't honor non-citrus fruits with this care. We add a "peel()" method to our base class:

```
class Fruit {
        int grams;
        int cals_per_gram;

        int total_calories ( ) { /* ... */ }
        void peel ( ) {System.out.println("peel a Fruit"); }
}
```

The subclass gets its own version of peel:

```
class Citrus extends Fruit {
        void squeeze() {  /* ... */ }
        void peel () {System.out.println("peel a Citrus"); }
}
```

The method peel() in Citrus replaces or overrides the superclass's version of peel() when the method is invoked on a Citrus object. C++ programmers will note that you do not need to specifically point out to the compiler (with the C++ "virtual" keyword) that overriding will take place. Here's an example:

```
class Example {
      public static void main(String args[]) {
          Fruit somefruit= new Fruit();
          Citrus lemon = new Citrus();

          somefruit.peel();
          lemon.peel();

          somefruit = lemon;
          somefruit.peel();
      }
}
```

If you try running this, you will note that when we apply the peel method to some-fruit, we get the base class version (it prints "peel a Fruit"). When we apply the peel method to lemon, we get the Citrus specialized version (it prints "peel a Citrus")

 When we apply the peel method to something which starts out as a general Fruit, but may have been assigned a Citrus at runtime, the correct peeling method is chosen at runtime, based on what the object is. And *that* is polymorphism. 🍒

> **The Difference Between Overloading and Overriding**
>
> Overloading, the trivial kind of polymorphism, is resolved by the compiler at compile time. Overloading allows several methods to have the same one name, and the compiler will choose the one you meant, by matching on argument types.
>
> Overriding, the fancy kind of polymorphism is resolved at runtime. It occurs when one class extends another, and the subclass has a method with same signature (exact match of name and argument types) as a method in the superclass. Question: which of them gets invoked? Answer: if it's an object of the subclass, the subclass one; if it's an object of the superclass, the superclass one. The reason this is "fancy" is that sometimes you cannot tell until runtime, so the compiler must plant code to work out which method is appropriate for whatever this object turns out to be, then call that at runtime.

The technical term for "choosing the correct method for whatever object this is at runtime" is "late binding" or "delayed binding." Polymorphism is the language feature that allows two methods to have the same name, such that late binding may be applied.

Some Light Relief

The Binary Burger—one byte is all you need.

Not too long ago, the fast food chain Burger King was proudly advertising the many choices they offered a customer. Burger King ads boasted of the 1024 ways a customer could order their Whopper burger.

Not "hundreds of ways" or "over 1000 ways," but "1024 ways." The number 1024 immediately jumps out at experienced programmers because it is 2^{10}, also known as a K, as in "They're offering a \$5K sign-on bonus at Flibbertigibbet Software, so I need you to at least match that, 'K?"

Naturally a few programmers with too much imagination and free time on their hands tried to decode what the ten binary variables were in the Burger King world of choices. Here's what we came up with:

- single or double
- mayo,
- lettuce,
- cheese,
- pickles,
- onion,
- tomato,
- mustard,
- ketchup

That's only nine. The tenth variable? It's something only a hacker would expect—it's the beef! Yep, one of the parameters that Burger King was apparently counting among its 1024 choices for the Whopper burger was "no burger." You heard it: go to Burger King and order a Veggie Burger and see what you get.

Even better, order a "double patty, with no patty." This kind of boolean confusion is precisely why Hamburger University just does not get the same kind of respect as, say, MIT or Caltech.

Glossary

class: a class is a user-defined type, just as int is a built-in type (some classes are predefined in Java, too). The built-in types have well-defined operations (arithmetic etc.) on them, and the class mechanism must allow the programmer to specify operations on the class types he or she defines, too. Anything in a class is known as a member of the class. Member functions of a class are also known as methods. Data members of a class are also known as fields.

object: an object variable is a reference to a specific instance variable of a class type.

data abstraction: refining out the essential data types to represent some real-world property.

encapsulation: encapsulation means grouping together the types, data, and functions that make up a class, and providing some information hiding to control access. In C, a header file provides a very weak example of encapsulation. It is a feeble example because it is a purely lexical convention, and the compiler knows nothing about the header file as a semantic unit.

inheritance: this means allowing one class to receive the data structures and functions described in a simpler base class. The extended class gets the operations and data of the superclass, and can specialize or customize them as needed. There's no example in C that suggests the concept of inheritance. C does not have anything resembling this feature.

polymorphism: reusing the same name for a related concept on different types. The system will choose which method is meant either by overloading (a compile-time match—which method has the matching argument types?) or by overriding (a run time match, which method was defined for this kind of object?)

Concept	Java term	C++ term
function in class	method	member function*
class that is expected to be extended	abstract	virtual
anything in class	member	member
parent relationship with another class	extend	inherit
class you extend	superclass	base class
extended class	subclass	derived class
initialization	constructor method	constructor
finalization method	finalizer (in part)	destructor

*("method" is also used)

Exercises

1. What are the four attributes that distinguish Object-Oriented Programming? What are some advantages and disadvantages of OOP?

2. Give 3 examples of primitive types, and 3 examples of pre-defined Java classes (i.e. object types).

3. What is the key difference between primitive types and object types? Show some code to illustrate the difference.

4. What is the default constructor, and when is it called? What is a no-arg constructor? Can the default constructor be an "arg" constructor?

5. Describe overriding, and write some code to show an example.

6. Consider the following three related classes:

```
class Mammal {}
class Dog extends Mammal { }
class Cat extends Mammal { }
```

There are these variables of each class:
```
Mammal m;
Dog d = new Dog( );
Cat c = new Cat( );
```

Which of these statements will cause an error at compile time, and why? Which of these statements may cause an error at run time and why?

```
m = d;
d = m;
d = (Dog) m;
d = c;
d = (Dog) c;
```

Some Answers to the Exercises

6. The first statement is the only one that is guaranteed both to compile and run without problems:

```
m = d;
```

The statement assigns from the specific (dog) to the general (mammal). All dogs are also mammals, so can be assigned to a variable that refers to mammals.

This statement fails to compile because a mammal is not necessarily a dog.

```
d = m;          // doesn't compile, needs cast.
```

It could be a cow, a pig or a cat. It could even be just a mammal in general, without being more specific. So to make this assignment, we need to use a cast, to assert that this "m" is a dog, and we are converting it (casting it) to be one as shown in the next statement.

This statement compiles without problems. It may fail at runtime however.

```
d = (Dog) m;        // may fail at runtime with
                       ClassCastException
```

At runtime, the class of "m" is checked. If it is not a dog or a subclass of dog (e.g., Dalmatian, Labrador, Chow), then the statement fails and throws a ClassCastException.

This statement fails to compile because a cat is not a dog.

```
d = c;          // doesn't compile, incompatible
                   type
```

This statement fails to compile because a cat is not a dog, even if you try to force it to become one by casting. The compiler is not fooled.

```
d = (Dog) c;    // doesn't compile, invalid cast
```

The general rules for casting classes are

- You can always assign parent = child; a cast is not needed, because a specific child class also belongs to its general parent class. You can assign several levels up the hierarchy, that is the "parent" may be a more remote ancestor.

- You can cast child = (child) parent, and it will be checked at runtime. If the parent is referring to the correct child type, the assignment will occur.

- You cannot cast between arbitrary unrelated classes.

Further Reading

The Tao of Objects

by Gary Entsminger

publ. M&T Books, Redwood City, CA 1990

ISBN 1-55851-155-5

An excellent beginner's guide to object-oriented programming. It features practical examples in C++ and Turbo Pascal (OK, that part is a bit dated) in a friendly, hands-on, jargon-free text.

Pitfalls of Object-Oriented Development

by Bruce F. Webster

publ M&T Books, New York 1995

ISBN 1-55851-397-3

Eiffel The Language

by Bertrand Meyer

publ. Prentice Hall, Herts England, 1992

ISBN 0-13-247925-7

A comprehensive reference, tutorial, and user's manual all rolled into one large book, describing the Eiffel language. Eiffel has been around for about a decade and has several interesting ideas. It is an improvement on C++ in several areas, such as generic classes, but is much less widely used. The book (and the language) does not flinch from offering challenging ideas.

Expert C Programming

by Peter van der Linden

Prentice Hall/SunSoft Press, 1994

ISBN 0-13-177429-8

Take a look at this book if you already know C pretty well and want to learn some of the tips and techniques used in Sun's compiler and OS kernel groups.

CHAPTER

3

- GIGO
- The Anatomy of an Application
- Identifiers
- Operators
- Evaluating Expressions

The Java Programming Language

"My friend George Mallory, who later disappeared close to the summit of Mt. Everest, once did an inexplicable climb on Mount Snowdon. He had left his pipe on a ledge, halfway down one of the Lliwedd precipices, and scrambled back by a shortcut to retrieve it, then up again by the same route. No one saw just how he did the climb, but when they came to examine it the next day for official record, they found it was an impossible overhang nearly all the way.

By a rule of the Climbers' Club, climbs are never named in honor of their inventors, but only describe natural features. An exception was made here. The climb was recorded as follows: "Mallory's Pipe, a variation on route 2; this climb is totally impossible. It has been performed once in failing light by Mr. G.H.L. Mallory."'

"Good-bye to All That," Robert Graves

Call me an old skeptic, but I've always had trouble swallowing the story of Mallory's Pipe. The details about "no one saw just how he did it" gives it away. I'll tell you just how Mallory did it—he was a young man with a robust sense of humor, and he intended to tweak the noses of the staid and proper Climbers' Club. So one evening, as everyone is exhausted after the day's climbing he "discovers" his pipe is missing, and "remembers" dropping it next to an alpine goat high on a crag. He announces he's going back to get it, and hurries off out of sight round the corner to wait for a decent interval before pulling the pipe out of his pocket and strolling back with a tale of an obviously impossible shortcut. The next morning, the goobers don't even realize they're being twitted and before he can stop them they've made public a proposal to name the climb in his honor! No backing down now, so he just has to go through with it. Mallory's Pipe should really be called Mallory's Leg-pull. The point is that things are not always what they seem, or what you are told.

Despite protestations that you may hear to the contrary, Java is not a small language, and is not well served by a small book. The Java language and libraries are extensive, and require some time to learn. The saving grace is that, while large, the system is not unduly complicated. The standard technique of dividing the whole into smaller parts and looking at each individually works well. If you already know C, you only have a little more to learn. If you already know C++, you only have a little to unlearn. No one part poses a huge challenge, and by the end of the text we will have studied all the parts. This technique is also known as "divide and conquer", which may bring to mind the association with the Pentium chip and its flawed division algorithm.

Ever since "The C Programming Language" was published in 1978 writers of programming text books have been using the "Hello World" program as the introductory example. Writers: get a clue! Programmers deserve a bit of innovation. To provide a refreshing change from the overexposed "Hello World" example we use a different program. Our example is the code snippet that exposes the defective division hardware in the Pentium chip.

GIGO: Garbage In, Garbage Out

In mid 1993, Intel launched the latest and greatest chip in its x86 family, the Pentium microprocessor. Intel spent millions of dollars to introduce the Pentium to the market and promote brand recognition using the slogan "Intel inside."

For about eighteen months everything went smoothly. Then on October 30, 1994, mathematics professor Thomas Nicely reported in a message on Compuserve that the Pentium gave an inaccurate result for some division operands. Professor Nicely had called Intel a week earlier to inform them of his findings, only to be told that no one else had complained. The bug was speedily reproduced and analyzed on several Usenet newsgroups, at which point the affair started to play out at high speed. Everything related to the Internet seems to happen at least seven times faster than the rest of life, which is why people refer to "Internet months" as being like "dog months."

After the matter was reported in the EE Times of November 7, 1994, instead of soothing Pentium-owners, Intel made matters far worse by implying that the problem wasn't important, that they'd known about it all along, and that most users didn't need accurate division. Pentium owners everywhere were outraged at the message that Intel had knowingly sold them a flawed chip, and didn't intend to do anything about it.

Public opinion shifted rapidly against the chip maker, and in a classic example of too little, too late, Intel announced on November 23 that it would supply replacement chips—but only to customers that it deemed worthy of accurate division. On December 12, IBM took the moral high road and increased the pressure on its rival by announcing that it was halting shipment of Pentium systems until error-free chips were available. At this point it became inevitable that Intel would be forced to support the consumer brand image they had created, or else cede the market to a more customer-driven organization.

Intel continued to be castigated on television and in numerous newspaper editorials. It managed to hold out until December 20, when mounting public pressure became intolerable. Intel's president Andy Grove reluctantly went public with sackcloth and ashes, and offered a free replacement Pentium to anyone who wanted one.

The surprising part of the affair wasn't the actual chip bug, but Intel's hubris and intransigence in dealing with it. All chip manufacturers encounter hardware problems of this kind. The accepted procedure is to mitigate the effects with compiler workarounds, and correct them in later revisions ("steppings") of the silicon. Intel's early failure to acknowledge the problem and offer users help with workarounds portrayed the company as recalcitrant, high-handed, and even dishonest. The initial failure to adequately address users' fears cost Intel dearly, $475M according to the San Jose Mercury News (Dec. 26, 1995). Many jokes circulated about "Intel inside" being a product liability warning, and so on.

The Pentium circuitry uses a subtractive division algorithm based on a radix-4 Booth SRT algorithm. It uses a table lookup to obtain an intermediate result. Five entries in the on-chip stored table of 2048 entries had bad values, causing some results that should have been accurate to seven significant figures to only be accurate to four significant figures.

Several people posted examples of operands that were known to produce inaccurate results. One was 1 / 12884897291. Another was 5505001 / 294911. It was a straightforward matter to write a small program that would output a bad result on a Pentium and the right answer on all other hardware.

This code was posted to Usenet by Thomas Koenig of the University of Karlsruhe in Germany. In C, it looks like this:

(C CODE)

```c
#include <stdio.h>
int main()
{
    double x,y,z;

    x = 4195835.0;
    y = 3145727.0;
    z = x - (x / y) * y;
    printf("result = %f \n",z);
    return 0;
}
```

On a defective Pentium, this program prints "256.000000"; on other machines Intel and non-Intel, it prints "0.000000". In Java the same program looks like:

(Java CODE)

```java
public class pentium {
    public static void main(String args[]) {
      double x,y,z;
      x = 4195835.0;
      y = 3145727.0;
      z = x - (x / y) * y;
      System.out.println("result = " + z);
    }
}
```

To compile this, put it in a file called "pentium.java" (it is important to use this exact filename and exact case of characters on case-sensitive systems) and issue the command:

```
javac pentium.java
```

When it has successfully compiled, run it by giving the command:

```
java pentium
```

We will analyze this program in the same way that you peel an onion, layer by layer. To start, note that we simply have the declaration of a class called "pentium."

```
class pentium {
    public static void main(String args[]) {
    double x,y,z;
    x = 4195835.0;
    y = 3145727.0;
    z = x - (x / y) * y;
    System.out.println("result = " + z);
    }
}
```

Inside the class is a single public method called "main"

```
    public static void main(String args[]) {
    double x,y,z;
    x = 4195835.0;
    y = 3145727.0;
    z = x - (x / y) * y;
    System.out.println("result = " + z);
    }
```

Right from the start, let's note a big difference between Java and C/C++. In Java, main() is defined to return a void (no value). In C, main() is defined to return an int. If you have declared any C programs as "void main(void)" go and correct them now, before anyone sees such sloppy coding.

Applications vs. Applets

Just as in C, the signature of this function is magic and it tells the runtime system to start execution here. It turns out that there are two different ways to run a Java executable:

- as a stand-alone program that can be invoked from the command line. This is termed an "application".

- as a program embedded in a web page, to be run when the page is browsed. This is termed an "applet". Just as a booklet is a little book, an applet is a little application.

The original intent was that applets would be small programs, but this distinction is going to be increasingly irrelevant. There's nothing in the Java system to establish any size limitations on applets.

Applications and applets differ in the default execution privileges they have, and also the way they indicate where to start execution. The example here shows an application; we will deal with applets in Chapter 7.

The Anatomy of an Application

Looking at the signature of main(),

```
public static void main(String args[]) {
```

the modifiers say that the function is public and static, namely visible everywhere (public), and can be called using the classname (static) without needing to instantiate.

Static methods are often used as the equivalent of global functions in C.

The main() routine where execution starts is a static method. It is associated with the class where the program starts, not any one instance object. So static makes sense for it. This leads to a very common and frustrating pitfall: trying to invoke an object method from the static (class) main method like so:

```
 ...
 public static void main () {//this is a static function
       SomeMethod();//NO! NO! NO!
   }

       void SomeMethod() {  }// NOT a static function
  // so can't be invoked from main ()

SomeClass.java:4: Can't make static reference to
            method void SomeMethod() in class SomeClass. 
```

There are two ways to get past this. The simplest way is to make the referenced field static too. But if the field has to be non-static because each object needs its own copy, then instantiate an object whose purpose is to be the "this" variable in the call. e.g.

```
       public static void main(String args[]) {
           // we want to invoke the instance
"SomeClass.someMethod()"
           SomeClass daffodil = new SomeClass();
           daffodil.someMethod();
```

It is a frequently-seen idiom to have the class that contains the main() function be instantiated inside the main() function, like this:

```
class pentium {
    void someMethod ( ...

    public static void main(String args[]) {
        pentium p = new pentium();     //weird looking, no?
```

```
    p.someMethod();
```

It looks weirdly recursive the first time you see it. Think of it this way: the class definition is a datatype. All you are doing is declaring an instance of that datatype at a point when you need one (which happens to be inside the original datatype definition).

Passing over the modifiers, the actual function is:

```
    void main(String args[]) {
```

Again, not that far away from C. It declares a function called "main" which has no return value, and takes just one argument called "args" (as in C, the parameter name doesn't matter, just its data type) which is an array of Strings. The empty bracket pair says that the function is not restricted to any one size of array. These Strings are the command line arguments with which the program was invoked. "String" is a class in Java, with more to it than just the nul-terminated character array it is in C.

An "argc" count is not needed, because all arrays have a length field which is a final variable (you cannot assign to it) holding the size of the array. In place of argc you would use "args.length"—the number of Strings in the args array, not the length of any one String in it, of course.

The zeroth argument in the args array is the first command line argument, *not* the program name as in C and C++. The program name is already known inside the program: it is the name of the class that contains the "main()" function. The name of this class will match the name of the file that it is in.

If you called it something different, change it. You will confuse yourself and parts of the Java compiler system. This framework is all that is needed to indicate the entry point program where execution will start.

The statements in main will be immediately clear to any programmer. Java has adopted wholesale the basic statements of C++, which in turn come directly from C. The first line of the body of main declares three double precision floating point variables, x, y, and z.

```
    public static void main(String args[]) {
        double x,y,z;
        x = 4195835.0;
        y = 3145727.0;
        z = x - (x / y) * y;
        System.out.println("result = " + z);
    }
```

The next two lines assign a couple of literal values. The third line is the one that exposes the Pentium flaw. If you examine the arithmetic expression, it should be clear that it cancels out to zero.

Finally, the last statement prints out the value. It refers to a library class called "System" that contains an object called "out" that has a method called "println". "out" does basic character output. You have to explicitly name at the top of your source file all packages that you use, with the exception of the built-in Java language package, which includes the class System used here.

> The first few lines of main () are just regular arithmetic, but in that last line Java uses the plus sign, +, as an operator to concatenate Strings. This is one of the places in the language where Strings are helped a little with some built-in support, without creating a general mechanism that can be applied to every user-defined type as well.
>
> Whenever a String appears as one operand of "+", the compiler does not do an arithmetic addition, but tries to convert the other operand to a String and then concatenates the two. In fact, concatenating an empty String with a value of a primitive type is a Java idiom to convert the value to a String, like so:
>
> ```
>         int i = 256;
>
>             ...
>
>
>         "" + i       // yields a String containing the value of i.
> ```
> That's much shorter than the obvious alternative of using the static method of the String class:
>
> ```
>         String.valueOf( i )
> ```
> In the case of the Pentium code, the variable z is converted to a String, and appended to the literal message. Then that entire String is passed as a single argument to the println() method, causing it to be printed to the system console.

The fact that the language features strict left-to-right evaluation makes a big difference here!

```
    "Your 2 values are:" + 2 + 3
```

evaluates to the String

```
    "Your 2 values are: 23"
```

But, putting the two integers first, like so

```
    2 + 3 + "are your 2 values"
```

evaluates to the String

```
"5 are your 2 values"
```

Be alert to this.

"Java means I won't have to learn C++!"

Libraries in the C sense are known as packages in Java, and like many things in Java, they are considerably simpler to use than the corresponding feature in other languages. Simplicity is a major advantage of Java. Programmers can devote all their brainpower to solving the problem, rather than trying to learn and remember the ten thousand complicated rules and the five thousand special cases of language or system. One of Silicon Valley's top programmers (and I mean really top programmers) confided to me "Thank heavens for Java—it means I won't have to learn C++." A lot of programmers share that sense of relief at being able to leapfrog over C++ and go directly to a simpler language that is fast replacing C++.

If the println in this program doesn't print zero, it's because the CPU arithmetic logic unit has returned an inaccurate result for one of the operations.

We're working from the middle out here. Having seen our first reasonable Java program, we'll next look at the small building blocks of individual tokens that the compiler sees.

Identifiers

Identifiers (names provided by the programmer) can be any length in Java. They must start with a letter, underscore, or dollar sign, and in subsequent positions can also contain digits.

Java has been designed with internationalization in mind, and it uses the 16-bit Unicode character set. So the character datatype takes 16 bits in Java, not the 8-bit byte that many other languages use. A letter that can be used for a Java identifier doesn't just mean upper- and lower-case A-Z. It means any of the tens of thousands of Unicode letters from any of the major languages in the world including Bengali letters, Cyrillic letters or Bopomofo symbols. Every Unicode character above hex C0 is legal in an identifier. The following are all valid Java identifiers:

Legal Java Identifiers

```
i
calories
$_99
Häagen_Dazs
déconnage
Puñetas
fottío
```

Java is going to be a major force pressuring OS vendors to adopt Unicode in the future.

Java and Unicode

The great majority of computer systems in use today employ the ASCII code set to represent characters. ASCII—the American Standard Code for Information Interchange—started out as a 7-bit code that represented upper and lower case letters, the digits 0 to 9, and a dozen or so control characters like NUL and EOT. As computing technology became pervasive in Western Europe, users demanded the ability to represent all characters in their national alphabets. ASCII was extended to 8 bits, with the additional 128 characters being used to represent various accented and diacritical characters not present in English. The extended 8-bit code is known as the ISO 8859-1 Latin-1 code set. It is reproduced for reference as an appendix at the end of this book.

But a more general solution was needed that included support for Asian languages, with their many thousands of ideograms. The solution that was chosen is Unicode. It is a 16-bit character set, supporting 65,536 different characters. About 21,000 of these are devoted to Han, the ideograms seen in Chinese, Japanese and Korean. The ISO Latin-1 code set forms most of the first 256 values, effectively making ASCII a subset of Unicode.

The two big disadvantages of Unicode are it is not compatible with existing Operating Systems that only support 8-bit characters, and it doubles the amount of storage needed for text files. Because of the compatibility problem Unicode is only supported well on new OS's, such as Microsoft's NT, Apple's ill-fated Pink, and Plan 9 from Bell. Various clever schemes (like the UTF approach in which characters are a variable number of bytes in length) have been tried to retrofit Unicode onto ASCII-based systems, but none of them are wholly satisfactory.

Java uses Unicode to represent characters internally. The external representation of characters (what you get when you print something, what you offer up to be read) is totally dependent on the services of the host operating system. On Unix,

Windows 95, and MacOS the character sets are all 8-bit based. When Java gets a character on these systems, the OS gives it 8 bits but Java immediately squirrels it away in a 16-bit datatype, and always processes it as 16 bits. This does away with the multibyte char complications in C, and special wide versions of the string-handling routines.

If at some future point the host system adopts Unicode, then only a few routines in the Java I/O library will need to be rewritten to accommodate it.

You can read more about the Unicode standard at http://www.unicode.org

However, be warned: For something that is conceptually so simple, the Unicode standard sets some kind of world record in obscurity, and all around lack of clarity. An example can be seen at http://www.unicode.org/unicode/standard/utf16.html, reproduced in the box below.

Extended UCS-2 Encoding Form (UTF-16)

The basic Unicode character repertoire and UCS-2 encoding form is based on the Basic Multilingual Plane (BMP) of ISO/IEC 10646. This plane comprises the first 65,536 code positions of ISO/IEC 10646's canonical code space (UCS-4, a 32-bit code space). Because of a decision by the Unicode Consortium to maintain synchronization between Unicode and ISO/IEC 10646, the Unicode Character Set may some day require access to other planes of 10646 outside the BMP. In order to accommodate this eventuality, the Unicode Consortium proposed an extension technique for encoding non-BMP characters in a UCS-2 Unicode string. This proposal was entitled UCS-2E, for extended UCS-2. This technique is now referred to as UTF-16 (for UCS Transformation Format 16 Bit Form).

Another way of saying all that is "Unicode characters are 16 bits, and UCS-4 characters are 32 bits. Right now, Unicode forms the least significant 16 bits of the 32-bit code, but that might get jumbled up in future in a new coding system called UTF-16." It's ironic (some programmers would say "predictable") that a standard whose purpose is to foster communication is so poorly written that it actually hinders the ready transmission of meaning.

Programming language standards are especially prone to being written in unintelligible gobbledygook. Programmers are too ready to excuse this, saying that "a standard is a formal contract between the language designer and compiler writers." As though that meant it couldn't be simple and clear too!

A language reference manual should be simple and clear enough that an average programmer can use it to learn the language. Alas, my request to transfer to the project to write the Java language specification was declined on the grounds that they "didn't want any light relief in it."

Comments

Java has the same comment conventions as C++.

Comments starting with //" go to the end of the line.

Comments starting with "/*" end at the next "*/".

Commenting out Code

Comments do not nest in Java, so to comment out a big section of code, you either put "//" at the start of every line, or you use "/*" at the front and immediately after every embedded closing comment, finishing up with your own closing comment at the end.

You can also use

```
if ( false ) {
    ...
}
```

around the section you want to temporarily delete. Each of these approaches has drawbacks. My preference is to use a smart editor that knows how to add or delete "//" from the beginning of each line. That way it is absolutely clear what is commented out. 🐾

There's a third variety of comment, one starting with "/**". This indicates text that will be picked up by javadoc, an automatic documentation generator. This is an implementation of the "literate programming" idea proposed by Donald Knuth. Javadoc parses the declarations and these special comments, and formats the text that it extracts into a set of HTML pages describing the API.

```
i = 0;  // the "to end-of-line" comment

/* the "regular multiline" comment
 */

/** the API comment for HTML documentation
    @version 1.12
    @author A.P.L. Byteswap
    @see SomeOtherClassName
    HTML tags can also be put in here.
 */
```

Try javadoc. Javadoc works on .java files, not .class files, because the .java files contain the comments. Run javadoc on any java source file that you created such as:

```
javadoc pentium.java
```

This will create a file called "pentium.html" which you can look at in your Web browser. It shows the chain of class inheritance, and all the public fields in the class. You can give javadoc an absolute pathname, or any pathname relative to a path in the CLASSPATH environment variable. Although CLASSPATH points to likely locations for .class files, the default behavior is to keep source and class files in the same directory. So javadoc can usually find .java files by following the CLASSPATH.

Whether you agree with the idea of using web pages to store program documentation or not (some people prefer to read documents bound in book form), it offers the compelling advantages that documentation automatically generated from the program source is much more likely to be (a) available, (b) accurate, (what could be more accurate than the documentation and the source being two views of the same thing?) and (c) complete. ❦

Keywords

Keywords are reserved words, and may not be overloaded for use as identifiers. ANSI C has only 32 keywords. Java has almost 60 keywords, including half-a-dozen reserved for future use, in case the language designers add to the language. The "gang of seven" in JavaSoft is kicking around some alternative proposals for templates (generic classes) at present. The keywords can be divided into several categories according to their main use:

Java keywords

Used for built-in types:

```
boolean   true      false
char
byte      short     int       long
float     double
void
```

Used in expressions:

```
null      new       this      super
```

Used in statements:

selection statements

```
if    else
switch    case    break    default
```

iteration statements

```
for    continue
do     while
```

transfer of control statements

```
return
throw
```

guarding statements (threads or exceptions)

```
synchronized
try    catch     finally
```

Used to modify declarations (scope, visibility, sharing etc.):

```
static
abstract    final
private     protected  public
transient   volatile
```

Used for other method or class-related purposes:

```
class       instanceof    throws    native
```

Used for larger-than-class building blocks:

```
extends
interface   implements
package     import
```

Reserved for possible future use:

```
cast        const       future     generic   goto
inner       operator    outer      rest      var
```

Operators

The operators in Java will be readily familiar to any programmer. The novel aspect is that the order of evaluation is well-defined. For many (not all) previous languages including C and C++, the order of evaluation of operands has been deliberately left unspecified. In other words the operands of a C expression like:

(C CODE)

```
i + a[i] + functioncall();
```

can be evaluated and added together in any order. The function may be called before, during (on adventurous multiprocessing hardware), or after the array reference is evaluated, and the additions may be executed in any order.

In the expression above if the "functioncall()" adjusts the value of "i", the overall result depends on the order of evaluation. This indeterminacy does not occur in Java.

Leaving the order of evaluation unspecified (as in C) is done for several reasons:

- Language philosophy. Since there is no reason to require L-to-R evaluation, the language neither promises nor forbids it.

- It makes it easier to write the compiler optimizer if it has complete freedom to change expressions into mathematically equivalent expressions. The generated code isn't necessarily faster, but the optimizer is easier to create and maintain.

- Common sub-expression elimination, and constant propagation are easier to identify. Often these opportunities arise from other optimizations like loop unrolling, rather than human code.

- It permits the compiler-writer the maximum opportunity to take advantage of values that are already in registers.

The trade-off is that some programs give different results depending on the order of evaluation. As professional programmers we know that such programs are badly written, but nonetheless they exist.

Java makes the trade-off in a different place. It recognizes that getting the same consistent results on all computer systems is more important than getting varying results a fraction faster on one system. In practice the opportunities for speeding up expression evaluation through reordering operands seem to be quite limited in many programs. As processor speed and cost has improved, it is appropriate that modern languages should optimize for programmer sanity instead of performance.

Note that the usual operator precedence still applies. In an expression like:

```
b + c * d
```

the multiplication is always done before the addition. It has to be done first, because the result is one operand of the addition.

What the Java order of evaluation says is that for all binary (two argument) operators the left operand is always fully evaluated before the right operand. Therefore, the operand "b" above must be evaluated before the multiplication is done (because the multiplied result is the right operand to the addition). 🍒

Left-to-right evaluation means in practice that all operands in an expression (if they are evaluated at all) are evaluated in the left-to-right order in which they are written down on a page. Sometimes an evaluated result must be stored while a higher precedence operation is performed. Although the Java Language Specification only talks about the apparent order of evaluation of operands to individual operators this is a necessary consequence of the rules.

Of course, some operands may not be evaluated at all. Evaluation of "||" and "&&" stops when enough of the expression has been evaluated to obtain the overall result. The point is that predictability in porting is a virtue that outweighs mathematical optimizations.

It's not just operands evaluation, but the order of everything else is defined in Java too. Specifically,

- The left operand is evaluated before the right operand of a binary operator. This is true even for the assignment operator, which must evaluate the left operand (where the result will be stored), fully before starting on the right operand (what the result is).

- In an array reference, the expression before the square brackets "[]" is fully evaluated before any part of the index is evaluated.

- A method call for an object has the general form
  object_instance.methodname(arguments);
  The "object_instance" is fully evaluated before the methodname and arguments are looked at. Then any arguments are evaluated one by one from left to right.

- In an allocation expression for an array of several dimensions, the dimension expressions are evaluated one by one from left to right.

The Language Specification uses the phrase "Java guarantees that the operands to operators *appear to be* evaluated from left-to-right." This is an escape clause that allows clever compiler-writers to do brilliant optimizations, as long as the appearance of left-to-right evaluation is maintained.

For example, compiler-writers can rely on the associativity of integer addition and multiplication. a+b+c will produce the same result as (a+b)+c or a+(b+c). This is true in Java even in the presence of overflow, because what happens on overflow is well-defined. The usual result of overflow when evaluating an integer expression is that you just get the low order bits that fit in an int.

If one of these subexpressions occurs in the same basic block, a clever compiler-writer might be able to arrange for its re-use. In general because of complications involving infinity and not-a-number (NaN)[1] results, floating point operands cannot be trivially reordered.

Associativity

Associativity is one of those subjects that is poorly explained in many programming texts, especially the ones that come from authors who are technical writers not programmers. In fact a good way to judge a programming text is to look for its explanation of associativity. Silence is not golden.

There are three factors that influence the ultimate value of an expression in any algorithmic language, and they work in this order: precedence, associativity, and order of evaluation. Precedence says that some operations bind more tightly than others. Precedence tells us that the multiplication in "a + b * c" will be done before the addition, i.e. we have "a + (b * c)" rather than "(a + b) * c". Precedence tells us how to bind operands in an expression that contains different operators.

Associativity is the tie breaker for deciding the binding when we have several operators of equal precedence strung together. If we have:

```
3 * 5 % 3
```

should we evaluate that as "(3 * 5) % 3" i.e. 15 % 3, or 0? Or should we evaluate it as "3 * (5 % 3)" i.e. 3 * 2, or 6? Multiplication and the "%" remainder operation have the same precedence, so precedence does not give the answer. But they are left-associative, meaning when you have a bunch of them strung together you start associating operators with operands from the left. Push the result back as a new operand, and continue until the expression is evaluated. In this case "(3 * 5) % 3" is the correct grouping.

"Associativity" is a terrible name for the process of deciding which operands belong with which operators of equal precedence. A more meaningful description

1.   See next chapter.

would be *"Code Order For Finding/Evaluating Equal Precedence Operator Text-strings."* Let me know if you find a good mnemonic for that in Java.

Note that associativity deals solely with deciding which operands go with which of a sequence of adjacent operators of equal precedence. It doesn't say anything about the order in which those operands are evaluated.

The order of evaluation, if it is specified in a language, tells us the sequence (for each operator) in which the operands are evaluated. In a strict left-to-right language like Java, the order of evaluation tells us that in "(i=2) * i++" the left operand to the multiplication will be evaluated before the right operand, then the multiplication will be done, yielding a result of 4, with i set to 3. Why isn't the auto-increment done before the multiplication? It has a higher precedence after all. The reason is because it is a <u>post increment,</u> so by definition the operation is not done until the operand has been used. In C and C++ this expression is undefined because it modifies the same i-value more than once. It is legal in Java because the order of evaluation is well defined.

In Java the ">>" operator does an arithmetic or signed shift, meaning that the sign bit is propagated. In C, it has always been implementation-defined whether this was a logical shift (fill with 0 bits) or an arithmetic shift (fill with copies of the sign bit). This occasionally led to grief as programmers discovered the implementation dependency when debugging or porting a system.

One new Java operator is ">>>" which means "shift right and zero fill" or "unsigned shift" (i.e. do not propagate the sign bit). This is not needed for shift left because there is no sign bit at the other end to propagate. It is not needed in C because it is implicitly achieved when shifting an unsigned quantity. Java does not have unsigned types apart from char.

The "&" takes two boolean operands, or two integer operands. It always evaluates both operands. For booleans, it ANDs the operands producing a boolean result. For integer types, it bitwise ANDs the operands, producing a result that is the promoted type of the operands (i.e. long, or int). " | " is the corresponding bitwise OR operation. "^" is the corresponding bitwise XOR operation.

The "&&" is a "conditional AND" which only takes boolean operands. It always avoids evaluating its second operand if possible. If a is evaluated to false, the AND result must be "false" and the b operand is not evaluated. This is sometimes called "short-circuited" evaluation. " | | " is the corresponding short-circuited OR operation. Possible mnemonic: The longer operators "&&" or " | | " try to shorten themselves by not evaluating the second operator if they can.

Java Operators

The Java operators and their precedence are shown in Table 3-1.

Table 3-1: Java operators and their precedence

Symbol	Note	Precedence	Coffeepot Property
names, literals	simple tokens	17	n/a
a[i]	subscripting	17	left
m(...)	method invocation	17	left
.	field selection	17	left
++ --	pre-increment, decrement	16	right
++ --	post-increment, decrement	15	left
~	flip the bits of an integer	14	right
!	logical not (reverse a boolean)	14	right
- +	arithmetic negation, plus	14	right
(typename)	type conversion (cast)	13	right
* / %	multiplicative operators	12	left
- +	additive operators	11	left
<< >> >>>	left and right bitwise shift	10	left
instanceof < <= > >=	relational operators	9	left
== !=	equality operators	8	left
&	bitwise and	7	left
^	bitwise exclusive or	6	left
|	bitwise inclusive or	5	left
&&	conditional and	4	left
||	conditional or	3	left
? :	conditional operator	2	right
= *= /= %= += -= <<= >>= >>>= &= ^= |=	assignment operators	1	right

Although the intent of the ">>>" operator is a zero filled shift right, it has a surprising—and very undesirable—twist in practice. The >> operator takes negative numbers and does an arithmetic shift on them, that is it sign-extends them so that the "new" bits from the left are filled with 1's to keep the sign negative.

In contrast the >>> operator is designed to fill in with 0's from the left in case you weren't using the operand as a "number", but as a bit mask. This works as expected on numbers of canonical size, ints and longs. But it is broken for short, and byte.

```
byte b = -1;
b >>>= 10;
```

If you have an 8-bit quantity, and you shift it right unsigned 10 bits, all the bits should fall off the right end, leaving zero. This does not happen. If you try it, you will see that b has the value –1.

The reason is the byte got promoted to an int before the shift took place. The int had the bit pattern 0xFFFFFFFF, and was shifted ten places right to yield 0x003FFFFF. That result was truncated to a byte, yielding a final result of 0xFF, or –1.

If you want to do unsigned shift on a short or a byte, an extra AND is required, in which case you can just use >>.

```
byte b = -1;
b = (byte)((b & 0xff) >> 4);
```

So because of the default operand promotion to a canonical size, >>> is useless on all negative byte and short operands. It is probably better not to use it at all, but to always use "&" to mask off the bits you require in a result. That way programs won't mysteriously stop working when someone changes a type from int to short. 🐛

Assignment operators result in values (as in C) not variables (as in C++). So this code fragment is legal in C++, but illegal in C and Java:

```
(a += 4)++;
```

In C the error will be a complaint that "operand is not a modifiable lvalue". Java thankfully lacks jargon like "modifiable lvalue" which was introduced into C to kludge around certain semantics of consts and arrays. In Java the error message is along the lines of "Invalid expression"—not the greatest but at least it doesn't include any words that have a special definition.

The other new operator is "instanceof". This is used with superclasses to tell if you have a particular subclass. For example, we may see:

```
class vehicle { ...
class car extends vehicle { ...
class convertible extends car { ...

vehicle v; ...
if (v instanceof convertible) ...
```

The "instanceof" operator is often followed by a statement that casts the object from the base type to the subclass, if it turns out that the one is an instance of the other. Instanceof lets us check that the cast is valid before attempting it.

Finally note that Java cut back on the use of the obscure comma operator. Even if you're quite an experienced C programmer you might never have seen the comma operator, as it was rarely used. The only place it occurs in Java is in "for" loops. The comma allows you to put several expressions (separated by commas) into each clause of a "for" loop.

```
for (i=0, j=0; i<10; i++, j++)
```

Why GIGO sometimes means "Garbage In, Gospel Out"

If you try the Pentium division Java program on a Pentium system with the flawed division implementation, you may be surprised to see that it actually prints out the correct answer—I certainly was! In fact "stunned" would be a better description.

How can that be, when the chip gives bad results? The answer lies in the compiler. Not the Java compiler, but the Microsoft Visual C++ library that is used to build Java on the Windows platform, and that provides runtime support. Whenever a chip manufacturer finds a hardware bug, and there are always some bugs in every design, it is the job of the compiler team to work around it. The compiler group must make sure that the generated code avoids or corrects the problem. In this case, within three months of the FDIV fault becoming public knowledge, Microsoft issued patch VCFDIV for Visual C++ 2.0.

The patch checks to see if the code is being run on a flawed Pentium. If it is, it checks if the operands are of the form that would hit the bad entries in the table. If so, it scales both operands (1200.0 / 100.0 gives the same result as 120.0 / 10.0) to avoid using that part of the lookup table. The process takes a little longer, but gives good results. The patch was folded into Visual C++ 2.1. Java on Windows is currently built with MS Visual C++ version 2.0 with the patch. When the Java interpreter finds a division operator, it passes it through to the native runtime routine (in this case the Microsoft msvcrt20.dll library which has the software workaround). You cannot see the flaw using a Java program, but it is not because of any Java quality, rather the runtime library that it uses.

To observe the Pentium division flaw, you need to run a C program that provides access to the raw hardware. I recommend the "Power C" ANSI C compiler for the PC available from Mix Software, in Richardson Texas. The compiler costs under $20, and comes with a properly bound book on C that is worth the price alone. Power C can be ordered by telephoning Mix at 1-800 333-0330. (telephone 214 783-6001 outside the U.S.) No, I don't own stock in Mix Software! My interest is in seeing more programmers use a good inexpensive unbloated ANSI C compiler system. Power C sells well to a lot of schools.

You can also download GnuC for the PC—a 32 bit C/C++ compiler for MS-DOS—for free. Take a look at web site http://www.delorie.com/djgpp.

Use GnuC if you want to study compiler internals.

Use Power C if you want to run C programs. 🐝

Some Light Relief
Animation Software

This is a story I got from the friend of a friend who works for a Hollywood special-effects company. In other words it's a FOAF-tale (Friend Of A Friend) and may have the same credibility gap as Burt Reynolds's toupee. Remember the cheesy 1970s tv series "Battlestar Galactica?" It did well enough to spawn a movie version with the same name.

When filming on the "Battlestar Galactica" movie began, the specification of the spaceship bridge set called for lots of CRT's with animated "wire-frame" displays. The displays should show pictures of various space craft and look futuristic, so the images had to rotate wildly.

When the staff at the special-effects company started to generate these displays, they discovered that programming real-time animated computer graphics is quite a bit more difficult than stop motion photography of claymation models. Shocking as it sounds, these people were not really programmers at all; what they mostly did was create motion-control sequences to "fly" model spaceships through combat maneuvers for the camera. Writing real software to display wire-frame images on the monitors was a venture into the unknown.

Their attempts to write code proved fruitless. So after a bit of thought they reverted to doing what they knew best: they got the model shop to build them some wire-frame models out of actual wire, sprayed them with fluorescent paint, and hooked them up to servomotors inside dummy CRT's that were illuminated with ultra-violet lamps; then they wrote a little code to run the servomotors. The wire models rotated and tilted up and down glowing brightly, and apparently looked very realistic on film even to people who knew what wire-frame graphics should look like.

All this cost only a small fraction more than it would have cost to learn the graphics programming, or to hire someone who already knew how to do it. But the great thing is that Hollywood's reputation was upheld for having, underneath all that fake tinsel and glitter, real tinsel and glitter. Battlestar Galactica was still a cheesy movie, but in this case at least it was real cheese.

Exercises

1. Identify two examples of a large company that is confronted with a public loss of confidence in its product. How has the company reacted? How did the organization's conduct affect public confidence?

2. How is an application distinguished from an applet?

3. What are the three kinds of comment in Java, and how is each used?

4. Compare the rules for forming Java identifiers to those of any other programming language you are familiar with. Compare the Java concept of a character as a 16-bit quantity to the more usual concept of a character as an 8-bit ASCII value.

5. Describe what precedence, associativity, and evaluation order are. How do they interplay in determining the value of an expression?

6. Write a Java program to demonstrate how the ">>>" unsigned shift operator does not in fact unsigned shift a negative **short** or **byte**. Account for this.

7. Write a Java program that uses the "instanceof" operator to check for appropriateness of subclass before attempting a cast.

Further Reading

The best description of the Pentium flaw appears in "Microprocessor Report," Dec. 26, 1994.

The Unicode site is http://www.unicode.org

The draft standard for Unicode HTML can be found at http://www.alis.com:8085/ietf/html/draft-ietf-html-i18n-01.txt

CHAPTER
4

- The Primitive Types and Built-in Classes
- The Java World of Objects
- Compilation Units: Coexisting With the Host System
- Interfaces

Java
Building Blocks

"There is no reason for any individual to have a computer in their home."

> *–Ken Olsen, President, Digital Equipment, 1977*

"640K ought to be enough memory for anybody"

> *–Bill Gates, 1981*

"Java is not for doing millions of lines of code, only applets"

> *–Ilog software co's CEO Pierre Haren,*
> *quoted in Unigram, Dec 25 1995*

T he first half of this chapter covers some more of the language basics: types, literals and statements. The second half is more outward-looking, providing details on how Java programs interact with libraries and the host system.

The Built-In Types and Declarations

Anyone who ever had to port a C program between a Unix system and a PC will know the problem: the basic types are completely different sizes on the different systems. You can't merely change every occurrence of "int" to "long" either—for one thing the usual type promotions all change when all your ints change to longs in C. For another, the implicit assumptions about the layout of structs will change. Yet a third problem is that any printf statements will need the format specifier changed.

How Long is a Long?

The same problem of "what size should types be?" was recently heatedly discussed by Unix workstation manufacturers as they move towards 64-bit architectures. The issue can be summarized as "we know we have to make pointers 64-bits, but where in the integer types do we bring in 64-bits: int, long, or long long?"

The three major competing approaches have adopted mysterious codenames because, well, because mysterious codenames are fun:

LP64: this group says "introduce 64-bitness at the top of the int range." "long"s and pointers should be 64-bits. Int stays at 32-bits. DEC and SGI are in this camp, and Sun recently switched to join them.

ILP64: this was the position taken by Hewlett-Packard. It says "Hey! Let's have a flag day, and change everything to 64-bits at once: ints, longs, and pointers. Users may squeak, but a change will be good for them. Programs that rely on ints and pointers being the same size will keep working when recompiled. You do have the source, don't you?" HAL Computers Inc. (they make excellent clones of Sun systems) chose the ILP64 model and will have to change eventually.

LLP64: this was the original position taken by Sun. It says "introduce 64-bitness *beyond* the top of the range, by having a 'long long' type. All the other existing integer types stay the size they are." Nobody else liked this position, and it got pretty lonely. Other folks inside Sun challenged some of the assumptions it was built on, so Sun switched.

The trade-offs involved in choosing the sizes of basic data types involve portability, compatibility with existing types, standards conformance, performance, and transition cost. Exactly the same issues were faced by the Java team, though the Java team had the luxury of putting a low value on some of these costs. All the approaches have advantages and drawbacks, but in the end all the vendors have committed to LP64.

The LP64 model is very close to the Java model, the only difference being that pointers are 32-bits in Java, not 64-bits. However there is nothing in the language that makes that visible to programmers. When the time for 64 bit pointers inevitably arrives (and it will be well before the turn of the Millennium) we should be able to merely recompile existing code and have it all "just work" on the new Java

Virtual Machine. The various "how much memory?" functions in lang/runtime.java already return long which is always 64-bits in Java. 🐦

The Primitive Types

Most high-level languages don't specify the sizes of data types. This allows compiler writers the freedom to select the best sizes on each architecture for performance. The freedom turns out to be a false economy since it greatly impedes program portability, and programmer time is a lot more expensive than processor time. Java does away with all the uncertainty by rigorously specifying the sizes of the basic types and making clear that these sizes are identical on all platforms.

There are eight built-in, non-object types, also known as primitive types. They are:

- boolean (for truth values)

- int, long, byte, short (for arithmetic on integers)

- double, float (for arithmetic on the real numbers)

- char (for character data, ultimately to be input or printed)

Let us examine the properties of each of these in turn.

boolean

This is the data type used for true/false conditions. Internally it takes up 32 bits.

range of values: false, true

literals: false, true. In the code below, the assignment will always occur.

```
if (true) x = 33;
```

You cannot cast a boolean value to any other type. However you can always get the same effect by using an expression:

```
i = (bool? 1:0); // set int according to bool value.
bool = (i==0? false:true); // set bool according to int value.
```

Note that expert programmers customarily write

```
boolean bean;
    ...
if (bean) ... // do something.
```

rather than

```
if (bean == true) ... // do something.
```

In Java, the boolean type is not based on integers. In particular, you cannot increment, decrement or add boolean values. To optimize memory access time, more than one bit is used to store a boolean value.

int

The type int is a 32-bit, signed, two's-complement number. This will be the type that you chose by default whenever you are going to carry out integer arithmetic.

range of values: −2,147,483,648 to 2,147,483,647

literals: a "literal" is a value provided at compile-time. Literals have types just like variables have types. Int literals come in any of three varieties:

- A decimal literal, e.g. 10 or −256

- With a leading zero, meaning an octal literal, e.g. 077777

- With a leading 0x, meaning a hexadecimal literal, e.g. 0xA5 or 0Xa5

Upper or lower case has no significance with any of the letters that can appear in integer literals. If you use octal or hexadecimal and you provide a literal that sets the leftmost bit in the receiving number, then it represents a negative quantity.

An integer literal is a 32-bit quantity. But provided its actual value is within range for a smaller type, an int literal can be assigned directly to something with fewer bits, such as byte, short or char. If you try to assign an int literal that is too large into a smaller type, the compiler will insist on a cast. Integer literals can be assigned to floating point variables without casting.

long

The type long is a 64-bit, signed, two's-complement quantity. It should be used when calculations on whole numbers may exceed the range of int. Using longs, the range of values is -2^{63} to $(2^{63}-1)$. Numbers up in this range will be increasingly prevalent in computing, and 2^{64} in particular is a number that really needs a name of its own. So in 1993, I coined the term "Bubbabyte" to describe 2^{64} bytes. Just as 2^{10} bytes is a Kilobyte, and 2^{20} is a Megabyte, so 2^{64} bytes is a Bubbabyte. Using a long, you can count up to half a Bubbabyte less one.

range of values: −9,223,372,036,854,775,808 to 9,223,372,036,854,775,807

literals: The general form of long literals is the same as int literals, but with an "L" or "l" on the end to indicate "long." However, never use the lower case letter "l" to indicate a "long" literal as it is just too similar to the digit "1." Always use the upper case letter "L" instead. The three kinds of long literals are:

- A decimal literal, e.g. 2047L or −10L

- An octal literal, e.g. 0777777L

- An hexadecimal literal, e.g. 0xA5L or OxABADCAFEDEADBE30L

All long literals are 64-bit quantities. A long literal must be cast to assign it to something with fewer bits, such as byte, short, int or char.

byte

The byte type is an 8-bit, signed, two's-complement quantity. The reasons for using byte are to hold a generic 8-bit value, to match a value in existing data files, or to economize on storage space (where you have a large number of such values). Despite popular belief, there is no speed advantage to bytes, shorts, or chars—modern CPUs take the same amount of time to load or multiply 8 bits as they take for 32 bits.

range of values: −128 to 127

literals: there are no byte literals. You can use, without a cast, char literals and int literals provided their values fit in 8 bits. You can use long and floating-point literals if you cast them.

You always have to cast a (non-literal) value of a larger type if you want to put it into a variable of a smaller type. Since arithmetic is always performed at least at 32-bit precision, this means that assignments to a byte variable must always be cast into the result if they involve any arithmetic, like this:

```
byte b1=1, b2=2;
byte b3 = b2 + b1; // NO! NO! NO! Causes error
byte b3 = (byte) (b2 + b1); // correct
```

People often find this unexpected. If I have an expression involving only bytes, why should I need to cast it into a byte result? The right way to think about it is that most modern computers do all integral arithmetic at 32-bit or 64-bit precision (there is no "8-bit add" on modern CPU's). Java follows this model of the underlying hardware. An arithmetic operation on two bytes potentially yields a bigger result than can be stored in a byte. The philosophy for casts is that they are required whenever you assign from a more capacious type to a less capacious type. The cast is the way in which the programmer tells the compiler "Yes, I acknowledge that there may be some loss of accuracy here." Use a cast where you need one, but don't use a cast unless that is a true message to convey.

short

This type is a 16-bit signed, two's-complement integer. The main reasons for using short are to match external values already present in a file, or to economize on storage space (where you have a large number of such values and they will be able to fit in the limited range of values).

range of values: −32,768 to 32,767

literals: there are no short literals. You can use, without a cast, char literals and int literals provided their values will fit in 16 bits. You can use long and floating-point literals if you cast them.

As with byte, assignments to short must always be cast into the result if the right hand side of the assignment involves any arithmetic.

The next two types, double and float, are the floating-point arithmetic types:

double

The type double refers to floating-point numbers stored in 64 bits, as described in the IEEE standard reference 754. The type double will be the default type you use when you want to do some calculations that might involve decimal places (i.e. not integral values).

range of values: These provide numbers that can range between about −1.7E308 to +1.7E308 with about 14 to 15 significant figures of accuracy. The exact accuracy depends on the number being represented. Double precision floating-point numbers have the range shown in Figure 4-1.

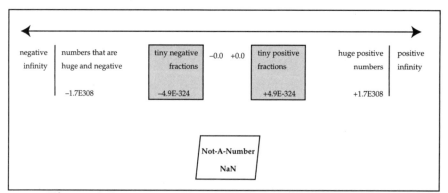

Figure 4-1: Type double should be used when calculations involve decimal places.

IEEE 754 arithmetic has come into virtually universal acceptance over the last decade, and it would certainly raise a few eyebrows if a computer manufacturer proposed an incompatible system of floating-point numbers now. IEEE 754 is the standard for floating point arithmetic, but there are several places where chip designers can choose from different alternatives within the standard, such as rounding modes. To get consistency on all hardware, Java specifies the alternative that must be used, where IEEE 754 allows choices. Instead of valuing the resultant portability, some number-crunching programmers actually complained about this! IEEE 754 has an ingenious way of dealing with the problem of representing on limited hardware the unlimited amount of infinite precision real-world numbers.

The problem is resolved by reserving a special value that says "Help! I've fallen off the end of what's representable and I can't get up." You're probably familiar with infinity, but the "Not-a-Number" might be new if you haven't done much numerical programming. Not-a-Number, or NaN, is a value that a floating point can take to indicate that the result of some operation is not mathematically well-defined, like dividing zero by zero.

If you get a NaN as an expression is being evaluated, it will contaminate the whole expression, producing an overall result of NaN—*which is exactly what you want!* The worst way to handle a numeric error is to ignore it and pretend it didn't happen.

Write, compile, and run a Java program that deliberately generates a NaN result, by dividing two floating-point numbers that both have the value 0.0. Print out the result of the division (just send it to System.out.println() as in earlier examples). What is the printable representation of NaN? Try using NaN in further arithmetic operations. 🍎

You may never see a NaN if your algorithms are numerically stable, and you never push the limits of your datasets. But it's nice to know that NaN is there, ready to tell you your results are garbage, if they head that way.

literals: It is easiest to show by example the valid formats for double literals:

```
1e1  2.   .3   3.14 6.02e+23d
```

The format is very easy-going. Just give the compiler a decimal point, or an exponent, and it will recognize that a floating-point literal is intended. A suffix of "D", "d", or no suffix, means a double literal. In practice, most people omit the suffix.

Make Mine a Double: How Large is 1.7E308?

The largest double precision number is a little bit bigger than a 17 followed by 307 zeroes.

How large is that? Well, the volume of the observable universe is about $(4pi/3)(15 \text{ billion light-years})^3 = 10^{85} \text{ cm}^3$. The density of protons is about 10^{-7} cm^{-3}, (this value seems so sparse because it is an average for all space— on a planet the value is much, much denser of course) so the number of protons in the observable Universe is about 10^{78}, or "only" 1 followed by 78 zeros, give or take two-fifty.

The largest double precision number is even bigger than a googol. A googol is the number description suggested by 9 yr. old Milton Sirotta in 1938 at the request of his uncle, mathematician Edward Krasner. A googol is 10^{100}, i.e. it is only a 1 followed by 100 zeroes. Is the largest double precision number bigger than Roseanne's capacity for self-promotion? No, we have to admit, it probably isn't that big.

It's possible to come up with problems where you want accuracy to 14 significant figures (e.g. figuring the national debt). But it is most unusual to need to tabulate numbers that are orders of magnitude greater than the number of protons in the universe.

It is also permissible to assign any of the integer literals or character literals to floats or doubles. The assignment doesn't need a cast, as you are going from a less capacious type to a more capacious type. So a line like this, while perverse, is valid:

```
double cherry = '\n';
```

It takes the integer value of the literal, 0x0a here, floats it to get 10.0d, and assigns that to "cherry." Don't ever do this.

float

The type float refers to floating-point numbers stored in 32 bits, as described in the IEEE standard reference 754.

The justification for using single precision variables used to be that arithmetic operations were twice as fast as on double precision variables. With modern extensively-pipelined processors and wide data buses between the cache and CPUs, the speed differences are inconsequential. The reasons for using floats are to minimize storage requirements when you have a very large quantity of them, or to retain compatibility with external data files.

range of values: The type float provides numbers that can range between about

−3.4E38 to 3.4E38 (i.e. 340,000,000,000,000,000,000,000,000,000,000,000,000) with about 6 to 7 significant figures of accuracy. The exact accuracy depends on the number being represented.

literals: The simplest way to understand what is allowed is to look at examples of valid float literals.

```
1e1f 2.f .3f 3.14f 6.02e+23f
```

A suffix of "F" or "f" is always required on a float literal. A common mistake is to leave the suffix off the float literal:

```
float cabbage = 6.5;
 Error: explicit cast needed to convert double to float.
```

The code must be changed to:

```
float cabbage = 6.5f;
```

Also, a double literal cannot be assigned to a float variable without a cast even if it is within the range of the float type. This is because some precision in decimal places may potentially be lost. The next section explains more about this interesting, and sometimes subtle, topic.

char

This type is a 16-bit, unsigned quantity that is used to represent printable characters. It is an integer-based type, and so all the arithmetic operators are available on it. Unlike all the other arithmetic types, char is unsigned—it never takes a negative value. You should only use char to hold character data or bit masks. If you want a 16-bit quantity for general calculations, don't use char, use short. This will avoid the possible surprise of converting between signed and unsigned types. Otherwise a cast of a negative value into char will magically become positive without the bits changing.

range of values: a value in the Unicode code set 0 to 65,535

You have to cast a 32- or 64-bit result if you want to put it into a smaller result. This means that assignments to char must always be cast into the result if they involve any arithmetic.

literals: Character literals appear between single quotes or in Strings. They can be expressed in four ways, and can be used for all of the types char, byte, short, int, and long.

- A single character, `'A'`

- A character escape sequence. The allowable values are:
  `'\n'` (linefeed) `'\r'` (carriage return) `'\f'` formfeed
  `'\b'` (backspace) `'\t'` (tab) `'\\'` (backslash)
  `'\"'` (double quote) `'\''` (single quote)

- An octal escape sequence. This has the form `'\nnn'` where nnn is one-to-three octal digits in the range 0 to 377. Note the odd fact that you can only set the least significant 8 bits of a 16-bit char when using an octal escape sequence. Examples: `'\0'` or `'\12'` or `'\277'` or `'\377'`

- A Unicode escape sequence. This has the form `'\uxxxx'` where xxxx is exactly four hexadecimal digits. Example:

  `'\u0041'` is the character A

How Accurate Are Calculations?

The accuracy when evaluating a result is referred to as the "precision" of an expression. The precision may be expressed either as number of bits (64 bits), or as the data type of the result (double precision, meaning 64-bit floating-point format). In Java, the precision of evaluating each operator depends on the types of the operands. Java looks at the types of the operands around an operator, and picks the biggest of what it sees of: double, float, long, in that order of preference. Both operands are then promoted to this type, and that is the type of the result. If there are no doubles, nor floats nor longs in the expression, then both operands are promoted to int, and that is the type of the result. This continues from left-to-right through the entire expression.

So a Java compiler follows this algorithm to compile each operation:

- If either operand is a double, do the operation in double precision.

- Otherwise, if either operand is a float, do the operation in single precision.

- Otherwise, if either operand is a long, do the operation at long precision.

- Otherwise, do the operation at 32-bit int precision.

In summary, Java expressions end up with the type of the biggest, floatiest type (double, float, long) in the expression. They are 32-bit integers otherwise.

Most programmers already understand that floating-point numbers are approximations to real numbers, and they may inherently contain tiny inaccuracies that may mount up as you iterate through an expression. (Actually, most program-mers learn this the hard way.) Do not expect 10 iterations of adding 0.1 to a float variable to cause it to exactly equal 1.0F! If this comes as a surprise to you, try this test program immediately, and thank your good fortune at having the chance to learn about it before you stumble over it as a difficult debugging problem.

```java
public class inexact1 {
    public static void main(String s[]) {
        float pear = 0.0F;
        for (int i=0; i<10; i++) pear = pear + 0.1F;

        if (pear==1.0F) System.out.println("pear is 1.0F");
        if (pear!=1.0F) System.out.println(
            "pear is NOT 1.0F");
    }
}
```

You will see this results in:

```
pear is NOT 1.0F
```

The reason is that 0.1 is not a fraction that can be represented exactly with powers of two, and hence summing 10 of them does not exactly sum to one. This is why you should never use a floating-point variable as a loop counter. A longer expla-nation of this thorny topic is in "What Every Computer Scientist Should Know about Floating Point" by David Goldberg, in the March 1991 (Vol 23 number 1) issue of *Computing Surveys*. Note that this is a characteristic of floating point num-bers in all programming languages, not a quality unique to Java.

Accuracy is not just the range of values of a type, but also (for real types) the num-ber of decimal places that can be stored. The type float can store about 6 to 7 digits accurately, so when a long (which can hold at least 18 places of integer values) is implicitly or explicitly converted to a float, some precision may be lost.

```java
public class inexact2 {
    public static void main(String s[]) {
        long  lasagna = 9000000000000000000L;
        float fructose = lasagna;
        lasagna = (long) fructose;
        System.out.println("fructose is: "+fructose);
        System.out.println(
            "lasagna (started as 9e18, assigned to float) is:"
            +lasagna);
    }
}
```

The output is:

```
fructose is: 9e+18
lasagna (started as 9e18, assigned to float) is:
9000000202358128640
```

As you can see, after being assigned to and retrieved back from the float variable, the long has lost all accuracy after six or seven significant figures. The truth is that if a float has the value shown, it could stand for any real value in the interval between the nearest representable floating-point number on each side. So the library is entitled, within the bounds of good taste and consistency, to print it out as any value within that interval. If all this makes you fidget uncomfortably in your seat, maybe you better take a look at that Goldberg article.

What Happens on Overflow?

 When a result is too big for the type intended to hold it, because of a cast, an implicit type conversion, or the evaluation of an expression, something has to give! What happens depends on whether the result type is integer or floating point.

Integer Overflow

When an integer valued expression is too big for its type, only the low end (least significant) bits get stored. Because of the way two's complement numbers are stored the wraparound means that adding one to the highest positive integer value gives a result of the highest negative integer value. Watch out for this (it's true for most languages, not just Java). It means arithmetic is effectively modulo-2^n arithmetic on the integer types. There is one case in which the calculation ceases and overflow is reported to the programmer: division by zero (using "/" or "%") which throws an exception. To "throw an exception" is covered in Chapter 5.

There is a class called `Integer` that is part of the standard Java libraries. It contains some useful constants relating to the primitive type `int`:

```
public static final int   MIN_VALUE = 0x80000000; // class Integer
public static final int   MAX_VALUE = 0x7fffffff; // class Integer
```

and there are similar values in the related class `Long`. Notice how these constants (`final`) are also `static`. If something is constant you surely don't need a copy of it in every object. You can use just one copy for the whole class, so make it static.

One possible use for these constants would be to evaluate an expression at long precision, and then compare the result to these int endpoints. If it is between them, then you know the result can be cast into an int without losing bits. Unless it overflowed long, of course . . .

Floating Point Overflow

When a floating-point expression (double or float) overflows, the result becomes infinity. When it underflows (reaches a value that is too small to represent) the result goes to zero. When you do something undefined like divide zero by zero, you get a NaN. Under no circumstances is an Exception ever raised from a floating-point expression.

The class `Float`, which is part of the standard Java libraries, contains some useful constants relating to the primitive type `float`:

```
public static final float POSITIVE_INFINITY;
public static final float NEGATIVE_INFINITY;
public static final float NaN;
public static final float MAX_VALUE = 3.40282346638528860e+38f;
public static final float MIN_VALUE = 1.40129846432481707e-45f;
```

One pitfall is that it doesn't help to compare a value to NaN, for NaN compares false to everything (including itself)! Instead, test the NaNiness of a value like this:

```
if (Float.isNaN( myfloat ) ) ... // It's a NaN
```

There are similar values in the class Double.

The Math Package

Let's note in passing that there is a class called `java.lang.Math` that has a couple of dozen useful mathematical functions and constants, including the trig routines (watch out, these expect an argument in radians, not degrees), pseudorandom numbers, square root, rounding, and the constants pi and *e*. You can review the source of this at

```
$JAVAHOME/src/java/lang/Math.java
```

All the routines in the Math package are static, so you typically invoke them using the name of the class, like this:

```
double cabbage = java.lang.Math.random(); // value 0.0..1.0
```

There is a way to shorten the method call to name just the class and method,

```
double cabbage = Math.random();
```

using the import statement, explained later. You usually cannot shorten it any further to just the method name.

However, there is a little trick that has been used to provide better name visibility. If a class doesn't need to inherit from anything else, a programmer may make it inherit from some other class whose methods he or she wishes to use directly. Making a class extend another class brings all the superclass methods into the subclass name space, without needing to prefix them with the name of the superclass. You can't use this trick in an applet, because you have to inherit from java.awt.Applet. It is recommended that you not do this, as it destroys the OOP design for the sake of some trivial naming advantage. It is only mentioned because you may see it in other people's code.

Convert degrees to radians with code like this:

```
    int degrees = ...
double radians =  (Math.PI * degrees / 180.0);
```

The Math.log() function returns a natural (base e) logarithm.

Convert natural logarithms to base 10 logarithms with code like this:

```
double nat_log = ...
    double base10log = nat_log / Math.log(10.0);
```

The full list of functions in the java.lang.Math class is:

```
public final class java.lang.Math extends java.lang.Object {
    public static final double E = 2.718282;
    public static final double PI = 3.141593;
    public native static double sin(double);
    public native static double cos(double);
    public native static double tan(double);
    public native static double asin(double);
    public native static double acos(double);
    public native static double atan(double);
    public native static double exp(double);
    public native static double log(double);
    public native static double sqrt(double);
    public native static double IEEEremainder(double,double);
    public native static double ceil(double);
    public native static double floor(double);
    public native static double rint(double);
    public native static double atan2(double,double);
    public native static double pow(double,double);
    public static int round(float);
    public static long round(double);
    public static synchronized double random();
    public static int abs(int);
    public static long abs(long);
    public static float abs(float);
    public static double abs(double);
    public static int max(int,int);
    public static long max(long,long);
    public static float max(float,float);
    public static double max(double,double);
    public static int min(int,int);
    public static long min(long,long);
    public static float min(float,float);
    public static double min(double,double);
}
```

Unicode

The type char holds Unicode values. As mentioned in the previous chapter, Unicode is an internationally-agreed 16-bit character set, just as ASCII is the *American Standard Code for Information Interchange* using an 8-bit character set. Java provides the framework that is capable of handling characters from just about any locale in the world. The cost is that we store and move 16 bits for each character instead of just 8 bits.

Full Unicode support in Java is limited by two things: I/O support in Java itself, and support from the underlying operating system. Both of these need to be in place, and both of these are currently deficient. At present, Java only supports the Latin-1 character set (i.e. the first 256 characters in Unicode). Although the general framework is in place and you can represent Cyrillic or other non-Latin-1 characters in a Java program, you cannot yet draw them on the screen. Better support for internationalization is introduced in the JDK 1.1 release, described in a later chapter.

Scanning

When a Java compiler reads in program source, the very first thing that it does, before even forming tokens out of the characters, is to look for any six character sequences of the form \uxxxx where xxxx is exactly four hexadecimal digits. e.g. \u3b9F. These six-character sequences are translated into the corresponding one Unicode character whose value is xxxx, which is pushed back into the input stream for rescanning. Because this early scanning takes place before tokens are assembled, the six character sequence \uxxxx will be replaced even if it appears in a quoted string or character literal. For most characters that is exactly what you want, but for characters that themselves affect scanning, you will get a bad result. Two characters that have the quality of affecting scanning are carriage return and line feed. If you try to put one of these in a quoted character literal like this:

```
char c = '\u000a';
```

the compiler will actually see this:

```
char c = '
';
```

causing two error messages about "invalid character constant"—one for each of the opening quotes it sees.

Choosing Unicode for the char type was a bold and forward-looking design choice. Although a few people complain about the cost and waste of using 16 bits per character, these are the same pikers who a few years ago didn't want to shift from 6-bit codesets to 7 bits, and who still hold onto their abacuses while they evaluate the "new technology" slide rules. Disk continues to get faster and cheaper every year. Designers of forward-looking systems like Java have a responsibility to include proper support for more than just Western alphabets. Especially if anyone wants to sell software outside Western Europe. Until all systems have adopted Unicode, handling it on an ASCII system is clumsy, so avoid sprinkling Unicode literals through your code.

String

Strings are not a primitive type like the types described up to now in this chapter. On the contrary, the type String is a class in Java, but it is important enough to have support for a couple of features built in to the language. The String literal is one of these features. The "+" string concatenation operator is another.

String objects hold a series of adjacent characters, as the name suggests. However it takes a method call (not an array reference, as in C) to pull an individual character out. String is a richly-featured class with methods and data. Java does not use the C convention that strings are just nul-terminated arrays of characters. You will use String instances a lot—whenever you want to store zero or more characters in a sequence, or do character I/O. Arrays of char do some of these things too, but String is a lot more convenient for comparing characters, and using literal values.

literals: A string literal is zero or more characters enclosed in double quotes, like this:

```
"" // empty string
"That'll cost you two-fifty \n"
"The first 3 letters of the alphabet are\t \101 \u0042 and C"
```

As the example shows, you can embed any of the character literals in a string.

Like all literals, string literals are immutable and cannot be modified after they have been created. String variables are also immutable—you cannot change a character in the middle of a String to something else. Of course, you can always discard any String and make the same reference variable refer to a different one in its place. You can even construct a new String out of pieces from another, so being unable to change a given String after it has been created isn't a handicap in practice. Each string literal behaves as if it is a reference to an instance of class String, meaning that you can invoke methods on it, copy a reference to it and so on. For the sake of performance the compiler can implement it another way, but it must be indistinguishable to the programmer.

If you have a long string literal, the way to continue it across several lines is to break it down into smaller strings, and concatenate them like this:

```
    "Thomas the Tank Engine and the naughty "
+ "Engine-driver who tied down Thomas's Boiler Safety Valve"
+ "and How They Recovered Pieces of Thomas from Three Counties."
```

String literals are a concession to programmer expectations. Although String is a class, you can create a new literal instance like this:

```
String peach = "Thomas the Tank Engine";
```

as an alternative to requiring the new keyword like this:

```
String peach = new String ("Thomas the Tank Engine");
```

String Concatenation

The previous chapter described how the "+" operator will concatenate any primitive type to a String. This magic of the "+" operator when one operand is a String also applies to objects. If you supply any object as the other operand to "+", the system will call a method with the name toString to create a String representation of that object and then concatenate the two Strings. You have two choices for the toString method for any class:

- You can provide a method with this signature:

  ```
  public String  toString()
  ```

  Usually, the method will print out the value of key fields, nicely formatted.

- Or you can let the inheritance hierarchy pick up the toString method from superclass Object. This will return a String containing the classname and something that looks like the address of the instance.

It's better to take the first alternative and provide more meaningful output. The method toString() will be invoked on any object that is concatenated with a String.

```
Citrus lemon = new Citrus();
   String s = "Your object is " + lemon;
// the + invokes method lemon.toString()
```

Defining toString for your classes, and printing an object this way is a useful debugging technique.

The following code shows the important methods of the String class. You can look at the entire source including the method bodies, as it is distributed with the JDK. The source for String is in file $JAVAHOME/java/src/lang/String.java

String Comparison

Compare two Strings like this:

```
      if ( s1.equals(s2)) ....
or    if ("Peter".equals(s2) ....
```

Not like this

```
      if (s1 == s2) ....
```

This ensures you compare <u>values</u> not <u>addresses</u> (explained later in this chapter). Failing to use "equals()" to compare two strings is probably the most common mistake made by Java novices.

```java
* A general class to represent character Strings. */
public final class String  {
    public String()
    public String(String value)
    public String(char value[])
    public String(char value[], int offset, int count)
    public String(byte ascii[], int hibyte, int offset, int count)
    public String(byte ascii[], int hibyte)
    public String (StringBuffer buffer)

    public int length()
    public char charAt(int index)
    public void getChars(int srcBegin, int srcEnd, char dst[], int dstBegin)
    public void getBytes(int srcBegin, int srcEnd, byte dst[], int dstBegin)
    public boolean equals(Object anObject)
    public boolean equalsIgnoreCase(String anotherString)
    public int compareTo(String anotherString)
    public boolean regionMatches(int toffset, String other, int ooffset, int len)
    public boolean regionMatches(boolean ignoreCase, int toffset, String other,
                                                     int ooffset, int len)
    public boolean startsWith(String prefix, int toffset)
    public boolean startsWith(String prefix)
    public boolean endsWith(String suffix)
    public int hashCode()
    public int indexOf(int ch)
    public int indexOf(int ch, int fromIndex)
    public int lastIndexOf(int ch)
    public int lastIndexOf(int ch, int fromIndex)
    public int indexOf(String str)
    public int indexOf(String str, int fromIndex)
    public int lastIndexOf(String str)
    public int lastIndexOf(String str, int fromIndex)
    public String substring(int beginIndex)
    public String substring(int beginIndex, int endIndex)
    public String concat(String str)
    public String replace(char oldChar, char newChar)
    public String toLowerCase()
    public String toUpperCase()
    public String trim()
    public String toString()
    public char[] toCharArray()
    public static String valueOf(Object obj)
    public static String valueOf(char data[])
    public static String valueOf(char data[], int offset, int count)
    public static String copyValueOf(char data[], int offset, int count)
    public static String copyValueOf(char data[])
    public static String valueOf(boolean b)
    public static String valueOf(char c)
    public static String valueOf(int i)
    public static String valueOf(long l)
    public static String valueOf(float f)
    public static String valueOf(double d)

}
```

String uses another built-in class called StringBuffer to help it operate. String-Buffer differs from String in that it supports character sequences that can be appended and inserted. It doesn't have any support for searching for individual characters or substrings. StringBuffer is widely used by the compiler to implement support for concatenating two Strings into a longer String. You'll probably use the class String a lot more than StringBuffer.

The Basic Statements

All statements in Java can be conveniently divided into four groups:

- Selection statements
- Iteration statements
- Transfer of control statements
- Guarding statements

We will describe the first three groups here, deferring consideration of the guarding statements until the sections on threads and exceptions in the next chapter. There's nothing particularly difficult or novel about guarding statements, it's just that they make more sense once the context in which they operate has been covered.

The selection, iteration, and branching statements are almost identical to their counterparts in C, and are readily recognizable to any programmer familiar with mainstream algorithmic languages. Accordingly we can limit our discussion to showing the general form of each statement.

Selection Statements

The general form of the "if" statement looks like this:

```
if ( Expression ) Statement  [ else  Statement ]
```

Statement Notes:

✔ The Expression must have boolean type. This has the delightful side-effect of banishing the old "if (a=b)" problem, where the programmer does an assignment instead of a comparison. If that typo is written, the compiler will give an error message that a boolean is needed in that context. Unless a and b are booleans. But at least you're protected for all the other types.

✔ The Statement can be any statement, in particular a block { ... } statement is fine.

✔ Since we are dealing with the "if" statement, we should also mention the " ? ... :"operator, as it is not very well known. It works in a very similar way to the "if" statement, but yields an expression, where the "if" statement does not. Compare:

if *(Expression)*   *Statement_when_true* else *Statement_when_false*
Expression?   *Expression_when_true* : *Expression_when_false*

When looked at this way, the conditional operator is a lot more understandable. You use it where you want to quickly choose between two alternative values, and you can fold it right into the expression, like this:

```
System.out.println(  "Your number is "
          + ((n%2)==0? "even" : "odd" ) );[1]
```

Never nest several conditional operators inside each other, as it causes unnecessary grief for whoever has to maintain the code (and it might be you).

The general form of the "switch" statement is impossible to show in any meaningful form in a syntax diagram with less than about two dozen production rules. That tells you something about the statement right there. If you look at Kernighan and Ritchie's C book, you'll note that even they were not up to the task of showing the syntax in any better way than:

switch *(Expression)* *Statement*

and neither has any C book since. Ignoring syntax diagrams, the switch statement is a poor man's "case" statement. It causes control to be transferred to one of several statements depending on the value of the Expression. It generally looks like:

```
switch (Expression) {

    case constant_1 : Statement; break;
    case constant_5 :
    case constant_3 : Statement; break;
           ...
    case constant_n : Statement; break;
           default : Statement; break;
    }
```

---

1.   You'd never really write a print statement this way, because it would make it much harder to localize the program to support natural languages other than English. But you get the idea.

Statement Notes:

✔ If you omit a "break" at the end of a branch, after that branch is executed control falls through to execute all the remaining branches! This is almost always *not* what you want.

 Looking through about 100,000 lines of the Java Development system source, there are about 320 switch statements. Implicit fall-through is used in less than 1% (based on a random sample of files). A statement in which you have to take explicit action to avoid something you don't want 99% of the time is a disaster. Death to the switch statement! 🐛

✔ There can only be one "default" branch, and it doesn't have to be last. The "default" branch can be omitted. If it is present, it is executed when none of the "case" values match the Expression.

✔ A Statement can be labelled with several cases. (This is actually a trivial case of fall-through).

✔ If none of the cases match, and there's no default case, the statement does nothing.

✔ Implicit fall-through (in the absence of "break") is a bug-prone misfeature.

Iteration Statements

At this point note that wherever you can have a statement in Java, you can also have a block of them. And you can also have a declaration of a local variable. As in C++ variable declarations count as statements.

The "for" statement looks like this:

for (*Initial; Test; Increment*) *Statement*

Statement Notes:

✔ Initial, Test, and Increment are all Expressions that control the loop. Any or all of them is optional. A typical loop will look like:

```
for( i=0; i<100; i++ ) { ...
```

A typical infinite loop will look like:

```
for (;;)
```

✔ As in C++, it is possible to declare the loop variable in the for statement, like this:

```
for( int i=0; i<100; i++ ) { ...
```

This is a nice feature done for programmer convenience. In a difference from most C++ compilers, the lifetime of the Java loop variable ends at the end of the for statement. The continued existence of loop variables in C++ was an artifact of the original implementations that simply translated the language to C. It was convenient to collect up all declarations and move them to the beginning of the block without trying to impose a finer granularity of scope. This sloppy approach is now being tightened up for ANSI C++.

✔ The comma separator "," is allowed in the Initial and Increment sections of loops so you can string together several initializations or increments, like this:

```
for(i=0,j=0; i<100; i++, j+=2 ) { ...
```

The "while" statement looks like this:

```
while ( Expression ) Statement
```

Statement Notes:

✔ While the boolean-typed expression remains true, the Statement is executed.

✔ This form of loop is for iterations that take place zero or more times. If the Expression is false on the first evaluation, the Statement will not be executed at all.

The "do while" statement looks like this:

```
do Statement while ( Expression ) ;
```

Statement Notes:

✔ The Statement is executed, and then the boolean-typed expression is evaluated. If it is false, execution drops through to the next statement. If it is true, you loop through the Statement again.

✔ This form of loop is for iterations that take place at least one time. If the Expression is false on the first evaluation, the Statement will already have executed once.

There may be "continue" statements in a loop. These look like:

```
continue;
```

```
continue Identifier;
```

Continue statements only occur in loops. When a continue statement is executed, it causes the flow of control to pass to the next iteration of the loop. It's as though you say "well, that's it for iteration N, increment the loop variable (if this is a "for" loop), do the test, and continue with iteration N+1."

The "continue Identifier" form is used when you have nested loops, and you want to break out of an inner one altogether and start with the next iteration of the outer loop. The loop that you want to continue with will be labelled at its "for" statement with the matching identifier, but don't be deceived into thinking that execution starts over at the beginning of that loop. It really does continue with the *next iteration*, even though the label is (confusingly) at the beginning, rather than labelling, say, the end of the loop. Here is an example "continue" statement:

```
months: for (int m=1; m<=12; m++) {
        // do something
        // nested loop
        for (int d=1; d<=31; d++) {
              // some daily thing
              if (m==2 && d==28) continue months;
              // otherwise something else
        }
        // more guff
}
```

There may be "break" statements in a loop or switch. These look like:

break

```
break;
```

```
break  Identifier;
```

Break is like a more dramatic version of continue. Break with no identifier causes control to pass to just after the end of the enclosing "for, do, while," or "switch" statement. The loop or switch statement is "broken out of." Break with no identifier can only appear in a statement by virtue of the whole thing being nested in an iteration or switch statement. You will break to the end of the iteration or switch, *not* the statement it's immediately nested in.

If an Identifier is included it must be an Identifier matching the label on some enclosing statement. The enclosing statement can be *any* kind of statement, not just an iterative or switch statement. In other words, it's OK to break out of any kind of enclosing block as long as you explicitly indicate it with a label. In practice, it's almost always a loop or switch that you break out of, not an if or block. Again, there is the slightly confusing feature that statements are labelled at their *beginning*, but "break" causes you to jump to their *end*. Here is an example:

```
months: for (int m=1; m<=12; m++) {

                // do something
                // nested loop
                for (int d=1; d<=31; d++) {
                        // some daily thing
                        if (cost > budget)  break months;
                }
        }
        cost=0;
```

Transfer of Control Statements

A "return" statement looks like:

```
                return;
```

```
        return  Expression;
```

Statement Notes:

- ✔ "Return" gets you back where you were called from.

- ✔ A "return *Expression*" can only be used with something that actually does return a value, i.e. never with a "void" method. There is another statement that causes transfer of control: the "throw" statement that raises an exception. We will cover this in the section in the next chapter that deals with exceptions.

There is a reserved word "goto" in Java, but there is no goto statement. The designers snagged the word to ensure that no-one uses it as a variable name, in case it later turns out to be convenient to support branching.

You can look at the java code that is output by the compiler by using the javap command, like this:

```
javap -c   class

javac pentium.java

javap -c   pentium
```

javap is an abbreviation for "java print." It can be instructive and fun to look at the bytecode output for various different java statements. 🍒

Review of Objects

This is a good point to review what we have seen of objects so far. The simplest form of data declaration looks like this:

```
type    variable;
```

If the type is a primitive type, the declaration provides you with a place to hold a value of that type. In contrast, if the type is an object type the declaration provides you with a place that holds a *reference* to an object. You do not yet have an object itself. This is a key difference from C++ and it's very important to understand the distinction. So,

```
int i;
```

gives you a variable that you can immediately do things with. But

```
Fruit melon;
```

merely gives you a location that can hold a (pointer to a) Fruit. It does not create a Fruit object. If you try to access any of the Fruit fields using melon, your program will fail.

I put "pointer to" in parentheses because the first Java white paper, "The Java Language Environment," unfortunately mentioned that "Java does not have pointers as they exist in C/C++." Too many people read the first half of that sentence without noticing the second half, and wrongly concluded that Java didn't have pointers and thus was useless for building dynamic data structures like linked lists or trees.

Java does have pointers and they are called "references." The declaration of melon I just mentioned makes melon a reference variable: it holds a pointer to a Fruit object. What Java does not have is pointer arithmetic, explicit memory deallocation (this is handled automatically for you), an "address of" operator, or anything that allows the programmer to turn a pointer into an int or back again.

Dynamic Data Structures

The first question that most programmers ask when they hear that Java does not feature pointer variables is "how do you create dynamic data structures?" How, for instance, do you create a binary tree class, in which objects of the class can point to each other?

The answer is that reference variables (which are implicit pointers) do this perfectly adequately. Here are the data members for a Tree class in C++:

```
class Tree {                    (C++ CODE)
    private:
          int     data;
          Tree    *left;
          Tree    *right;
          ...
```

Here is how the same data structure is written in Java:

```
class Tree {                    (Java CODE)
    private Object data;
    private Tree left;
    private Tree right;
          ...
```

By allowing arithmetic on pointers, unchecked deallocation, dangling pointers, pointers into the stack, and other evils, C/C++ gives the programmer too much rope. Sooner or later, most of us end up tying ourselves in knots with it. Java makes pointers implicit, and all object access is through a reference type. The compiler can automatically de-reference when an object is needed, and use the pointer when a pointer is needed (e.g. to pass an object as a parameter, or make a reference variable point to a different object).

The more general form of data declaration is:

```
    visibility_modifiers  type   [] variable  = initializer;
```

You can actually have as many bracket pairs (meaning "array of") as you like to signify multi-level arrays of arrays. You can declare several variables at once in a comma-separated list. None or any of them can be set to an initial value. The basic declaration of an object reference, combined with an initializer that creates ("instantiates") an object, looks like this:

```
    Fruit melon = new Fruit();
```

The initializer is a call to a constructor in the fruit class. Whenever you see "Someclass variable" think to yourself "variable holds a reference (initially null) to a Someclass object." Null is actually a literal value, meaning "references nothing."

Initialization

All data fields in a class have a well-defined initial value. If you did not explicitly initialize a field, it is given a default "zero-bits" value according to its type: 0, null, false, " ", 0.0, etc.

Contrast this with primitive variables declared local to a method. These have an undefined initial value. Note for those familiar with compiler internals: It's too big a performance hit to keep clearing stackframes, so it's not done, and local variables can pick up any old junk as their initial values. This won't happen for objects because objects are never allocated on the stack. All objects are allocated on the heap.

(Nearly) Everything is an Object

We come now to a brief discussion about the philosophy of Java. In some ways Java goes further than C++ in its object-oriented nature. In C++ you have several ways to structure data other than making a class out of it. You could put it in a struct for instance. Java does not have structs. The major way to group data items together in Java is to put them into a class. We also have arrays which are important enough to have their own section in the next chapter. Arrays are presented to the programmer as a class, too.

It's convenient and easy to put things in Java classes and so people do. This is really a central principle of Java: (nearly) everything is an object. Apart from the primitive types everything is object-oriented. The "main()" routine is a static method of a class, exceptions are objects, threads are objects, the GUI is built out of objects that you extend, applets are objects and of course Strings are objects.

Object

We've mentioned a couple of times that there is a class called "Object" that is the ultimate superclass of all other classes in the system. The methods that exist in Object are thus inherited by every class in the system. We have already heard of the toString() method of Object. There are also a couple of variations on the standard OS synchronization primitives wait() and notify(). These are further described in the chapter on Threads. The remaining methods in Object, and thus in every class, are listed as follows:

```
public native int hashCode ()
```

> A hashcode is an identifying value, ideally unique for every object in a program. It's used as a key in the standard java.util.Hashtable class. A hashcode could be implemented as anything, but in current compilers it looks a lot

like an address. We'll return to the subject of hashtables later. This and the next method go together.

`public boolean equals(Object obj)`

There are two philosophies for equality comparison—something may have the same reference as what you're comparing it to (i.e. you are asking "is it at the same address?"), or it may have the same value (i.e. you are asking "are these bits here the same as those bits there?") The Object version of this method returns true when the two objects being compared are actually the same one object. This is also the precise comparison that is done by the "==" operator. However, you can override equals with your own version, to give it a weaker definition. This has been done for String, because two Strings are usually considered equal if they contain the exact same sequence of characters, even if they are different objects. When you override equals(), you'll want to override hashCode() to make certain equal Objects get the same hashcode.

`protected void finalize() throws Throwable`

The method finalize() is just a hook you can override to help with memory management. See the next chapter on garbage collection. That "throws Throwable" is an indication of what error conditions (exceptions) this method can potentially raise. See the next chapter on exceptions.

`protected native Object clone() throws CloneNotSupportedException`

Java supports the notion of cloning, meaning to get a complete bit-for-bit copy of an object. The subtlety comes in when a class has data fields that are other classes. Do you simply copy the reference, and share the referenced object (a "shallow clone"), or do you recursively clone all referenced classes too (a "deep clone")? Java does a shallow clone by default, but providing this in class Object and making it overridable allows you to choose the behavior you want. You can disallow any kind of clone, or you can override clone as public (so anyone can clone) rather than the default protected (outside this package, only subclasses can clone).

Note that clone() returns an Object. The object returned by clone() is almost always immediately cast to the correct type, as in this example:

```
Vector v = new Vector();
Vector v2;

v2 = (Vector) v.clone();
```

Not every class should support the ability to clone. If I have a class that represents unique objects, such as employees in a company, the operation of cloning doesn't make sense. But methods in Object are inherited by all classes. So, the system places a further requirement on classes that want to be cloneable—they need to implement the cloneable interface to indicate that cloning is valid for them. Implementing an interface is described at the end of this chapter.

```
public final native Class getClass()
```

Java maintains a run time representation for all classes, known as RTTI or "run time type identification." This method gets that information, which is of type "Class," and which has several methods to tell you more about the class that an arbitrary object belongs to. You invoke this method in the usual way:

```
Class which = myobject.getClass();
```

Class

Here's where the terminology starts to get really confusing. The RTTI is stored in objects whose class is called "Class." It could certainly use a better, less self-referential, name. The major use of Class is to help with dynamically loading new classes. This is a systems programming activity unlikely to occur in your programs, but providing Class makes it easy to program without stepping outside the Java system.

There are several methods in class Class to access the run time information identifying other classes. All of these operate on an object of type Class (of course), so it's common to first get the Class, and then call one of its methods:

```
Class which = myobject.getClass();
String name = which.getName();
```

However the strict left-to-right evaluation of Java allows these two calls (and any such calls where the result of one method is the reference used in the next) to be written in one statement, like so:

```
String name = myobject.getClass().getName();
```

It can be useful to print out the names of classes while debugging code that deals with arbitrary objects. This and other popular methods of class are:

```
public native String getName();
```

> Returns the name of the Class.

```
public static native Class forName(String className)
    throws ClassNotFoundException
```

> This method takes a String which should be the name of a class, and retrieves the Class (RTTI) object for that class. It's an alternative to get-Class(), used when you have the name of the class in a String, rather than having any objects of it.

```
public native Object newInstance()
    throws InstantiationException, IllegalAccessException
```

> This is a surprising method—it allows you to create an object of the class for which this is the RTTI. Coupled with the forName() method, this lets you create a object of any class whose name you have in a String. Highly dynamic! The no-arg constructor of the appropriate class will be called, so it better have one.
>
> ```
> String s = "Fruit";
> ...
> Object f = Class.forName(s).newInstance();
> ```
>
> If you have an instance of a class, and you cast it to the class that you know it is, you can call its methods!

Other built-in classes

You have already seen the basic types boolean, char, int, long, etc. For each of these, there is also a class as shown in Table 4-1

Table 4-1: For every Basic type there is a corresponding class.

Basic type	Corresponding Class (in java/src/lang)
boolean	Boolean
char	Character
byte	Byte
short	Short
int	Integer
long	Long
float	Float
double	Double

The classes for Byte and Short were added in JDK 1.1.

The class version of each basic type provides an object wrapper for data values, and often a few named constants. A wrapper is useful because most of Java's utility classes require the use of objects. Since variables of these built-in types are not objects in Java, it's convenient to provide a simple way to "promote" them when needed. Note that once one of these objects has been created with a given value, that value cannot be changed. You can throw away that object and create a new one, but the object itself doesn't change its identity once assigned.

Here is an example of moving an int to an Integer object and an Integer to an int, using methods from the Integer class.

```
// changes int to Integer and back
Integer mango;
int i=42;

mango = new Integer(i);   // to Object
i = mango.intValue();     // to int
```

The Building Blocks: Compilation Units

This section covers the mechanics of how java code co-exists with the host system. It explains what gets created when you compile something, and in a larger sense how a group of such "somethings" form a Java package.

Java does away with all the aggravation of header files, forward declarations, and ordering declarations. You can think of javac as a two-pass compiler: On the first pass, the source code is scanned, and a table built of all the symbols. On the second pass, the statements are translated and since the symbol table already exists, there is never any problem about needing to see the declaration of something before its use. It's already right there in the symbol table. So any field in a class can quite happily reference any other field, even if it doesn't occur until later down the page or in another file. There is some fine print covering initialization order for pathological cases.

A source file is what you present to a Java compiler, so the contents of a complete source file are known as a "Compilation Unit." (Think of it as the unit of compilation, just as the gram is a unit of weight).

Automatic Compilation

Java tries hard not to let you build a system using some components that are out-of-date. When you invoke the compiler on a source file, the compiler does not just translate that in isolation. It looks to see what classes it references, and tries to determine if they are up-to-date. If the compiler decides another class needs compiling it adds it in, and recursively applies the same procedure to it.

In other words, Java has a "make"-like utility built into it. Say the class you are compiling makes reference to a class in another file. That utility is capable of noticing when the second .class file does not exist, but the corresponding .java does, and of noticing when the .java file has been modified without a recompilation taking place. In both these cases it will add the second .java file to the set of files it is recompiling.

Here is an example. This is the contents of file plum.java

```
public class plum {
    grape m;

}
```

And this is the contents of file grape.java

```
public class grape {}
```

If we now compile plum.java, the compiler will look for grape.class, check that it is up-to-date with respect to its source file, and if not, it will recompile grape.java for you!

Here is the output from such a compilation:

```
javac -verbose plum.java
[parsed plum.java in 602ms]
[checking class plum]
[parsed .//grape.java in 44ms]
[wrote plum.class]
[checking class grape]
[wrote .//grape.class]
```

[done in 2347ms]

As you can see, grape.java got compiled as well, creating grape.class.

There is a "-depend" option to the java compiler to tell it to consider the freshness of all classes this depends on directly and indirectly, and recompile as needed. There is a related "–cs" option when running an application, to check that the source has not been updated after the bytecodes were generated. If the source is newer, it will recompile it:

```
java –cs myApp
```

will achieve this. 🐾

File Name Is Related To Class Name

Java emphasizes the idea that the name of a file is related to its contents, and understanding this is the key to understanding how to build programs out of more than one file or library. What we're explaining here is how the rules work when you use the default case of source and object files in the same directory. If you use the "-d" option to javac to make your class files be written in a different directory to the source, then the rules below are modified correspondingly.

A compilation unit (source file) has several rules:

1. It can start with a "package" statement, identifying the package (a library) that the class will belong to.

   A package statement looks like

   ```
   package mydir;
   ```
   When starting out, it's simplest not to use packages. Your class files will be visible to other classes in the same directory, and belong to a default anonymous package.

2. Next can come zero or more "import" statements, each identifying a package or a class from a package, that will be available in this compilation unit.

   An import statement looks like

   ```
   import java.io.*;
   ```
   The predefined package "java.lang.*" is automatically imported into each compilation unit for every compilation. Java.lang contains the classes Float, Long, etc. discussed above and other classes as well.

3. The rest of the compilation unit consists of Class declarations and Interface declarations. Interfaces are skeletons of Classes showing what form the Class will take when someone implements it.

4. At most one of the classes in the file can be "public." This class must have the corresponding name as the file it is in, as shown in Figure 4-2.

   ```
   public class plum     must be in file plum.java.
   ```

The underlying host system should allow filenames with the same form as Java classnames: unbounded length, contain "$" or "_" as well as Unicode alphabetics, and case sensitive. The more restrictions there are on filenames on your host system, the more restrictions there will be on the classnames you can use. This will form a practical impediment to the total portability of software. Avoid using characters in classnames that are problematic for any host file systems.

Each of the classes in a .java file will create an individual .class file to hold the generated byte codes. If you have three classes in a source file, the compiler will create three . class files.

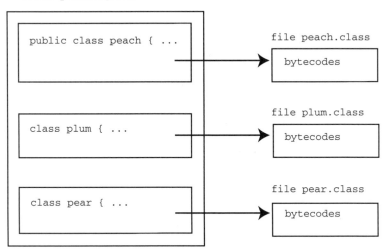

Figure 4-2: Classes and corresponding file names

The Building Blocks: Packages

Right up front, let's make it clear that the java term "package" means a collection of individual .class files in a directory. So a package is both a directory and a library. A package is the way we group several (usually related) class files together. They are grouped together in the file system as files in the same directory. Just as java classnames must match the source file name, so too must package names match the directory name.

As well as being a way of grouping multiple classes together, a package also has implications for the visibility of classes and fields. The default access modifier (i.e. not mentioning "public," "private" or "protected") means the element is visible to everything else in the same package and nothing in other packages. For that reason, some people call this unnamed visibility "package access." Public things are visible in other packages. Protected things are visible in subclasses regardless of package boundaries.

Package names (which match directory names), classnames (which match file names), and the CLASSPATH environment all work together to pinpoint which classes are pulled into a compilation. You need to understand all three together.

When you start to build bigger systems you will use a "package" statement at the top of each source file to say which package the class belongs to. The package name must match the directory name. You can also prefix it with the name of the parent directory, and so on, up the directory hierarchy (as high as you need to go to represent the structure of your system). The package name is concatenated with the class name and stored as the full name of the class.

In the example above, if our source file "peach.java" is in a directory:

```
/home/linden/Java/Code/Examples
```

then some choices for package name in the package statement would be:

```
package Examples;
package Code.Examples;
package Java.Code.Examples;
```

and so on.

Another way to think about this, is to take the pathname to a given source file, say "/a/b/c/d.java". The endmost component forces the public class in the Java file to be called "d". For example:

```
public class d {
```

The name of the package is formed by taking the rest of the pathname, and substituting dots for the file separator character "/" (or "\" on Windows systems). If the compilation unit above starts with a package statement it can only be one of these alternatives (in this example):

```
        package a.b.c;
or      package    b.c;
or      package    c;
```

This requirement that package name match the source file directory name also means that any given directory can contain files of at most one named package (see Figure 4-3). It could also contain a few files compiled into the default anonymous package as well, but we assume that if you are building a big system across several directories, you are going to take care to make sure everything ends up in a named package.

Using the host filesystem to structure a Java program, and particularly to help organize the program namespace, is a very good idea. It avoids unnecessary generality, and it provides a clear model for understanding.

If you let your directory naming match components in your Internet domain name (sorted from most general to least general, e.g. "com.sun.engineering"), you can also easily create package names that will be unique across the entire Internet (because domain names have this quality). This allows different vendors to provide class libraries with no danger of namespace collisions.

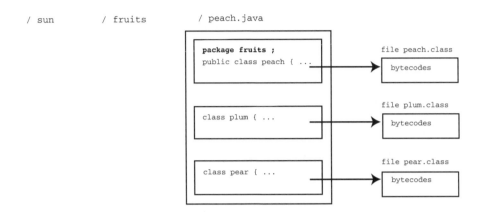

Figure 4-3: How package names relate to directory names

Classpath

CLASSPATH is an environment variable, typically set in the autoexec.bat file (on Windows) or in a shell initialization file (on Unix). CLASSPATH is not required from JDK 1.1 on, unless you are creating your own packages. In fact, you'll confuse the compiler if you do set it unnecessarily, so remove any reference to it left from any previous version of the JDK. The CLASSPATH will be set to a list of one or more pathnames separated by ";" (Windows) or ":" (Unix). It may look like this, for instance on Windows:

```
SET CLASSPATH = c:\sun;c:\project\test\source;.
```

It may look like this on a Unix system using c-shell:

```
setenv CLASSPATH /sun:/project/test/source:.
```

The CLASSPATH tells the class loader all the possible starting places to begin looking for Java packages to import or to load at runtime. The look-up algorithm will do this:

- Take the full name of the class we are looking for, including the package name, e.g. "java.lang.Math"

- Replace the dot (".") characters with directory separator characters and suffix it with ".class." In this example, we will get "java/lang/Math.class" on Unix, "java\lang\Math.class" on Windows.

- Take that pathname from step 2, concatenate it onto each element of the CLASSPATH, and look that up in the filesystem. Here we would consecutively look for:

```
/sun/java/lang/Math.class
/project/test/source/java/lang/Math.class
./java/lang/Math.class
```

One of these had better be a match, or else the compilation will fail with "Class not found." The first match found is the class it is looking for.

To summarize, CLASSPATH, package, and classnames are related to the filesystem names in this manner:

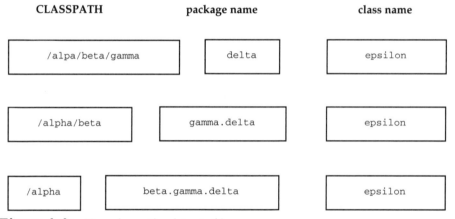

Figure 4-4: How classpath relates to filenames

The three lines above show three alternatives for CLASSPATH and package names in order to identify the same one filename:

```
/alpha / beta / gamma / delta / epsilon.java
```

CLASSPATH is used when executing programs too. If you try

```
java foo
```

you will get back the error message "can't find class foo" if "foo" isn't in any of the directories pointed at by your CLASSPATH.

This can be very frustrating if your CLASSPATH doesn't include the current working directory, and you want to execute something in there. You list the directory contents, and there is "foo.class." Why can't java see it!? Answer: it uses a different algorithm for looking for class files than you do. It doesn't know to look in the current directory unless the CLASSPATH tells it to. 🐾

The CLASSPATH can also be given as a compiler option, but most people will find it simpler to set it once, rather than mention it on each compiler invocation. It is possible to use the "-d pathname" option with the Java compiler to cause the class files to be written to a different directory than the one the source resides in. As the name suggests, the CLASSPATH is only used to hunt for .class files. Normally they reside with the corresponding source, but if you have caused them to go elsewhere, then modify the advice above appropriately.

Import

You never have to use the "import" statement. Its effect is to allow you to use a class name directly, instead of fully qualifying it with the package name. So these are your two alternatives:

```
class Pie {
        java.util.Date      whenmade;
        double              weight;
    }
```

or

```
import java.util.Date;
class Pie {
        Date       whenmade;
        double     weight;
    }
```

An import statement can either name an individual class file that is being imported, or a series of them like this

```
import fruits.peach;
import fruits.orange;
import fruits.prune;
```

Or it can specify that all public files in that package are to be imported, with a statement like this:

```
import fruits.*;
```

An "import" statement always has at least two components, like so:

```
import    package.classname
```

The final component is either a class name, or a "*" meaning all classes in that package.

Some people say "just use the 'import all classes' form," others recommend that you only import the minimum number of packages and libraries that you require. It provides clear documentation on what the actual dependencies are.

Whatever you import, only the code that is needed gets written to the .class file. Superfluous imports are discarded.

All compilations import the standard Java package `java.lang.*` without specifically naming it. It contains the standard I/O streams, objects representing some of the built-in types, predefined exceptions, and mathematical operations, among other useful items.

Here is a diagram showing how the "import" statement works and interacts with "package" and "CLASSPATH" for files that are split across different directories.

How Import Names Relate to Package and Directory Names

Using a CLASSPATH that includes the path "/sun", the import statement "import fruits.*" tells the compiler to make available all public class files from the package found in directory /sun/fruits. In Figure 4-5 there is only one public class file from that directory, namely, the class "peach," and it will be usable in class runner, under the name "fruits.peach," or simply "peach." The scope of any imported classes is the entire compilation unit (file).

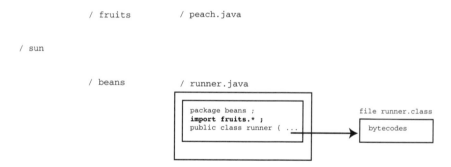

Figure 4-5:   One public class file representing the class peach

Zip files were introduced in December 1995 for classes. A zip file is a collection of .class files all grouped together in one physical file, as can be done on Windows with the standard Windows zip software. Jar files replaced zip files in the JDK 1.1 release. Jar files are in zip format, and can contain an extra "manifest" file listing all the files in the jar.

The standard java and Sun libraries now come all wrapped up in one zip file called "java/lib/classes.zip". This blows the import model a little, in that you have to make the CLASSPATH environment variable contain the name of the actual zip file, rather than the path to it, like this:

(Unix): `setenv CLASSPATH /java/lib/classes.zip:.:/mycode`

(Windows): `set CLASSPATH=c:\java\lib\classes.zip;.;c:\mycode`

Think of the justification as "the zip file contains an archive of class files, so in some theoretical sense it is a directory." Or don't think of it at all if it makes your head hurt. It is convenient for a browser opening a connection to a remote URL applet. The browser only need open one connection for a package, not one for each class. Since opening the TCP/IP connection often takes more time than transmitting the data this is a win. Zip files are a performance enhancement aimed mostly at browsers. ❧

Visibility Revisited

With this new knowledge of how classes are organized and referenced by the compiler, let us revisit the (nontrivial) field modifiers that we first listed in Chapter 2. Java has field modifiers that support four levels of accessibility. In order of most accessible to least accessible, they are:

1.   **public**—world access

2.   **protected**—accessible in this package (think "directory") and also in subclasses in other packages

3.   Default—package access (any class in the package)

4.   **private**—accessible only in this class

Java has no exact equivalent of the C++ "protected" modifier that says "this field can only be accessed by this class and its subclasses." The Java "protected" modifier has a slightly different meaning that says "this field can only be accessed by this class and its subclasses, plus anything else in the same package." Java has no equivalent of C++ "friend." ❧

The interaction between classes and subclasses, along with things in the same package and things in other packages can be downright confusing. Figures 4-6 through 4-9 are designed to illustrate the interaction of public, protected, default (package), and private.

Note that the access modifiers for a method can come in any order: static public is the same as public static.

However, the return type of a method must be next to the method name. Otherwise you will get this error:

```
void public init() {
         ^
```

```
alice.java:8: Invalid method declaration; return type required.
```

The correct way to write this is:

```
public void init() {❧
```

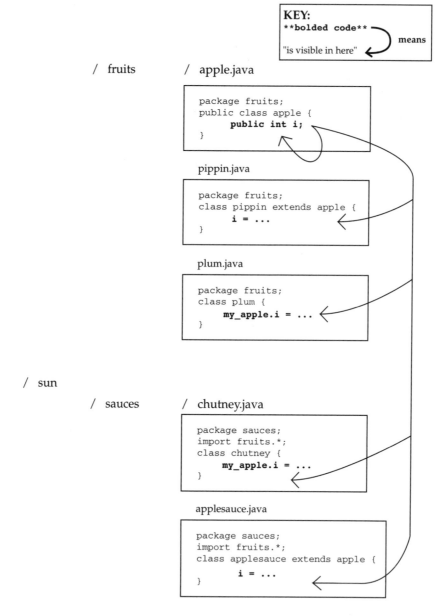

KEY:
bolded code
"is visible in here"
means

/ fruits   / apple.java

```
package fruits;
public class apple {
    public int i;
}
```

pippin.java

```
package fruits;
class pippin extends apple {
    i = ...
}
```

plum.java

```
package fruits;
class plum {
    my_apple.i = ...
}
```

/ sun

/ sauces   / chutney.java

```
package sauces;
import fruits.*;
class chutney {
    my_apple.i = ...
}
```

applesauce.java

```
package sauces;
import fruits.*;
class applesauce extends apple {
    i = ...
}
```

Figure 4-6:   Public—visible everywhere

/ fruits   / apple.java

```
package fruits;
public class apple {
    protected int i;
}
```

pippin.java

```
package fruits;
class pippin extends apple {
    i = ...
}
```

plum.java

```
package fruits;
class plum {
    my_apple.i = ...
}
```

/ sun

/ sauces   / chutney.java

```
package sauces;
import fruits.*;
class chutney {

}
```

applesauce.java

```
package sauces;
import fruits.*;
class applesauce extends apple {
    i = ...
}
```

Figure 4-7:   Protected—visible in same package, and subclasses anywhere

/ fruits   / apple.java

```
package fruits;
public class apple {
             int i;
}
```

pippin.java

```
package fruits;
class pippin extends apple {
             i = ...
}
```

plum.java

```
package fruits;
class plum {
      my_apple.i = ...
}
```

/ sun

     / sauces   / chutney.java

```
package sauces;
import fruits.*;
class chutney {

}
```

applesauce.java

```
package sauces;
import fruits.*;
class applesauce extends apple {

}
```

Figure 4-8: Default (package)—visible in this package

/ fruits / apple.java

```
package fruits;
public class apple {
    private int i;
}
```

pippin.java

```
package fruits;
class pippin extends apple {

}
```

plum.java

```
package fruits;
class plum {

}
```

/ sun

/ sauces / chutney.java

```
package sauces;
import fruits.*;
class chutney {

}
```

applesauce.java

```
package sauces;
import fruits.*;
class applesauce extends apple {

}
```

Figure 4-9:   Private—not accessible outside this class

Terminology

Packages and classes have members. The members of a package are the subpackages and classes. The members of a class are the fields (data) and methods (code).

What Happens When Names Collide?

If a variable in the subclass has the same name as a variable in the superclass, then it supersedes ("hides") the superclass one. The visible, subclass variable is said to "shadow" (put in the shade) the superclass variable. The superclass one is still available by giving its full name, e.g. "Fruit.grams" or using the "super" keyword "super.grams." The reason Java allows hiding is to allow new fields to be added to superclasses without breaking existing subclasses.

A variable may have the same name as a method in its own class or superclass, without either hiding the other. Name duplication should be rare, because the Java Language Specification says that method names should be based on verbs, while field names should be based on nouns (JLS, sect. 6.8). And for the sake of completeness, note that the case of a method with the same name in both the superclass and the subclass is dealt with in the section in Chapter 2 on polymorphism.

Interface Declarations

Interfaces are an important concept in Java. Let's motivate a discussion of interfaces by explaining that interfaces are in the language mainly to provide much of the functionality of multiple inheritance, but without the difficulties. In C++, a class can inherit from multiple superclasses, as shown in Figure 4-10.

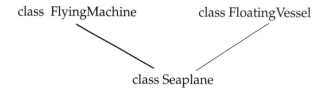

Figure 4-10: Multiple Inheritance

Problems arise when there are name clashes in the base classes. Class FlyingMachine may have a method called navigate() which does navigation in three dimensions. Class FloatingVessel may have a method with the same name, but which only navigates in two dimensions. Seaplane inherits both methods, which immediately results in a name clash error. You don't want to be forced to change the names in one base class because of names in some other base class. Worse, there is no general way to say which of the two navigate() methods Seaplane should have and which it should forget.

Interfaces avoid this kind of problem. An interface is a skeleton of a class, showing the methods the class will have when someone implements it. An interface
may look like this:

```
interface FlyingMachine {
        int navigate(Point from, Point to);
        void land();
        void takeoff(double fuel);
    }
```

The declarations in an interface are always public, even if you don't label them so.
The methods aren't labelled public here to avoid cluttering up the examples, but it
is always preferred to label fields with their actual modifiers. You can declare data
in an interface but only constant data. Even if you don't label it "final," this is
assumed for you.

An interface is thus a way of saying "you need to plug some code in here for this
thing to fully work." The interface specifies the exact signatures of the methods
that must be provided. A later class implements the interface by defining those
methods including their bodies. If two interfaces should happen to demand a
method of the same name in a class, it isn't a problem. It merely says that both
interfaces are making the same demand for a method of that name in the class.
Here's an example implementation of the FlyingMachine interface:

```
class Helicopter implements FlyingMachine {
        double fueltank;
        int engine_rpm;
        int rotors;

        int navigate(Point from, Point to) {
                // full body of code appears here
        }

        void land() {
            for( ; engine_rpm>0; engine_rpm--) ;
        }

        void takeoff(double fuel) {
            fueltank += fuel;
            for( ; engine_rpm<6000; engine_rpm++) ;
        }

        void hover() {
                // full body of code appears here
        }

        // other methods can be in the class too.
    }
```

Several different classes can implement the same interface, each in their own special way. A class may implement several interfaces at once, leading people to say that Java has multiple inheritance of interfaces, but not of implementations. The FloatingVessel interface may look like:

```
interface FloatingVessel {
        int navigate(Point from, Point to);
        void dropAnchor();
        void weighAnchor();
}
```

The class Seaplane may then implement the methods promised by both the FloatingVessel and the FlyingMachine interfaces, like this:

```
class Seaplane implements FloatingVessel, FlyingMachine {
        double fueltank;
        int engine_rpm;
        int anchorline;

        void dropAnchor(){
            anchorline = 200;
        }

        void weighAnchor(){
            anchorline = 0;
        }

        int navigate(Point from, Point to) {
            // full body of code appears here
        }

        void land() {
            for( ; engine_rpm>0; engine_rpm--) ;
            dropAnchor();
        }

        void takeoff(double fuel) {
            weighAnchor();
            fueltank += fuel;
            for( ; engine_rpm<6000; engine_rpm++) ;
        }

        // other methods can be in the class too.
}
```

One reader of the previous edition wondered how you could implement a Seaplane if FloatingVessel and FlyingVessel had already been coded as classes, not interfaces. One answer is to define the Seaplane class to contain an instance of both those vessels, and to use the methods as desired.

An interface is used to specify the form that something *must* have, but not actually provide the implementation. In this sense, an interface is a little like an abstract class, that must be extended in exactly the manner that its methods present. An interface differs from an abstract class in the following ways:

- An abstract class is an incomplete class. An interface is a specification or prescription for behavior.

- A class can implement several interfaces at once, whereas a class can only extend one parent class.

- An interface doesn't have any overtones of specialization that are present with inheritance. It merely says "well, we need something that does 'foo' and here are the ways that users should be able to call it."

- Interfaces can be used to support call backs. (Inheritance doesn't help with this). This is a most important and significant coding idiom. It essentially provides a pointer to a function, but in a type-safe way. The next section explains call-backs.

Here's the bottom line: you'll probably use interfaces a lot more than abstract classes. Use an abstract class when you want to initiate a hierarchy of more specialized classes. Use an interface when you just want to say "I want to be able to call methods with these signatures in your class."

Using Interfaces Dynamically

So far the examples of interfaces have all been solving compile time issues. There is an additional way that an interface can be used to obtain more dynamic behavior. Once we have defined an interface, we can use it as the type of some parameter to a method. Inside the method we can use that parameter to invoke the operations that the interface promises. Whenever we make a call to that method, we can pass it a class that implements the interface, and it will call the appropriate method of that class. The following four steps should make this a little clearer.

1. Define an interface, which promises a method called "run," like this:

```
interface runnable {
    public void run();
}
```

2. Now sprinkle calls to "run" throughout our code, even though we don't yet have anything that fulfills the interface.

```
void vitalSystemThing(runnable r) {
    r.run();
}
```

This code can be compiled and put in a library.

3. At a later time and in another file entirely, we provide a class (or several classes) that implements the following interface:

```
class myCode implements runnable {
    public void run() {
        System.out.println("You called myCode.run()");
    }
    // other code ...
}
```

4. Finally, we pass myCode object to the vitalSystemThing

```
myCode myobj = new myCode()
vitalSystemThing( myobj );
```

This results in myCode.run() being called back, hence this is known as a "callback." It's a longwinded way of doing what you do with a function pointer in C or C++, and the obscurity of it has led some people to call for function pointers to be added to Java. Java callbacks are type-safe, but function pointers might not be.

The main reason for writing your code this way is that it decouples the calling routine from the called back routine. You could have several different classes that implement the runnable interface. Callbacks allow any or all of them to be sent to the vitalSystemThing, and hence called back. The correct class is called back, based on the type at runtime.

There actually is a built-in Java interface, called "Runnable" (with a capital "R") that is used in this way for threads. It is described in Chapter 5. The use of an interface allows the runtime system to schedule and control threads which you implement and compile later. Here is another example of an interface used as a callback.

```
interface runnable {
    public void run();
}

public class VeryDynamic {
    public static void main(String args[]) {
        runnable r;
        try {
            Class unknown = Class.forName(args[0]);
            r = (runnable) unknown.newInstance();
            r.run();
        } catch (Exception e){ e.printStackTrace();}

    }
}

class Coffee implements runnable {
    public void run() { System.out.println("Coffee.run called"); }
}

class Tea implements runnable {
    public void run() { System.out.println("Tea.run called"); }
}
```

Ignore the try and catch statements for now—they are required here to accommo-date the exceptions that the enclosed statements might cause. If you compile this program, you can run it like this:

```
java VeryDynamic Tea
```

Try executing it with an argument of "Coffee" and an argument of "Bogus." The three lines in bold simply get the runtime type information for the class whose name you give as an argument. Then create an instance of that class that is cast to runnable and call the run() method of that class.

There's another way to use an interface, that's not really what it was intended for, but which forms a useful programming idiom.

If you have a group of related constants, perhaps of the kind you would put in an enumerated type (if the language had enumerated types), you might gather them in a class like this:

```
public class FightingWeight {
    public static final int          flyweight = 100;
    public static final int        bantamweight = 113;
    public static final int      featherweight = 118;
    public static final int         lightweight = 127;
    public static final int        welterweight = 136;
    public static final int        middleweight = 148;
    public static final int lightheavyweight = 161;
    public static final int         heavyweight = 176;
}
```

Then to use the constants in another class, you would have to do something like this:

```
static int title = FightingWeight.heavyweight;
```

If however, you make FightingWeight an *interface*, like this:

```
public interface FightingWeight {
    public static final int          flyweight = 100;
    public static final int        bantamweight = 113;
    public static final int      featherweight = 118;
    public static final int         lightweight = 127;
    public static final int        welterweight = 136;
    public static final int        middleweight = 148;
    public static final int lightheavyweight = 161;
    public static final int         heavyweight = 176;
}
```

Then you can reference the names directly. Wow!

```
class gooseberry implements FightingWeight {
    ...
static int title = heavyweight;
```

Don't tell anyone you heard it from me, at least not until the gods of programming have smiled upon it.[2] This works for classes too, but it's poor style to extend a class just to get better name visibility.

An interface can only extend another interface. A class can legally implement an interface but only implement some of the methods. It then becomes an abstract class that must be further extended (inherited) before it can be instantiated.

---

2. The gods of programming have now officially granted their benediction to this technique of opening up name visibility.

Some Light Relief

To close out a chapter that has dealt at length with naming, it's appropriate to consider two other examples of naming, and the confusion that can arise. The first one is computer-related, the second one pertains to confectionery. But they are both instructive.

There's a pervasive legend that the antihero computer HAL in the film "2001: A Space Odyssey" was so-named to indicate that he was one step ahead of IBM. Alphabetically "H" "A" "L" precede "I" "B" "M" by one letter.[3]

The author of 2001, Arthur C. Clarke emphatically denies the legend in his book "Lost Worlds of 2001," claiming that "HAL" is an acronym for "Heuristically programmed algorithmic computer." Clarke even wrote to the computer magazine *Byte* to place his denial on record.

Certainly the claims of an involved party are one piece of evidence, but there is no particular reason why they should be uncritically accepted as complete truth; consider them rather in the context of all pieces of evidence. This is what happens in courts of law every day. Clarke's protestations are a little unconvincing. For one thing "Heuristically programmed algorithmic computer" is a contrived name that does not properly form the desired acronym. For another, most of the working drafts of the 2001 story had HAL named "Athena," and it would have remained so had not Clarke deliberately rechristened it. The chances of him accidentally fastening on to the one name that mimics one of the world's largest computer companies are one in a few thousand.

Why would Clarke deny it if it were true? IBM logos appear in several places in the movie, and the filmmakers clearly cut a deal with IBM for product placement. It may be that Clarke decided to assert some artistic independence and decided on the name change as a subtle dig at IBM, in that HAL is a homicidal maniac who goes berserk. Or he may just have been suggesting that his creation was one step ahead of IBM. Later, when the story got out, Clarke realized he would look foolish, or at the very least ungracious by lampooning them. So he denied the connection.

An interesting question is why was the name changed at all? If Clarke provided an explanation of *that* along with his denials, then the denials would have more credibility.

---

3. People say the same thing about Windows NT (WNT) being one step away of VMS. Dave Cutler designed VMS when he was at Digital, and then joined Microsoft to become the chief architect of Windows NT. I believe that the name was chosen with this in mind.

Lessons in Naming: the disgusting case of the Baby Ruth Candy Bar

A similar confusion over naming has arisen in the case of the Baby Ruth candy bar. The matter was thoroughly researched by my colleague David Mikkelson who wrote the following summary of his findings.

> The Curtiss Candy Company was founded in Chicago in 1916 by Otto Schnering. Schnering, who wanted a name more "American-sounding" than his own for the company—German surnames not being much of an asset during World War I—used his mother's maiden name instead.
>
> The Curtiss Candy Company's first product was a confection known as Kandy Kake, which featured a pastry center topped with nuts and coated with chocolate. This candy bar was only a moderate success until 1921, when Schnering reintroduced it as a log-shaped bar made of caramel and peanuts, covered with chocolate. Schnering named his new confection the "Baby Ruth" bar, priced it at five cents a bar (half the cost of other bars), and soon had one of the hottest-selling candy bars on the market.

Three explanations have since been offered concerning the origins of the "Baby Ruth" candy bar's name:

1. The bar was named after "Baby" Ruth Cleveland, the first-born daughter of President Grover Cleveland.

2. The bar was named after baseball slugger George Herman "Babe" Ruth.

3. The bar was named for a granddaughter of Mrs. George Williamson, Mrs. Williamson being the wife of the president of the Williamson Candy Company and one of the developers of the "Baby Ruth" bar formula.

Explanation #1 is the "official" explanation that has been proffered by the Curtiss Candy Company since the 1920s.

Explanation #2 is the "obvious" explanation; the one assumed by persons who have heard no explanations.

Explanation #3 is an alternate explanation whose origins are unknown, but it can be readily dismissed. The Williamson Candy Company—producer of the "Oh! Henry" bar—was a direct competitor of Curtiss' and would have been most unlikely to supply a product name and formula to a rival. Furthermore, the Curtiss Candy Company has never claimed this as an origin of their candy bar's name.

The claim that the "Baby Ruth" bar was named after Ruth Cleveland is found dubious by many because Ruth Cleveland died of diphtheria in 1904, over seventeen years before the "Baby Ruth" bar was first produced. Naming a candy bar after the long-dead daughter of a former president would certainly be a curious choice. Moreover, the notion that a candy bar called "Baby Ruth" should appear on the market just when a baseball player named Babe Ruth had suddenly become the most famous person in America is perceived as a rather striking coincidence.

If the Curtiss Candy Company did indeed appropriate Babe Ruth's name without permission, they would have had a motive for developing a fabricated yet believable explanation in case a challenge arose over the candy bar's name. Curtiss did indeed have to fight off at least one challenge to their name, when a competitor—with the full approval of Babe Ruth—attempted to market a candy named the "Babe Ruth Home Run Bar." Curtiss, claiming that their candy bar was named for Ruth Cleveland, was successful in forcing the competing candy bar off the market because its name too closely resembled that of their own product. Nobody ever said life was fair, and that's the way things are in the brutal world of children's candy marketing.

The fact that Curtiss successfully fought off a challenge to their candy bar's name does not prove that they were untruthful, however. Merely showing that they had a reason to lie is not evidence that they did lie and are still lying; it must be demonstrated that Curtiss actually has been untruthful about the origins of the "Baby Ruth" name. Although it may not now be possible to prove that Curtiss was less than honest when they were fighting off the challenge of the "Babe Ruth Home Run Bar," it can certainly be demonstrated that they have been dishonest about the origin of the name "Baby Ruth" in the years since then.

First of all, the official Curtiss position maintained for many years is that their "candy bar made its initial appearance in 1921, some years before Babe Ruth . . . became famous." In 1919, Babe Ruth was a standout pitcher for the Red Sox, but not yet well-known outside of Boston and the baseball world. Sold to the New York Yankees prior to the 1920 season, Ruth soon established himself as an outfield star and was nationally famous by the end of the year. By 1921 his name was featured more prominently on the front pages of afternoon newspapers than President Harding's. The claim that he was not famous until "some years" after 1921 is nothing but absurd. This misstatement could merely be a mistake on Curtiss' part due to shoddy record-keeping or research, but the claim has been offered for so many years and is so easily verifiable that it is hard to explain as anything other than dissembling.

Another claim made by the Curtiss Candy Company is much harder to forgive as mere bad record-keeping, though. Part of the official statement about the "Baby Ruth" name offered by Curtiss has been that Ruth Cleveland "visited the Curtiss Candy Company plant years ago when the company was getting started and this largely influenced the company's founder to name the candy bar 'Baby Ruth'." Ruth Cleveland died at age twelve in 1904; no amount of bad record-keeping can place her in the factory of a company that wouldn't exist until more than a decade after her death. The conclusion is clear.

See how many books you can find which have the inaccurate version of the Baby Ruth candy bar story. The story is commonly re-told with the Curtiss cover story being presented as fact. I have yet to find a reference work where the author has actually done some independent analysis, and concluded that Curtiss is full of it. Kudos to David Mikkelson for setting the record straight.

Exercises

1. What advantages are there in requiring all Java implementations to share the same data sizes for the primitive types? What disadvantages are there?

2. Write a short program that clearly demonstrates floating-point arithmetic is inexact.

3. Why do we have a primitive type boolean, and reference type Boolean?

4. Why does every class have a toString() method? Where does it come from and for what is it useful?

5. Describe what the class Class provides.

6. Describe how the CLASSPATH variable is combined with package and class names to locate a class file.

7. What are two common uses for interfaces?

8. Take any class that you have written, and make it cloneable by making it implement the Cloneable interface. The Cloneable source code is at $JAVAHOME/src/java/lang/Cloneable.java. Write some code to clone an object of your class. Override Object.clone() to do a deep copy for your class.

Sources:

Bob Broeg, "At Microphone, Plate, Reggie's A Real Blast" <u>St. Louis Post-Dispatch</u>, 7 August 1993.

Ray Broekel, <u>The Great American Candy Bar Book</u> (Boston: Houghton Mifflin, 1982), p. 23

Tom Burnam, <u>More Misinformation</u> (New York: Lippincott & Crowell, 1980), p. 13

Sharon Kapnick, "Sweet Beginnings; How Some Famous Chocolate Treats Evolved to Stand the Taste of Time" <u>The Arizona Republic</u>, 13 February 1993.

Richard Sandomir, "Legacy of Earning Power; Babe Ruth: Dead 41 Years, He Lives on in Endorsements That Bring Heirs Hundreds of Thousands" <u>Los Angeles Times</u>, 22 December 1989

Kal Wagenheim, <u>Babe Ruth: His Life and Legend</u> (New York: Praeger Publishers, 1974), p.86

Further Reading

"What Every Computer Scientist Should Know About Floating-Point Arithmetic"

by David Goldberg Computing Surveys, March 1991, published by the Association for Computing Machinery.

It explains why all floating-point arithmetic is approximate, and how errors can creep in. The paper was reprinted and is distributed in postscript form with the compilers sold by Sun Microsystems.

ANSI/IEEE Standard 754-1985 for Binary Floating-Point Arithmetic

Institute of Electrical and Electronic Engineers, New York, published 1985. Reprinted in SIGPLAN 22(2) pages 9-25.

"The C Programming Language, Second Edition"

by Brian W. Kernighan and Dennis Ritchie Published by Prentice-Hall Inc., New Jersey, 1988

ISBN 0-13-110163-3

The first edition of this book was the ground-breaking work from which so much has flowed in the past twenty years. Like C itself, this book set a standard which many have aspired, but few others have achieved. The text (and the language) is not perfect, few things of human construction are, but it has served well over the years.

CHAPTER 5

- All About Arrays

- Exceptions and their Purpose

- What are Threads

- Collecting Garbage

More Sophisticated Techniques

London's gangland underworld was dominated during the 1960s by two brothers who were career criminals from the East-end, Ronnie and Reggie Kray. The Kray twins were eventually sentenced to life terms in prison for the chaos and mayhem they created.

FACT: The UK government Meteorological Office has two Cray supercomputers used to simulate chaotic systems such as weather fronts. These twin Crays are therefore affectionately named "Ronnie" and "Reggie"—the Cray twins.

I n this chapter we address the topic of arrays, and how to build dynamic data structures in a language without pointers. We then go on to cover the functionality of exceptions (runtime error handling) and threads (light weight processes). We finish up with some notes on the automatic reclaiming of memory that is no longer in use.

Arrays

It is a little misleading to claim as some people have done that "support and syntax for arrays is much the same in Java as it is in C." Any similarities are superficial ones based on syntax alone. The key to understanding C arrays is understanding the interaction between arrays and pointers. But Java does away with all that guff.

Java has neither the complexities, nor the "size fixed at compile time" of C arrays. The Java array model is more like that of Ada: arrays of arbitrary bounds as parameters, and dynamically-allocatable arrays, each carrying around information about its own length.

Arrays are regarded as objects in Java. Here are some ways in which arrays *are* like objects:

- Because the language says so
- Arrays are a reference type
- Arrays are always allocated on the heap, never on the stack
- Arrays inherit from Object, and support methods such as toString()
- Arrays are allocated with the "new" operator.

On the other hand, here are some ways arrays *are not* like objects:

- They have a different syntax from other object classes
- You can't subclass and extend arrays
- You can't define your own methods for arrays
- An array can't implement an interface or be cloned.

There is, however, a method `java.lang.System.arraycopy()` that will copy part or all of an array. On the whole, the right frame of mind is to regard arrays as a funny kind of object that shares some key characteristics of regular objects. Most importantly, arrays are a reference type.

When you declare what looks like an array, you actually get a variable that can hold a reference to an array. You still have to create the array. The simplest form of array declaration is this:

```
int carrot [];
```

Note that the size is not given. In fact you may not specify the array dimension in a declaration like this.

You never specify the size of an array in a C-style declaration like this:

```
int carrot [256];                // NO! NO! NO!
```

The array's size is set when you assign something to it, either in an initializer or a regular assignment statement. Once an array object has been created with a given size, it cannot change for that array, although you can replace it by assigning a differently-sized array object to it.

The array can be created like this:

```
int carrot [] = new int[256];
```

This creates a 256 element array, with the default initialization of 0; you can create and initialize an array in one declaration, like this:

```
int carrot[] = {1,2,3,4,5,6};
float beet[]  = { 5.5F, p, q, 2.2F, };
```

Note that a superfluous trailing comma is allowed in an initialization list—an unnecessary carryover from C. The permissible extra trailing comma is claimed to be of use when a list of initial values is being generated automatically. The claim is like Dick van Dyke's cockney accent in the film "Mary Poppins"—it starts off as unlikely, then rapidly becomes totally unbelievable the more you hear it.

Array constants (a series of values in braces) can only be used in initializers, not in later assignment statements. There's no good reason for this restriction.

Because an array is an object, all the usual object-y style things apply. Operations that are common to all objects can be done on arrays. Operations that require an object as an operand can be passed an array. The length of an array (the number of components in it) is a data field in the array class. So you can get the size of an array by referencing:

```
a.length      // yes
```

People always want to treat that as a method call, and write

```
a.length()    // NO! NO! NO!
```

Think of it this way: for an array, length is just a final data field, set when the array object is created. There is no need to have the overhead of a method call. There is no need for a "sizeof" operator, and Java does not have one.

You may be wondering how to get the length of the array (the total number of Strings) versus the length of a given String in the array when there is an array of Strings. This situation frequently occurs when you need to find out something about the String arguments to the main() routine. Here is some code that demonstrates the two scenarios.

```
public static void main(String args[]) {
    int i=0;
    System.out.println( "number of Strings: " + args.length );
    System.out.println( "length of i'th String:" + args[i].length() );
}
```

Contrast how "length" is a data field for arrays, and is a method for the class String. This is a frequent point of confusion for beginners.

For non-C programmers: array subscripts *always* start at 0.

People coming to Java (or C or C++) from another language often have trouble with that concept. After all, when you're counting anything, you always start "one, two, three"—so why would array elements be any different?

The answer is that this is one of the things carried over from C. C was designed by and for systems programmers, and in a compiler a subscript is translated to "offset from base address." You can save a step in subscript-to-address translation if you disallow subscripts with an arbitrary starting point. Instead directly use offset-from-base-address, and the first offset is zero.

Watch out! It means that when you declare:

```
int day[] = new int[365];
```

valid subscripts for "day" are in the range 0 to 364. A reference to "day[365]" is invalid. If this causes distress in terms of program readability (e.g. you want days numbered from 1 to 365 to match the calendar) then simply declare the array one larger than it needs to be, and don't use element zero. ❦

Array indexes are all checked at runtime. If a subscript attempts a reference outside the bounds of its array, it causes an exception and the program ceases execution rather than corrupt memory. Exceptions are described later in this chapter. ❦

Arrays of Arrays

The language specification says there are no "multidimensional" arrays in Java, meaning Java doesn't use the convention of Pascal or Ada of putting several indexes into one set of subscript brackets. Ada allows multidimensional arrays like this:

```
banana : array(1..12, 1..31) of real;
```
Ada code for multi-dimensional array

```
banana(i,j) = 3.14;
```

Ada also allows arrays of arrays, like this:

```
type carrot is array(1..31) of real;        Ada code for array of arrays

banana : array(1..12) of carrot;
banana(i)(j) = 3.14;
```

Pascal, too, allows both forms, and treats them as one:

```
var banana : array[1..12] of array[1..31] of real;    Pascal code
banana[i][j] = 3.14;                                   for arrays
                                                       of arrays.
```

it is usual to abbreviate this as:

```
var banana : array[1..12, 1..31] of real;    Pascal code
banana[i, j] = 3.14;                          for multi-
                                              dimensional
                                              arrays
```

Pascal blurs the distinction by saying that arrays of arrays are equivalent to and interchangeable with multidimensional arrays [Pascal User Manual and Report, Springer-Verlag, 1975, page 39]. Java just has arrays of arrays.

What "Multidimensional" Means in Different Languages

The Ada standard explicitly says arrays of arrays and multidimensional arrays are different. The language has both.

The Pascal standard says arrays of arrays and multidimensional arrays are the same thing.

The ANSI C standard says C has what other languages call arrays of arrays, but it also calls these "multidimensional."

The Java language only has arrays of arrays, and it only calls these arrays of arrays.

Arrays of arrays are declared like this:

```
int cabbage [] [] ;
```

Array "cabbage" is composed of an array which is composed of an array whose elements are integers.

Because object declarations do not create objects, you will need to fill out or "instantiate" the elements in an array before using it. If you have an array of arrays, like this:

```
int cabbage[][];
```

you will need to instantiate both the top-level array, and at least one bottom level array before you can start storing ints. The bottom level arrays do not have to all be a single uniform size. (This is true for C too—the classic example being the argv array of strings declared in main.)

Here is one way you could create a triangular array of arrays, and fill it with initial values:

```
int cabbage[][] = new int[5][];

int slice0[] = {0};
int slice1[] = {0,1};
int slice2[] = {0,1,2};
int slice3[] = {0,1,2,3};
int slice4[] = {0,1,2,3,4};

cabbage[0] = slice0;
cabbage[1] = slice1;
cabbage[2] = slice2;
cabbage[3] = slice3;
cabbage[4] = slice4;
```

We introduce the variables slice0 etc. because array literals, like "{0,1,2,3}" can only be used in an initializer, not in a statement. Here is another way to do it, that provides an equivalent result in cabbage.

```
int cabbage[][] = new int[5][];

for( int i=0; i<cabbage.length; i++) {
    int tmp[] = new int [i+1];

    for (int j=0; j<=i; j++)
        tmp[j]=j;

    cabbage[i] = tmp;
}
```

Yet a third way is to lump all the initializers together in a big array literal like this:

```
int cabbage[][] = {  {0},
                     {0,1},
                     {0,1,2},
                     {0,1,2,3},
                     {0,1,2,3,4}
                   };
```

Note that if you instantiate the dimensions at different times, you must instantiate the most significant dimensions first. So,

```
int cabbage[][] = new int[5][];   // ok
int cabbage[][] = new int[5][3];  // ok
```

but

```
int cabbage[][] = new int[][3];   // NO! NO! NO!
```

Remember that declarations do not create objects!

An object declaration merely sets aside the space, for when you do get around to creating ("instantiating") it. This is just as true when you have arrays of objects, as it is with individual objects.

```
Integer beer[]  = new Integer[10]; // note: class Integer, not int.
```

does not give you an array full of Integer objects. It gives you an array full of elements that can reference an Integer object. If you reference beer[3] before filling out that value in the array with either of:

```
beer[3] = new Integer(n);
beer[3] = SomeExistingIntegerObject;
```

you will of course get a null pointer exception. Note the contrast with an array of a primitive type

```
int cider [] = new int[10]
```

does give you an array into which you can start storing ints immediately. 👟

Arrays with the same element type, and the same number of dimensions (in the C sense, Java doesn't have multidimensional arrays) can be assigned to each other. The arrays do not need to have the same number of elements because what actually happens is that one reference variable is copied into the other.

For example:

```
int eggs[] = {1,2,3,4};
int ham[] = {1};
ham = eggs;
ham[3] = 0;     // OK, because ham now has 4 elements.
```

This doesn't make a new copy of eggs, it makes ham and eggs reference the same array object.

So changes made to the array through references by one variable will be seen by references through the other variable.

```
// show example of what is a copy, and what is a ref.
     Integer beer[] = new Integer[10];
     Integer lager[];

     beer[3] = new Integer(3);

     lager = beer;

     beer[3] = new Integer(256);

     if (lager[3].intValue() == 256)
          System.out.println("It just copied the reference" +
                          " -- they point at same Object" );
```

In this code example, the assignment "lager=beer" simply copies the beer reference variable into the lager reference variable. When one element of the array that beer points at is changed, naturally the change is seen by both, and so the println message will be printed out.

In diagram form, before the assignment of "lager=beer" we have Figure 5-1:

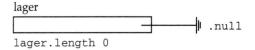

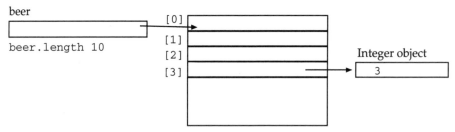

Figure 5-1:   Pre-"lager=beer" assignment

After the assignment of "lager=beer" we have the Figure 5-2:

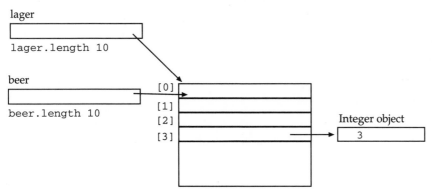

Figure 5-2: "lager=beer" has been assigned

After the assignment of "beer[3] = new Integer(256)" we have the diagram shown in Figure 5-3:

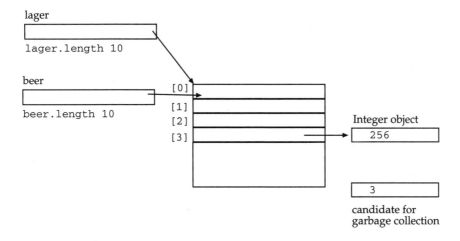

Figure 5-3: Post-assignment of "beer[3] = new Integer (256)

If instead, it was your intention that a fresh copy of all the objects referenced by the array beer be put into the array referenced by lager, then you would have to do something like this:

```
// create an array for lager
lager = new Integer[10];

// copy the elements of beer into lager array
System.arraycopy(beer,0,lager,0,beer.length);
```

This would allow you to assign something different to beer[3], and not see any change in lager[3]. After the "System.arraycopy()" we will have Figure 5-4:

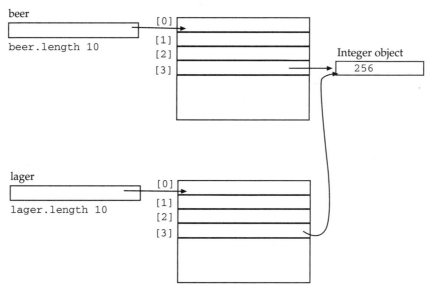

Figure 5-4: A change to beer[3] without affecting lager[3]

And finally, if you then assign "beer[3] = new Integer(3);" the diagram will look like Figure 5-5:

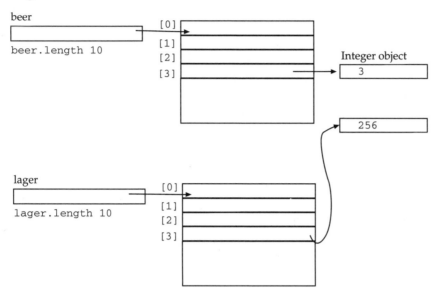

Figure 5-5: beer[3] = new Integer(3)

Have Array Brackets, Will Travel

There is a quirk of syntax in that the array declaration bracket pairs can "float," to be next to the element type, next to the data name, or in a mixture of the two. These are all valid array declarations:

```
int a [] ;
int [] b = { a.length, 2, 3 } ;

char c [][] = new char[12][31];
char[] d [] = { {1,1,1,1}, {2,2,2,2} }; // creates d[2][4]
char[][] e;

byte f [][][] = new byte [3][3][7];
byte [][] g[] = new byte [3][3][7];

short [] h, i[], j, k[][];
```

If array brackets appear next to the type, they are part of the type, and apply to *every* variable in that declaration. In the code above, "j" is an array of short, and "i" is an array of arrays of short.

This is mostly so declarations of functions returning arrays can be read more normally. Here is an example of how returning an array value from a function would look following C rules (you can't return an array in C, but this is how C syntax would express it if you could):

```
int funarray()[] { ... }
```
Pseudo-C CODE

Here are the alternatives for expressing it in Java, (and it is permissible in Java), first following the C paradigm:

```
int ginger ()[]  { return new int[20]; }
```
Java CODE

A better way is to express it like this:

The latter allows the programmer to see all the tokens that comprise the return type grouped together.

Arrays are never allocated on the stack in Java, so you cannot get into trouble returning an array stack variable. In C, it is too easy to return a pointer to an array on the stack that will be overwritten by something else pushed on the stack after returning from the method.

Programmers cannot make this programming error in Java, as arrays are never allocated on the stack. If you write an array as a local variable, that actually creates a reference to the array. You need a little more code to create the array itself, and that will allocate the array safely on the heap.

Indexing Arrays

Arrays may be indexed by "int" values. Arrays may not be indexed by "long" values. That means arrays are implicitly limited to no more than the highest 32-bit int value, namely 2,147,483,647. That's OK for the next couple of years—but the lack of 64-bit addressing will eventually make itself felt in Java.

Values of types "byte", "short", and "char" are promoted to "ints" when they are used as an index, just as they are in other expression contexts.

When to use char[ ] vs. String vs. StringBuffer

There are three types that store character sequences available to programmers: String, StringBuffer, and char[]. How do you choose which to use? The answer is to look at the operations available on each and choose the type that most closely matches what you want to do.

String

Once a String is created, the characters in it cannot be modified, although you can always make a different String using pieces from the String you have. This class supports:

- Literal strings in double quotes

- Comparisons against the entire string or a substring

- Finding where particular characters occur in the string

- Constructing a String out of other types including StringBuffer and array of char

StringBuffer

You might use this class if you know you are going to be appending a large number of characters or changing characters in the middle—and you expect to do this more than you will do comparisons. This class supports:

- Inserting and appending various types onto a StringBuffer

- Setting the length of the StringBuffer.

char [ ]

This class is an array type so it doesn't have any methods. You can only load and store individual array elements. However, you do have random access by subscripting to any character in the array, and you can set or change it as needed. Once created, the number of characters in the array cannot change. It is convenient and efficient to access successive elements using a loop counter as the array subscript.

Keep in mind that you cannot extend String or StringBuffer because they are both *final* classes. This is for security and performance reasons. When a class is final, the compiler doesn't need to dynamically look up which method should be invoked based on the runtime class of the object. The method is fixed at compile time, allowing the code in the method to be placed inline, saving the overhead of a procedure call. This can be more of an effort than just the cost of a "push parameters and jump to a subroutine." On modern RISC processors, a branch to a new location forces the CPU to empty all the instruction and data pipelines (called "stalling the processor"). This prevents instructions from being executed in the overlapped style necessary for top speed. Most programmers don't need to worry about this, but compiler writers certainly do.

In contrast to finding the length of an array, getting the length of a String or StringBuffer variable does require a method call:

```
String s = "scrofulous";
int i = s.length();
```

You might remember this by thinking "Strings" support more operations than mere character arrays. So Strings use a method to calculate their length whereas character arrays can just use a "length" field. On the other hand, since Strings are fixed in size once created, why isn't length just a final data field?

The thinking seems to be that it is better for String to be consistent with String-Buffer (which has to do it via a method as that is the only way to give users read access to the length field without also granting them write access).

A shortcut to the normal "new" operator is allowed when giving Strings an initial value. You can say:

```
String s = "crapulent";
```

This works as well as the equivalent:

```
String s = new String("crapulent");
```

This is a concession to the existing expectations of programmers.

Exceptions

At several points in the preceding text I have mentioned exceptions, only to defer discussion. This is where I deliver on the promise of describing the purpose and use of exceptions following this order:

1. The purpose of exceptions

2. How to cause an exception (implicitly and explicitly)

3. How to handle ("catch") an exception within the method where it was thrown

4. Handling groups of related exceptions

5. How the exception propagates if not handled in the method where it was thrown

6. How and why methods declare the exceptions that can propagate out of them.

7. Fancy Exception stuff

The Purpose of Exceptions

Exceptions are for changing the flow of control when some important or unexpected event, usually an error, has occurred. They divert processing to a part of the program that can try to cope with the error, or at least die gracefully. The error can be any condition at all, ranging from "unable to open a file" to "array subscript out of range" to "no memory left to allocate" to "division by zero." Java exceptions are adapted from C++ which itself borrowed them from the language ML. Java exception terminology is presented in Table 5-1.

Table 5-1: Exception Terminology of Java

Note	Java	Some other languages
An error condition that happens at run time	Exception	Exception
Causing an exception to occur	Throwing	Raising
Capturing an exception that has just occurred, and executing statements to resolve it in some way	Catching	Handling
The block that does this	Catch clause	Handler
The sequence of call statements that brought control to the method where the exception happened	Stack trace	Call chain

An exception can be set in motion explicitly with the "throw" statement, or implicitly by carrying out some illegal or invalid action. The exception then diverts the normal flow of control (like a goto statement). If the programmer has made provision, control will transfer to a section of the program that can recover from the error. That section can be in the same method, in the method that called the one where the exception occurred, or in the one that called that method. It can continue up the stack of calls that were made at runtime. If it gets to the top, where your program execution started—and no handler for this exception has yet been found—then program execution will cease, with an explanatory message.

Therefore, the places that you can jump to are strictly limited. You even have to explicitly stipulate "in this block, I will listen for and deal with this type of exception."

How To Cause An Exception (implicitly and explicitly)

Exceptions are caused in one of two ways: the program does something illegal (usual case), or the program explicitly generates an exception by executing the throw statement (less usual case). The throw statement has this general form:

```
throw ExceptionObject;
```

The *ExceptionObject* is an object of a class that extends the class java.lang.Exception.

Triggering an Exception

Here is a simple program that causes a "division by zero" exception.

```
class melon {
    public static void main(String[] a) {
        int i=1, j=0, k;

        k = i/j;     // Causes division-by-zero error
    }
}
```

Compiling and running this program gives this result:

```
> javac melon.java
> java melon
    java.lang.ArithmeticException: / by zero
        at melon.main(melon.java:5)
```

There are a certain number of predefined exceptions, like ArithmeticException, known as the runtime exceptions. Actually, since *all* exceptions are runtime events, a better name would be the "irrecoverable" exceptions. They mean "runtime" in the sense of "thrown by the runtime library code, not your code." This contrasts with the user-defined exceptions which are generally held to be less severe, and in some instances can be recovered from. If a filename cannot be opened, prompt the user to enter a new name. If a data structure is found to be full, overwrite some element that is no longer needed. You don't have to make provision for catching runtime exceptions. You do have to make provision for catching other exception types.

Some Predefined Exceptions and their class hierarchies

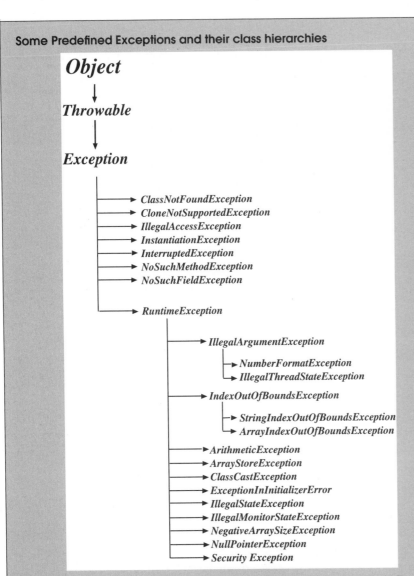

The names are intended to suggest the condition each represents. The source files for these can be found in $JAVAHOME/src/java/lang.

Why is there a class "Throwable." Why doesn't Exception extend Object directly? The reason is that there is a second class called "Error," which also extends Throwable. In other words, both Exceptions and Errors can be thrown, but Errors are not meant to be caught. They usually indicate some catastrophic failure. Typical Errors are: LinkageError, OutOfMemoryError, VerifyError and IllegalAccessError.

User-Defined Exceptions

Here is an example of how to create your own exception class by extending System.exception:

```
class OutofGas extends Exception {}

class banana {
      :

    if (fuel < 0.1) throw  new OutofGas();
}
```

Any method that throws a user-defined exception must also either catch it, or declare it as part of the method interface. What, you may ask, is the point of throwing an exception if you are going to catch it in the same method?

The answer is that exceptions don't *reduce* the amount of work you have to do to handle errors. Their advantage is they let you collect it all in well-localized places in your program, so you don't obscure the main flow of control with zillions of checks of return values.

How to Handle ("Catch") an Exception
Within the Method Where It Was Thrown

Here is the general form of how to catch an exception.

```
try          block
                    There must be at least one (or both) of
                    the two choices below.

[ catch (arg)  block  ]←—— there can be zero or many of these
[ finally      block  ] ←—there can be zero or one of these

                    A "block" is a group of statements
                    in curly braces.
```

The "try" statement says "try these statements, and see if you get an exception." The "try" statement must be followed by at least one "catch" clause or the "finally" clause.

Each "catch" says "I will handle any exception that matches my argument." Matching an argument means that the thrown exception could legally be assigned to the argument exception. There can be several successive catches, each looking for a different exception. Don't try to catch *all* exceptions with one clause, like this:

```
catch (Exception e) { ...
```

That is way too general to be of use: you might catch more than you expected. You'd be better off letting the exception propagate to the top and give you a reasonable error message.

The "finally" block, if present, is a "last chance to clean up" block. It is always executed—even if something in one of the other blocks did a "return!" The "finally" block is executed whether an exception occurred or not, and whether it was caught or not. It is executed after the catch block if present, and if one of them caught an exception or not.

The finally block can be useful in the complete absence of any exceptions. It is a piece of code that will be executed irrespective of what happens in the "try" block. There may be numerous paths through a large and complicated "try" block. The "finally" block can contain the housekeeping tasks that must always be done (counts updated, locks released, etc.) when finishing this piece of code.

Here is an example of an exception guarding statement in full, adapted from the window toolkit code.

```
try {
        a[i] /= j;

        comp.paintAll(cg);
    }

  catch (ArithmeticException e) {
            System.out.println("you doofus");
        }

  catch (ArrayIndexOutOfBoundsException e) {
            System.out.println("bad subscript");
        }

finally {
            cg.dispose();
        }
```

 Supply enough of a context to the code above such that it will compile and run. Put the code in a loop, and have one iteration cause a division by zero, and when you try it again cause an array index out-of-bounds exception. Make up null methods for paintAll() and dispose() and for the objects cg and comp. This example is adapted from code in the Java window toolkit (Easy).

After the whole *try ... catch ... finally* series of blocks are executed, if nothing else was done to divert it, execution continues after the last catch or finally (whichever is present). The kinds of things that could make execution divert to elsewhere are the regular things: a continue, break, return, or the raising of a different exception. If a "finally" clause also has a transfer of control statement, then it is the one that is obeyed.

Handling Groups of Related Exceptions

We mentioned before that "matching an argument" means that the thrown exception can legally be assigned to the argument exception. This permits a subtle refinement. It allows a handler to catch any of several related exception objects with common parentage. Look at this example:

```
class Grumpy   extends Exception {}
class TooHot    extends Grumpy {}
class TooTired extends Grumpy {}
class TooCross extends Grumpy {}
class TooCold  extends Grumpy {}

    .
    :

    try {
      if ( temp > 40 ) throw (new TooHot() );
      if ( sleep < 8 ) throw (new TooTired() );
    }
    catch (Grumpy g) {
        if (g instanceof TooHot)
           {System.out.println("caught too hot!"); return;}
        if (g instanceof TooTired)
           {System.out.println("caught too tired!"); return;}
    }
    finally {System.out.println("in the finally clause.");}
  }
```

The catch clauses are checked in the order in which they appear in the program. If there is a match, then the block is executed. The instanceof operator can be used to learn the exact identity of the exception.

How The Exception Propagates If Not Handled In The Method Where It Was Thrown

If none of the catch clauses match the exception that has been thrown, then the finally clause is executed (if there is one). At this point (no handler for this exception), what happens is the same as if the statement that threw the exception was not nested in a try statement at all. The flow of control abruptly leaves this method, and a premature return is done to the method that called this one. If that call was in the scope of a try statement, then we look for a matching exception again, and so on.

Figure 5-6 shows what happens when an exception is not dealt within the routine where it occurs. The runtime system looks for a try . . . catch block further up the call chain, enclosing the method call that brought us here. If the exception propagates all the way to the top of the call stack without finding a matching exception handler then execution ceases with a message. You can think of this as Java setting up a default catch block for you, around the program entry point that just prints an error message and quits.

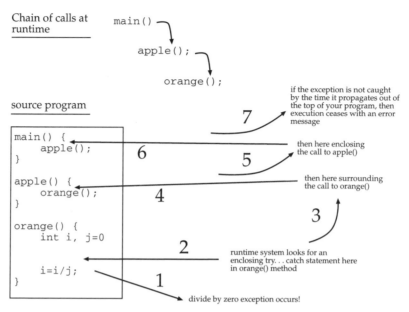

Figure 5-6: The result of an exception not dealt within the occuring routine

There is no overhead to putting some statements in a "try" statement. The only overhead comes when an exception occurs.

How and Why Methods Declare The Exceptions That Can Propagate Out of Them

Earlier we mentioned that a method must either catch the exceptions that it throws or declare it as part of its signature, meaning it must announce the exception to the outside world. This is so that anyone who writes a call to that method is alerted to the fact that an exception might come back instead of a normal return. This allows the programmer who calls that method to make the choice between handling the exception, or allowing it to propagate further up the call stack. Here is the general form of how a method declares the exceptions that might be propagated out of it:

```
modifiers_and_returntype name (params)  throws e1, e2, e3  { }
```

The names e1... etc. must be exception or error names (i.e. any type that is assignable to the predefined type Throwable). Note that, just as a method signature specifies the return *type*, it specifies the exception *type* that can be thrown (rather than an exception object).

An example, taken from the Java I/O system is:

```
 byte readByte() throws IOException;
short readShort() throws IOException;
 char readChar() throws IOException;

 void writeByte(int v) throws IOException;
 void writeShort(int v) throws IOException;
 void writeChar(int v) throws IOException;
```

The interesting thing to note here is that the routine to read a char, can return a char—not the int that is required in C. C requires an int to be returned so that it can pass back any of the possible values for a char, plus an extra value (traditionally –1) to signify that the end of file was reached. Some of the Java routines just throw an exception when the EOF is hit. Out-of-band-signalling can be effective in keeping your code well-organized. The EOF exception is a subclass of the IOException so the technique suggested above for handling groups of related exceptions can be applied.

The rules for how much and what must match when one method that throws an exception overrides another, work in the obvious way. Namely, if you never do this, you will never be obviously bothered by it. Well, OK, another way to think about it is to consider the exception as an extra parameter that must be assignment-compatible with the exception in the class being overridden.

Fancy Exception Stuff

When you create a new exception, by subclassing an existing exception class, you have the chance to associate a message string with it. The message string can be retrieved by a method. Usually the message string will be some kind of message that helps resolve the problem or suggests an alternative action.

```
class OutofGas extends Exception {
    OutofGas(String s) {super(s);}  // constructor
}


   ...
// in use, it may look like this
  try {
       if (j<1) throw  new OutofGas("try the reserve tank");
      }
catch ( OutofGas o) {
        System.out.println( o.getMessage() );
      }
   ...


//At runtime it will look like this:
  try the reserve tank
```

Another method that is inherited from the superclass Throwable is "printStack-Trace()." Invoking this method on an exception will cause the call chain at the point where the exception was thrown (not where it is being handled) to be printed out. For example:

```
// catching an exception in a calling method
class test5p {
    static int slice0[] = {0,1,2,3,4};
    public static void main(String[] a) {
        try {
            bob();
        } catch (Exception e) {
            System.out.println("caught exception in main()");
            e.printStackTrace();
        }
    }

    static void bob() {

        try {
          slice0[-1] = 4;
        }
        catch (NullPointerException e) {
           System.out.println("caught a different exception");
        }

    }
}
```

At runtime it will look like this:

```
caught exception in main()
java.lang.ArrayIndexOutOfBoundsException: -1
        at test5p.bob(test5p.java:19)
        at test5p.main(test5p.java:9)
```

Summary of Exceptions

- Purpose: safer programming by providing a distinct path to deal with errors.

- Use them. They are a useful tool for organized error handling.

- The main use is getting a decent error message out explaining what failed and where and why. It's a bit much to expect recovery. Graceful degradation is often about the most you can obtain.

Threads

Multithreading is not a new concept in software, but it is new to come into the limelight. People have been kicking around experimental implementations for a dozen years or more, but it is only recently that desktop hardware (especially desktop multiprocessors—if you don't have one ask your boss for it today!) became powerful enough to make multithreading popular. There is a POSIX document P1003.4a (ratified June 1995) that describes a threads API standard. The threads described by the POSIX model and the threads available in Java do not exactly coincide. Java threads are simpler, take care of their own memory management, and do not have the full generality (or overhead) of POSIX threads. The Java designers didn't use POSIX threads because the POSIX model was still being cooked when they implemented Java.

Everyone is familiar with time sharing: a computer system can give the impression of doing several things simultaneously, by running each process for a few milliseconds, then saving its state and switching to the next process, and so on. Threads simply extend that concept from switching between several different programs, to switching between several different functions executing simultaneously within a single program. A thread isn't restricted just to one function. Any thread in a multi-threaded program can call any series of methods that could be called in a single-threaded program.

Instead of the costly overhead of saving the state (virtual memory map, file descriptors, etc.) of an entire process, a low-overhead context switch (saving just a few registers, a stack pointer, the program counter, etc.) within the same address space is done. Threads can actually achieve the counterintuitive result of making a program run faster, even on uniprocessor hardware. This occurs when there are calculation steps that no longer have to wait for earlier output to complete, but can run while the I/O is taking place.

Threads (an abbreviation of "threads of control," meaning control flow) are the way we get more than one thing to happen at once in a program. Why is this a good idea? The example that is often related is a web browser, and it's a good example. In an unthreaded program (what you have been using to date in Java, and what you have always used in Fortran, Pascal, C, Basic, C++, COBOL, and so on), only one thing happens at a time.

Threads allow a program to do more than one thing at a time. There are three reasons why you would do this:

- So you can really do more than one thing at a time. This is becoming more and more common. You might have one thread controlling and responding to a GUI, while another thread carries out the tasks or computations requested, while a third thread does file I/O, all for the same program. This means that when one part of the program is blocked waiting on some resource, the other threads can still run and are not blocked.

- Some programs are easier to write if you split them into threads. The classic example is the server part of a client/server. When a request comes in from a client, it is very convenient if the server can spawn a new thread to process that one request. The alternative is to have one server program try to keep track algorithmically of the state of each client request.

- Some programs are amenable to parallel processing. Writing them as threads allows the code to express this. Examples include some sorting and merging algorithms, some matrix operations, and many recursive algorithms.

Alternative Ways to Obtain a New Thread

There are two ways to obtain a new thread of control in Java. One tends to be used inside an application, and the other is used inside an applet.

The first way can only be used if your class doesn't extend any other class (as Java disallows multiple inheritance).

1. extend class "java.lang.Thread" and override "run()"

```
class mango extends Thread {
    public void run() { ... }
}
```

or

2. implement the "Runnable" interface, (the class "Thread" itself is an implementation of "Runnable")

```
class mango implements Runnable {
    public void run() { ... }
}
```

Your applets extend class Applet by definition, so threads in applets must always use the second way. Of course, if the thread doesn't have to run in the Applet object, it can use the first approach.

Figure 5-7 shows how a class Thread is created by extending Thread.

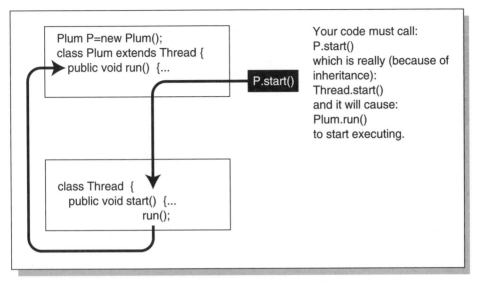

```
Plum P=new Plum();
class Plum extends Thread {
    public void run() {...

                                    P.start()


class Thread {
    public void start() {...
                    run();
```

Your code must call:
P.start()
which is really (because of
inheritance):
Thread.start()
and it will cause:
Plum.run()
to start executing.

Figure 5-7:   Class Thread created by an extending Thread

Creating a thread by extending class Thread looks confusing, because you have to start the thread running by calling a method that you do not have, namely the subclass.start(). You extended Thread to obtain subclass, so this will default back to Thread.start(this) and all will be well. It looks most confusing in the source code however.

Then declaring an object of class Plum gives you a new thread of control, whose execution will start in the method "run()." Declaring two Plums (or more likely a Plum and a Peach) will give you two independently executing threads of control, and declaring and filling an array of Plums will give you an entire array.length threads of control.

New Threads do not start executing on creation. For some applications, programmers (or maybe the runtime system—we'll talk about this in Chapter 7 on applets) want to create threads in advance, then explicitly start them when needed, so this has been made the way it works. When a thread has been created like so:

```
Plum p = new Plum();
```

you start it running by calling the "start()" method, like so:

```
p.start();
```

Or create and start it in one step, like this:

```
new Plum().start();
```

Execution will then begin in the "run()" method, from whence you can call other methods in this and other classes as usual. Remember: "run()" is the place where it starts. And "start()" will get it running. Arrrgh! Perhaps another way to think of this is that "run()" is the equivalent of "main()" for a thread. You do not call it directly, but it is called on your behalf. There's a lot of this in Java! 🐛

A Few Words on Runnable

The Runnable interface just looks like this:

```
public interface Runnable {
    public abstract void run();
}
```

A class that implements the Runnable interface works in much the same way as a class that extends Thread, but with one big difference. The class Thread has many other methods, as well as run(). It has methods to stop(), sleep(), suspend(), resume(), setPriority(), getPriority(), and more besides. These can only be invoked on an object that belongs to a (sub)class of Thread.

None of these methods exist in the Runnable interface, so none of them are available to objects that implement Runnable. Here is the kludge around that. To obtain them, you instantiate a Thread object, and pass it an argument of an object that implements the Runnable interface, like this:

```
class Pear implements Runnable {
   public void run() { ... }
}


   ...


   Thread t1 = new Thread(new Pear());
```

That allows the use of all the Thread methods such as:

```
      t1.start();
      t1.stop();
```

In fact, you have to call start() to get the Runnable implementation executing (just as with a thread). It's common to instantiate and start in one statement like this:

```
      new Thread (new Pear()).start();
```

However, you cannot have statements *within the Runnable interface implementation* of "run()" that operate on the thread itself, like "sleep()" or "getName()" or "setPriority()." This is because there is no Thread "this" in Runnable, whereas there is in Thread. This perhaps makes an implementation of Runnable slightly less convenient than a subclass of Thread. There is a simple workaround shown after this code example.

```
// Show the two ways to obtain a new thread
//   1.  extend class java.lang.Thread and override run()
//   2.  implement the Runnable interface,

class example {
    public static void main(String[] a) {

        // alternative 1
        ExtnOfThread t1 = new ExtnOfThread();
        t1.start();

        // alternative 2
        Thread t2 = new Thread (new ImplOfRunnable());
        t2.start();
    }
}

class ExtnOfThread extends Thread {
    public void run() {
        System.out.println("Extension of Thread running");
        try {sleep(1000);}
        catch (InterruptedException ie) {return;}
    }
}

class ImplOfRunnable implements Runnable {
    public void run() {
        System.out.println("Implementation of Runnable running");

// next two lines will not compile
//          try {sleep(1000);}
//          catch (InterruptedException ie) {return;}
    }
}
```

You can only call Thread methods if you have a Thread object to invoke them on. You don't get this automatically in a class that implements Runnable. Instead, you call the static method `Thread.currentThread()` whose return value is simply the currently running thread. Once you have that, you can easily apply any thread methods to it, as shown in the example below:

```
class ImplOfRunnable implements Runnable {
   public void run() {
        System.out.println("Implementation of Runnable running");
        Thread t = Thread.currentThread();
        try { t.sleep(1000); }
        catch  (InterruptedException ie) { return; }
   }
}
```

A call to currentThread() can appear in any java code, including your main program or whatever. Once you have that thread object you can invoke the thread methods on it.

The official word from the Java team is that the Runnable interface should be used if the "run()" method is the only one you are planning to override. The thinking is that, to maintain the purity of the model, classes should not be subclassed unless the programmer intends to modify or enhance the fundamental behavior of the class.

Confidentially, this is one place where most programmers will say "nuts to the purity of model," and go on subclassing Thread where it is convenient.

As with exceptions, you can provide a string argument when you create a thread subclass. As with exceptions, if you want to do this, you must provide a constructor to take that string and pass it back to the constructor of the base class. The string becomes the name of the object of the Thread subclass, and can later be used to identify it.

```
class Grape extends Thread {
   Grape(String s){ super(s); } // constructor

   public void run() { ... }
}
   . . .
  static public void main(String s[]) {
       new Grape("merlot").start();
       new Grape("pinot").start();
       new Grape("cabernet").start();
       . . .
```

You cannot pass any parameters into the "run()" method, because then its signature would differ from the version it is overriding in Thread. A thread can however get the string that it was started with, by invoking the "getName()" method. This string could encode arguments, or an index into a static array of arguments as needed.

You have already seen enough to write an elementary Java program that uses threads. So do it.

Write two classes that extend Thread. In one the run() method should print "I like tea" in a loop, while the other prints "I like coffee." Create a third class with a main() routine that instantiates and starts the other two threads. Compile and run your program. ☙

The Lifecycle of a Thread

We have already covered how a thread is created, and how the "start()" method inherited from Thread causes execution to start in its run() method. An individual thread dies when execution falls off the end of "run()" or otherwise leaves the method (an exception or return statement).

A thread can also be killed with the "stop()" method. This stops the thread executing and destroys the thread object. To restart it again, you would need to create a new thread object, and start it again. If you want to temporarily halt a thread and have it pick up again from where it was, then suspend()/resume() are the calls to use.

Priorities

Threads have priorities that can be set and changed. A higher priority thread executes ahead of a lower priority thread if they are both ready to run.

Java threads are preemptible, meaning that a running thread will be pushed off the processor by a higher priority thread before it is ready to give it up of its own accord. Java threads might or might not also be time-sliced, meaning that a running thread might or might not share the processor with threads of equal priority.

A Slice of Time

Not guaranteeing time-slicing may seem a somewhat surprising design decision as it violates the "Principle of Least Astonishment"—it leads to program behavior that programmers find surprising (namely threads suffer from CPU starvation). There is some precedent, in that time-slicing can also be missing in a POSIX-conforming thread implementation. POSIX specifies a number of different scheduling algorithms, one of which (round robin) does do time-slicing. However another scheduling possibility allows a local implementation. In the Solaris case of POSIX threads only the local implementation is used, and this does not do any time-slicing.

Many people think that the failure to require time-slicing is a mistake that will surely be fixed in a future release.

Since a programmer cannot assume that time-slicing will take place, the careful programmer assures portability by writing threaded code that does not depend on time-slicing. The code must cope with the fact that once a thread starts running, all other threads with the same priority might become blocked. One way to cope with this is to adjust thread priorities on the fly. That code is going to cost you plenty in software maintenance though.

A better way is to yield control to other threads very frequently. CPU-intensive threads should call the "yield()" method at regular intervals to ensure they don't hog the processor. This won't be needed if time slicing is made a standard part of Java. Yield allows the scheduler to choose another runnable thread for execution.

In the 1.0 version of Java, priorities run from 1 (lowest) to 10 (highest). Threads start off with the same priority as their parent thread, and the priority can be adjusted like this:

```
t1.setPriority ( getPriority() +1 );
```

On Operating Systems that have priorities, most users cannot adjust their processes to a higher priority (because they may gain an unfair advantage over other users of the system).[1] There is no such inhibition for threads, because they all operate within one process. The user is only competing with himself or herself for resources.

Thread groups

A thread group is (big surprise!) a group of Threads. A Thread group can contain a set of Threads as well as a set of other Thread groups. It's a way of lumping several related threads together, and doing things like suspend and resume to all of them with a single method invocation.

There are methods to create a thread group and add a thread to it. Applets are not allowed to manipulate threads outside the applet's own thread group. So you may want to save a reference to that group for later use:

```
public class Apples extends Applet{
    private ThreadGroup mygroup;
    public void init(){
        mygroup=Thread.currentThread().getThreadGroup();
}
```

Thread groups exist because it turned out to be a useful concept in the runtime library. There was no reason not to just pass it through to application programmers, too.

---

1.   Hence the infamous message from the system operator "I've upped my priority, now up yours."

How many Threads?

Sometimes programmers ask "how many threads should I have in my program?" Ron Winacott of Sun Canada has done a lot of thread programming, and he compares this question to asking "how many people is it reasonable to fit in a car?"

The problem is that so much is left unspecified. How big is the car, is it a minibus or a compact? How large are the people, are they children, or 300 pound wrestlers? And how many are needed to get to where you want to go in this car (e.g., driver, mechanic, navigator, someone to buy the fuel.)? In other words, how many people are required to operate the vehicle?

The bottom line is this. Each thread has a default stack size of 400Kbytes in the JDK current release. It will also use about 0.5Kbytes to hold its internal state, but the stack size is the limiting factor. A Unix process (Unix is the most capable of all the systems that Java has been ported to) effectively has a 2Gbyte address space, so in theory you could have around 5000 threads. In practice you would be limited by CPU availability, swap space, and disk bandwidth before you got up there. In one experiment, I was able to create almost 2000 threads before my desktop system ground to a halt. Just create them, I'm not making any claims about them doing any useful work.

Now, back to the real question. Overall there is no unique correct answer. How many is "reasonable?" There is only one person who can accurately answer this question, and that is the programmer writing the threaded application.

The best estimate is "the number of threads needed to perform the task." If this number is too high for the address space, or the CPU power, then you must redesign the tasks (and the number of threads) to use what is available. Use threads where you can achieve concurrency, or to gain overlapping I/O. Do not try to create a new thread for every method, class, or object in your program. 🍃

Four Kinds of Threads Programming

Coordination between different threads is known as "synchronization." Programs that use threads can be divided into the following four levels of difficulty, depending on the kind of synchronization needed between the different threads.

1. Unrelated Threads

2. Related But Unsynchronized Threads

3. Mutually-Exclusive Threads

4. Communicating Mutually-Exclusive Threads

The following sections describe how each of these can be written in Java. Figure 5-8 is the key for all illustrations presented in this section.

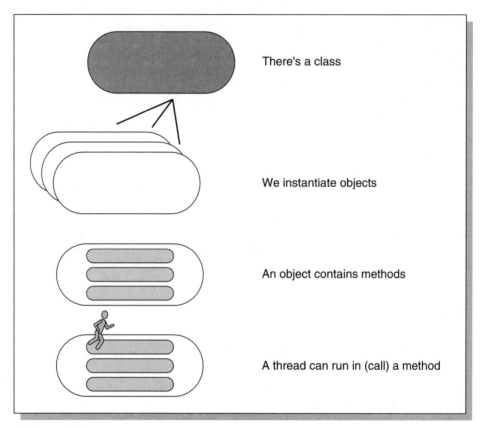

There's a class

We instantiate objects

An object contains methods

A thread can run in (call) a method

Figure 5-8:   Key to threads diagrams

Unrelated Threads

The simplest threads program involves threads of control that do different things and don't interact with each other.

A good example of unrelated threads is the answer to the programming challenge set a few pages back.

The code is:

```java
public class drinks {
    public static void main(String[] a) {
        Coffee t1 = new Coffee();
        t1.start();
        new Tea().start();   // an anonymous thread
    }
}

class Coffee extends Thread {
    public void run() {
        while(true) {
            System.out.println("I like coffee");
            yield();   // did you forget this?
        }
    }
}

class Tea extends Thread {
    public void run() {
        while(true) {
            System.out.println("I like tea");
            yield();
        }
    }
}
```

When you run this program, you will see the output:

> I like coffee
> I like tea
> I like coffee
> I like tea
> I like coffee
> I like tea

It is repeated over and over again, until you press control-C or otherwise interrupt program execution. This type of threads programming is easy to get working. See Figure 5-9.

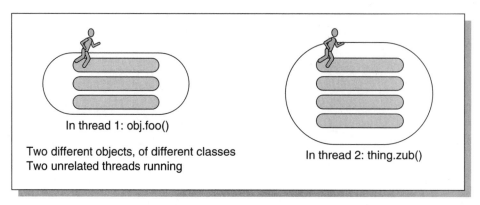

Figure 5-9: Unrelated Threads

Related But Unsynchronized Threads

This level of complexity has threaded code to partition a problem, solving it by having multiple threads work on different pieces of the same data structure. The threads don't interact with each other. Here, threads of control do work that is sent to them, but don't work on shared data, so they don't need to access it in a synchronized way.

An example of this would be spawning a new thread for each socket connection that comes in. Threads that just do "work to order" like that are termed *demon* or *daemon* threads—their only purpose is to serve a higher master. See Figure 5-10. You can mark a thread as being a demon thread with the `setDaemon(true)` method. The advantage being that a program will terminate if the only thing left running in it are daemon threads.

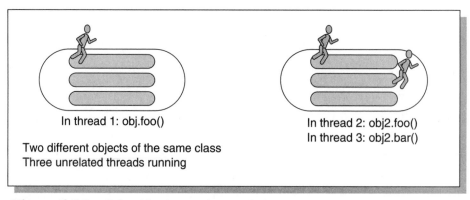

Figure 5-10: Related but Unsynchronized Threads

A less common but still interesting example of related but unsynchronized threads involves partitioning a data set, and instantiating multiple copies of the same thread to work on different pieces of the same problem. Be careful not to duplicate work, or even worse, to let two different threads operate on the same data at once.

Here is an example program that tests whether a given number is a prime number. That involves a lot of divisions so it's a good candidate for parcelling the work out among a number of threads. Tell each thread the range of numbers it is to test-divide into the possible prime. Then let them all loose in parallel. The driver code is:

```
// demonstrates the use of threads to test a number for primality

public class testPrime {

    public static void main(String s[]) {
        long possPrime = Long.parseLong(s[0]);
        int centuries = (int)(possPrime/100) +1;

        for(int i=0;i<centuries;i++) {
            new testRange(i*100, possPrime).start();
        }

    }
}
```

This main program gets its argument, which is the value to test for primality, and then calculates how many 100s there are in the number. A new thread will be created to test for factors in every range of 100. So if the number is 2048, there are twenty 100s. Twenty one threads will be created. The first will check whether any of the numbers 2 to 99 divide into 2048. The second will check the range 100 to 199. The third will check 200 to 299, and so on, with the 21st thread checking the numbers 2000 to 2100.

The line "new testRange(i*100, possPrime).start();" instantiates an object of class testRange, using the constructor that takes two arguments. That object belongs to a subclass of Thread, so the ".start()" jammed on the end starts it running. This is a java idiom. The class testRange follows.

```
class testRange extends Thread {

    static long possPrime;
    long from, to;

    // constructor
    //    record the number we are to test, and
    //    the range of factors we are to try.
    testRange(int argFrom, long argpossPrime) {
        possPrime=argpossPrime;
        if (argFrom==0) from=2; else from=argFrom;
        to=argFrom+99;
    }

    public void run() {
        for (long i=from; i<=to && i<possPrime; i++) {
            if (possPrime%i == 0) {  // i divides possPrime exactly
                    System.out.println(
                            "factor "+i+" found by thread "+getName());
                    this.stop();
            }
            yield();
        }
    }

}
```

The constructor just saves a copy of the number we are to test for primality, and it saves the start of the range of potential factors for this thread instance to test. The end of the range is the start plus 99.

All the run() method does is count through this range, trying each divisor. If one divides the number exactly, then print it out and stop this thread. We have the answer that the number is not prime. There are many possible improvements to the algorithm (for instance, we need only test for factors up to the square root of the possible prime). These improvements have been omitted so as not to clutter up the code example. A sample run of this program might look like this:

```
% java testPrime 2048
  factor 2 found by thread Thread-4
  factor 512 found by thread Thread-9
  factor 1024 found by thread Thread-14
  factor 128 found by thread Thread-5
  factor 256 found by thread Thread-6
```

So 2048 is not a prime number and five of the 21 threads found factors. The default name for the first thread you create is Thread-4 (not Thread-1) because there are already several threads running in your program, including the garbage collector and your main program.

Mutually-Exclusive Threads

Here's where threads start to interact with each other, and that makes life a little more complicated. In particular we use threads which need to work on the same pieces of the same data structure. You may not believe this or see why if I just state it, so we will motivate the discussion with some code, which you should type in and run.

These threads need to take steps to stay out of each others' way so they don't each simultaneously modify the same piece of data leaving an uncertain result. Staying out of each other's way is known as *mutual exclusion*.

This code simulates a steam boiler. It defines some values (the current reading of a pressure gauge, and the safe limit for that gauge), and then instantiates 10 copies of a thread called "pressure" storing them in an array. The main routine concludes by waiting for each thread to finish (this is the "join()" statement) and then prints the current value of the pressure gauge. Here is the main routine:

```
public class p {
 static int pressureGauge=0;
 static final int safetyLimit = 20;

 public static void main(String[]args) {
 pressure []p1 = new pressure[10];
 for (int i=0; i<10; i++)   {
    p1[i] = new pressure();
    p1[i].start();
 }
 try{ for (int i=0;i<10;i++) p1[i].join(); } catch(Exception e){}

 System.out.println("gauge reads "+pressureGauge+", safe limit is 20");
 }

}
```

Now let's look at the pressure thread. This code simply checks if the current pressure reading is within safety limits, and if it is, it waits briefly, then increases the pressure. Here is the thread:

```
class pressure extends Thread {

   void RaisePressure() {
     if (p.pressureGauge < p.safetyLimit-15) {
       // wait briefly to simulate some calculations
       try{sleep(100);} catch (Exception e){}
       p.pressureGauge += 15;
     } else ; // pressure too high -- don't add to it.
   }

   public void run() {
     RaisePressure();
   }
}
```

If you haven't seen this kind of thing before, it should look pretty safe. After all, before we increase the pressure reading we always check that our addition won't push it over the safety limit. Stop reading at this point, type in the two dozen lines of code, and run them. Here's what you may see:

```
% java p
  gauge reads 150, safe limit is 20
```

Although we always checked the gauge before increasing the pressure it is over the safety limit by a huge margin! Better evacuate the area! So what is happening here?

This is a classic example of what is called a *data race* or a *race condition*. A race condition occurs when two or more threads update the same value simultaneously. What you want to happen is:

- Thread 1 reads pressure gauge

- Thread 1 updates pressure gauge

- Thread 2 reads pressure gauge

- Thread 2 updates pressure gauge

But it may happen that thread 2 starts to read before thread 1 has updated, so the accesses take place in this order:

- Thread 1 reads pressure gauge

- Thread 2 reads pressure gauge

- Thread 1 updates pressure gauge

- Thread 2 updates pressure gauge

In this case, thread 2 will read an erroneous value for the gauge, effectively missing the fact that thread 1 is in the middle of updating the value based on what it read. For this example we helped the data race to happen by introducing a tenth-of-a-second delay between reading and updating. But a data race can occur even in statements that follow each other consecutively, whenever you have different threads updating the same data.

In this example we have highlighted what is happening and rigged the code to exaggerate the effect, but in general data races are among the hardest problems to debug. They typically do not reproduce consistently and they leave no visible clues as to how data got into an inconsistent state.

To avoid data races, follow this simple rule: Whenever two threads access the same data, they must use mutual exclusion. You can optimize slightly, by allowing multiple readers at one instant. A reader and a writer must never be running at the same time. Two writers must never be running at the same time. As the name suggests, mutual exclusion is a protocol for making sure that if one thread is touching some particular data, another is not. The threads mutually exclude each other in time.

In Java, thread mutual exclusion is built on data Objects. Every Object in the system has its own mutex semaphore (strictly speaking this will only be allocated if it is used), so any Object in the system can be used as the "turnstile" or "thread serializer" for threads. You use the "synchronized" keyword and explicitly or implicitly provide an Object, any Object, to synchronize on. The runtime system will take over and apply the code to ensure that, at most, one thread has locked that specific object at any given instant as shown in Figure 5-11. The "synchronized" keyword can be applied to a class, to a method, or to a block of code. In each case, the mutex (mutual exclusion) lock of the named object is acquired, then the code is executed, then the lock is released. If the lock is already held by another thread, then the thread that wants to acquire the lock is suspended until the lock is released.

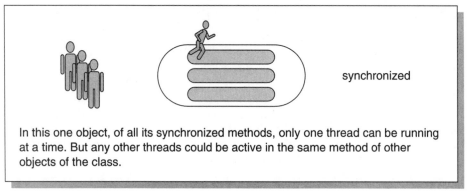

synchronized

In this one object, of all its synchronized methods, only one thread can be running at a time. But any other threads could be active in the same method of other objects of the class.

Figure 5-11: Mutually-exclusive Threads

The Java programmer never deals with the low-level and error-prone details of creating, acquiring and releasing locks, but only specifies the region of code and the object that must be exclusively held in that region. You want to make your regions of synchronized code as small as possible, because mutual exclusion really chokes performance. Here are examples of each of these alternatives of synchronizing over a class, a method, or a block, with comments on how the exclusion works.

Mutual exclusion over an entire class

This is achieved by applying the keyword "synchronized" to a class method (a method with the keyword "static"). Making a class method synchronized tells the compiler "add this method to the set of class methods that must run with mutual exclusion." See Figure 5-12. Only one "static synchronized" method for a particular class can be running at any given time. The threads are implicitly synchronized using the class object.

In the preceding pressure example, we can make RaisePressure a static synchronized method, by changing its declaration to this:

```
static synchronized void RaisePressure() {
```

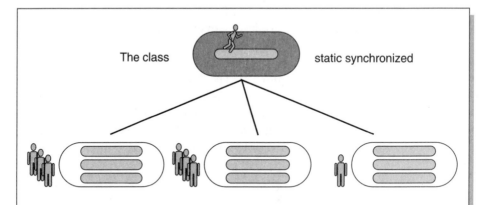

The class   static synchronized

Only one thread can be running in a synchronized static (class) method at a time, no matter how many objects of the class there are.

There is one lock for static synchronized methods, and a different lock for synchronized methods. So a thread could have exclusive access to a static synchronized method, while another thread has exclusive access to a synchronized method, for a given class and object. Yet other threads could be running in methods that are not marked as synchronized at all.

Figure 5-12:   Mutual exclusion over a class

Since there is only one of these methods for the entire class, no matter how many thread objects are created, we have effectively serialized the code that accesses and updates the pressure gauge. Recompiling with this change, and rerunning the code will give this result (and you should try it):

```
% java p
gauge reads 15, safe limit is 20
```

Mutual exclusion over a block of statements

This is achieved by attaching the keyword "synchronized" before a block of code. You also have to explicitly mention in parentheses the object whose lock must be acquired before the region can be entered. Reverting to our original pressure example, we could make the following change inside the method RaisePressure to achieve the necessary mutual exclusion:

```
void RaisePressure() {
    synchronized(O) {
      if (p.pressureGauge < p.safetyLimit-15) {
            try{sleep(100);} catch (Exception e){} // delay
            p.pressureGauge += 15;
      } else ; // pressure too high -- don't add to it.
    }
}
```

We will also need to provide the object O that we are using for synchronization. This declaration will do fine:

```
static Object O = new Object();
```

We could use an existing object, but we do not have a convenient one at hand in this example. The fields "pressureGauge" and "safetyLimit" are ints not Objects, otherwise either of those would be a suitable choice. It is always preferable to use the object that is being updated as the synchronization lock wherever possible. Recompiling with the change, and rerunning the code will give the desired exclusion:

```
% java p
gauge reads 15, safe limit is 20
```

Mutual exclusion over a method

This is achieved by applying the keyword "synchronized" to an ordinary (non-static) method. Note that in this case the object whose lock will provide the mutual exclusion is implicit. It is the "this" object on which the method is invoked.

```
synchronized void foo { ...  }
```

is equivalent to

```
void foo {
  sychronized (this) {
      ...
  }
}
```

Especially note that making the obvious change to our pressure example will not give the desired result!

```
// this example shows what will NOT work
synchronized void RaisePressure() {
    if (p.pressureGauge < p.safetyLimit-15) {
        try{sleep(100);} catch (Exception e){} // delay
        p.pressureGauge += 15;
    } else ; // pressure too high -- don't add to it.
}
```

The reason is clear: The "this" object is one of the 10 different threads that are created. Each thread will successfully grab its own lock, and there will be no exclusion between the different threads at all. Synchronization excludes threads working on the <u>same</u> one object; it doesn't synchronize the same method on different objects.

Synchronized methods are useful when you have several different methods that might be called simultaneously on the same one object. It ensures that at most one of all the methods designated as synchronized will be invoked on that one object at any given instant. In this case we have the reverse: one method in several threads that is called simultaneously on several different objects. Note that synchronized methods all exclude each other, but they do not exclude a non-synchronized method, nor a (synchronized or non-synchronized) static (class) method from running.

Communicating Mutually-Exclusive Threads

Here's where things become downright complicated until you get familiar with the protocol. The hardest kind of threads programming is where the threads need to pass data back and forth to each other. Imagine that we are in the same situation as the previous section. We have threads that process the same data, so we need to run synchronized. However, in our new case, imagine that it's not enough just to say "don't run while I am running." We need the threads to be able to say "OK, I have some data ready for you" and to suspend themselves if there isn't data ready. There is a convenient parallel programming idiom, known as "wait/ notify" that does exactly this. Figure 5-13 shows this in four stages.

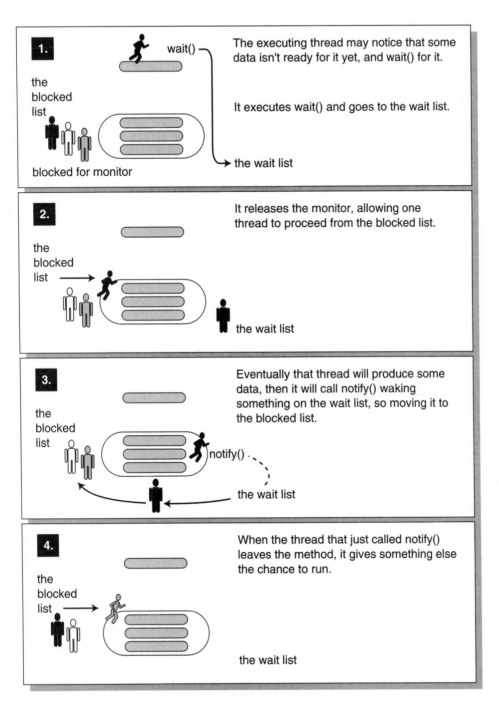

Figure 5-13: Communicating mutually-exclusive threads

Wait/notify is a tricky language-independent protocol that has been developed by ingenious minds. You just need to accept it as the right solution to this problem. Wait/notify is used when synchronized methods in the same class need to communicate with each other. The most common occurrence of this is a producer/consumer situation—one thread is producing data irregularly, and another thread is consuming (processing) it.

Methods in the threads are only ever called from within synchronized code, which means they are both only ever called when a mutex lock is held. However, simple synchronization is not enough. The consumer might grab the lock and then find that there is nothing in the buffer to consume. The producer might grab the lock and find that there isn't yet room in the buffer to put something. You could make either of these spin in a busy loop continually grabbing the lock, testing whether they can move some data, releasing the lock if not. But busy loops are never used in production code. They burn CPU cycles without any productive result.[2] The correct approach lies in the two method calls wait() and notify().

- Wait() says, "Oops, even though I have the lock I can't go any further until you have some data for me, so I will release the lock, and suspend myself here. One of you notifiers carry on!"
- Notify() says, "Hey, I just produced some data, so I will release the lock and suspend myself here. One of you waiters carry on!"

The pseudo-code for the way the producer works is:

```
// producer thread
enter synchronized code (i.e. grab mutex lock)
produce_data()
notify()
leave synchronized code (i.e. release lock)
```

The pseudo-code for the consumer is

```
// consumer thread
enter synchronized code
while( no_data )
    wait()
consume_the_data()
leave synchronized code
```

The consumer waits in a loop because a different consumer may have grabbed the data, in which case it needs to wait again. As we have already seen, entering and

2. Well, OK, one of my colleagues pointed out a research paper that showed a brief busy loop followed by a wait/notify was superior to either used alone. Let's leave research papers out of this for now.

leaving synchronized code is trivially achieved by applying the keyword "syn-chronized" to a method, so the templates become like this:

```
// producer thread
produce_data()
notify()

// consumer thread
while( no_data )
    wait()
consume_the_data()
```

Usually the producer is storing the produced data into some kind of bounded-buffer, which means the producer may fill it up and will need to wait() until there is room. The consumer will need to notify() the producer when something is removed from the buffer. The pseudo-code is:

```
// producer thread—produces one datum
while( buffer_full )
    wait()
produce_data()
notify()

// consumer thread—consumes one datum
while( no_data )
    wait()
consume_the_data()
notify
```

The reason we walked through this step-by-step is that it makes the following program a lot easier to understand. So if you didn't follow the pseudo-code above, go back over the previous section again. This code directly implements the pseudo-code, and demonstrates the use of wait/notify in communicating mutu-ally-exclusive threads.

There are three classes below. The first is a class that contains a main driver pro-gram. It simply instantiates a producer thread and a consumer thread and lets them go at it.

```
public class plum {
  public static void main(String args[]) {
      Producer p = new Producer();
      p.start();

      Consumer c = new Consumer(p);
      c.start();
  }
}
```

The second class is the Producer class. It implements the pseudo-code above, and demonstrates the use of wait/notify. It has two key methods: one that produces data (actually just reads the number of millisecs the program has been running) and stores it into an array. The other method, called consume(), will try to return successive values from this array. The value of this set-up is that produce() and consume() can be called from separate threads: they won't overrun the array; they won't get something before it has been produced; they won't step on each other; neither ever gets in a busy wait.

```java
class Producer extends Thread {
    private String [] buffer = new String [8];
    private int pi = 0;   // produce index
    private int gi = 0;   // get index

    public void run() {
        // just keep producing
        for(;;) produce();
    }

    private final long start = System.currentTimeMillis();
    private final String banana() {
        return "" + (int) (System.currentTimeMillis() - start);
    }

    synchronized void produce() {
        // while there isn't room in the buffer
        while ( pi-gi+1 > buffer.length ) {
            try {wait();} catch(Exception e) {}
        }
        buffer[pi&0x7] = banana();
        System.out.println("produced["+(pi&7)+"] " + buffer[pi&7]);
        pi++;
        notifyAll();
    }

    synchronized String consume() {
        // while there's nothing left to take from the buffer
        while (pi==gi) {
            try {wait();} catch(Exception e) {}
        }
        notifyAll();
        return buffer[ gi++&0x7 ];
    }
}
```

Produce () puts a datum in the buffer, and consume () pulls something out to give it to the consumer.

Those expressions like "pi&0x7" are a programming idiom to mask off the bits of the subscript we want. In this case it is cheap way to let the subscript be incremented without limit, but always get the value modulo 8. It requires the buffer size to be a power of two, which we can easily arrange. If this coding idiom makes you uneasy, change the program to use subscripts that are incremented modulo the buffer size. You'll see it is actually simpler this way.

Finally, the third class is another thread that will be the consumer in this example. It starts off with a common Java idiom: another class is passed into the constructor, and all the constructor does is save a copy of this object for later use. This is the way that the consumer can call the consume() method of the producer.

```
class Consumer extends Thread {
    Producer whoIamTalkingTo;
    // java idiom for a constructor
    Consumer(Producer who) { whoIamTalkingTo = who; }

    public void run() {
        java.util.Random r = new java.util.Random();
        for(;;) {
            String result = whoIamTalkingTo.consume();
            System.out.println("consumed: "+result);
            // next line is just to make it run a bit slower.
            int randomtime = r.nextInt() % 250;
            try{sleep(randomtime);} catch(Exception e){}
        }
    }
}
```

The idiom of passing an object into a constructor that saves the reference to it, for later communicating something back, is a common idiom. You should make especial note of it. Make sure you understand the example above, to see how this is written and used.

The run method of this consumer simply repeats over and over again a get, printing what it got, followed by a sleep for a random period. The sleep is just to give the producer some work to do, in adapting to an asynchronous consumer.

When you compile these three classes together and try running them, you will see output like this:

```
% java plum       produced[0] 12
      produced[1] 18
      produced[2] 20
      produced[3] 22
      produced[4] 24
      produced[5] 26
      produced[6] 29
      produced[7] 31
      consumed: 12
      produced[0] 47
      consumed: 18
      produced[1] 213
      consumed: 20
      produced[2] 217
```

And so on. Notice that the producer filled up the buffer before the consumer ran at all. Then each time the slow consumer removed something from the buffer, the producer re-used that now empty slot. And always the consumer got exactly what was stored there with no data race corruption. If this explanation of wait/notify seems complicated, your impression is correct. Programming threaded code is hard in the general case and these methods supply a specialized feature that makes one aspect of it a little easier. The good news is that, for simple producer/ consumer code, you don't have to bother with any of this. Two classes, PipedInputStream and PipedOutputStream, in the I/O library can be used in your code to support simple asynchronous communication between threads. We will look at this later.

Wait and notify are methods in the basic class Object, so they are shared by all objects in the system. There are several variants:

```
public final native void notify();
public final native void notifyAll();

public final void wait() throws InterruptedException;
public final void wait(long time, int nanos) throws InterruptedException;
public final native void wait(long timeout) throws InterruptedException;
```

The difference between notify() and notifyAll() is that notifyAll() wakes up all threads that are in the wait list of this object. That might be appropriate if they are all readers or they are all waiting for the same answer, or can all carry on once the data has been written. In the example there is only one other thread, so notify() or notifyAll() will have the same effect. There are three forms of wait, including two that allow a wait to timeout after the specified period of milliseconds or milliseconds and nanoseconds(!) have elapsed. Why have a separate wait list or 'wait set' for each object, instead of just blocking waiting for the lock? Because the whole point of wait/notifying is to take the objects out of contention for systems resources until they are truly able to run! A notify notifies an arbitrary thread in the wait list. You can't rely on FIFO order.

Let Sleeping Threads Lie

Now we have all that theory behind us, let's explain the minor point of what statements like this mean:

```
try {sleep(randomtime);} catch(Exception e){}
try {wait();} catch(Exception e) {}
```

It's quite easy. One thread can interrupt another sleeping thread by calling its `interrupt()` method. This will make the interrupted thread wake up and take the exception branch. The thread really needs to be able to tell the difference between waking up because it has been "notified" and waking up because it has been "interrupted." So the second case is detected by raising the exception `InterruptedException` in the thread. Statements like sleep() and wait() that are potentially prone to being interrupted in the middle need to catch this exception or declare that their method can throw it.

Two further points. I have used the parent type Exception here, instead of the correct subtype, InterruptedException. This was to minimize the size of the lines in the example. Always catch the narrowest type of exception you can or you may catch more than you bargained for. And do something sensible with it, like print an error message. Finally, note that the interrupt() method was not implemented in the first major release of the JDK.

Synchronized code isn't a perfect solution, because a system can still get into deadlock. Deadlock or "deadly embrace" is the situation where there is a circular dependency among several threads between resources held and resources required. In its simplest form, Thread "A" holds lock "X" and needs lock "Y," while Thread "B" holds lock "Y" and is waiting for lock "X" to become free. Result: that part of the system grinds to a halt. This can happen all too easily when one synchronized method calls another. The "volatile" keyword may also be applied to data. This informs the compiler that several threads may be accessing this simultaneously. The data therefore needs to be completely refreshed from memory (rather than a value that was read into a register three cycles ago) and completely stored back on each access. Volatile is also intended for accessing objects like real time clocks that sit on the memory bus. It is convenient to glue them on there, because they can be read and written with the usual "load" and "store" memory access instructions, instead of requiring a dedicated I/O port. They can return the current time via a single cycle read, but the value will change unpredictably due to actions outside the program. Volatile isn't really intended for general use on arbitrary objects in applications. The keyword isn't used anywhere in the current version of the runtime library.

Generalized thread programming is a discipline in its own right, and one that will become increasingly significant now that Java makes it so easy. The Solaris OS kernel is a multi-threaded implementation, and multi-threaded is definitely the future trend. Consult the threads books listed at the end of this chapter for a thorough grounding in the topic of threads programming.

Garbage Collection

Languages with dynamic data structures (structures that can grow and shrink in size at runtime) must have some way of telling the underlying Operating System when they need more memory. Conversely, you also need some way to indicate memory that is no longer in use (e.g. threads that have terminated, objects that are no longer referenced by anything, variables that have gone out of scope, etc.), this can amount to a large amount of memory in a nontrivial program or a program that runs for an extended period of time. Once acquired from the OS, memory is usually never returned to it, but retained for re-use by the program. This will all be taken care of by a storage manager. One subsystem of the storage manager will be a "garbage collector." The automatic reclaiming of memory that is no longer in use is known as "garbage collection" in computer science.

Compiler writers for algorithmic languages have the concept of a "heap" and a "stack." The stack takes care of dynamic memory requirements related to procedure call and return. The heap is responsible for all other dynamic memory. In Java, that's a lot because object allocation is always from the heap. The only variables allocated on the stack are the local variables of a method.[3]

Java is going to give a powerful boost to doctoral dissertations on the subject of speeding up garbage collector algorithms.

In the C language, malloc() allocates memory, and free() makes it available for re-use. In C++, the new and delete operators have the same effect. Both of these languages require explicit deallocation of memory. The programmer has to say what memory to give back, and when. In practice this has turned out to be an error-prone task. It's all too easy to create a "memory leak" by not freeing memory before overwriting the last pointer to it; then it can neither be referenced nor

---

3. Java actually has multiple stacks: it starts out with one for Java code and another stack for C native methods. Additional stacks are allocated for every thread created. This aspect of Java requires a virtual memory mapping system to operate efficiently.

freed. Some X-Windows applications are notorious for leaking even more than Apple Computers' board of directors.

Why do we need Garbage Collection?

Java takes a different approach. Instead of requiring the programmer to take the initiative in freeing memory, the job is given to a runtime component called the garbage collector. It is the job of the garbage collector to sit on top of the heap and periodically scan it to determine things that aren't being used any more. It can reclaim that memory and put it back in the free store pool within the program.

Making garbage collection an implicit operation of the runtime system rather than a responsibility of the programmer has a cost. It means that at unpredictable times, a potentially large amount of behind-the-scenes processing will suddenly start-up when some low-water mark is hit and more memory is called for. This has been a problem with past systems, but Java addresses it somewhat with threads. In a multi-threaded system, the garbage collector can run in parallel with user code and has a much less intrusive effect on the system. It still carries some runtime performance cost however.

Taking away the task of memory management from the programmer gives him or her one less thing to worry about, and makes the resulting software more reliable in use. It may take a little longer to run compared with a language like C++ with explicit memory management because the garbage collector has to go out and look for reclaimable memory rather than simply being told where to find it. On the other hand, it's much quicker to debug and get the program running in the first place. Most people would agree that in the presence of ever-improving hardware performance, a small performance penalty is an acceptable price to pay for more reliable software.

We should mention at this point that there is almost no direct interaction between the programmer and garbage collection. It is one of the runtime services that you can take for granted, like keeping track of return addresses, or identifying the correct handler for an exception. The discussion here is to provide a little more insight into what takes place behind the scenes.

Garbage Collection Algorithms

A number of alternative garbage collection algorithms have been proposed and tried over the years. Three popular ones are "reference counting," "mark and sweep," and "stop and copy."

Reference counting keeps a counter for each chunk of memory allocated. The counter records how many pointers directly point at the chunk or something inside it. The counter needs to be kept up-to-date as assignments are made. If the reference count ever drops to zero, nothing can ever access the memory and so it can immediately be returned to the pool of free storage. The big advantage of reference counting is that it imposes a steady constant overhead, rather than needing aperiodic bursts of the cpu. The big disadvantage of reference counting is that in its simplest incarnation it is fooled by circular references. If A points to B, and B points to A, but nothing else points to A and B they will not be freed even though they could be. It's also a little expensive in multi-threaded environments because reference counts must be locked for mutual exclusion before reference counts are updated.

You can turn off garbage collection in your application, by starting java with this option:

```
java -noasyncgc  ...
```

One reason for doing this might be to experiment and see how much of a difference in performance it makes, if any. You should not turn off garbage collection in a program that may run for an extended period. If you do it is almost guaranteed to fail with memory exhaustion sooner or later.

Alternatively, you can call the method

```
system.gc();
```

to run the garbage collector at any point you choose.

The current Java implementation from Sun uses the "mark and sweep" garbage collection algorithm. The marker starts at the root pointers. These are things like the stack, and static (global) variables. You can imagine marking with a red pen every object that can be accessed from the roots. Then the marker recursively marks all the objects that are directly or indirectly referenced from the objects reachable from the roots. The process continues until no more red marks can be placed. The entire virtual process may need to be swapped in and looked at, which is expensive in disk traffic and time. A smart garbage collector knows it doesn't have to bring in objects that can't contain references like large graphics images and the like. Then the "sweep" phase starts, and everything without a red mark is swept back onto the free list for re-use. Memory compaction also takes place at this point. Memory compaction means jiggling down into one place all the memory that is in use, so that all the free store comes together and can be merged into one large pool. Compaction helps when you have a number of large objects to allocate.

The current Java implementation from Microsoft is based on the source licensed from Sun. Microsoft did change the garbage collector to one that uses the "stop and copy" algorithm. As the name suggests, it stops all other threads completely and goes into a garbage collection phase, which is simplicity itself. The heap is split into two parts: the currently active part and the new part. Each of these is known as a "semi-space." It copies all the non-garbage stuff over into the new semi-space and makes that the currently-active semi-space. The old currently-active semi-space is just discarded completely. Non-garbage is identified by tracing active pointers, just as in mark and sweep.

The advantage of "stop and copy" is that it avoids heap fragmentation, so periodic memory compaction is not needed. Stop and copy is a fast garbage collection algorithm, but it requires twice the memory area. It also can't be used in real time systems as it makes your computer appear to just freeze from time to time. More about that in the Light Relief section coming up.

Finalizers

A "finalizer" is a Java term, related to but not the same as a C++ destructor. When there are no further references to an object, its storage can be reclaimed by the garbage collector.

A finalizer is a method from class Object that any class may override. If a class has a finalizer method, it will be called on dead instances of that class before the memory occupied by that object is re-used. The programmer makes this possible by providing a body for the method finalize() in the class. It will look like this:

```
class Fruit {

        protected void finalize() throws Throwable {
           // do finalization ...
};
```

It must have the signature shown (protected, void, and no arguments).

The Java Language Specification says:

> *"The purpose of finalizers is to provide a chance to free up resources (such as file descriptors or operating system graphics contexts) that are owned by objects but cannot be accessed directly and cannot be freed automatically by the automatic storage management. Simply reclaiming an object's memory by garbage collection would not guarantee that these resources would be reclaimed."*

Finalization was carried over from the Oak language, and justified on the grounds that it would help provide good resource management for long running servers.

If present, a class's finalizer is called by the garbage collector at some point after the object is first recognized as garbage and before the memory is reclaimed, such that the object is garbage at the time of the call. A finalizer can also be called explicitly. In JDK 1.0 there is no guarantee that an object will be garbage collected, and hence there is no guarantee that an object's finalizer will be called. A program may terminate normally without garbage collection taking place. So you could not rely on a finalizer method being called, you cannot use it to carry out some essential final housekeeping (release a lock, write usage statistics, or whatever). Java 1.1 will guarantee that finalizers are run, if the method `System.runFinalizersOnExit()` is called (and accepted by the Security-Manager) before exit. 🐛

Finally (uh...) don't confuse "final" (a constant) or "finally" (a block that is always executed after a "try()" with "finalize"—the three concepts are unrelated.

Some Light Relief

The Robot Ping-Pong[4] Player

Computer scientists are always looking for hard new problems to solve. They want the problems to be hard enough to be worth tackling, preferably capable of eventual solution, yet easy to describe (so that you don't have to spend too long educating grant-making organizations on what you'll do with their money).

Constructing a robot that could play ping-pong was proposed years ago as a particularly difficult computer science problem requiring solutions in vision, real-time control, and artificial intelligence.

Various other robots have been proposed and constructed over the years: robots that walk on jointed legs, robots that try to learn from their environment, robots that recognize facial expressions and so on. None has quite achieved the popularity of the ping-pong playing robots. A number of them have been built in the engineering labs of the finest universities around the globe. The researchers even published the official rules of robot ping-pong so they could have tournaments. Several of these were organized by Professor John Billingsley, of the E.& E.E. Department at Portsmouth University.

---

4.   "Ping-Pong" is a trademark of Parker Brothers

> **Extracts From The Official Rules of Robot Ping-Pong**
>
> Rule 11: Those parts of the robot visible to the opponent must be black including absorption of infrared in the region of 1 micron wavelength.
>
> Rule 17: The judges may disqualify a robot on the grounds of safety, or penalize it for serious breaches of sportsmanship.

Naturally the students at M.I.T. built their share of robot ping-pong players. Some of the best work was done there, in the Artificial Intelligence labs, where they used Lisp as the implementation language.

> **Cheaters Never Prosper?**
>
> Table tennis is full of surprises. In one world championship after the Cultural Revolution communist China seemed absolutely unbeatable at table tennis. They won every competition in sight, dominating their opponents with surprising spin shots.
>
> Later the truth came out; they were cheating, or at least stretching the rules to breaking point. The communist regime had equipped its teams with special bats. Both sides of the bat looked identical, but they were made out of very different materials. One side of the bat would give a regular shot, the other would help impart a fierce spin. Opponents didn't even know about the trick bats, and had no way of knowing what kind of a shot was coming at them.
>
> The tournament rules were changed. Trick bats were still allowed, but the faces had to be different colors. Communist Chinese domination of the sport came to an end.

A story, probably apocryphal, is told of an early prototype at M.I.T. After several months of hard work, the students finally coaxed the robot into accurately serving a series of balls from its ball magazine. Eagerly the students reloaded it, and fetched their professor to witness the accomplishment. When the balding professor arrived, he stood expectantly at the far end of the table from the robot and gave the signal to proceed.

As soon as the robot started, it launched a series of hard accurate lobs directly at the professor's cranium. No matter how the professor twisted and ducked, the machine kept him in its sights until at last it was out of balls. When all the tears and laughter had finally stopped, the students were cleared of any wrongdoing. It seems that the robot had been set up to target a large illuminated white patch on the wall representing the opponent, and when the luckless teacher stood within range, his bald brow showed up on the vision system as larger, whiter and shinier, so was preferred. This incident allegedly led to the aforementioned rule 11. No word on whether the robot was nailed under rule 17.

The name of Professor Marvin Minsky of MIT is often attached to this story. Professor Minsky is adamant that he was never bombarded with ping pong balls, but he concedes that an early ball catcher robot did once make a grab for his head. That seems to be the origin of this story.

There is an equally apocryphal coda to this story. It seems that the students went on to enter the robot in one of the tournaments where it played quite well for the first 15 minutes. Suddenly, unaccountably, the robot froze completely and let several successive balls from the opponent bounce off its chest without even attempting a return serve. Then equally suddenly it started playing again. A furious debugging session was started, only to pinpoint the cause of the problem almost immediately. The robot was driven by Lisp software. It ran perfectly for a quarter hour until it had exhausted its free memory. At that point the garbage collector kicked in. Nothing else could run until the garbage collector had done its thing, not even the code to return a ball. That's why single threaded systems aren't very good at real-time processing. The workaround was simple: reboot the processor immediately prior to each tournament match.

Exercises

1. Write a program to read the arguments provided on the command line and print the characters of each in reverse order.

2. If you had to read in and sort a file of five hundred words, would you use String, StringBuffer or char[]? Explain your choice.

3. How do the "runtime exceptions" differ from exceptions you define? Give six examples of runtime exceptions and explain how each might be generated.

4. Give three examples of when threads might be used to advantage in a program. Describe a circumstance when it would not be advantageous to use threads.

5. What are the two ways of creating a new thread in java?

6. Take your favorite sorting algorithm, and make it multi-threaded. *Hint*: a recursive partitioning algorithm like quicksort is the best candidate for this. Quicksort simply divides the array to be sorted into two pieces, then moves numbers about until all the numbers in one piece are smaller (or at least no larger) than all the numbers in the other piece. Repeat the algorithm on each of the pieces. When the pieces consist of just one element, the array is sorted.

Further Reading

Threads Primer: A Guide to Multithreaded Programming

by Bil Lewis/Daniel J. Berg

published by SunSoft Press/Prentice Hall, 1995.

ISBN: 0-13-443698-9

The definitive introduction to threads programming.

There is a survey of garbage collection techniques at

ftp://ftp.cs.utexas.edu/pub/garbage/bigsurv.ps

A Robot Ping-Pong Player: an experiment in real-time intelligent control

by Russell L. Andersson,

published by the M.I.T. Press, Cambridge, MA, 1988

ISBN: 0-262-01101-8

A rather stuffy book that completely shies away from the essential levity of the subject matter, in favor of dragging in a lot of guff about polynomials and trajectories. Doesn't mention either of the two stories above, but the system was written in C and the book includes several interesting C listings.

Programming with Threads

by Steve Kleiman, Devang Shah, and Bart Smaalders

published by SunSoft Press/Prentice Hall, 1996

ISBN: 0-13-172389-8

Written by senior threads development engineers at Sun Microsystems, this is a comprehensive reference work on threads. This book was introduced in February 1996.

Design Patterns—Elements of Reusable Object-Oriented Software

by Erich Gamma, Richard Helm, Ralph Johnson, John Vlissides

published by Addison Wesley, 1994

ISBN 0-201-63361-2

The design patterns book is of particular interest, as it describes an area of emerging OOP technology. As the authors explain, design patterns describe simple, repeatable solutions to specific problems in OO software design. They capture solutions that have been made better over time, hence they aren't typically the first code that comes to mind unless you know about them. They are code idioms writ large. They are not unusual or amazing, or tied to any one language.

By giving the common idioms names, and describing them, it helps reuse. Some common idioms/design patterns are shown in Table 5-2.

Table 5-2: Common idioms/design patterns

Design Pattern	Purpose and use
Factory Method	Supplies an interface to create any of several related objects, without specifying their concrete classes. The Factory figures out the precise class that is needed, and constructs one of those for you.
Adapter	Converts the interface of a class into another interface that the client can use directly. Adapter lets classes work together that couldn't otherwise. Think "hose to sprinkler interface adapter."
Observer	Defines a many-to-one dependency between objects, so that when the observed object changes state, all the Observers are notified and can act accordingly. Think "monitoring the progress of something coming in over the network."
Strategy	Defines a family of algorithms, and make them interchangeable. Strategy lets the agorithm vary independently from the clients that use it. Think "let the client specify if speed or space is the preferred optimization."

The recommended book describes a couple of dozen design patterns. It will repay further study.

CHAPTER

6

- Anagram Program

- Core Java APIs

- Basic Utilities

- Native Methods

- Properties

Practical Examples Explained

> "As a matter of fact a high tree makes a wretched sniping post, and I rarely allowed one to be used on our side. But we found that the German sense of humor appears to be much tickled by seeing, or thinking that he sees, a Britisher falling out of a tree. When our sniping became very good, and the enemy consequently shy of giving a target, a dummy in a tree worked by a rope sometimes caused Fritz and Hans to show themselves unwisely. One had to be very careful not to go too far in this sort of work or trickery, lest a minenwerfer should take his part in the duel."
>
> Major H. Hesketh-Prichard, DSO, MC
> "Sniping in France"

This chapter contains a nontrivial Java program annotated with a running commentary. The program source appears on the CD accompanying this book, so you can look at it without the annotation, and you can try compiling and running it without typing it in.

The program generates anagrams (letter rearrangements). You give it a word or phrase, and it comes back with all the substring combinations that it can find in the dictionary. You need to provide it with a wordlist that it will use as a dictionary,[1] and you can also specify the minimum length of words in the anagrams that it generates.

For any phrases more than a few letters long, there are a lot more anagrams than you would ever think possible.

Case Study Java Program

Here is an example of running the program on the infamous "surfing the Internet" phrase, specifying words of length four or longer. It finds dozens and dozens of them, starting like this:

```
java anagram "surfing the internet" 4
reading word list...
main dictionary has 25144 entries.
least common letter is 'f'

fritter shunt engine
fritter hung intense
surfeit Ghent intern
surfeit ninth regent
furnish greet intent
furnish egret intent
furnish tent integer
further stint engine
further singe intent
further tinge tennis
further gin sentient
freight nurse intent
freight runt intense
freight turn intense
freight run sentient
freight nun interest
freight sen nutrient
freeing Hurst intent
    ...
```

If you specify a length argument, it will try to use words with at least that many characters, but the final word it finds to complete the anagram may be shorter. This program is written as an application, so there is no issue about accessing files.

---

1. If you don't have such a word list (e.g. in your spellchecker), there are several alternatives available for downloading, e.g. at: http://web.soi.city.ac.uk:8080/text/roget/thesaurus.html, or, http://math-www.uni-paderborn.de/HTML/Dictionaries.html. Both of these sites contain links to several dictionaries. On Unix, just use the file /usr/dict/words.

Here is the annotated program source:

```
/*
 * Usage: anagram string-to-anagram [[min-len] wordfile]
 * Java Anagram program, Peter van der Linden Jan 7, 1996.
 */

import java.io.*;
```

Note, the "using an interface to hold useful constants" idiom was explained in Chapter 4.

```
interface UsefulConstants {
    public static final int MAXWORDS = 50000;
    public static final int MAXWORDLEN = 30;
    public static final int EOF = -1;
```

Note the way a reference variable can be used to provide a shorter name for another object.

We can now say "o.println()" instead of "System.out.println()".

```
    // shorter alias for I/O streams
    public static final PrintStream o = System.out;
    public static final PrintStream e = System.err;
}

class Word {
    int mask;
    byte count[]= new byte[26];
    int total;
    String aword;
```

This is an important data structure for representing one word. We keep it as a string, we note the total number of letters in the word, the count of each letter and a bitmask of the alphabet. A zero at bit N means the letter that comes Nth in the alphabet is in the word. A one means that letter is not in the word. This allows for some fast comparisons later on for "how much overlap is there between these two strings?"

```
Word(String s)   // construct an entry from a string
{
    int ch;
    aword = s;
    mask = ~0;
    total = 0;
    s = s.toLowerCase();
    for (int i = 'a'; i <= 'z'; i++) count[i-'a'] = 0;

    for (int i = s.length()-1; i >= 0; i--) {
        ch = s.charAt(i) - 'a';
        if (ch >= 0 && ch < 26) {
            total++;
            count[ch]++;
            mask &= ~(1 << ch);
        }
    }
}
```

The program has the following steps:

1. Read in a list of real words, and convert each word into a form that makes it easy to compare on the quantity and value of letters.

2. Get the word or phrase we are anagramming, and convert it into the same form.

3. Go through the list of words, using our helpful comparison to make a second list of those which can be part of a possible anagram. Words that can be part of a possible anagram are those which only have the same letters as appear in the anagram, and do not have more of any one letter than appears in the anagram.

4. Go through our extracted list of candidate words. Choose the most difficult letter (the one that appears least often) to start with. Take words with it in, and call the anagram finder recursively to fill out the rest of the letters from the candidate dictionary.

The class "Word" above is the class that deals with one word from the wordlist and puts it in the special "easy to compare" form.

In several places in this program, characters are used as the basis for an index into an array. The line below, from the Word() constructor is an example of this.

```
for (int i='a'; i <= 'z'; i++) count[i-'a'] = 0;
```

In C, this is the classic example of something that would work on a system with an ASCII codeset, but fail on an EBCDIC machine since the alphabetic letters are not contiguous in EBCDIC. Java's use of Unicode ensures that this idiom works on all systems. On say a Sun Ultra workstation, the code

```
int i='a';
System.out.println("i = " + i);
```

gives the expected "i = 97" because that is the decimal value that represents lower case A in both ASCII and Unicode. However, you would even get the same result on an IBM System/390 where an EBCDIC 'a' is decimal 121, as Java guarantees and requires the internal representation of a character to be 16-bit Unicode. The runtime system will need to do the translation from/to EBCDIC on input/output.

IBM and the Java Ports

IBM is the only company of any consequence still using EBCDIC, which is a holdover from the days when its mainframe computer systems ruled the earth. However the issue of EBCDIC is of more than theoretical interest as IBM has announced that it is porting Java to its MVS mainframe operating system (to slow the migration of "right-sizing" applications to workstations).

IBM finally delivered a Windows 3.1 port of Java. The port is admittedly more arduous because the underlying system does not have threads, and does not support proper filenames (limiting them to 8 characters and a 3 character extension).

Their port of JDK 1.0.2 to Windows 3.1 became available in August 1996 and can be downloaded from http://www.alphaWorks.ibm.com

Netscape also launched a Java-enabled browser for Windows 3.1 in early 1997. Look at http://www.netscape.com

---

The class "WordList" below is the one that reads in a word list, and builds up an entire dictionary of all words in the special format:

```
class WordList implements UsefulConstants {
    static Word[] Dictionary= new Word[MAXWORDS];
    static int totWords=0;

    static void ReadDict(String f)
    {
```

The half dozen lines that follow are a very common idiom for opening a file. This can throw an exception, so we either deal with it here or declare it in the method. It is usually easiest to deal with exceptions closest to the point where they are raised, if you are going to catch them at all.

Here we catch the exception, print out a diagnostic, then re-throw a RuntimeException to cause the program to stop with a backtrace. We could exit the program at this point, but re-throwing the exception ensures that it will be recognized that an error has occurred. We throw RuntimeException rather than our original exception because RuntimeException *does not have to be handled or declared.* Now that we have printed a diagnostic at the point of error, it is acceptable to take this shortcut:

```
FileInputStream fis;
try {fis = new FileInputStream(f)};
catch (FileNotFoundException fnfe) {
    e.println ("Cannot open the file of words '" + f + "'");
    throw new RuntimeException();
}
e.println("reading dictionary...");
```

It is better not to have any arbitrary fixed size arrays in your code. This one is done for convenience. Removing the limitation is one of the programming challenges at the end of this example. The buffer holds the characters of a word as we read them in from the word list and assemble them.

```
char buffer[] = new char[MAXWORDLEN];
String s;
int r =0;
while (r!=EOF) {
    int i=0;
    try {
        // read a word in from the word file
        while ( (r=fis.read()) != EOF ) {
            if ( r == '\n' ) break;
            buffer[i++] = (char) r;
        }
    } catch (IOException ioe) {
        e.println ("Cannot read the file of words ");
        throw new RuntimeException();
    }
```

This simple looking constructor to create a new Word object actually does the complicated conversion of a string into the form convenient for further processing (the dozen or so lines of code in class Word).

```
                s=new String(buffer,0,i);
                Dictionary[totWords] = new Word(s);
                totWords++;
        }

        e.println("main dictionary has " + totWords + " entries.");
    }

}
```

An example of a class that is both a subclass and an implementation follows. It extends and implements:

```
class anagram extends WordList implements UsefulConstants {

    static Word[] Candidate = new Word[MAXWORDS];
    static int totCandidates=0,
            MinimumLength = 3;
```

We just made it implement UsefulConstants to show that a class can implement and extend at the same time. In practice, since anagram's parent class implements UsefulConstants, that namespace is already present in the subclass.

This is the main routine where execution starts:

```
    public static void main(String[] argv)
    {
        if ( argv.length < 1 || argv.length > 3) {
            e.println("Usage: anagram  string-to-anagram "
                        + "[min-len [word file]]");
            return;
        }
        if (argv.length >= 2)
            MinimumLength = Integer.parseInt(argv[1]);
```

If the name of a words list isn't explicitly provided as an argument, the program expects to find a file called "words.txt" in the current directory. This will simply be an ASCII file with a few hundred or thousand words, one word per line, no definitions or other information.

```
    // word filename is optional 3rd argument
    ReadDict( argv.length==3? argv[2] : "words.txt" );
    DoAnagrams(argv[0]);
}

static void DoAnagrams(String anag)
{
    Word myAnagram = new Word(anag);

    myAnagram.mask = ~myAnagram.mask;
```

The next couple of lines go through the list of words that we read in, and extract the ones that could be part of the phrase to anagram. These words are extracted into a second word list or dictionary, called "Candidates." The dictionary of Candidate words is sorted.

```
    getCandidates(myAnagram);

    int RootIndexEnd = sortCandidates(myAnagram);
```

This call says "Find an anagram of the string "myAnagram," using this working storage, you're at level 0 (first attempt), and considering candidate words zero through RootIndexEnd".

```
    FindAnagram(myAnagram, new String[50],  0, 0,
RootIndexEnd);

    o.println("----" + anag + "----");
}
```

This is how a word becomes a candidate:

1. The candidate must only have letters that appear in the anagram (this is the fast overlap test that a bit mask representation provides).

2. It must also be no shorter than the minimum length we specified.

3. It must not be too long.

4. And it must not have more of any one letter than the anagram has.

If the word meets all these conditions, add it to the candidates dictionary.

```
    static void getCandidates(Word d)
    {
        for (int i = totCandidates = 0; i < totWords; i++)
            if (    (  (Dictionary[i].mask | d.mask) == (int)~0)
                && (    Dictionary[i].total >= MinimumLength    )
                && (    Dictionary[i].total + MinimumLength <= d.total
                     || Dictionary[i].total == d.total)
                && ( fewerOfEachLetter(d.count,
                    Dictionary[i].count) )   )

                    Candidate[totCandidates++]=Dictionary[i];

        e.println(
          "Dictionary of words-that-are-substring-anagrams has "
                 + totCandidates + " entries.");
//      PrintCandidate();
    }


    static boolean fewerOfEachLetter(byte anagCount[], byte
entryCount[])
    {
        for (int i = 25; i >= 0; i--)
            if (entryCount[i] > anagCount[i]) return false;
        return true;
    }

    static void PrintCandidate()
    {
        for (int i = 0; i < totCandidates; i++)
            o.print( Candidate[i].aword + ", "
                    + ((i%4 == 3)?"\n":" " ) );
        o.println("");
    }
```

Here's where we start trying to assemble anagrams out of the words in the candidates dictionary.

```
static void FindAnagram(Word d,
                        String WordArray[],
                        int Level, int StartAt, int EndAt)
{
    int i, j;
    boolean enoughCommonLetters;
    Word WordToPass = new Word("");

    for (i = StartAt; i < EndAt; i++) {
      if ( (d.mask | Candidate[i].mask) != 0) {
         enoughCommonLetters = true;
         for (j = 25; j >=0 && enoughCommonLetters; j--)
            if (d.count[j] < Candidate[i].count[j])
                enoughCommonLetters = false;

         if (enoughCommonLetters) {
           WordArray[Level] = Candidate[i].aword;
           WordToPass.mask = 0;
           WordToPass.total = 0;
           for (j = 25; j >= 0; j--) {
```

The cast to (byte) is needed whenever a byte receives the value of an arithmetic expression. It assures the compiler that the programer realizes the expression was evaluated in at least 32 bits and the result will be truncated before storing in the byte.

```
             WordToPass.count[j] = (byte)
               (    d.count[j] -
                    Candidate[i].count[j] );
             if ( WordToPass.count[j] != 0 ) {
                WordToPass.total +=
                    (int)WordToPass.count[j];
                WordToPass.mask |= 1 << j;
             }
           }
           if (WordToPass.total == 0) {
              /* Found a series of words! */
              for (j = 0; j <= Level; j++)
                  o.print(WordArray[j] + " ");
              o.println();
           } else if (WordToPass.total < MinimumLength) {
                ; /* Don't call again */
           } else {
```

The recursive call to find anagrams for the remaining letters in the phrase.

```
                    FindAnagram(WordToPass, WordArray, Level+1,
                         i, totCandidates);
              }
          }
       }
     }
  }


static int SortMask;

static int sortCandidates(Word d)
{
    int [] MasterCount=new int[26];
    int LeastCommonIndex=0, LeastCommonCount;
    int i, j;

    for (j = 25; j >= 0; j--) MasterCount[j] = 0;
    for (i = totCandidates-1; i >= 0; i--)
        for (j = 25; j >= 0; j--)
            MasterCount[j] += Candidate[i].count[j];

    LeastCommonCount = MAXWORDS * 5;
    for (j = 25; j >= 0; j--)
        if (    MasterCount[j] != 0
            && MasterCount[j] < LeastCommonCount
            && (d.mask & (1 << j) ) != 0  ) {
            LeastCommonCount = MasterCount[j];
            LeastCommonIndex = j;
        }

    SortMask = (1 << LeastCommonIndex);

    quickSort(0, totCandidates-1 );

    for (i = 0; i < totCandidates; i++)
        if ((SortMask & ~Candidate[i].mask) == 0)
            break;
```

The root breadth is the first word in the sorted candidate dictionary that doesn't contain the least common letter. Since the least common letter will be hard to match, we plan to start out by using all the words with it in as the roots of our search. The breadth part is that it represents the number of alternatives to start with.

```
        e.println("least common letter is '"
                + (char)(LeastCommonIndex+'a') + "'" );
        e.println("words with least common letter: " + i + " words");
        return i;
    }
```

Sort the dictionary of Candidate words, using the standard quicksort algorithm from any Algorithm book. This one was adapted from page 87 of K&R Edition 2. Again, it shows that recursion is fine in Java.[2]

```
    static void quickSort(int left, int right)
    {
        // standard quicksort from any algorithm book
        int i, last;
        if (left >= right) return;
        swap(left, (left+right)/2);
        last = left;
        for (i=left+1; i<=right; i++)   /* partition */
            if (MultiFieldCompare( Candidate[i],
                                   Candidate[left] ) == -1 )
                swap( ++last, i);

        swap(last, left);
        quickSort(left, last-1);
        quickSort(last+1,right);
    }


    static int MultiFieldCompare(Word s, Word t)
    {
        if ( (s.mask & SortMask) != (t.mask & SortMask) )
            return ( (s.mask & SortMask)>(t.mask & SortMask)? 1:-1);

        if ( t.total != s.total )
            return (t.total - s.total);

        return (s.aword).compareTo(t.aword);
    }

    static void swap(int d1, int d2) {
        Word tmp = Candidate[d1];
        Candidate[d1] = Candidate[d2];
        Candidate[d2] = tmp;
    }
}
```

2. This anagram program was based on a C program that my colleague Brian
    Scearce wrote in his copious free time.

When I wrote the above Java code, my first version had a bug in it. In the following code, I had omitted to subtract 1 from the String length, (also I did not check that the character was alphabetic before putting it in the data structure). Instead of looking like this:

GOOD CODE

```
for (int i = s.length()-1; i >= 0; i--) {
            ...s.charAt(i)...
```

I had it like this:

BAD CODE

```
for (int i = s.length(); i >= 0; i--) {
            ...s.charAt(i)...
```

In a C program, this would cause no anagrams to be found, but the program would run to completion. There would not be any indication that an error had occurred, or where. A naive tester would report that the program worked fine. Works fine? Ship it!

In my java program, this was the output from my first test run:

```
java.lang.StringIndexOutOfBoundsException: String index out of
range: 4
        at java.lang.String.charAt(String.java)
        at Word.<init>(anagram.java:35)
        at WordList.ReadDict(anagram.java:77)
        at anagram.main(anagram.java:104)
```

It told me an error had occurred, what the error was, why it was an error, where in the program it happened, and how execution reached that point. Some other languages have this kind of comprehensive runtime checking (Ada comes to mind), but Java is the only one that is also both object-oriented and has a C flavor. At that moment, as they say, I became enlightened. 🍎

Core Java APIs

As chapter one explained, the Java system comes with more than a few libraries. Some of these libraries are required to be present on every Java system, so programmers can always count on them being there. Other libraries are optional, but if the implementation supports that feature at all (e.g., telephony) it must be supported in the standard way.

Just for the record, the core libraries that must be present in every Java 1.1 system are listed in Table 6-1. Some of these APIs started out as optional extensions, and were moved into the core JDK as they were proved by practical use.

Table 6-1: Core Java APIs.

Library	Library size	Purpose
java.lang	77 classes	The java.lang package provides basic runtime support for language features that require them, such as threads, reflection, and exceptions.
java.applet	4 classes	The java.applet classes support applet execution.
java.awt	141 classes	The java.awt classes implement the windowing operations.
java.util	44 classes	A package of utility data structures. Very useful.
java.io	71 classes	The java.io package supports input/output for files.
java.rmi	48 classes	The java.rmi package provides remote method calls to Java programs running on other computers.
java.sql	17 classes	The java.sql library contains support for Java Data-Base Connectivity (JDBC).
java.security	40 classes	The java.security package provides programmers with the ability to digitally sign applets and supports coding and decoding data.
java.net	31 classes	The java.net library provides programmers with a wide variety of UDP, IP, and TCP/IP networking classes.
java.beans	23 classes	The java.beans API supports "component software" allowing rapid application development through the easy connection and reuse of existing program fragments.

Table 6-1: Core Java APIs. *(continued)*

Library	Library size	Purpose
java.text	41 classes	The java.text package is concerned with internationalization and localization. It handles the most common kinds of text that are localized: dates, times, currency, etc.
java.math	2 classes	The java.math class is provided to match the SQL database types DECIMAL and NUMERIC. Don't confuse this package with the more general java.lang.Math class.

These libraries are present on every Java 1.1-based system. The libraries are shown here roughly in the order in which a new Java programmer will use them, most frequent first.

The one dozen core APIs contain a total of 539 classes and interfaces. That's a lot of classes! We do not cover the beans and text packages in detail in this book (although we present examples of common uses of java.text). Component software, as expressed in the Beans API (and the java.lang.reflect package), is a large topic that requires book-length treatment of its own. Reflection means "what I see when I look in the mirror," and the reflect API is a class that you can use to find out at runtime the methods and data fields that are in any class. Finding out dynamically the methods and data in a class is a key part of making software components work together. Component software is an area of emerging software technology, and looks likely to be very important. After you finish this book, you may want to study a JavaBeans book. The java.text library helps programmers to localize strings in the course of internationalizing software. We show some examples in the I/O chapter, but again, internationalizing software is a specialized topic that really takes a book of its own.

Here we'll give a summary of what each of the other core packages does, and a more detailed description of the packages you will use most frequently. Inside your programs, these core (required) packages all have package names starting with "java" such as "java.io" or "java.applet." That name indicates that these are all part of the Java implementation. Some of the packages are multi-level packages. We have classes in java.awt.*, and there are also classes in java.awt.event.* and java.awt.image.*. When you import a package, you do not automatically also import any packages it contains. In other words "import java.awt.*;" does not also bring in "java.awt.event.*;" The java.lang package is the only package that is included by default in all your programs, so you can use those classes without any "import" statement.

As part of its Java Development Kit, Sun Microsystems even supplies the source code for these libraries (another reason to use Sun's JDK rather than some other Java compiler). As a programmer you can and should review the source code, and you should become practiced at consulting the code to answer any questions you may have.

When you installed the JDK that accompanies this book, you set up an environment variable called $JAVAHOME that pointed to the root of the JDK on your disk. The file $JAVAHOME/src.zip may need to be unzipped, or it may have already been done as part of the installation (it varies from platform to platform). The source code for these runtime libraries is at $JAVAHOME/src/java. Following the regular rules for package names mirroring pathnames, the IO library source is in directory $JAVAHOME/src/java/io. Take a minute to cd (change directory) to $JAVAHOME/src/java and find these source files.

We will now expand on some of these libraries at greater length. Most of the rest of this book is concerned with explaining the libraries and showing examples of their use. Let's point out the sections in this book where individual libraries are covered (see Table 6-2).

Table 6-2: Java libraries

Library	Covered in
java.lang	chapters 3, 4, and other places
java.math	this chapter (chapter 6)
java.util	this chapter (chapter 6)
java.applet	chapter 7
java.security	chapter 7
java.sql	chapter 8
java.rmi	chapter 8
java.awt	chapters 9 and 10
java.io	chapter 11
java.net	chapter 12

First we will cover the java.math API, new in JDK 1.1. The remainder of this chapter is concerned with the java.util API.

The `java.math` API

The java.math package is simple to understand and use. It was added to JDK 1.1 for three reasons. First, for use in the java.security Digital Signature Algorithm interfaces. Second, to complete the support for all SQL types used in database programming, and to allow arithmetic on types larger than long and double. If you do database programming, you'll be comfortable with the two classes java.math.BigDecimal and java.math.BigInteger which can represent the SQL types DECIMAL and NUMERIC. Third, even if you don't use cryptography or database programming, you can still use these classes for arithmetic on numbers of arbitrary size.

As the names suggest, BigInteger deals with integers of unbounded size, and BigDecimal deals with unbounded numbers with fractional parts. BigDecimal is essentially BigInteger with some extra code to keep track of the scale (where the decimal point is). If you want to manipulate a number that takes a megabyte to store all its decimal places, you can. BigInteger provides versions of all of Java's primitive integer operators, and all relevant static methods from java.lang.Math. Additionally, BigInteger provides operations for modular arithmetic, GCD calculation, primality testing, prime generation, single-bit manipulation, and a few other odds and ends.

Here's an example of BigInteger used to perform a calculation that is listed in the 1989 Guinness Book of World Records under "Human Computer."

```
BigInteger bi1 = new BigInteger("7686369774870");
BigInteger bi2 = new BigInteger("2465099745779");
bi1 = bi1.multiply(bi2);
System.out.println( "The value is "+ bi1 );
```

When compiled and run, the correct answer appears:

```
The value is 18947668177995426462773730
```

BigInteger naturally does it quite a lot faster than the human record holder who took 28 seconds. *It must be stressed that record-breaking mental arithmetic is an extremely hazardous activity and should only be attempted by trained professionals and not using a Pentium computer.* (I copied that warning out of the Guinness book. They print a version of it next to all the people who set records for wrestling alligators, sword swallowing, parachute freefall, etc).

Here's an example of BigDecimal used to round a number with many decimal places of precision.

```
BigDecimal bd1 = new BigDecimal( java.lang.Math.PI );
System.out.println( "The value is "+ bd1 );

int digsrightofradix = 4;
bd1 = bd1.setScale(digsrightofradix, BigDecimal.ROUND_HALF_UP);
System.out.println( "The value is "+ bd1 );
```

When compiled and run, the output is

```
The value is 3.141592653589793115997963468544185161590576171875
The value is 3.1416
```

Class BigDecimal also contains many other options for rounding numbers. Don't confuse the big numbers available from package java.math with the generalized math and trig operations available in class java.lang.Math.

Utilities

There are some built-in utilities in the package java.util such that a class for the data structure you want may already exist. There is a utility class called Vector, for instance. The class java.util.Vector presents an array into which you can insert elements. The array will be grown behind the scenes as necessary to hold whatever you add to it. This does the job of a linked list, but is even better because you also have random access to the individual elements.

Here's how you can time your Java code:

```
long start = System.currentTimeMillis();
    :   // do the work here
    :
long stop = System.currentTimeMillis();
System.out.println("Run time: " + (stop-start) +
                                "millisecs" );
```

Take a look at the other routines available in $JAVAHOME/src/java/lang/System.java. Contrast the Java situation of many utility packages, and guaranteed interoperability, with that of C++. When C++ first became available, there were few utility classes, but everyone used the same compiler (cfront from AT&T). Later when utility libraries became available from third parties, there were sometimes several alternative compilers available for a given platform. That turned out to cause problems. The lack of a C++ Application Binary Interface (ABI) that specified details like name-mangling, exception handling, and argument passing meant that software from different compilers was usually *not* interoperable.

The Guilty Secret of C++: lack of interoperability

A C++ binary package you bought to support linked lists will not work with just any compiler. And it might not work with a different library you bought from another vendor. To stand a reasonable chance of getting libraries to work together you either need access to the source to recompile it in your own environment or you need the library vendor to maintain a special version just for the compiler you are using. The C++ language has been handicapped by this dirty secret for several years. Until there is a standard, stable C++ language, it's hard to have a standard, stable ABI.

The standard API and ABI, fixed for all platforms, is an important part of the basic design of Java. It will avoid the "every compiler shows a different interface" problem. Table 6-3 shows some of the Java utility classes that exist in every implementation:

Table 6-3: Java Utility Classes

java.util.*	Notes
BitSet.java	An array of bits indexed by subscript. The collection grows as you need to add more bits.
Date.java	A class to hold timestamps in a system independent way. Gives access to year, month, day, hour, minute and second.
Calendar	Translates between internal form timestamps and the day, month, year, hour, etc. fields.
GregorianCalendar	Creates timestamps of arbitrary times.
Enumeration.java	An interface that specifies two methods to help count through a set of values.
Hashtable.java	A very useful class! This class maintains a hash table that holds object-and-key pairs. This class lets you impose some order and storage capability on arbitrary objects.
Properties.java	Persistent properties class. Can save a hash table to a stream, and read one back in again. It is an extension of the Hash table class. This is also used for the System properties (used instead of environment variables).
Random.java	Generates pseudo-random numbers in various useful forms and types. Can be completely different each time, or provide the same sequence of random numbers (for testing).
Stack.java	Implements a last-in/first-out stack of objects.
StringTokenizer.java	Does simple lexing (separation into individual tokens removing white space) on a text string.

Table 6-3: Java Utility Classes *(continued)*

java.util.*	Notes
Vector.java	Data structure that can hold a collection of arbitrary objects, and provide immediate access by subscript to them. The array will be extended as needed as more objects are added to it.

Hash Table Explanation

A symbol table in a compiler is often maintained as a hash table. When a name is first read in from the source program, it is hashed (converted to a hash-key value, say 379, by an algorithm designed to spread the values around the table) and entered in the table at location 379 along with all its characteristics (type, scope, etc.). Then when you get the same name again, it is hashed, and the same result, 379, is used as a subscript for immediate access to all its details in the hash table. It is marvellous that a hash table is a library data structure in Java!

Why is a hash table better than just maintaining a sorted list or vector? Because hashing is fast, and sorting is slow.

 Go to the directory with the Java library source on your system ($JAVAHOME/ src/java) and change directory into the util subdirectory, then follow these three steps:

1. List the directory contents. These are the java source files for the utility programs.

2. Look at the source of any five programs there. Read all the methods. Look at the implementation. Why does it do what it does? If your boss offered you a 10,000 zloty bonus to make one of these methods faster, which one would you select and how would you do it?

3. Run javadoc on a five different source files and read the resultant html files. (Medium). 🐛

Basic Utilities

The utility classes are used throughout the Java system, and can be found in the java.util package. You can review the source files at $JAVAHOME/src/java/util. The widely-used classes in the util package, and their purposes are shown in the following paragraphs.

BitSet

This class maintains a set of bits that are identified by the value of an integer, like an array index. You can have up to about 2 billion individual bits in a set (if you have enough virtual memory), each of which can be queried, set, cleared and so on. The bit set will be increased dynamically as needed to accommodate extra bits you add to it.

```
public BitSet(); // constructor
public BitSet(int N); // constructor for set of size N bits

public void or (BitSet s); // OR's one bit set against another.

public void set (int i); // sets bit number i.

public int size(); // returns the number of bits in the set.
```

Date

This class attempts to represent dates and times, but has been criticized for its poor design. Among its other questionable features are that:

- It numbers months starting at 0 (rather than 1 as used on planet earth). Day-of-the-month starts at 1 as expected.

- It will happily construct dates out of invalid input like January 32 (the code author proudly announces that this "feature" allows you to find the difference between two days).

- It fails to parse certain RFC822 style dates, namely those with negative time zone offsets, like: "Thu, 5 Sep 1996 17:44:11 -0700." These occur in e-mail headers.

- The documentation claims that it limits itself to years after the year 1900. So most of history can't be stored or computed.

- The external representation of a year is "years since 1900," so the year 2001 will be given to the programmer as the year 101, which is counter-intuitive to say the least, as it no longer matches the least significant digits of the full year.

The source for Date has a half page comment in the front yammering about leap seconds. It serves as a reminder that even excellent programmers can occasionally turn out substandard code when their work isn't adequately reviewed. Fortunately, Date is not a final class, so it can be overridden and fixed up a bit. This was done by the database crowd to get an implementation of Date that mapped onto SQL.

You can instantiate Date with no arguments, to represent the current moment. You used to be able to provide arguments (year, month, day, hour, etc.) to say "build me a Date that represents this date/time." That use is now deprecated (officially disapproved) and you should use the class GregorianCalendar instead. See the shaded box below for information about "deprecated features."

Deprecated Features

There have only been two major releases of Java: 1.0.2, and 1.1, though there have been many small maintenance releases. Compatibility between all releases is a major goal of JavaSoft's. In most cases this works very well, but there are a small number of cases where an API has had to be changed. The new event model of the window system is the most well known of the API changes, and there are a few others too.

When an API is replaced by a different one, JavaSoft assures software compatibility by leaving the old API in place, and marking it as "deprecated." To deprecate something means to disapprove of it. Deprecated features will eventually be removed from the API. When you compile a program that uses a deprecated API, the compiler will issue a single line error message, like this:

```
% javac foo.java
Note: foo.java uses a deprecated API.  Recompile with "-
deprecation" for details.
1 warning
```

The purpose of this warning is to tell you that you are using an old interface that has been replaced. The warning will not cause compilation to fail, but it reminds you that the class will eventually be removed from the JDK and you need to bring your code up to date. Only one deprecation warning is issued for a compilation, even if you use dozens of outmoded classes or methods. To view the full list of deprecated features that you have used, compile like this

```
% javac -deprecation foo.java
 foo.java:4: Note: The constructor
java.util.Date(int,int,int)
 has been deprecated.
 Date d1 = new Date(97,12,2);
              ^
 Note: foo.java uses a deprecated API.
 Please consult the documentation for a better alternative.
 3 warnings
```

This tells you the deprecated feature, in this case one of the constructors in java.util.Date. You then look at the source code to see the suggested replacement. In this case, that piece of code refers you to java.util.Calendar. The Calendar class is the replacement for some methods in the Date class.

Doing something with dates sometimes involves a mixture of classes. The Date class itself is still used to represent an instant in time. You get a Date representing the current point with

```
Date d = new Date();
```

Java uses a 32-bit int to represent an instant in time. The value is interpreted as "milliseconds since Jan 1 00:00:00, 1970." Earlier dates can be represented by negative numbers, which gives a range extending back to Dec 13 1901, and forward to January 19, 2038.

Calendar and GregorianCalendar

The class Calendar translates between an instant in time, and individual fields like year, month, day, hour, etc. Date used to do this, but it did it in a way that didn't properly internationalize, so those methods have been deprecated. Calendar holds dates internally in two forms: the "milliseconds since the epoch" (annoyingly held as a long int, rather than a Date object) form, and the "several ints individually representing day, month, year, hour, etc." form. In a striking example of bad-code design, updating one of these forms does not update its twin.

Calendar also knows about time zones, and hence things like summer time. The time zone information has a class of its own: TimeZone. There is also a DateFormat class that provides elementary Date formatting.

Calendar is an abstract base class, which is meant to be overridden by a subclass that implements a specific calendar system. It's a dumb approach: it makes the common case of simple date processing un-obvious. But at least Yak-herders in Syria can now use Java to calculate their birthday under the Babylonian calendar. Most of the world uses the Gregorian calendar (named after the Pope who established it in 1582).

The class java.util.GregorianCalendar extends Calendar and provides more methods. Since Calendar is an abstract class, and the parent of GregorianCalendar, I recommend that you simply use GregorianCalendar all the time. Here is how you would get a date of a particular value.

```
GregorianCalendar g = new GregorianCalendar(61,7,13);
```

That represents the day the Berlin wall was constructed, August 13 1961 in the European Central Time (ECT) zone. So a more accurate way to construct that date is to first set the correct time zone, then set the date.

```
TimeZone z_ect = TimeZone.getTimeZone("ECT");
GregorianCalendar g = new GregorianCalendar(z_ect);
g.set(61,7,13);
```

Note that (rather stupidly) months are on the range 0 to 11, and years are represented by the 4-digit year less 1900. If you don't specify a time zone, Gregorian-Calendar defaults to the time zone where the program is running. For example, for a program running in Japan, the default is Japanese Standard Time (JST). A list of all time zones can be found by looking in the source for java.util.Time-Zone.java.

You can pull the individual values out of a date like this

```
int year = g.get(Calendar.YEAR);
int month = g.get(Calendar.MONTH);
int date = g.get(Calendar.DATE);
int day = g.get(Calendar.DAY_OF_WEEK);
```

You can also check if one date is before or after another date. There is no simple way to get the amount of time between two dates. There are two "helper" classes: TimeZone and SimpleTimeZone. Again, SimpleTimeZone is a concrete subclass of TimeZone, and can be used exclusively. You can create a time-zone object for any time zone you want, and then pass it to GregorianCalendar so it will work with values in that time zone.

```
TimeZone z_ect = TimeZone.getTimeZone("ECT");
GregorianCalendar g2 = new GregorianCalendar(z_ect);
g2.set(89, 10, 9, 19, 0); // Berlin Wall Down  Nov 9 1989 7pm
```

You can print out a date as a String with methods from java.text.SimpleDateFormat. You provide a format String argument to the constructor, in which different letters represent different fields of a date (day, hour, year, am or pm, etc.) and the style you want to see them in. Then you call the format() method with your date as the argument, and it passes it back as a String of the requested form. The class SimpleDateFormat is in package java.text rather than java.util because it is mostly concerned with internationalized and localized ways of formatting the date. Date-Format has an interesting feature (bug): it always defaults to Pacific Standard Time. The bug was probably overlooked because that's the TZ containing the JavaSoft programmers. Use `public void setTimeZone(TimeZone zone)` to set the correct time zone. The Calendar, DateFormat, and TimeZone classes will default to the time zone of your system.

Between you and I, the whole time zone/date/calendar thing is riddled with more special cases than the United States Supreme Court. As computer consultant Roedy Green says, "Dates are the lemon of Java." The best approach is to use dates as little as possible and hope that somebody fixes up this mess in a future JDK release. The database crowd fixed up date a little in java.sql.Date by overriding java.util.Date, and making it just deal with dates, not times as well. That's another possibility for you to use.

Enumeration

This is an interface that specifies just two methods. A class will implement these methods to supply a way to enumerate or count through, all its objects, or all the values held in one object, whichever makes the most sense for you to implement. For an array, enumeration is simply going from a[0] to a[n-1], but for a binary tree a little more effort is needed. The Enumeration interface allows that effort to be encapsulated and hidden from user classes. The methods are:

```
boolean hasMoreElements();

Object nextElement();
```

The method above returns the next element of the enumeration. It will throw the runtime exception NoSuchElementException if there is no next element. Here is how a class might implement Enumeration:

```java
import java.util.*;
public class el implements Enumeration {

    private int a[] = {9,1,8,2,4,7};

    private int i=0;

    public boolean hasMoreElements(){
        return (i<a.length);
    }

    public Object nextElement() {
        if (i>=a.length) throw new NoSuchElementException();
        return new Integer( a[i++] );
    }
}
```

Notice how we have to wrap each int in an Integer to send it back as we enumerate. Enumerations only work on objects. A class that uses class el can easily "thumb through" each element of the array using the enumeration. A class that implements Enumeration is offering a service to other classes—it provides an easy way to step through every data item belonging to an object, along these lines:

```java
while( o.hasMoreElements() )
    doSomethingWith( o.nextElement() );
```

The example above uses an array because these are easy to understand But, the real value of enumerations is in using them on data structures that don't already provide trivial access to all the elements such as trees, hash tables, graphs and the like. The Enumeration class is an example of the "iterator" design pattern.

You can only enumerate an object once. If you need to list all the elements of an enumeration twice, save any references to them in a Vector as they go by.

Hashtable

A supremely useful class. It allows you store together an arbitrary number of arbitrary objects. Instead of storing items with index values 0,1,2,3 as you would in an array, you provide the key which is to be associated with the object.

Then in future, you only need provide that key again, and voila, out pops the right object. If you cast your mind back to the class Object, you'll recall that each object in a Java system can call hashCode(), because this is a method in Object. You will usually use Object.hashCode or your overridden version of it, as the key. If you override hashCode for one of your classes, you must make sure that the method equals() is still consistent with it (namely, if two different Objects compare equal, they must also have the same hashCode()). This is because hashCode() and equals() are both used when accessing data in a hash table. Another way to state the requirement is that you should only overload equals() and hashCode() as a matched pair.

The type String is one class where hashCode() and equals() are both overridden. Rather than the default definition of equal of "is at the same address as," we want two Strings to be equal if they have the same characters in the same order. Accordingly, hashCodes for Strings are calculated by number-crunching the characters in the string. Strings with the same contents will then have the same hashcode. Typical Hash Table methods are:

```
public Hashtable();    // constructor

public synchronized boolean contains(Object value);
        // says whether this value is already in the table.

public synchronized Object put(Object key, Object value);
        // puts this object in the table with this key

public synchronized Object get(Object key);
        // retrieves the object for this key
```

There is a good example of the use of a HashTable on the CD that comes with this book. It is in the origami program which displays how to fold a piece of paper for interesting effects.

When I wrote the Origami applet (this appears as an example on the CD), I simply had it read the parameters that were lists of coordinate points, and draw lines between the pairs of points. If you drew the lines right, they looked like a sheet of paper being folded. The parameter file might contain "70 90 100 125," that tells the program to draw line from (70,90) to (100,125).

A typical origami creation might contain two dozen folds, each made up of a dozen lines. If so, the data becomes almost unreadable to a human. The way to simplify this is to allow names to be associated with a line by using the String as a key and storing the four numbers (a coordinate pair for each end of the line) as the hash table entry. Then I could refer to that line symbolically by name for the rest of the parameter file. When the program found the definition of a name, it would put the coordinates in the hash table using the name as the key. When it just found the name it could retrieve the coordinates with a single statement.

```
Hashtable        H = new Hashtable(100);
   ...

String s = theName;   // get the word
//look it up in the hashtable
CoordPair cp = (CoordPair) H.get(s);

if (cp==null) {
    //if not in hash table, add it.
        cp = new CoordPair(ax,ay,bx,by);
        try{
            H.put(s, cp);
        } catch(Exception e){}
}

// now we can draw using the cp coordinates
```

It was a very simple amendment to the applet, and the code worked the very first time (after years of programming in C, this is a refreshingly novel and frequent experience in Java). It allowed the parameter file to contain lines like "top-side," instead of the coordinates "70 90 150 90" corresponding to the line, along the top.

Note that only Objects can be stored in a HashTable. If you want to put primitive types in (as I did above) you have to wrap them in an object wrapper. That is the purpose of the CoordPair class.

Properties

As you were reading the description for HashTable, the remark about key/ value pairs may have reminded you of the System Properties sometimes seen in applets. The Properties class is really just an instance of HashTable with a few extra methods wrapped around it. The concept of properties is in some other languages too, like Lisp and Forth. The Java system comes with a whole set of predefined properties holding information about the implementation. These are shown in a section at the end of the chapter.

This utility class has two purposes: First, it allows a property table to be read in and written out via streams. And, second, it allows programmers to search more than one property table with a single command. If you don't need either of these benefits, then just use a HashTable instead of a Properties table. Typical methods are:

```
public String getProperty(String key);

public synchronized void load(InputStream in)
    throws IOException;
// reads key/value pairs in from a stream, stores them in this

public synchronized void save(OutputStream out, String
header);
// writes the key/value pairs out as text
// the header is just a comment string you provide to label
the
// the property table. The current date is also appended to
it.
```

To put entries in a Properties object, just use the put(Object key, Object element) method inherited from HashTable. So that you don't feel obliged to start adding to the predefined system property table, there's a feature that you can provide an existing properties table to a constructor. This creates an empty properties list that you can populate. Whenever you do a getProperty, it will search your table. If nothing is found, it will go on to search the table provided to the constructor. Here is an example:

```
Properties sp = System.getProperties();
Properties mytable = new Properties(sp);
mytable.list(System.out);
```

The first line gets the standard predefined properties table. The second line piggybacks it onto a second Properties table that we create and can fill with a call like: mytable.put ("propertyname", "propertyvalue"). When we do a lookup in mytable, it will look up first in mytable and then in the system properties table. The third line prints mytable out (intended for debugging, but it's not clear why you can't just use the save() method). The method public String getProperty(String key, String default); will return the default String if there is no entry for this key in the table.

Random

This is a class to provide pseudo-random numbers. We call them "pseudo-random" rather than random because the source of bits is an algorithm. To the casual observer it looks like a random stream of bits and for most applications we can pretend that they are. The numbers aren't really random, though, and sequences tend to get stuck in repetitive cycles after a large number of iterations.

If you just quickly want a random number between 0.0 and (just less than) 1.0, then package Math has a method random, which is just a wrapper for instantiating Random one time, and then supplying values. You would call it like this:

```
double d = Math.random();   // 0.0 .. 1.0
```

Typical methods of the package Random are:

```
public Random(long seed);
// using the same seed gives the same sequence of numbers.

public int nextInt();      // returns a random int
public long nextLong();    // returns a random long
public double nextDouble();  // returns value in range 0.0 to 1.0

public synchronized double nextGaussian();
// a Gaussian distribution has mean 0.0, standard deviation 1.0.
```

This provides numbers symmetrically distributed around zero, and successively unlikelier to be picked the further away from zero you get. If we collected a group of these numbers and plotted them, they would form the shape of a bell curve.

Exercise: Convince yourself of this by writing a program to actually do it. *Hint:* You'll find it easier plot a graph using ASCII text if you generate the values first, save them in an array, and sort the array into order before plotting the values.

The algorithm used here for taking random values from a Gaussian distribution is from "The Art of Computer Programming" by Donald Knuth, Section 3.4.1 Algorithm C.

To get a random int value in a certain range (say, 1 to 6) to simulate the cast of a die, you would use:

```
Random r = new Random();
int myturn = 1 + Math.abs(r.nextInt()) % 6;
```

To get a random double value in a certain range (say, 0.0 to 100.0) to simulate a percentage, you would scale it up with multiplication:

```
double mypercent = r.nextDouble() * 100.0;
```

You can instantiate Random with or without a seed. If you don't give it a seed, it uses the current reading from the day/time clock (the millisecond part of this is going to be pretty close to random). If you choose to supply the seed, you will get the same series of random numbers every time you supply that same seed. This is useful in testing and debugging code.

If pseudo-randomness isn't good enough, believe it or not you can buy CDs full of truly random numbers for use in one-time pad encryption and other applications.

Vector

The Vector class should be thought of as an array that grows without bounds, as needed to store the number of elements you want to put there. You don't index it with the array brackets "[...]," instead there are several methods to get and set the elements at particular indices.

"Under the covers" this class is implemented as a regular array. When you want to add an element and the array is already full, a new, larger array is allocated to make room, and the old array is copied over. To cut down on incremental reallocation, you can provide hints to the runtime system as to how many elements the array should grow by. Typical methods are:

```
public Vector(int startSize, int growthIncrement); // a constructor

public final synchronized void addElement(Object o);
// adds the object to the next highest location in the vector.

public final synchronized void insertElementAt(Object o, int index);
// adds the object to the vector at the given index.

public final int size();  // the number of objects in the vector.

public final synchronized Object elementAt(int index);
// returns the object in the vector at the given index.

public final synchronized Enumeration elements();
// returns an enumeration object for this vector, allowing every
// object in the vector to be looked at in one pass
```

There are a dozen other methods, as well, that will clear the vector, set its size, turn it into a string and so on.

Stack

The stack class maintains a "last-in-first-out" stack of Objects. You can push (store) objects to arbitrary depth. The methods are:

```
public Object push(Object item);   // add to top of stack.

public Object pop();   // get top of stack.
```

In addition there are 3 other methods not usually provided for stacks.

```
public boolean empty(); // nothing on the stack?

public Object peek();   // returns top Object without popping it.

public int search (Object o); // returns how far down the stack
// this object is (1 is at the top), or -1 if not found.
```

The author of this class made an interesting mistake. He made Stack a subclass of Vector, so that he would get the vector behavior of allowing unbounded input. He failed to notice that it meant all the methods of Vector would be available in Stack—including inappropriate methods like removeElementAt() to pull something out of the middle of a vector. So Stack does not guarantee Last-In-First-Out behavior. Hans Rohnert from Germany pointed this out to me in email. As Hans put it, it is not true that Stack "is a" Vector, rather it should "have a" Vector in which to store.

The usual way to "hide" unwanted methods from a base class is to override them with private versions, or empty versions or versions that throw a run time exception. In this case, Vector.removeElementAt(int) is final, and final methods can't be overriden. Some of these utility packages were written very quickly by skilled programmers who were more interested in getting the code working than achieving a perfect design. It's easier to find flaws in code than it is to write faultless software. Pointing out the occasional defect here is meant to instruct, not to denigrate the work of others.

StringTokenizer

The fundamental idea of StringTokenizer is to instantiate it with a string, and it will then break that string up into islands of characters separated by seas of white space. If you gave it the string "Noel Bat is a fossil," successive calls to nextToken would return the individual strings "Noel" followed by "Bat" then "is" then "a" then "fossil" then a further call would throw the NoSuchElementException.

Actually you can specify the delimiters for the substring, and they don't have to be white space. One of the constructors allows for new delimiting characters to be set and also takes a boolean saying whether the delimiters themselves should be returned. The representative methods are:

```
public   StringTokenizer(String words_to_breakup); // constructor

public   StringTokenizer(String words_to_breakup,
                         String delimiting_chars,
                         boolean return_delims); // constructor

public boolean hasMoreTokens();

public String nextToken();
```

You may have noticed that tokenizing a string is a pretty similar operation to enumerating all the elements in it. The StringTokenizer class does in fact implement the Enumeration interface, and provide bodies for hasMoreElements() and nextElement(). They are alternatives to the token methods, and return exactly the same objects. In the case of nextElement the return type is Object not String, but the Object it returns is a String. The StringTokenizer is simpler than the StreamTokenizer we met earlier. StringTokenizer just breaks things up into Strings. StreamTokenizer does this and also tries to classify them as numbers, words, etc.

Observer and Observable

These two are a matched pair. Together they provide a general interface for one thread to communicate a state change to another. We'll start with Observer, because it is simpler.

Observer is an interface that looks like this:

```
public interface Observer {
    void update(Observable o, Object arg);
}
```

Any object that wants to look at (observe) something else asynchronously can declare that it is an observer and provide its own body for update. The update() method is just a callback, so let's give an example of use. When you ask an image file to load, the method returns at once and in the background (as soon as it's sure you want it) starts reading the file off disk. That incoming file is an observable event. The thread that asked to load it is an observer.

When the thing that it's looking at has something to communicate, it will call update. Since the observer might be keeping an eye on several observable objects, update needs to be told which of them is calling it. That is the purpose of the first argument. The second argument is an object to permit just about anything at all to be passed in. The body of update will do whatever needs doing when that observable object says "look at me."

In our JPEG file example, there will be a number of times when there is enough information to call observer.update(). It may be called when the image file header has been read, when we have decoded enough to know the height of the image, when we know the width, and when the entire transfer has been completed.

Now lets take a look at Observable. The class Observable is intended to be extended by classes you write. The key methods that Observable provides are:

```
public synchronized void addObserver(Observer o);
// this is how an Observer registers its interest
// with the Observable thing.

protected synchronized void setChanged();
// only subclasses have the privilege of saying something
// observable has changed.

public void notifyObservers();
public void notifyObservers(Object arg);
```

If the *changed* flag is true, then these two routines call the update() method of all Observers. It's done this way (with an extra flag) so the observable thing has precise control over when notification really takes place.

Observer/observable is another example of a design pattern. You could think of it as an alternative, more general, version of a wait( )/notify( ). Like wait/notify, observer/observable is always used with threads. Unlike wait/notify observer.update( ) is called rather than just allowed to contend for the lock.

There are also methods to delete one or all Observers, and set, clear, or query an internal "changed" flag that an Observer may look at.

Note: Having justified Observer and Observable in terms of loading image files, you should be aware that image loading actually uses its own special version of Observer, called ImageObserver. It works in exactly the same way as Observer and it's unclear why the general mechanism was defined, only to be passed over in favor of a special purpose implementation for image files.

One common use of Observer/Observable is in sending a message from a dialog window back to its parent Frame. The parent implements Observer, the dialog class contains an Observable object, and a method to return the text. Then, when the dialog captures some relevant information, it sets its own changed bit and calls notifyObservers().

Note on the Java Native Interface

The Java Native Interface is an API that allows you to make calls into C and C++ programs from Java. You can also make calls into any other programming language that can follow the C calling and linking conventions. Non-Java code is refered to as "native" code, hence it is a native interface. Much of the Java runtimes (e.g., window operations, I/O, networking) are supported by native code on each platform. With the JNI you can get outside the JVM and access the underlying platform in your own code.

If you use the JNI, you destroy portability, which is the major benefit of Java. The JNI should only be used as a last resort under special circumstances. Most programs don't need it and won't use it. For this reason we will only summarize the JNI here. Readers who want to put JNI into practice can browse to the JavaSoft web page at

```
http://java.sun.com/products/jdk/1.1/docs/guide/jni/index.html
```

If this has moved, use the search facility on the home page, http://www.java.sun.com.

Under the native-code support in JDK 1.0.2, it was just assumed that C and Java would share the same view of how objects were laid out in memory. That is an unjustified assumption. JNI was introduced with JDK 1.1. It replaced the earlier, more ad-hoc feature, with one that is more consistent between different JDK implementations. Now your C code can obtain a pointer to a class, and using that pointer, access the Java method, constructor or data field that you want. Before making any calls to native routines, you must load the native library that contains them. This is usually done in the main() routine, or in a static block somewhere (to ensure it is only done once). The actual code will be something like

```
System.loadLibrary("mylib"); // loads mylib.dll
```

Although you can call from Java to C, and expose the Java objects to C, there is no easy way to have a C program as the main routine which invokes Java subroutines as necessary. The only other details we will provide here are tables showing the JNI signatures. These are one character abbreviations or encodings of the standard Java types, used to describe the signatures of Java methods when you have a C function that has been invoked from Java and needs to call back into Java. You may also see these in debugging Java code, or in stack traces. These tables help you decode them.

Table 6-4: These abbreviations are used for things relating to Objects.

Java type	JNI signature
a class	L followed-by-full-classname ;
array	[followed-by-element-type
method	(list-of-parameters) return-type
constructor	<init>

Note how the array signifier lacks a closing "]". No spaces are allowed in the abbreviations; we have shown them with spaces here for readability.

Table 6-5: How primitive types can be represented.

Java type	JNI signature
boolean	Z
byte	B
char	C
short	S
int	I
long	J
float	F
double	D
void	V

The object-related description always comes before the primitive types if it is present at all.

The C routine will first make a JNI call to get the Class containing the method. It will then use this as an argument to a second JNI call, along with a string containing the encoded signature (using Tables 6-4 and 6-5) of the desired method. This call returns a method ID that can be used to make the actual call into Java (see Table 6.6).

Table 6-6: Some examples of how these JNI signatures can represent Java types.

Description	Java thing	Corresponding JNI signature
int	int i;	I
int array	int []i2;	[I
String	String s1;	Ljava/lang/String
String array	String s2[];	[Ljava/lang/String
method with three parameters returning long	long foo(byte, char, int)	(BCI)J
method returning String array	String [] foo()	()[Ljava/lang/String
method taking String array parameter	void main (String[])	([Ljava/lang/String)V

Only use native methods when you really have to.

Properties

Java has a platform-independent way to communicate extra information at runtime to a program. Known as "properties" these do a job like environment variables. Environment variables aren't used because they are too platform-specific. A programmer can read the value of a property by calling getProperty() and passing an argument string for the property in which you are interested.

```
String dir = System.getProperty("user.dir");
```

A long list of predefined properties appears in the file java/lang/System.java and is reproduced below. Some properties are not available in applets for security reasons. You can also define a property on the command line when you invoke the program like this:

```
java -Drate=10.0 myprogram
```

That value "10.0" will be returned as a string when querying the property "rate." It can then be converted to a floating-point number and used as a value in the program. In this case, it's an alternative to a command line argument, but it's value is visible everywhere, not just in main.

Table 6-7 lists the predefined properties, guaranteed to have a value on every Java client.

Table 6-7: Predefined Properties

Property name	Explanation	Visible in Applet
java.version	version number of the Java system	yes
java.vendor	vendor specific string	yes
java.vendor.url	vendor URL	yes
java.home	Java installation directory	no
java.class.version	Java class version number	yes
java.class.path	Java classpath	no
os.name	Operating System Name	yes
os.arch	Operating System Architecture	yes
os.version	Operating System Version	yes
file.separator	File separator ("/" on Unix)	yes
path.separator	Path separator (":" on Unix)	yes
line.separator	Line separator ("\n" on Unix)	yes
user.name	User account name	no
user.home	User home directory	no
user.dir	User's current working directory	no

Most programs don't need to access these properties at all. But when they do, it's nice to be able to do it in a platform-independent way.

This tip is so useful, you'll use it almost everyday!

Some of these Java library routines can be a bit confusing. What order do the parameters come in for all the varieties of PixelGrabber? Here's an easy way to check.

Just run javap on any class name (*not* class file name), whether your own or one in the java.*.* packages, and it will print out the class, its methods, and the parameters.

javap java.lang.Math

```
Compiled from Math.java
public final class java.lang.Math extends java.lang.Object {
    public static final double E = 2.718282;
    public static final double PI = 3.141593;
    public native static double sin(double);
    public native static double cos(double);
    public native static double tan(double);
    public native static double asin(double);
    public native static double acos(double);
    public native static double atan(double);
    public native static double exp(double);
    public native static double log(double);
    public native static double sqrt(double);
    public native static double IEEEremainder(double,double);
    public native static double ceil(double);
    public native static double floor(double);
    public native static double rint(double);
    public native static double atan2(double,double);
    public native static double pow(double,double);
    public static int round(float);
    public static long round(double);
    public static synchronized double random();
    public static int abs(int);
    public static long abs(long);
    public static float abs(float);
    public static double abs(double);
    public static int max(int,int);
    public static long max(long,long);
    public static float max(float,float);
    public static double max(double,double);
    public static int min(int,int);
    public static long min(long,long);
    public static float min(float,float);
    public static double min(double,double);
}
```

Excellent! Now it's really easy to check the method signatures of any classes.

Some Light Relief

There's an old story to the effect that "the people at Cray design their supercomputers with Apple systems, and the Apple designers use Crays!" Apart from this being a terrific example of recurring rotational serendipity (what goes around, comes around) is there any truth to it?

Like many urban legends, this one contains a nugget of truth. In the 1991 Annual Report of Cray Research Inc. there is a short article describing how Apple used a Cray for designing Macintosh cases. The Cray is used to simulate the injection molding of the plastic enclosure cases. The Mac II case was the first Apple system to benefit from the modelling, and the trial was successful. The simulation identified warping problems which were solved by prototyping thus saving money in tooling and production. Apple also uses their Cray for simulating air flow inside the enclosure to check for hot spots. The Cray house magazine reported that the Apple PowerBook continues to use supercomputer simulations. (CRAY CHANNELS, Spring 1992 pp.10-12 "Apple Computer PowerBook computer molding simulation").

The inverse story holds that Seymour Cray himself used a Mac to design Crays. The story seems to have originated with an off-the-cuff remark from Seymour Cray himself, who had a Mac at home, and used it to store some of his work for the Cray 3. Common sense suggests that the simulation of discrete circuitry (Verilog runs, logic analysis, etc.) which is part of all modern integrated circuit design, is done far more cost-effectively on a supercomputer than on a microprocessor. Cray probably has a lot of supercomputer hardware laying around ready for testing as it comes off the production line.

It's conceivable that a Macintosh could be used to draft the layout of blinking lights for the front of a Cray, or choose some nice color combinations, or some other non-CPU intensive work. A Macintosh is a very good system for writing design notes, sending email, and drawing diagrams, all of which are an equally essential part of designing a computer system.

The good folks at Cray Research have confirmed in a Cray Users Group newsletter that they have a few Macs on the premises. So while it's extremely unlikely that they run logic simulations on their Macs, we can indeed chalk it up as only-slightly-varnished truth that "the people at Cray design their supercomputers with Apple's systems, and the Apple designers use Crays," for some value of the word "design"!

Exercises

1. After it's completed one anagram, make the program go back and prompt for more. Don't make it reload the wordlist! (Easy)

2. Modify the program so it doesn't use arrays of fixed size, but uses the Vector class from package "java.util" to grow arrays as needed at runtime. (Easy) Add this line to the start of the program:

```
import java.util.Vector;
```

3. What is the "C++ interoperability problem?" How does it handicap the use of libraries in C++? Is Java any different? Why?

4. Create a version of the program that has the word list compiled into it. You'll probably want to first write a java program that reads a word list and prints out the array initialization literals for you to edit into your source program. What difference does this make to program start-up time? Run time? Size? (Medium)

5. Create a version of the program that uses several threads to sort the candidate words. Use a heuristic like "if the partition is larger than 4 elements, spawn a thread to sort it using quicksort, otherwise sort it directly by decision tree comparison." Decision tree comparison means

```
if ( a>b )
    if ( a>c )
        if (a>d)  // a is largest
        else      // d is largest, then a
            if (b>c) // order is d,a,b,c
            else     // order is d,a,c,b
// and so on
```

This challenge is of medium complexity.

6. What needs to be changed in the anagram program to make it capable of dealing with alphabets other than English? (Easy) Make it so. (Medium to Hard, depending on whether you select a specific non-English alphabet or "all of them").

7. Have several threads calculating anagrams at once. This challenge is hard to get working correctly so the threads know how to stop when they reach the point of overlap.

Further Reading

Alice in Wonderland

by Lewis Carroll

This text is the best book on mathematics for the layman, because (as Professor Perlis pointed out) it's the best book on anything for the layman.

CHAPTER
7

- Embedding a Java program in a Web page

- Starting applet execution

- Passing Parameters to applets

- Security issues and the SecurityManager

- ZIP files

- Signing a Java program

All
About
Applets

"People say you can't compare apples and oranges. But why not? They are both hand-held, round, edible, fruity things that grow on trees."

—anonymous

J ava is a fine general purpose programming language. It can be used to good effect to generate stand-alone executables, just as C, C++, Visual Basic, Pascal or Fortran can.

Java offers the additional capability of writing code that can live in a web page and then get downloaded and executed when the web page is browsed. Opinions differ on which is the more important role of Java, but it's a debate without much value. If you want to write applications, write applications. If you want to write applets and put them in web pages, write applets and put them in web pages. This chapter explains how to do that.

There are a number of special considerations that apply to applets. These considerations include connecting a class file to a web page, starting execution, screen appearance, parameter passing, and security. Let's take these one by one.

Embedding a Java Program in a Web Page

As mentioned in Chapter 3 when we touched on this topic, an applet is a Java program that is invoked not from the command line, but rather through a web browser reaching that page, or equivalently through the appletviewer that comes with the Java Development Kit. We will stick with the appletviewer in this chapter because we are trying to teach the language not the use of a browser.

> **Reminder on Applets**
>
> There are two different ways to run a Java executable:
>
> - as a stand-alone program that can be invoked from the command line. This is termed an "application."
>
> - as a program embedded in a web page, to be run when the page is browsed. This is termed an "applet."
>
> Applications and applets differ in the execution privileges they have, and also the way they indicate where to start execution.

The first thing to understand about applets is how they get run from a web browser, because the numerous methods that applets can override follow from that.

Web browsers deal with HTML (the HyperText Markup Language we mentioned in Chapter 1). There are HTML tags that say "set this text in bold," "break to a new paragraph" and "include this GIF image here." There is now an HTML tag that says "run the Java applet that you will find in this .class file." Just as a GIF image file will be displayed at the point where its tag is in the HTML source, so the applet will be executed when its tag is encountered. The applet will start running even if it is on a part of the page that is scrolled off the screen.

An example of the HTML code that invokes an applet is shown below:

```
<title>
The simplest applet
</title>
<applet code=pentium.class width=300 height=50>
</applet>
```

The width and height fields are mandatory, and they are measured in units of pixels (dots of resolution on the computer monitor). Applets run in a window object called a panel, and you have to give the browser a clue as to how big a panel the applet should start with.

Since this is HTML, put the prior example in a file called foo.html, Figure 7-1 shows how it will be run. The class needs to be found somewhere along the CLASSPATH environment variable or from the CODEBASE defined in the HTML tag. CODEBASE specifies a different directory or URL that contains the applet's code. This is to help applets located on remote servers be accessed just as easily as those stored locally.

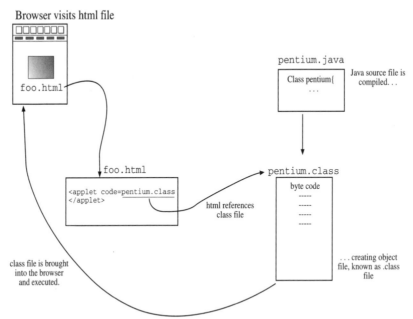

Figure 7-1:   example.html will run like this

The full list of tags that can be used for applets is:

```
<applet
     code=classfilename
     width=integer_pixels
     height=integer_pixels
     [archive=archivefile [,archivefile]]
     [codebase=applet-url]
     [vspace=integer_pixels]
     [hspace=integer_pixels]
     [align=alignment]
     [name=some_name]
[alt=some_text]
>
```

The applet tag can be followed by zero or more parameter tags, with the general form of attribute name/value pairs.

```
<param name=param_name  value=param_value >
```

The parameter tag will be described a little later. You can also put some alternate html here, which will only be formatted if the browser doesn't understand the applet tag. Finally, the applet ends with an "end applet" tag:

```
</applet>
```

Confusingly, letter case is not significant for any html tags or attribute names, but it is significant for some of the arguments they take (e.g. the name of the class file). When in doubt make all uses of upper and lower case consistent.

The attributes have the following meanings:

CODE=*CLASSFILENAME*

> This attribute is required, and names the class file that is to be executed. Note: this must just be a single file name, with no part of a longer path prefixed to it: So "foo.class" is good, but "bin/foo.class" is bad.

WIDTH=*INTEGER_PIXELS*
HEIGHT=*INTEGER_PIXELS*

> These two attributes are required, and say how large a space in the browser the applet takes up.

All the remaining attributes are optional.

ARCHIVE=*ARCHIVEFILE* [*,ARCHIVEFILE*]

> This attribute allows an applet to bundle all its class files and media files into one ZIP archive. The browser will retrieve the entire in one big transaction, rather than many slow, smaller transactions.

CODEBASE=*APPLET-URL*

> This attribute allows you more flexibility in where applet class files are located. You can provide a URL identifying a directory where the browser should look for the class files this applet loads. Since it is a URL, the directory can be specified anywhere on the Internet, not just on the server or client system. If this attribute is omitted (a common occurrence) the class files must be in the same directory as the html file.

VSPACE=*INTEGER_PIXELS*
HSPACE=*INTEGER_PIXELS*

> These two attributes allow you to specify the size of the blank margin to leave around the applet in the browser. These two tags and the one below are similar to the attributes of the same names used with the <IMG> tag.

ALIGN=*ALIGNMENT*

> This attribute allows you to control where the applet appears on the page. There are several possible alignment values: "left," "right," "top," "middle" are popular choices.

NAME=*SOME_NAME*

> The name provided here is associated with the applet, and can be used by other applets running on the same page to refer to the applet and communicate with it.

`ALT=SOME_TEXT`
> This attribute specifies the text to be displayed in the (unlikely) event that the browser understands the applet tag, but does not understand Java.

The <applet> tag was invented specifically for Java, but it is possible that people will want to download other types of executable content. It would be a poor idea to have to invent a new tag for each new type of downloadable program. Accordingly, the <embed> tag has been proposed to replace the <applet> tag. The main difference is that <embed> allows you to put a full URL on the beginning of the "class=" attribute (and it calls it "src=," not "class="). As a result the codebase attribute is not needed.

 While we wait for all browsers to become Java-capable (and pretty soon you won't be able to give away a browser unless it understands Java), here's a useful tip.

All browsers ignore HTML tags that they don't understand. And they also ignore HTML tags that they do understand when they appear in unexpected places. These two facts together make it possible to write an HTML file that will invoke an applet in a Java-capable browser, and provide an alternative text or image for an incapable browser. Between the <applet> and </applet> tags, only a few tags, including <param> tags are recognized by applet-aware browsers. Browsers that cannot run Java will ignore these applet-specific tags.

So the HTML below will run the java applet if the browser can, and will display the alternative image instead if the browser is not Java capable.

```
<applet  code=anagram.class  width=500, height=500>
    <param   name="target"   value="surfing the net">
    <param   name=wordlist   value="words.txt">
    <param   name=minsize    value="2">

    <img src="NoJava4U.JPG">

</applet>
```

Starting Applet Execution

We've just seen that applets are started up in a different manner from applications. The difference is more than just command-line vs. HTML file. Applications start execution in a public function called "main()" similar to the convention used in C. Applets have a different convention, involving overriding certain pre-named functions.

The first thing to note is that an applet is a *window object* that *runs in a thread object,* so every applet will be able to do window-y kind of things and thread-y kind of things. (We mean window in the general sense rather than Java-specific sense. In the Java-specific sense, an Applet is a Panel.) An applet's execution starts using the thready kind of methods that we have already seen in Chapter 5. You create an applet by extending the Java class Applet, and providing your own versions of some of the methods. You can override the start()/stop() methods, but you do not call them yourself. This funny stuff exists because of the funny context that applets live in. They are loaded once, then subject to the kind of repeated execution that a hypertext Web browser makes. The diagram in Figure 7-2 shows how.

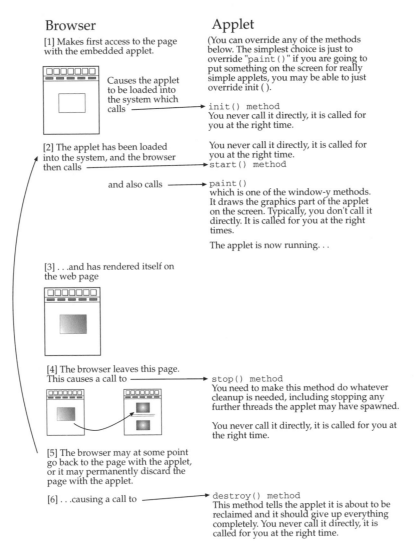

Figure 7-2: Repeated execution caused by a hypertext Web browser

You can almost always leave "destroy()" alone. The method "init()" is a good place to create GUI objects and threads. Similarly you will only override the methods "start()" and "stop()" if you have something that actually needs to be started and stopped, namely threads. If your applet doesn't start up any threads of its own, there's no need to supply your own version of start and stop. On the other hand, if your applet does create some threads, start() is probably where you will want to start them. And it is most important that you override stop() and explicitly stop all threads—otherwise they will continue to run even after you leave the page. If you want a thread to suspend when the browser leaves the page and resume where it left off if the browser returns, then use suspend() in method stop() and resume() in method start(). Obviously, you'll need to create the thread the first time through.

Table 7-1 lists a summary of Methods Useful in Applets, and when they are called.

Table 7-1: Summary of Useful Methods

Method	Description
void init()	Called when the applet is first loaded into memory. Typically you override it with one-time initialization code.
void start()	Called each time the browser visits the page containing this applet. Typically you override it to start or resume any threads the applet contains.
void paint(Graphics g)	Will be called by the window system when the component needs to be redisplayed. You will not call this. You will override this if you dynamically change the appearance of the screen, and want to see it appear.
void stop()	Called when the browser leaves the page containing this applet. Typically you override it to stop or suspend any threads the applet contains.
void run()	Nothing to do with applets—this is the main routine in which thread execution starts.

There is more housekeeping associated with threads in applets than in applications, because of the way pages (including their embedded running applets) are left behind and possibly revisited. An applet gets the ability to override all these thread method names for free—it does not need to import anything explicitly. However, the window-y stuff needs to be imported ("import java.awt.*;") so that you can display window objects like menus and buttons.

> **Magic methods**
>
> These magic methods init(), start(), stop(), and destroy() are defined in
> src/java/applet/Applet.java. These are exactly the methods that a thread has
> (see them in src/java/lang/Thread.java). What methods does an application
> have that correspond to these? None! An application isn't run under a
> browser, so it isn't liable to be stopped and started unpredictably as the
> browser moves to new pages.
>
> The paint() method is a window-y thing, available to all window components.
> See Chapter 9.

Screen Appearance of an Applet

Here is an example of the minimal applet:

```
import java.awt.Graphics;
public class Message extends java.applet.Applet {
    public void paint(Graphics g) {
        g.drawString("Yes!", 15, 25);
    }
}
```

An HTML suitable for this program might be

```
<applet code=Message.class width=200 height=100>
</applet>
```

Now put it in a file called Message.html. Compile the java program. When you
run it under the appletviewer with the command

```
appletviewer Message.html
```

you will see a window like the following appear.

Figure 7-3:   A minimal applet

If you don't see this, step through the installation instructions again, checking that you have done everything correctly.

Because an applet is a windowing thing (we will get back to more formal terminology eventually), it does not use the standard I/O that we have been using up till now for interactive I/O. Instead it uses the facilities that are available to windows, like drawing a string at particular coordinates. The coordinate system of every window has the origin in the top left as shown in Figure 7-4.

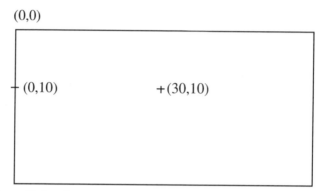

Figure 7-4:   Every window's coordinates originate in the top left corner

What are the other facilities that are available to windows? We will discuss these in greater depth in a later chapter which deals with the Abstract Window Toolkit. For now you can code review the classes that make up the AWT in directory $JAVAHOME/src/awt. The file Container.java contains the superclass from which Applet is (eventually) derived. Container has the method "paint()" which is called by the Window toolkit whenever the applet panel needs to be refreshed. By providing our own version of paint, we override Container's version.

You can look at the source for method drawString() in file java/src/awt/Graphics.java. This class has many methods concerned with rendering a shape, line, or text onto the screen. It will also let you select colors, and fonts.

The convention throughout Java is that class names begin with a capital letter, and method names start with a lower case letter, but subsequent words in the name are capitalized. This leads to odd looking names like "drawString" that make it seem as though someone had a previous job writing ransom notes wItH rAndOmlY caPitALiZeD LeTteRs. ("wE HaVe yOuR MiSsinG piXeL. seNd $10K iN sMaLL BilLS. dO nOt TeLl tHe PolICe. ThEy'Re sTuPId.")

When the compiler complains that it can't find one of the library methods, your first thought should be "did I get the capitals right?" It is not always consistent in that we have "MenuBar" and yet "Scrollbar" in the window toolkit. Especially watch out for the "instanceof" operator that uses no capitals. In cases like this, it's better to always be consistent or always be inconsistent, but not keep changing between the two.

Set up the "pentium flaw" program as an applet. Modify the program so that it extends Applet and make sure that the class is public. Use g.drawString() instead of println(), in this method:

```
public void paint(Graphics g) {
    g.drawString("text to display", x_pos, y_pos);
}
```

Write some html that points to the class. Invoke it through the appletviewer, and then try a Java capable web browser. (Medium).

Back in Chapter 5 we mentioned that some programs need to explicitly start threads, rather than have them created and started in one operation. An applet running in a web browser is one of those programs. It allows a closer fit to the "go back to a page you already visited, and which is likely to still be loaded" model. That is why init() (one-time initialization) is separated from start() (called every time the page is accessed).

Browser Summary

The browser will automatically instantiate an object of your Applet subclass, and make certain calls to get it running.

You can overload some of the called methods. The methods "init() and "paint()" are the ones you will mostly overload, unless you have threads in the applet, when you will want to overload "start()" and "stop()" too.

Typically you never call any of these methods. They are called for you by the window system/browser at appropriate times. As the browser visits pages and moves away from them these predefined Applet methods are invoked.

Build in Debugging Help

You can put a main method in any class—even a class that runs as an applet or a class that isn't the main routine of your application. Like any other method that isn't called, it doesn't do any harm.

Some programmers recommend adding a main() routine to all classes. This main should just be a test driver to check the functionality of that class. When you are

Cut down the number of files you need. When you start creating applets, you usually need at least three files before anything can happen: a .java source file, a .class bytecode file, and a .html file. If you aren't careful with your naming, you'll lose track of what's where.

One suggestion (for experts only) useful while the code is under development is to put the HTML commands in the java source file, inside a comment, like this:

```
// <applet  code=Message.class  height=100  width=100>
// </applet>
import java.awt.Graphics;
public class Message extends java.applet.Applet {
    public void paint(Graphics g) {
        g.drawString("Yes!", 10,10);
    }
}
```

It offers two advantages: First, you cut out the need for a separate html file (so you don't waste time flipping back and forth between HTML file and source file in the editor); and secondly, you can put the parameters for the applet right in the file with the applet code (so it's easy to check you've got them right). Then you invoke appletviewer on the source file

```
appletviewer  Message.java
```

This works because browsers just read arbitrary text files, looking for tags. They don't care if the file contains source code as well.

debugging your system, you'll find it most convenient to test individual classes this way. Just leave it there—it won't hurt in the finished version of the system.

Alternatively, you can use a main() routine in a different class as a different entry point to your program allowing the program to do slightly different things depending on which class you tell the interpreter to start in. You can vary this from run to run. 🍂

Passing Parameters to Applets

Just as we have command line arguments for applications, there is a similar feature for passing arguments from the HTML file to the applet it invokes. Parameters are indicated by an HTML tag of the form

```
<param    name=namestring    value=valuestring>
```

The param tags come after the <applet> tag, and before the </applet> tag. An example of some actual parameters in the applet version of the anagram program might be:

```
<applet  code=anagram.class  width=500, height=500>
    <param    name="target"    value="surfing the net">
    <param    name=wordlist    value="words.txt">
    <param    name=minsize     value="2">
</applet>
```

It does not matter if strings are quoted or not, unless the string contains embedded white space. Inside the program you call getParameter with the name as an argument, and it returns the string representing the value. If there isn't a parameter of that name, it returns null. Here is an example:

```
String s = getParameter("minsize");
// parse to an int.
int minsize = Integer.parseInt(s);
```

Notice that this follows the same conventions as "main(String argv[])"—all arguments are passed as strings, and programmers need to do a little processing to get the values of arguments that are numbers.

To pass a double as a parameter to an applet, the html tag would look like this

```
<param name=peach    value="3.1" >
```

The code to retrieve it would be:

```
String s = getParameter("peach");
double d = Double.valueOf(s).doubleValue();
```

This differs from the int code because the class Double does not have a parseDouble method to create a double from a String. Instead we have to create a double object from the String, then extract the double value from that.

Security Issues of Applets

The term "security" means controlling the resources of your computer system: the files, screen, peripherals and CPU cycles. Even on a single-user system, like Windows 3.11, this is an issue because a computer virus can destroy your valuable work. Some form of security check is especially needed with applets because they are executed automatically on your behalf. Just by browsing a web page embedded applets are sent over and executed on your system. Without a security check an applet could, either through maliciousness or poor programming, corrupt your files or transmit the contents to points unknown.

Viruses are already too prevalent in the PC world. A virus was recently detected that even infected the MS-Word word processor by taking advantage of an "execute macros on start-up" feature. MS-DOS, Windows 3.11, and Windows 95 have little-to-no security. The Microsoft ActiveX framework has security in terms of identification through signing, but no security in terms of resource access permission. This makes ActiveX unsuitable for use across the Internet.

Right from the start, Java improves on this situation by defining and supporting several levels of resource access control. Some of Java's security is user-configurable, and some of it (to avoid a breach of security) is not.

The SecurityManager is a built-in class in package java.lang with about a dozen methods each of which checks access to a particular resource: threads, properties, socket connections, reading a file, and so on.

The java.lang.SecurityManager class contains these public methods:

```
class SecurityManager {
    public void checkCreateClassLoader();
    public void checkAccess(java.lang.Thread);
    public void checkAccess(java.lang.ThreadGroup);
    public void checkExit(int);
    public void checkExec(java.lang.String);
    public void checkLink(java.lang.String);
    public void checkRead(java.io.FileDescriptor);
    public void checkRead(java.lang.String);
    public void checkRead(java.lang.String,java.lang.Object);
    public void checkWrite(java.io.FileDescriptor);
    public void checkWrite(java.lang.String);
    public void checkDelete(java.lang.String);
    public void checkConnect(java.lang.String,int);
    public void checkConnect(java.lang.String,int,java.lang.Object);
    public void checkListen(int);
    public void checkAccept(java.lang.String,int);
    public void checkPropertiesAccess();
    public void checkPropertyAccess(java.lang.String);
    public void checkPropertyAccess(java.lang.String,java.lang.String);
    public boolean checkTopLevelWindow(java.lang.Object);
    public void checkPackageAccess(java.lang.String);
    public void checkPackageDefinition(java.lang.String);
    public void checkSetFactory();
    public boolean getInCheck();
    public java.lang.Object getSecurityContext();
}
```

All but the last 3 methods have names that are self-explanatory; they scrutinize some specific form of resource access. So checkRead(java.io.FileDescriptor) will return normally if a read may be done using this file descriptor, and throw an exception if it should not. The last three methods carry out this processing:

`checkSetFactory()` check whether an applet can set a networking-related object factory. A "factory" is a java term for a class that creates objects of another class. Usually classes are responsible for their own constructors, but sometimes it is convenient to manage this from another class, especially when one of several subtype classes might be needed.

`getInCheck()` simply says whether a check is currently taking place.

`getSecurityContext()` returns an implementation-dependent Object which holds enough information about the current execution environment to perform some of the security checks later.

You never call these checking methods, they are called at appropriate times by the Java runtime. When a Java system first starts executing, the security manager is set to null and the only access restrictions are those imposed by the underlying OS. In other words, anything goes.

To change that, you can write your own class that extends SecurityManager, and provide new methods to override the checking method for the resources you are interested in. The body of each new method contains your algorithm for deciding whether to grant access or not. It will either return or throw a security exception. Returning without throwing an exception means the access is allowed. If you install a new security manager of your own, then every resource not controlled in your new manager is disallowed. Here is an example that allows access to all System properties and nothing else.

```
class MySecurityManager extends SecurityManager {

    public void checkPropertyAccess(String key) {
        return;
    }

}


public class foo {
    public static void main(String s[]) {

        SecurityManager msm = new MySecurityManager();

        try {
            System.setSecurityManager(msm);
        } catch(Exception e){}

    }
}
```

A SecurityManager can be set at most once during the lifetime of a Java runtime. There is no way to install a new SecurityManager that includes permission to keep installing new SecurityManagers: it's a one shot deal and cannot later be replaced, changed, or overridden. In an application, you the programmer can define the level of security for your program. In an applet, the browser must do this (and applets must be unable to impose a new security manager).

Different browsers have imposed slightly different SecurityManager policies, and they can take into account whether an applet was loaded from a local file or from browsing over the net. Local files only exist on your system because you put them there, so they are presumed to have more privileges. Table 7-2 is a matrix of broswer characteristics extracted from the JavaSoft site http://www.javasoft.com/sfaq.

Table 7-2:   Capabilities of an untrusted Applet

Capabilities	Ns/net	Ns/local	Av/net	Av/local	Applic
read or write a file in /home/me with access control list set	no	no	yes	yes	yes
read the user.name property	no	yes	no	yes	yes
connect to port on client	no	yes	no	yes	yes
connect to port on 3rd host	no	yes	no	yes	yes
load library	no	yes	no	yes	yes
exit(-1)	no	no	no	yes	yes
create a popup window without a warning	no	yes	no	yes	yes

Key:
- •Ns/net: Netscape Navigator 3.x, loading applets over the Net
- •Ns/local: Netscape Navigator 3.x, loading applets from the Local file system
- •Av/net: Appletviewer, JDK 1.x, loading applets over the Net
- •Av/local: Appletviewer, JDK 1.x, loading applets from the Local file system
- •Applic: Java Standalone applications

A sandbox is like a room built out of firewalls. Applets are executed inside a sandbox by default, so they cannot access the private or vulnerable resources of your system. This is a representative but not exhaustive list of the restrictions on remotely accessed applets.

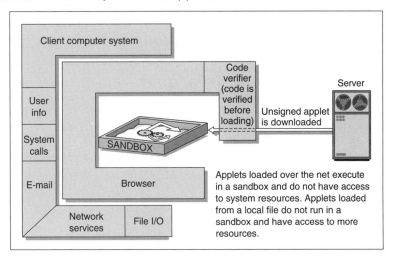

By default, an applet accessed over the net:
- cannot read or write files;
- cannot open a socket connection, except to the server that it came from;
- cannot start up a program on your system;
- cannot call native (non-Java) code.

Applets accessed from a local file system (rather than over the net) are allowed more privileges. They can only be on your local file system with your permission, so it is presumed that you trust them.

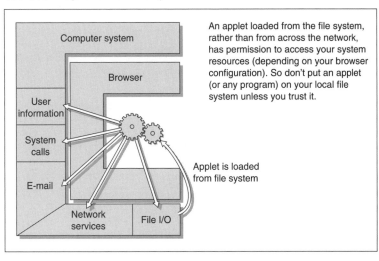

The restrictions mean that an applet loaded from over the net:

- Can really read and write files if an access control list file permits it, and you run the applet using Appletviewer.

- Cannot make network connections to hosts other than the one it came from

- Cannot start a program on your system by using the equivalent of the system() call in C. An application or local applet can do this with the method "java.lang.Runtime.exec()".

- Cannot load a library

- Cannot execute native code

Some browsers may impose other restrictions on top of these. The eventual aim is to provide support for recognizing and executing trusted applets with more capabilities even over the net, without jeopardizing system security.

Default Capability Differences

Note that there is a difference in default capabilities between an applet loaded from over the net, and an applet loaded from the local file system. Where an applet comes from determines what it is allowed to do. An applet brought from over the net is loaded by the applet class loader, and it is subject to the restrictions enforced by the applet security manager.

An applet stored on the client's local disk and accessible from the CLASSPATH is loaded by the file system loader. These applets are permitted to read and write files, load Java libraries and exec processes. Local applets are not passed through the bytecode verifier, which is another line of defence against code from the net.

The verifier checks that the bytecode conforms to the Java language specification and looks for violations of the type rules and name space restrictions. The verifier looks at individual instructions to ensure that:

- There are no stack overflows or underflows.

- All register accesses and stores are valid.

- The parameters to all bytecode instructions are correct.

- No illegal type conversions are attempted.

Netscape Navigator 3.x disables all privileges for applets browsed over the net. It allows a small number of privileges for applets loaded from a local file system, such as the ability to load a library or read the user.name property.

You can configure the Sun appletviewer to read and write files on your local disk by editing the file .hotjava/properties. This file is in your home directory on Unix (note its name starts with a dot, so it is not usually visible when you list the directory). Under Windows, the files is in the root directory of the drive you installed java on (the file might be C:\.hotjava\properties).

Then you can set the acl.read and acl.write properties to point to the files or directories that you will allow applets to read or write. For example, if I add these two lines to my ~/.hotjava/properties file, (or my C:\.hotjava\properties file on Windows)

```
acl.read=/home/linden
acl.write=/tmp
```

then applets are allowed to read any files in /home/linden or to write to any files in the /tmp directory. ACL stands for "Access Control List"—a mainframe feature for providing fine-grained control of resources like files.

Here's an applet that you can run under Sun's appletviewer to confirm this.

```java
// <applet code=show.class  height=100 width=200> </applet>
import java.io.*;
import java.awt.*;
import java.applet.Applet;
public class show extends Applet {

    public void Read() throws IOException {

        DataInputStream dis;
        String s, myFile = "show.java";

        dis = new DataInputStream(new FileInputStream(myFile));
        s = dis.readLine();
        System.out.println("line> "+s);
    }

    public void paint(Graphics g) {
        try {
            Read();
            g.drawString("Success in read", 10, 10);
        }
        catch (SecurityException e) {
            g.drawString("Caught security exception in read", 10, 10);
        }
        catch (IOException ioe) {
            g.drawString("Caught i/o exception in read", 10, 10);
        }
    }
}
```

Don't worry about the I/O details—that will be covered in full in the next chapter. For now the purpose is to demonstrate that browsers control the resources accessed by applets, and that file I/O is possible from an applet using the applet-viewer.

Zippy-de-Doodah

This section explains how you can group together any number of files into one zip file. There are two reasons for doing this: a small reason and a big reason. The small reason is that, if you have a Java program that consists of five `.class` files, three `.jpg` files, four `.au` files, and a GIF file, that's a lot of files to remember to move onto your web server. It's much more convenient for passing the program around if you can roll all the pieces up into one large archive file, just as the Windows ZIP or the Unix tar utilities do.

The second, more important reason, for grouping together lots of little files into one large file is that HTTP (the protocol used between a web server and a client browser) is an inefficient protocol. It takes a large amount of effort on both server and client side to set up an HTTP connection. For files of just a few Kbytes, the time and effort to set up the connection can easily outweigh the time to transmit the file. And not just by a little, but by a lot. As with disk I/O, one large read of 100N bytes is far less time and effort than the sum of 100 small reads of N bytes each. For an individual client, the applets arrive and start running faster. At the server end, the server can handle many more client requests at a time, and throughput rises.

JDK 1.0.2 lets you wrap up several class files in a `.zip` file, using the standard PKZIP format popularized on PCs. Zip file format is a combination of compression and aggregation, though file compression was not supported in JDK 1.0.2. An example of the use of zip files in JDK 1.0.2 is the core Java libraries which were put into a file called `classes.zip`, to which your $CLASSPATH environment variable had to point. We won't dwell on zip files in JDK 1.0.2 because things are better and easier in JDK 1.1.

PKZIP stands for Phil Katz ZIP. The zip part just means "bringing things together speedily" as a clothing zip fastener does. Phil Katz was the programmer who, several years before Java, developed the zip file format, the compression format, and `.zip` file extension and put it all in the public domain for the benefit of everyone in the industry. Java now has a built-in API to read and write zip files; some examples of this are in the I/O chapter later in the book.

Keep Your Software in a Jar

In JDK 1.1, the format was extended to a JAR, or "Java ARchive." A jar file contains a group of files in zip format, with compression turned on. You can create your own jar files by using standard WinZIP, other software, or the `jar` utility that comes with JDK 1.1. The `jar` program has a command line that looks like this in general form

```
jar [ options ] [manifest] destination input-file [input-files]
```

The options that `jar` takes are similar to those of `tar`—the Unix tape archive utility—but the formats are different, and tar files are not used in Java. To create a compressed archive of all the class files and .jpg files in a directory, you would use the command

```
jar cvf myJarFile.jar *.class *.jpg
```

An example of the applet tag used with a jar file is

```
<APPLET ARCHIVE=myfile.jar
        CODE=myapplet.class
        WIDTH=600   HEIGHT=250> </APPLET>
```

These lines will use an applet called myapplet that can be found in the jar file `myfile.jar`. You can supply several jar file names in a comma-separated list.

Removing the Contents from a Jar

As we mentioned earlier, a jar file can contain media files as well as code. The class files will be extracted automatically when the class loader sees an applet tag such as:

```
<applet
    archive=Example.jar
    code=Example.class   height=200 width=250>
</applet>
```

However the noncode files like .gif, .au, or .jpg must be extracted a slightly different way. The method `getImage (getCodeBase(), image_name)`, which works for individual image files in the HTML directory, doesn't work when the file is in a jar. This applet example shows how to pull a media file out of a jar file. The key idea is to use the class runtime-type information to create a URL for the media file (this line is shown in bold in the example). The rest of the code is the magic associated with displaying an image and is described in the chapter on graphics programming. The approach also works for .au (sound) files and .gif files.

First create our example source file called `view.java`, with this HTML and code inside it.

```
/* <applet
       archive=view.jar    code=view.class
       width=350           height=450>
   </applet>
*/
import java.net.*;
import java.awt.*;
import java.awt.image.*;
import java.applet.*;

public class view extends Applet {
    String MyFileName = "titan.jpg";
    URL MyURL;
    Image MyImg;
    ImageProducer MyImgProd;

    public void init() {
        Toolkit tool = Toolkit.getDefaultToolkit();
        MyURL = getClass().getResource(MyFileName);
        try {
            MyImgProd = (ImageProducer) MyURL.getContent();
        } catch (Exception ex) {
            System.out.println(ex.getMessage());
        }
        MyImg = tool.createImage( MyImgProd );
    }

    public void paint(Graphics g){
        g.drawImage(MyImg, 10, 10, this);
    }
}
```

The code is on the CD under `book/ch07`. Compile the code, and create the JAR file by entering these commands

```
% javac view.java

% jar -cvf view.jar  view.class titan.jpg
adding: view.class (in=1418) (out=781) (deflated 44%)
adding: titan.jpg (in=59698) (out=59340) (deflated 0%)
```

Then, you can run the program by using the appletviewer:

```
% appletviewer view.java
```

The applet will successfully read and execute the code from the jar file. It will then extract the jpeg file from the jar and display it on the screen like this:

Figure 7-5: Displaying a JPEG extracted from a JAR file.

Be warned: the appletviewer may just wait forever if you send it to look for a file that isn't there. You must make sure that your applet tags, jar name, and file names are all absolutely correct.

Also, if you are using the programmer's shortcut of placing the HTML into the source file, then it's better to use a /* to open a comment at the beginning, and a */ to close a comment at the end of all the tags. The browsers and applet viewers get confused if they find a // on lines interspersed with applet tags.

Finally, don't forget that once you put some code in a jar, it's not enough to recompile when you change something. You must also rebuild the jar file with the new .class; otherwise, you'll continue to get the old version of the program. 🍒

Signing an Applet

Now that we have seen how to put Java applets into jars, the next step is to describe how jars can be used to convey the notion that an applet is trusted. Since an applet can be downloaded from anywhere on the Internet just by browsing a URL, the default security model needs to be very strict. JDK 1.1 introduced support for signing an applet, which gives the browser the opportunity to identify who wrote the applet and so lets that applet access more system resources on a graduated and controlled basis.

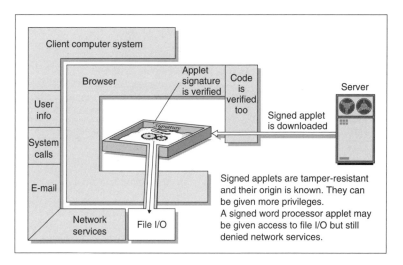

Figure 7-6: Signed Applets Have More Privileges

Signing an applet is like signing a bank check. It means labeling it with a tamper-proof identifying mark saying where it came from. Don't we already know this? Doesn't it come from the URL we are browsing? The answer is, "We are not sure enough to trust the applet with our system." Applets start running by virtue of visiting a page; there need not be any visible indication that the page contains an applet. Secondly, although an applet is hosted on a page, it is not necessarily located on that page. The "codebase" applet tag can point to a URL anywhere else on the Internet. Finally, with enough effort, it is possible to spoof (masquerade as) web servers. If the stakes are high enough people could do this to make a malicious applet appear to come from http://mother.teresa.org.

Why Graduated Security Is Needed

The "graduated and controlled" basis is the piece that ActiveX™ (a technology to download MS Windows-only executables) lacks and cannot be given. Within a couple of months of the launch of ActiveX, a programmer in Washington had written an ActiveX program that switched off any Windows computer that browsed its web page. An ActiveX control can be signed to identify where it came from, but once a user accepts it as trusted, it can, deliberately or through bugs, do anything to the user's system.

The Hamburg-based Chaos Computer Club went one better and wrote an ActiveX program that caused your computer to transfer money to an arbitrary bank account. The ActiveX program created a secret extra transaction for the Quicken™ financial software which is on many PCs. Next time the user dialed up to his bank, the extra transaction was submitted along with all the valid ones. With ActiveX, the permission is all or nothing. There is no way to say "this executable can access files in /tmp and nowhere else" Because of its fatal security deficiency and its Windows-only nature, ActiveX is quickly dropping from use, just like the Microsoft Bob software did. The Java model supports a fine granularity of applet access to system resources.

This is typically configured through the browser.

We can write our signature on a check because it is a physical piece of paper. For an applet in a jar file, we add an extra file saying what the origin is. Obviously, it wouldn't be good enough just to put an ASCII text file in there saying "Software from Honest Software Corporation," since the bomb-building, drug-peddling porno-terrorists that the FBI says are all over the Internet could easily forge that file on their own applets.

Instead, we use computer encryption to sign a file. Here is a summary of the basic steps:

1. Do all the one-time preparation necessary to set yourself up for encrypting files. The preparation consists of generating your code keys, registering them with the java database, and a couple of other things.

2. Put all the files that make up the applet into a JAR file. We have already seen how to do this in the previous section.

3. Create a directives file to use in signing. The directives file is an ASCII file that says who the software comes from.

4. Sign the JAR file, using the directives file. The javakey signing utility looks up your code in the java database and runs it over a hash of the

jar file and the directives file. Then, it adds the coded result to the jar. Anyone can look at it, and anyone can change it, but if they do, the results won't match the encoded hash   value, and the tampering will be obvious.

5.   Change the applet tag to reference the newly created `.sig` file instead of the old `.jar` file.

6.   Put the signed applet jar file on your web page, and let people have at it.

This process makes the applet trusted. Let's step through it at length, using an actual example. The longest part of the process is the one-time setup, which is explained in the next section. To help you keep track of the steps and substeps, the following sections are numbered corresponding to the steps above.

What Do All Those Cryptographic Terms Mean?

We don't present a general tutorial on computer cryptography in this text. Bruce Schneier does that in his excellent book referenced at the end of the chapter, and it takes 750 pages. The pages are packed with information and stories that will keep you reading and learning. (OK, Bruce, that'll cost you a dollar for every referral ;-))

You don't have to know how computer cryptography works in order to sign Java applets. But most readers will be very interested to find out more details. Cryptography is a truly fascinating topic, with an engaging blend of intrigue, high finance, and technical challenges. If you get caught up in it, it might even become your career!

Step 1: Setup for Applet Signing (One-Time)

We'll start by listing the bits and pieces involved in registering yourself with the Java system as a person or organization that can sign code. Note that you can sign applications as well as applets just by putting them in a jar file. It's more usual to sign applets because their signatures are checked automatically for you by the browser.

- Public and private keys—Java uses public key cryptography which involves two keys, one private and one public. Anyone can use your public key, but only you know your private key. There is no practical way to discover one key from the other, but either key can turn a message into seemingly random bits, and the other key can recover it.
  Encrypting something is like translating it into Martian—the encryption key is an English-to-Martian dictionary, and the decryption key is a Martian-to-English dictionary. Only instead of Martian, we use mathematical ciphers that are a lot harder to search exhaustively.

- Certificates—Anyone can generate their own keys, and anyone can claim to be whoever they like. To provide better assurance that you are who you say you are, we use X.509 certificates (bit files) in the on-line world.

- The `javakey` database—This repository holds records of all users, their certificates, and the pairs of code keys that each has. There is one `javakey` database on each system.

- The `javakey` utility—You'll be relieved to hear that there is only one utility used to do all this key generation and database registration. It has lots of different options, but there's only one command: `javakey`.

Now that we know the players, let's go over the rules of the game shown in Table 7-3.

Table 7-3: How to Prepare for Signing your Applets

Step 1a	Register yourself in the Java crypto database.
Step 1b	Generate your pair of keys.
Step 1c	Generate or buy an X.509 certificate
Step 1d	Register your keys and certificate with the Java database.

When you have completed these four steps, you will be able to sign applets. Although the process may seem cumbersome, remember that these four steps only have to be done once and then you can do any amount of code signing.

Step 1a: Register yourself in the Java crypto database

As we mentioned, there is only one utility, `javakey`, to do all the preparatory work, and it has several different options which you can see if you type:

```
%    javakey
l    list of the identities in the database.
c    create a new identity.
r    remove an identity from the database.
i    import a public key, a key pair, etc.
g    generate a key pair, a certificate, etc.
d    display a certficate.
```

For more information, see documentation.

Additional option letters can be used with each of these main options. We use a command of the form

```
javakey -cs yourname   true
```

to say "create a new signer called 'yourname,' who is regarded as trusted (true)." For example, the actual command and output might be:

```
javakey -cs lemon   true
```

```
Created identity [Signer]lemon[identitydb.obj][trusted]
```

You'll find it more convenient to use your own user ID or last name. We use the example name `lemon` so that you can easily see what is a command option and what is a name you supply.

At any time, you can use the command

```
javakey -li lemon
```

to list identity information on the named user. Try it now and you will see.

```
Identity: lemon
[Signer]lemon[identitydb.obj][trusted]
        no keys
        no certificates
        No further information available.
```

Step 1b: Generate your pair of keys

The next step is to generate the private and public keys for this user. As always, we use the `javakey` command, this time with the `-gk` (generate keys) option.

```
javakey -gk lemon  DSA 768  lemon.key.public  lemon.key.private
```

The `DSA 768` argument tells `javakey` to use the Digital Signature Algorithm (a royalty-free digital signature algorithm standardized by the US Government as NIST FIPS PUB 186 in May 1994) with a key length of 768 bits. An alternative to DSA is PGP, the Pretty Good Privacy algorithm. You would need to install the PGP software on your computer before using it. Another option is SHA (the Secure Hash Algorithm). The longer a DSA key, the more secure the encryption. A key length of 512 is regarded as wimpy. A key length of 1024 is regarded as secure for a few years. The U.S. export laws currently bar the export of an encryption algorithm using a key of more than 40 bits without a special license.

The last two arguments are just file names, telling `javakey` where to dump the results. Generating keys involves mathematical wizardry using prime numbers and exponential functions. Expect it to take a few seconds to run.

Step 1c: Generate or buy an X.509 certificate

Anyone can generate their own keys, and anyone can claim to be whoever they like. To provide better assurance that you are who you say you are, we use X.509 certificates (bit files) in the on-line world.

X.509 is an ISO standard for computer authentication. There are companies in business simply to check your credentials and issue you an unforgeable X.509 certificate in the form of an encrypted file. One such company is Verisign of Mountain View, California, reachable at `http://www.verisign.com`.

You prove who you are to a certification authority, using real-world documents, show them your public key, and they issue you a certificate. An X.509 certificate is like a passport, only better because it's harder to forge. An X.509 certificate works like a notary public: you identify yourself to the notary public and sign something, then the notary affixes an official seal to guarantee your signature.

Buying an X.509 certificate from a certification authority is more reliable for your users and will make your code accepted in more places. Generating our own certificate is good enough for this example. First create a certificate file, called `lemon.cert.directives`, for user `lemon` with these contents:

```
# info about the Certification Authority
issuer.name=lemon
issuer.cert=1

# info about the subject
subject.name=lemon
subject.real.name=Myers Tangy
subject.org=Honest Software Co
subject.org.unit=Software development
subject.country=USA

# info about the certificate
start.date=6 May 1997
end.date=6 May 1998
serial.number=42

# the file to write the cert in
out.file=lemon.cert
```

The certificate file is just a kind of directives file that saves you providing masses of information on the command line. Notice how the file just looks like a Java properties file. The contents shown are fairly typical, though the actual values will change.

Now, generate a certificate for user `lemon` by typing the command

`javakey -gc lemon.cert.directives`

```
Generated certificate from directive file lemon.cert.directives.
```

You can display a certificate in human-readable form by using the command

`javakey -dc lemon.cert`
```
[
    X.509v1 certificate,
    Subject is CN=Myers Tangy, OU=Software development,
        O=Honest Software Co, C=USA
    Key:  Sun DSA Public Key

        ... some lengthy key information omitted ...

    Issuer is CN=Myers Tangy, OU=Software development
    Issuer signature used [SHA1withDSA]
    Serial number =      2a
]
```

Generating a certificate involves about the same amount of work as generating the keys. It can take a few seconds to complete, so be patient and don't break in prematurely.

Step 1d: *Register your keys and certificate with the Java database*

Finally, the last step of the one-time setup process is to import your keys and certificate into the java `crypto` database.

```
javakey -ic  lemon    lemon.cert
```

```
Imported certificate from lemon.cert for lemon.
```

If you run the `javakey -li lemon` command again at this point, you will see that the database now holds data for this user.

Step 2: Put all the files that make up the applet into a jar file

We saw how to put the class files and other resources into a jar file earlier in this chapter. Here is the example code we will use. It is an applet that attempts to write to a local file on the client. Untrusted applets do not have permission to write to local files.

```
/* <applet
        archive=write.jar      code=write.class
        width=120              height=75>
    </applet>
*/
import java.io.*;
import java.awt.*;
import java.applet.*;

public class write extends Applet {

    public void init() {
        try {
            FileWriter fw = new FileWriter("score.txt");
            fw.write("new high score: 14 \n");
            fw.close();
        } catch (IOException ioe) {System.out.println(ioe);}
    }

    public void paint(Graphics g){
        g.drawString("Have written the file", 10, 10);
    }
}
```

Compile the applet and put the class in a jar file:

```
% javac write.java
```

```
% jar -cvf write.jar  write.class
```

The applet attempts to open a file and write to it. When you try to run the applet, it will fail with a security error. Untrusted applets are not permitted access to the client file system.

```
% appletviewer write.java
sun.applet.AppletSecurityException: checkwrite
at sun.applet.AppletSecurity.checkWrite(AppletSecurity.java:427)
at java.io.FileOutputStream.<init>(FileOutputStream.java)
at java.io.FileWriter.<init>(FileWriter.java)
at write.init(write.java:15)
at sun.applet.AppletPanel.run(AppletPanel.java:287)
    at java.lang.Thread.run(Thread.java)
```

Next we will sign it and try again.

Step 3: Create a directives file to use in signing

To sign a jar file, we first need to create a directives file. The directives file is an ASCII file that says who the software comes from. A typical directives file might look like this:

```
# who is signing this
    signer=lemon

    # the certificate number to use.  A large organization might
    # have several certificates.
    cert=1

    # the "chain" of related certificates to include
    # currently an unsupported but required technicality
    chain=0

    # the name to give the signature file and
    # signature block within the signed jar file
    signature.file=writesig
```

As you probably realize, a # in a directives file makes the line into a comment. The chain line is required but not yet supported. It refers to how many additional, related certificates should be used in the generation of this signature.

The `signature.file=writesig` directive allows you to choose a name for the signature information that is going to be added to the jar file to create the signed file. This allows you to choose a name that won't conflict with a file that is already in the jar. There is currently a limitation of eight characters for the name you choose.

Assume that you called this directives file `write.sig.directives`. The next step is to sign your jar file, using the directives file you just created.

Step 4: Sign the jar file, using the directives file

The `javakey` signing utility reads the directive file and looks up the entry in the java `crypto` database for that user. It then runs the signing algorithm on the jar file and adds a few more files in a new subdirectory. The general form of the command is

```
javakey -gs  directives-file   jar-file
```

The option `-gs` of course means "generate signature." In this case, the command is

```
javakey -gs write.sign.directives write.jar
```

You will see the output

```
Adding entry: META-INF/MANIFEST.MF
Creating entry: META-INF/WRITESIG.SF
Creating entry: META-INF/WRITESIG.DSA
Adding entry: write.class
Signed JAR file write.jar using directive file write.sig.directives.
```

The directory that is added is called META-INF because it contains "meta-information"—information about the information in the archive. The MANIFEST.MF file is named in the same sense that a manifest is a list of the cargo on a ship. It specifies the files to be found in the archive.

Step 5: Change the applet tag

Now we change the applet tag in our HTML file to refer to the signed version of the jar file. We want users to reference the newly created .sig file instead of the old .jar file.

The new tag will look like this

```
<applet
        archive=write.jar.sig
        code=write.class
        width=120
        height=75>
    </applet>
```

Step 6: Put the signed applet jar file on your web page, and let people have at it

A signed applet takes longer to start because the browser must check the signature information before accepting the code. On the other hand it will usually download faster.

This whole process makes the applet trusted. If you try running the example now in the appletviewer, you will see that this time the applet runs successfully and the `score.txt` file is created in the user's directory.

Note that signing an applet gives the browser some additional information about the applet. The user can still choose not to grant that applet any privileges or the privileges it wants. In this event, the applet will still fail with a security exception. At the time of writing (Summer 1997), Netscape does not have a browser that handles signed applets. Sun's HotJava™ browser and the JDK appletviewer do handle signed applets.

By the time this book gets into the hands of readers, more browsers are expected to support configurable applet security. One need is to be able to configure browsers to accept or refuse certain Certification Authorities. You'll want to be able to tell your browser "accept applets that are accompanied by certificates from these five companies, and ask me explicitly about any others."

Some Light Relief

Did Apple Copy Xerox?

The Apple Macintosh is a marvellous personal computer that featured a windowing interface right from its introduction in 1984.The Mac popularized the use of windows, menus, and mouse pointing devices very effectively. But where did the Mac team get the idea from?

There's a story in wide circulation that the Mac GUI was ripped off wholesale from Xerox! Before starting the Macintosh project, Steve Jobs visited the Xerox Research Center in Palo Alto California (PARC), and was shown a GUI interface running on the Xerox Star computer. Conspiracy theorists then claim that Steve Jobs realized the potential of the Xerox technology and pinched the ideas (and later some of the people) for the Mac.

How shocking. But what are the facts? One indication that things might not have happened quite that way, is the marked lack of innovation at Apple since Steve Jobs was pushed out in 1985. (In a surprise move, he was pushed back in again in December 1996. It's hard to keep up with the latest developments at Apple!) The stagnation at Apple without Jobs suggests that Jobs may well have been an innovator rather than a copier. On the other hand, it might just mean that it is really hard to get anything new done in a huge corporation. Since Jobs and many of his key developers left, the product improvement focus at Apple has largely centered around more memory/bigger screen/newer processor. These are just pedestrian "mid-life kickers" as we call them in Silicon Valley. The one totally new product, the Newton personal digital assistant, was an unmitigated disaster. Ironically, the failure of the Newton led to the firing of John Sculley, the Pepsi executive who had pushed Jobs out. Users don't want small products of increased complexity.They want decreased complexity in existing products.

But to come back to the Macintosh GUI. The man who started the Macintosh project (and named it for his favorite type of eating apple, modified to avoid trademark issues—those fruit farmers are apparently fanatically litigious) was Jef Raskin. The Mac project started early in 1979, long before Jobs ever visited Xerox. In fact, the reason Jobs finally went to PARC was that Raskin asked him to, to help convince Jobs that a WYSIWYG environment was the way to go.

Raskin had been a professor and computer center director at the University of California at San Diego and a visiting scholar at the Stanford Artificial Intelligence Laboratory (SAIL). Raskin was often a visiting academic at the Xerox Research Center in its first few years, but to avoid any possible conflict of interest Raskin stopped visiting PARC after he joined Apple in 1978.

Raskin was an early originator of the idea that user interface and graphics were of primary importance to the future of computing. His 1967 Computer Science thesis argued that computers should be all-graphic, that we should eliminate character generators and create characters graphically and in various fonts, that what you see on the screen should be what you get, and that the human interface was more important than mere considerations of algorithmic efficiency and compactness. The thesis was titled "The Quickdraw System" which is the name of the Mac GUI drawing toolbox.

At Apple, Raskin built on his own earlier work to create click-and-drag for moving objects and making selections. Xerox used a click-move-click paradigm that was prone to error. Raskin hired a former student of his, Bill Atkinson, who extended Raskin's work to pull-down menus.

Larry Tesler was the first PARC ex-employee to join Apple, and some people have claimed that he brought the selection-based editor with him. In reality the concept dates back to an editor Raskin had designed many years before in 1973 while at Bannister & Crun. However, Raskin had discussed his ideas with those of similar interests at Xerox, so perhaps some of the technology transfer was actually from future Apple employee to Xerox!

Summary: Contrary to the widely-accepted version, Steve Jobs didn't totally rip off the Mac GUI from a visit to Xerox. On the contrary, key elements of the design came from Jef Raskin, a computer science professor who had evangelized WYSI-WYG designs for many years, including inside Xerox. Other parts of the Mac interface originated with Bill Atkinson and Bud Tribble who had been students at UCSD when Raskin taught there.

The moral of this story is ... what—you expect every story to end with a moral? Too bad. This one doesn't have one. Raskin did comment on the inaccuracies in the common story, and tried to get his perspective down on paper in the fourth reference below. The only other point to mention is that Raskin gave his three children Palindromic names: Aza, Aviva, and "Sums are" Erasmus (not sure about that last one...)

Exercises

Make the anagram application into an applet.

(Medium) 🐛

1. The scheme for passing parameters to applets from HTML is very flexible, and in fact allows you to pass an arbitrary number of parameters. If you give your HTML parameters names that end with a number in sequence, like this

    ```
    <param  name=myparam1   value="some value" >
    <param  name=myparam2   value="another value" >
    <param  name=myparam3   value="25.2" >
    ```

    it's easy to concatenate a count onto the name, as an argument to get-Parameter like this:

    ```
    next = getParameter( "myparam"+i );
    i++;
    ```

    That way you can keep retrieving parameters until you get a null returned. Write a program with the two statements above in a loop to demonstrate this. Print out the value of the parameters received.

2. Write an applet that reads a file. Run it in the appletviewer and set the properties so it will run successfully. Then sign it and configure a browser to run it.

3. Distinguish between "init()" and "start()" in an applet.

4. Does HTML have to be in a file with the extension .html or .htm? Where else might you put it and why?

Further References

1. "Down With GUIs!" Wired, December 1993, pg. 122. Jef Raskin

2. "Hubris of a heavyweight. A review of Steve Jobs & the NeXT Big Thing" Randall E. Stross, IEEE Spectrum, July 1994 pp. 8-9.

3. "Intuitive Equals Familiar." Communications of the ACM. 37:9 September 1994 pg. 17, Jef Raskin

4. "Holes in the Histories" Interactions 1.3, July 1994 pg. 11, Jef Raskin

5. "Applied Cryptography, 2nd Edition," by Bruce Schneier, John Wiley and Sons, 1996, ISBN 0-471-11709-9 (paperback)
    A wonderful book. The author has gone to considerable trouble to explain a complicated mathematical topic so that any programmer can follow it. More technical books should be written like this one.

CHAPTER

8

- What's New in JDK 1.1

- Java APIs: Present and Future

- Delving Into Remote Method Invocation

- All About JDBC

Utilities and Libraries

"There's a tomato in every automaton."

—*Professor Rudolph's Big Book of Finite*
State Machines and Fruit Fancies

At first, Java came with only a dozen or so basic classes that implemented common data structures and operations. As Java began to grow in popularity, it grew in size too as JavaSoft and other interested parties hurried to announce and support more libraries. This chapter provides an overview of the utility classes and libraries that accompany Java.

The Java libraries and products can be divided into three broad categories:

- Utilities bundled with the JDK
- Optional additions to the JDK
- Other Java-related products and services

There are so many additional libraries and packages announced for Java at this point, that aspect alone would make a topic for a pretty thick book. What we'll do here is provide an overview of everything that has been announced at the time of this writing. We will also provide a complete working example of Remote Method Invocation, and of Java database access using the JDBC.

New Features of the Java Development Kit 1.1 Release

The following is a summary of everything new that was introduced with the JDK 1.1 release.

Java Archive (JAR) Files. These are intended to solve two problems. First, address poor http performance due to making a socket connection for every individual file to be downloaded. Second, they support individual files being signed to authenticate their origin. JAR files combine several files into one Java archive, and support compression of the individual files. JAR files use a new applet tag, called the *archive* tag, as in:

```
<applet archive="Nuclear.jar"
   code="NuclearPlant.class"
   width=680 height=473   >
```

The system will bring the entire Nuclear.jar file over, and start executing in the NuclearPlant class.

Better Support for Internationalization. There is now some support for localized applets, so that the same program can display its messages in German in Germany, in French in France, and so on. There is also support for obtaining the date and time in the right format for the locale. This can be different even when the language is the same. In the United States the date is written as month.day.year, but in Britain the usage is day/month/year.

Security. The introduction of libraries to support cryptography and digital signatures. Developers will be able to build cryptography into their products. Additionally the features are used internally to sign files of code, data and images. The first support comes in with JDK 1.1, and more will be phased in with later releases.

Abstract Windowing Toolkit (AWT) Improvements. Much work has been done to raise the quality and performance of the AWT. The programming model for receiving window events is very different. Several new widgets have appeared: scroll panes, pop-up menus, cursors per component, and some clipboard support. There is now a way to print the screen from within the AWT.

Network Enhancements. Some BSD-style options for sockets have been added, along with some new subclasses of SocketException for better error reporting.

The class MulticastSocket has moved from the vendor hierarchy sun.net into the standard Java.net.

Remote Method Invocation. Remote Method Invocation (RMI) is best described as "RPC for Java." It allows a client system to make calls into another computer system. To the client it just looks like invoking a method within its own process, but it actually executes code on another system. There is a fuller description of this later in the chapter.

Object Serialization. This means that there are now ObjectOutputStream and ObjectInputstream classes, just as there are DataInputStream and DataOutput-Stream. You can now write objects into files or sockets for persistent storage or transmission across the ether. RMI uses object serialization.

Reflection. Reflection is a way for Java code to find out what methods and fields are in any loaded class. It can then construct new instances of classes and arrays, and call methods on the classes. Reflection is useful to have when you are building component frameworks, such as Java Beans. It is reflection in the sense of "what I see when I look in the mirror."

Byte, Short, and Void Classes. These just round out the standard classes for the primitive types. They are needed now that we have serialization and reflection. The class void is a wrapper class, which Javasoft has yet to describe detail. The name suggests it is used when you want to pass any general object around, but the class Object already does that.

Database Connectivity. Now there is a standard way to access SQL databases from Java. The Java Database Connectivity (JDBC) library provides uniform access to a wide range of relational databases. A complete example is given later in this chapter.

New Native Method Interface. There is a new interface for calling code written in C or other non-Java language. The main goal is to get binary compatibility of all native method libraries on a given VM. This means that Hot Java, Internet Explorer, and Netscape Navigator should not each require a different convention for the same Java-to-C call. To a user, it means that code containing native methods can be executed in any browser (once signed classes make it feasible to execute native methods from a browser). Microsoft has refused to support this common interface, preferring its own incompatible "Raw Native Interface".

A Standard Interface for the Just-in-Time Compiler Crowd. This is intended for tool implementors, and essentially documents the interfaces that people were already using, bringing them to an official standardization.

Nested Classes. Nested classes are a technique allowing a simpler syntax for a nested class. This gives Java the lexical scoping used in block structured languages like Pascal.

General Performance Improvements. The JDK 1.1 release includes many bug fixes, and many performance improvements. The AWT peer class was re-implemented for Windows 95. On the Macintosh, fragmented heaps were allowed (the heap does not have to be all in one place). On Windows 95 and Solaris/SPARC, a critical portion of the inner loop of the interpreter was recoded in assembler. A compile time option now allows the use of native threads on Solaris.

Never in the past has a language evolved as rapidly as Java. The FCS release is not even past its first birthday, and it has already gained a road map that will make it the most richly-featured portable language in computer history. The JDK 1.1 release is a big first step in that direction.

Overview of All APIs

This section provides a list of everything that will eventually be in Java, and in some cases is already here. In an amazingly short space of time, a rich variety of Java tools, APIs, and services has already sprung up. Sun has taken the unusual step of providing a complete road map showing how future libraries will be added to enable Java to evolve from a programming language to a full operating environment. The initiative is clearly aimed at moving Java to become a complete software solution, scalable from the smallest applet to the biggest corporate data center.

We're going to be using the term API a lot in this section, so let's review the meaning. An API is an *Application Programmer Interface*. It is a specification of a software library, detailing all the function calls, arguments, and results you get back from them. An API exists on paper and is just a design. To actually use an API, you need a real library that implements the API.

Chapter 7 of the ANSI C specification is an API describing many functions like printf() in the C runtime library. On Unix, the file libc.so is the library that implements the API. An API promises some services on paper, a library delivers them in code.

When Jorge Luis Borges commented that "I have always imagined that paradise will be a kind of library," he surely had the JDK road map in mind.

Some of these libraries are being shipped with JDK 1.1, while others are planned to come in future releases. The new libraries shipped with JDK 1.1 will be described at length in this chapter. It's helpful to start by providing a thumbnail description of all of them. When your boss thunders into your office and demands to know if you can integrate Java programs with the various CORBA implementation, you'll be able to give the right answer: "Certainly. Java is aligned with CORBA and may even adopt IIOP as its "over-the-wire" protocol in future."

There are about one dozen families, each containing several new APIs. The APIs are classified as either a *core* API or a *standard extension* (in most cases all the APIs in a family are classified the same way). A core API is one that comes with the JDK, is part of Sun's standard implementation, and must be supported by every Java system. A standard extension is a library that does not have to be supported, but if the feature is supported, it must be done in exactly that standard way. Some of these software components, like the JDBC, moved into the core Java Development Kit with the 1.1 release. More will migrate in over time. The API families are shown in Table 8-1.

Table 8-1: The API family tree

Core	Standard Extension
JDK 1.0.2 and JDK 1.1	Java Media API (some core)
Java Enterprise (some standard extension)	Java Commerce (some core)
Java Beans	Java Server (some core)
Java Security	Java Management (JMAPI)
Java Enterprise	Personal Java
Java Foundation Classes (JFC)	Embedded Java

Several of the APIs are complete now, one or two are available in early form, and the rest are currently under development. Sun is developing these APIs using an open process that is unprecedented in the industry.

The API proposals are being drafted in partnership with industry leaders in each area. Lucent Technologies (the new name for Bell Labs) is working on the telephony API. The 2D graphics API in the Media family is based on Adobe's Bravo document imaging system. Intel and Silicon Graphics assisted in the development of a media framework API covering audio, video, and MIDI.

The results of these collaborative efforts will be available for public comment and review before the specifications are finalized. Most of these specifications will be published by the end of 1996. The extensions to the Java Media API are more complicated, and will be published in 1997. Everything will be completed by the end of 1997.

Now let's look at these API families in greater detail.

Java Enterprise

These APIs allow Java applications to be integrated with corporate database and legacy applications. Within Java Enterprise, four APIs have been designed:

- JDBC. A standard SQL database access interface, providing access to many different relational databases.

- Java IDL. Implements the OMG Interface Definition Language specification, as a language-neutral way to specify an interface between an object and a client on a different platform. It allows Java to call out to other object frameworks.

- Java RMI. A remote method invocation between peers, or between client and server, when both ends are written in Java. RMI is an object-oriented protocol that does the same kind of thing as RPC. RMI is built on Object Serialization. Object Serialization is a new I/O library to turn an object into a byte stream, usually written to disk, and later reconstitute it back into an object.

- Java Naming and Directory Interface (JNDI). The API supports a standard for connection to and use of different enterprise-wide naming and directory services, such as LDAP or Banyan Vines.

The Java Enterprise APIs make it easy to create large-scale commercial and database applications that can share multimedia and other data with applications inside an organization or across the Internet.

Java Commerce (Java Wallet)

The Java Commerce APIs will (finally!) bring secure purchasing and financial management to the Web. These APIs, also called *Java Wallet*, are the first step towards the goal. It defines and implements a client-side framework for credit card, debit card, and electronic cash transactions. Java Wallet will provide a purchasing framework for consumers to buy goods, and pay for them using a payment-service API. The merchant APIs will provide shopping-cart and billing capabilities to vendors.

The term Java Wallet is carefully chosen. You don't pay for things with your wallet itself. Your wallet is the place you safely keep the objects that really pay for things: credit cards, money, check book. And so it is with the Java Wallet: a secure receptacle for holding electronic financial instruments known as "cassettes" (because they plug in like tape cassettes). Java Wallet builds on the *Java Security* family described in the next paragraph.

There is a tremendous profit waiting for the first organization to bring simple and secure financial transactions to the Net. So the competition is heating up. Netscape already has a proposal in place, and Microsoft is not far behind.

Java Security

Java Security APIs are a framework to let developers put security-related features in their applets and applications. The features include cryptography with digital signatures, encryption, and authentication. Respectively, these allow you to say who you are, secretly, and have other people believe it.

Instead of every programmer having to implement an authentication class, the class will be part of a library. The design provides a clean interface between applications and the cryptography, so that developers (or users) can plug in one of several alternative cryptographic algorithms. This simplifies matters for US vendors, as the US Government currently insists on putting cryptographic software in the same category as machine guns, bazookas, and artillery pieces, and forbids export under Arms Trade regulations.

US computer companies usually bear the expense of preparing two versions of their products: one with cryptography for the domestic market, and one with no or weaker cryptography for export. Now systems developers will use the Java Security APIs, and provide the receptacle into which alternative encryption modules can easily be placed.

If you agree with the current position of the US Government that software (like Netscape Navigator and the Unix operating system) is a munition, that cryptography should be restricted so the US Government can break it, and that the US Government should have a "back door" key to read anyone's encoded messages (including yours), then here are some things to consider:

- *Do not* visit the URL http://www37.netscape.com/eng/US-Current/itar.hmtl and read the International Traffic in Arms Regulations.

- *Do not* look at the Usenet newsgroups alt.security.pgp, talk.politics.crypto, or sci.crypt.

- *Do not* download and use PGP (Pretty Good Privacy), a package of strong encryption available for all popular systems, written by Phil Zimmermann. Do *not* visit http://web.mit.edu/pgp, and follow the directions to download. Overseas readers should avoid visiting the alternative site http://www.ifi.uio.no/~staalesc/PGP/language.html. in Norway.

- *Do not* buy Phil Zimmermann's books available in many bookstores. Do not specify "The Official PGP User's Guide," by Philip Zimmermann, from MIT Press, 128 pages, ISBN 0-262-74017-6, $14.95. Nor should you read "PGP Source Code and Internals" by Philip Zimmerman, published by MIT Press 1995, ISBN 0-262-24039-4. This book contains the entire source code for PGP, and almost put the US Government in the medieval position of banning the sale and distribution of a book.

Note that everybody in the world already has access to the Data Encryption Standard (DES), the strong encryption technique standardized by the US Government in 1977. Prohibiting its export doesn't keep it out of any nation's hands. So why do it? Some people speculate that the real agenda driving the NSA is their fear that bundling DES in popular American software products will encourage routine use of good cryptography both inside and outside the US; this makes traffic analysis much harder for them.

Therefore (the theory runs), the US Government wants cryptography to be awkward to deploy, not because they can't break it, but because they want to discourage people inside the US from using better products by default. If you spend a long time in the counter intelligence world, I guess that's how you end up thinking.

There is genuinely a certain amount of nonsense or misinformation fed to the media, who are all too ready to report it unquestioningly. *Parade Magazine* of Sept. 29, 1996 printed a reader's letter that asked "If we know so much, how come we can't catch terrorists?" *Parade* printed an answer from "an expert" claiming "they started using codes on the Internet." Needless to say, this is such complete nonsense, one can only presume they are trying to soften up public opinion to accept restrictions on privacy on the Internet.

For three years, Zimmermann was the target of a US Customs criminal investigation to determine if he violated federal export laws after he programmed, and gave away free, the PGP software. Finally in 1996, after years of expense and strain for Zimmermann, the Feds dropped the case against the computer programmer. If you want to read some press stories about the case, see the following references:

Steven Levy, "The Encryption Wars: Is Privacy Good or Bad?" Newsweek, 24 April 1995, page 55.

Vic Sussman, "Lost in Kafka Territory," US News and World Report, 3 April 1995, page 32.

Ken Hoover, "Indictment Possible in Cyberspace Privacy Case," San Francisco Chronicle, 29 May 1995, page A15.

William Bulkeley, "Cipher Probe," Wall Street Journal, Thursday 28 April 1994, front page.

John Markoff, "Federal Inquiry on Software Examines Privacy Programs," New York Times, Tuesday 21 Sep 1993, page C1.

Steven Levy, "Battle of the Clipper Chip," New York Times Magazine, Sunday 12 Jun 1994, page 44.

John Markoff, "Cyberspace Under Lock and Key," New York Times, Sunday 13 Feb 1994.

Philip Elmer-DeWitt, "Who Should Keep the Keys," Time, 14 Mar 1994, page 90.

An excellent source of general information on cryptography and algorithms is the book "Applied Cryptography, 2nd Edition," by Bruce Schneier, published by John Wiley and Sons, 1995.

Java Beans

After the Enterprise API family, Java Beans is probably the most significant API. It is also the least well-defined at this point. It is a component object model that ties all the other APIs together.

It's a little hard to describe something this abstract, but the Java Beans family defines a portable, platform-neutral set of APIs for software components to talk to each other. Java Beans are little fragments of programs that can be joined together at runtime to form complete programs. A bean can inspect other beans and call its services. A few typical functions that can be put into beans include sorting, searching, drawing graphs, spreadsheets, printing services and so on. Java Beans are an example of component software which has been popularized in the PC world with Borland's Delphi product. Several benefits are claimed for components, including rapid application development (RAD) and software development by users. It is an area that is still evolving, and it shows great promise.

Java Beans will make it easier for developers to write applications that use a common framework to blend programs seamlessly. The usual example people give is embedding a spreadsheet in a word processor document, and a chart program in the spreadsheet. The application is much wider and more significant than that. If the promise of Beans is fulfilled it could provide a complete desktop component environment largely independent of the underlying operating system (OS). See Figure 8-1. It could even replace the underlying OS on a single-user system, just as Netscape ultimately desires its browser to be the universal GUI.

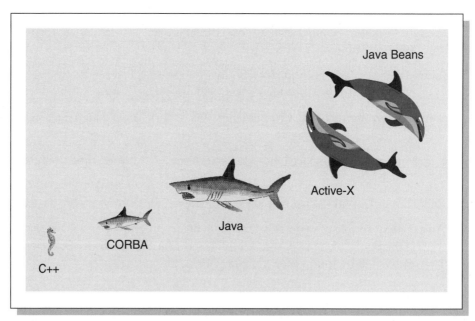

Figure 8-1: A strange food chain can be found in the ocean

Java Beans required some refinement of the AWT. JDK 1.2, coming at the end of 1997, will support Drag and Drop, and integration with the clipboard (a place to paste and temporarily save information).

When Sun Microsystems licensed Java to Microsoft back in December 1995, many industry commentators wondered if Microsoft would try to subvert the language in some way. The answer wasn't long in coming. Microsoft's plan was to retain their desktop monopoly by taking every possible opportunity to undermine, or weaken the portable, platform-independent nature of the language and protocols. One opportunity involves using the proprietary ActiveX library so that Java programs wouldn't be portable to non-Microsoft desktops. The Java beans initiative was born to counter Microsoft's plan, and provide the benefits of software components to all platforms in an even-handed way.

In late 1996 Microsoft launched a strident marketing campaign to try to win people over to the ActiveX lock-in. Part of the campaign involved handing just enough of the ActiveX specification to run the Windows client side to a standardization body (The Open Group, needing a new mission in life, accepted the technology, along with a fat check). But ActiveX has fatal flaws. Not only is it unportable, it lacks proper security. These two deficiencies make ActiveX useless for the Internet. The Wall Street Journal described ActiveX as "withering on the 'Net" outnumbered sevenfold by Java (August 8 1997). ActiveX is a dead end, best avoided by developers.

Java Media

Java Media API is designed to deliver multimedia over the Internet. The simpler media support is part of the core system, and the more advanced features are initially intended as standard extensions. In greater detail, the APIs cover these areas:

- Java Speech provides Java-based speech recognition in real time, and speech synthesis (the conversion of text strings to audio output).

- Java Collaboration provides for sharing of applications among multiple users, such as a shared white board. The collaboration API will consist of two parts: one to enable applications that are already collaboration-aware, and a second, later, API to retro-fit this ability to other applications.

- Java Animation provides for motion and transformations of 2D objects. It makes use of the Java Media Framework for synchronization, composition and timing.

- Java Media Framework has clocks for synchronizing sound, vision and external events. It also has media players for playing audio, video and MIDI. You will be able to play MPEG video by virtue of having Java on your system, and will not need to download additional plug-ins. The framework will allow users to do full audio and video streaming. Programmers will be able to create applications with moving backgrounds, foregrounds, and sprites. Intel is working on implementing the API, and the first implementation will be for the Windows platform.

- Java Telephony integrates telephones with computers. It provides basic functionality for a full range of telephone services including simple phone calls, teleconferencing, call transfer, caller ID and *dual tone multifrequency* (DTMF) decode/encode. Java applications will be able to interact with the phone system to place calls, automatically identify incoming calls, and interface with voice mail systems—all in a standard way. ISVs and companies that build communications cards have expressed great interest in JavaTel. It ties in well with recent interest in TCP/IP as a network control interface. People are also experimenting with using Internet to carry voice traffic. JavaTel will handle call control both for the desktop and for enterprise-wide telephony. It is a layer over other computer-telephony integration middleware such as Microsoft's TAPI, Novell and Lucent's TSAPI, and the Sun's own SunXTL.

- Java 3D provides an abstract, interactive imaging model for behavior and control of 3D objects. Objects can be viewed in light or shade, rotated to view from different angles, and seen as solid or wire frames.

Java Server

JavaSoft marketing literature says that the Java Server API is "an extensible framework that enables and eases the development of a whole spectrum of Java-powered Internet and Intranet servers. The APIs provide uniform and consistent access to the server and administrative system resources required for developers to quickly develop their own Java *servlets*—executable programs that users upload to run on networks or servers."

In English, that means "this is going to replace CGI." You'll be able to write your server code and client code in the same language. The APIs will let developers create servlets that run on servers, much like applets run on clients. Servlets are directly invokable via URL, and are activated by the server formerly known as Jeeves[1] on demand. A servlet may be automatically uploaded from the net, so there must be support for an "untrusted servelet" to run without compromising the server.

---

1. Trademark problems forced a name change. That's why we pay the lawyers the big bucks.

The server API doesn't have a GUI (since it's on the server), but file access, controlled by ACLs is important. There may be additional access to network administration and server system data.

When an applet accesses a servelet, a dynamically created document will be returned. If the servelet was browsing financial data in a company, it could provide different levels of access, depending on the applet making the query. If the applet was associated with a clerk, it would give access to individual invoices. If it was associated with the company accountant, it would provide overall totals as well.

Java Management

The short insight into this API family is that there will be some libraries to allow network administrators to use Java tools to manage their networks. The marketing talk is the usual guff about "a rich set of feature-full extensible object-oriented libraries to ease and enable" etc., etc., etc. What that means is that you'll have the libraries to talk *Simple Network Management Protocol* (SNMP), and thence to build applets that manage an enterprise network over Internet. The API includes support for events, topology discovery and access to SNMP through use of a Java SNMP proxy.

The Management API should really be called the Network Management API. It has been developed jointly with a broad range of industry leaders including AutoTrol, Bay Networks, BGS, BMC, Central Design Systems, Cisco Systems, Computer Associates, CompuWare, LandMark Technologies, Legato Systems, Novell, OpenVision, Platinum Technologies, SunSoft, Tivoli Systems, and 3Com.

Personal Java

The Personal Java API is for personal consumer devices that are occasionally connected to the network. It includes palm-tops, set-tops, games devices, and high-end smart telephones. A goal of Personal Java is to fit the JVM plus the subset libraries plus the user bytecode into 2Mb of ROM plus 2Mb of RAM (about $13 worth of memory at August 1997 prices).

Embedded Java

The Embedded Java API is for devices even lower than Personal Java devices. It caters to high volume real-time embedded systems such as those found in network routers, pagers, process control systems, or office peripherals. It specifies how the Java API may be further reduced or divided into a subset for embedded devices that can't support the full Java Core API. The Embedded API is based on java.lang, java.util and parts of java.io. It also defines a series of extensions for networking and GUIs.

At least two telephone companies are building Java chips into phones. If you think about it, a cell phone has a CPU, a network interface (to the telephone exchange), a keyboard (strictly a keypad), and a screen (LED display).The embedded API will allow everyone to program to the same feature subset. The embedded API is useful for much more than phones. It can be expected in almost every device that has, or could have, a CPU, such as cars, video cameras, printers, or copiers.

It doesn't take much imagination to see that if every intelligent appliance had a $5 serial port in it, and the Java Embedded API in ROM, you could program them and get them all working the way you want. If your VCR had this, you could hook it up to your computer and write a program to record shows, change channels, play tapes, or adjust the color balance automatically when needed. If your stereo had this, you could get it to talk to your TV, or even call you at work to play you soothing music. Devices that were formerly programmed in obscure ways can now have a public API that any Java programmer can use.

Object Communication Middleware

This section contains a description of some Java-related products. It provides useful background information on non-Java object software.

CORBA

If you read the object-oriented trade press, one term you may have seen more and more is CORBA. CORBA is the *Common Object Request Broker Architecture*. In a single sentence, it is a framework to let objects on one computer to talk to objects on another computer, just as Unix RPC (Remote Procedure Call) lets processes talk to one another. CORBA is a true object-oriented distributed processing framework. The "common" part means that it is not tied to any one language, or any one hardware vendor, but can inter-operate among all. CORBA was designed over the course of several years in an open industry-wide process, with the main participants being the Unix hardware vendors: DEC, H-P, Sun, and IBM.

Why do you want objects on different computers to talk to each other? Because it allows you to build much more complicated and capable systems that support true distributed processing. It's not intended for a single programmer working on a lone PC. It is highly useful in a large enterprise with Terabytes of data distributed in databases on dozens of mainframe class systems.

CORBA implementations have just started to be deployed. Sun has an implementation known as NEO. Like all CORBA implementations, NEO is language-neutral, and it achieves this by having an interface language (it looks close to C) that other languages must map into. Making CORBA language independent was a very far-sighted decision on the part of the original designers, and it means there is a place for CORBA in the Java world.

CORBA implementations were often deployed with C++, but with the right "glue" or interface definition language (IDL), they can talk to Java programs and supply object services across a Net.

When you want objects to communicate across different systems, there are two main reasons for using CORBA instead of just using Java's RMI:

- CORBA provides an object framework that is language independent. If you're using multiple languages, or you wish to leave that option open for the future, or you want to access C++ legacy systems, CORBA makes it easy.

- The CORBA initiative started before Java, and the CORBA code is further along. CORBA ORBs are sophisticated pieces of middleware that can schedule, route, queue and despatch incoming object requests. System administrators can inspect queues and do load-balancing across servers.

The overlap between Java RMI and CORBA is still being worked on. Everyone is converging on IIOP (the Internet Inter-ORB Protocol allowing different CORBA implementations to talk to one another). Netscape adopted IIOP in Fall 1996, and is folding it into its browser products. IIOP and RMI are being aligned more closely to provide a common solution to industry, and the details are still being worked out.

CORBA is a big industrial-strength language-independent object communication system. Java's RMI is a smaller, simpler system that can only be used when both endpoints are written in Java. CORBA gives you compatibility with legacy code, Java's RMI provides simplicity of remote communication. The two are converging into a single Java solution.

IDL

IDL or *Interface Definition Language* is the way CORBA achieves language-neutrality. You describe in IDL the signature of the methods and data that CORBA will pass back and forth for you. IDL looks somewhat like C, but it is purely for describing interfaces, not writing actual programs. IDL is only for people using

CORBA. Many Java systems won't see the CORBA framework directly, so many Java programmers will not need to bother with IDL.

NEO and Joe

Sun has a CORBA implementation named NEO. Joe is the productization of the IDL technology, specialized for the NEO product. In other words, the Joe libraries let Java run in the NEO Object Request Broker. Joe integrates Java applications with Solaris NEO object servers. A Java ORBlet is automatically downloaded to a client browser to support Java client requests.

Remote Method Invocation

Remote Method Invocation (RMI) is a java-specific version of a CORBA. RMI means that an object on one system can call a method in an object somewhere else on the network. It will send over parameters, and get a result back automatically. It all happens invisibly, and just looks like the invocation of a local method (it may take a little longer time of course). RMI directly supports client/server systems in Java. Clients can truly make procedure calls directly to their server

How does this differ from opening a socket to the server? It's a higher-level interface (RMI is actually built on top of sockets). A socket just lets you pass data to the server. RMI lets you call a method on the server, and pass objects in and out. This *is* a very big deal!

For those familiar with Remote Procedure Calls (RPC), RMI is RPC with an object-oriented flavor. It is also very simple to set up and use, compared to what it offers. Let's think about the problem for a second, show a diagram in Figure 8-2, and use that to lead into a description of how it works, with a code example. What we are trying to do is allow an object in a Java program on one system to call a method in a Java program on another system. Furthermore, we want this to look as similar as possible to a method calling a method in the same program.

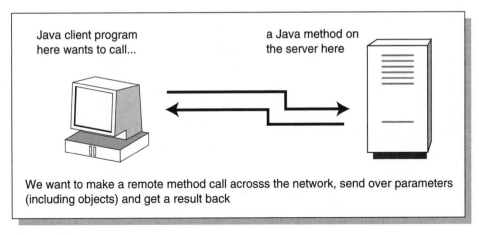

Java client program
here wants to call...

a Java method on
the server here

We want to make a remote method call acrosss the network, send over parameters
(including objects) and get a result back

Figure 8-2:   What RMI does

Not only does RMI look like RPC, it is implemented in a similar way to this established, and ingenious software. We know that it is not possible to make the desired call directly, so we break the problem down into smaller pieces that can be done directly. We make the client call a local routine which looks just like the one it wants to call remotely. We call this local dummy routine a *stub*. The stub is responsible for getting the incoming arguments and transmitting them over to its buddy on the server machine. It does this by opening a socket, serializing the objects, and passing the data across.

The buddy routine on the server machine is called a *skeleton* because it's just the bare bones of a routine. It doesn't do anything except unmarshal the data passed to it, and call the real server routine. The algorithm is then reversed to communicate the result back to the method on the client machine. And so a remote method has been invoked on one system by another, as shown in Figure 8-3.

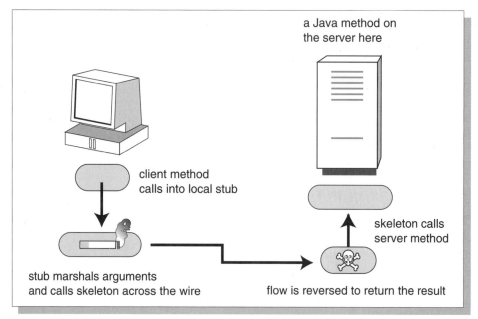

Figure 8-3: How RMI does it

Various extra cleverness takes place to support sending Objects across the network, including sending the exact type of the object arguments with the data. If that class doesn't exist on the receiving side, the corresponding class object itself is also loaded over the network.

Outline of our RMI System

Let's look at a code example to make this abstract description a little more concrete. Suppose we have a computer system that is physically connected to all sorts of weather-monitoring equipment: rain gauges, thermometer, anemometer, barometer, and so on. This will be our server system. We will abstract an interface of this, that describes the methods that can be called remotely.

The remote method we want to invoke is getWeatherReadings(). We need to provide an implementation of this on the server, and we need to provide an interface for it on the client, so it can compile against it. The next section describes this server interface

The Interface to the RMI Remote Server

The interface WeatherIntf is compiled on the client, and it describes the service (method calls) that we will be accessing remotely. The interface looks like this:

```
package met;
public interface WeatherIntf extends java.rmi.Remote {
    public String getWeatherReadings()
          throws java.rmi.RemoteException;
}
```

It is only a few lines long. We are going to compile it into a package called "met" ("met" stands for "meteorological office"). It is recommended that you always compile remote servers and interfaces into a named package, and not try to lazily squeak by using the anonymous package as we have to date.

The interface says that it extends (i.e. includes all the methods promised by) the java.rmi.Remote interface. WeatherIntf promises one method of its own "getWeatherReadings()" that returns a String, and may throw a RemoteException. There's nothing too special about RemoteException. It can be caught like any other exception. Rather than try to propagate arbitrary exceptions across the ether, we just have the one RemoteException type, and build into its string message some indication of what went wrong remotely.

Next we will look at the client code that uses this remote interface.

The RMI Client

The client code is straightforward. It looks like this:

```
import met.WeatherIntf;
import java.rmi.*;

public class RMIdemo {

  public static void main(String[] args) {
    try {
      Remote robj = Naming.lookup("//localhost/WeatherServer");
      WeatherIntf weatherserver = (WeatherIntf) robj;

      String forecast = weatherserver.getWeatherReadings();

      System.out.println("The weather will be " + forecast );

    } catch (Exception e) {System.out.println(e.getMessage());}
  }
}
```

The only new thing in this code is these two lines:

```
      Remote robj = Naming.lookup("//localhost/WeatherServer");
      WeatherIntf weatherserver = (WeatherIntf) robj;
```

The first line creates a `Remote`. This is the counterpart of an `Object`, but it represents a reference to something that can be anywhere outside this Java virtual machine. The naming lookup takes a string that looks something like a URL. It describes:

- the name of the server—localhost (use a different system once you have this working locally)

- the service to look for—the service called "WeatherServer"

Figure 8.4 illustrates how everything fits together.

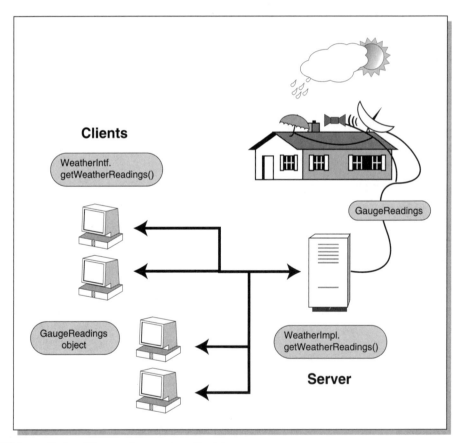

Figure 8-4: The weather station client/server

Everyone who wishes to communicate with a server has to agree on the name of the server and the name of the service. For this example I am running server and client all on one machine, so I just use the special name `localhost` (a TCP/IP standard meaning "this system". I made up the name "WeatherServer" for the service.

Our Remote object implements the WeatherIntf interface. As a result, we can cast it to that interface, and use it issue the "getWeatherReadings()" call that the interface promises. We catch any exceptions (there shouldn't be any) and print out the String that we receive back. This example uses a String object to represent the gauge readings, but you can pass back and forth objects of arbitrary complexity, both as arguments and return values.

Apart from the references to Remote, there is nothing at all in this code that is different from a wholly local system. What a marvellous advantage to have code that works the same way in the local case and when distributed across a network.

The RMI Remote Server Code

Finally we come to the server code that has some (a very little) RMI magic dust sprinkled over it to make everything work. The code looks like:

```
package met;
import java.rmi.*;
import java.rmi.server.UnicastRemoteObject;
public class WeatherServer extends UnicastRemoteObject
                           implements WeatherIntf {

    public WeatherServer ()  throws java.rmi.RemoteException {
        super();
    }

    public String getWeatherReadings() throws RemoteException {
        return Math.random()>0.5? "sunny" : "rainy";
    }

    public static void main(String[] args) {

        System.setSecurityManager(new RMISecurityManager());

        try {
            WeatherServer myWeatherServer = new WeatherServer();
            Naming.rebind("/WeatherServer",myWeatherServer);
        }catch (Exception e) {
            System.out.println(e.getMessage() );
        }
    }
}
```

Here we extend the `java.rmi.server.UnicastRemoteObject` class. This tips off the system that clients will expect to talk to and treat instances of this class as Remote objects. We extend the WeatherIntf. This promises that we will provide an implementation of the getWeather() method. Sure enough, we do. The getWeatherReadings() method just looks at a random number to decide whether to predict sunshine or rain, exactly the same as professional weather forecasters do. Alternatively, the software could actually be wired to all those instruments up on the roof through a serial port interface.

We set a security manager (this is required in a server). It allows us to customize the kind of accesses and services that we are going to provide. Then we create an instance of this class simply so we can pass the object as an argument to the Naming.rebind. Rebind is the way a server announces its service to the registry.

There is a central table called the Registry on each server. It contains a list of service names paired with (essentially) socket connections. It is not the Windows Registry, but it does a similar job: acts as a central place to ask for information.

Compiling and Running the Code

Here, alas, is where things get a little complicated. As part of moving to JDK 1.1, the RMI system was changed around a little, and the rules for locating stub classes became a little confused. In particular, the sensible defaults for the CLASSPATH have not yet made it into the RMI tools, so you still have to set those explicitly. The two RMI demo programs that ship with the JDK did not actually work in all releases from JDK 1.1 to JDK 1.1.3 for this reason. In addition, we have the added factor of compiling into a named package.

As a result it is very easy to screw up and find that your efforts to reproduce this example don't work. To help prevent that I will present numbered steps to compile and run this example, and I recommend you follow them exactly. You'll need three command windows: one each for the registry, the server, and the client (on Unix you could run them all in the background out of one window if you wanted).

1. Create a directory hierarchy to contain your code

   ```
   mkdir top
   mkdir top/met
   ```

2. Put the RMIdemo.java source file in the directory called top. Put the WeatherServer and WeatherIntf.java files in the top/met subdirectory.

3. change directory to be in the top dir, and compile the programs. Compile the server first because the client will use it.

```
cd top
javac met/WeatherIntf.java
javac met/WeatherServer.java
javac RMIdemo.java
```

4.   Generate the stub and skeleton files for the server

```
rmic -classpath $JAVAHOME/lib/classes.zip:. -d . met.WeatherServer
```
The "-d *path*" option says where to put the resulting classes. You should still be in the "top" directory when you issue this command

5.   Make sure that "." is in your CLASSPATH variable.

```
setenv CLASSPATH $JAVAHOME/lib/classes.zip:.
```

6.   Make sure that you are in directory "top" and start the registry by entering the JDK command:

```
rmiregistry
```
at the command line in a shelltool you are not otherwise using.

7.   Remove your classpath environment variable

```
unsetenv CLASSPATH
```

8.   Start the remote server:

```
java WeatherService
```

9.   Then start the client:

```
java RMIdemo
```

10.   Electrons will whizz back and forth across the ether for a second or two, and then you will get the weather forecast:

```
The weather will be sunny
```

A common mistake results in this error message:

```
Unexpected exception; nested exception is:
java.lang.ClassNotFoundException: met/weather/WeatherServer_Stub
```

It means that it can't find the server stub code, probably because you haven't set the CLASSPATH correctly. Log out and start again from the beginning.

It is common to get this error message:

```
Unexpected exception; nested exception is:
java.io.NotSerializableException:
```

Any classes whose objects are sent remotely must implement java.io.Serializable. This is a change between JDK 1.0 and JDK 1.1.

RMI is a very powerful technique for building large systems. The fact that the technique can be described, along with a working example, in just a few pages, speaks volumes in favor of Java. RMI is tremendously exciting and it's simple to use. You can call to any server you can bind to, and you can build networks of distributed objects. RMI opens the door to software systems that were formerly too complex to build.

Object Serialization

Serializing an object just means writing the values of all its data fields into a stream of bytes. You already know how to serialize an array or a String. The two new classes let you serialize/serialize other objects too.

Once you can turn an object into a stream, you can write it to a file (which gives you a persistent object that lives on after the program in which it was created), print it, pipe it to a thread, or even send it down a socket to another system on the other side of the world. All of these are useful things.

Object serialization is in the java.io class, along with all the other classes that process streams shown here. The new classes are:

```
public class java.io.ObjectOutputStream
    extends java.io.DataOutputStream implements
                    java.io.ObjectOutput {
  public java.io.ObjectOutputStream(java.io.OutputStream);

  public final void writeObject(java.lang.Object);
}
```

```
public class java.io.ObjectInputStream
    extends java.io.DataInputStream implements java.io.ObjectInput {
  public java.io.ObjectInputStream(java.io.InputStream);
  public final java.lang.Object readObject();
  public synchronized void registerValidation(java.io.ObjectInputValidation,int);
}
```

A whole slew of exceptions can be thrown by the readObject routine, namely ClassNotFound Exception, MethodMissingException, ClassMismatchException, StreamCorruptedException, and of course IOException. The method writeObject can throw MethodMissingException, ClassMismatchException, and IOException. Primitive data types can be written directly, and object data types can be written by applying the routine recursively. If an object points to other objects, those objects are saved too, and so on.

The registerValidation() method lets you register an object to be validated before the entire graph is handed back to you. Validating an object means checking that it still points to all the things it pointed to before.

The new keyword *transient* marks data as not having a value that is saved when the class is serialized. One example would be anything whose value is only valid at a given moment in time, like:

```
transient int current_speed
```

The serializer knows it has to reserve space for the value, but it doesn't save the soon-to-be outdated value there. For this reason, transient fields should usually be marked private too, as you don't want other objects using the values they find there. Static (class-level) data is not serialized either.

Do you want to serialize something from the class? You already have. That's what a class file is. You don't have to write out methods, because you already have those in the.class file, and can get them by loading it at any time. Different data values are what distinguish two objects of the same class. To indicate a class is serializable, it should implement java.io.Serializable. Like Cloneable, this is an empty interface that just says "I'm allowed to do this".

Class Versioning

If you just use write out the data values, you've got no guarantee that someone hasn't since modified its class and recompiled it, so the serializer calculates a hash value on the class and saves that too. The saved hash value from the object you bring in must match the hash value for the class in memory.

You will also find that Java protects you against classes that evolve. Say you serialize an object, then add a couple more methods to the class, recompile and use it. Then you want to read in one of the old objects. It won't match with the system's current definition of that class, and you'll get an exception like this:

```
java.io.InvalidClassException:
MyClass; Local class not compatible at
java.io.ObjectStreamClass.setClass(ObjectStreamClass.java:219)
```

How do you avoid this? With the "serialver" utility that comes with the JDK. You run "serialver" on your new class file and it will provide you a version id to add to the class in a declaration like this:

```
static final long serialVersionUID = 4021215565287364875L;
```

The first version of class doesn't need this field, but any later versions do if you are going to be serializing and deserializing them. The version id lets Java identify the classes.

Note that when you read an object back in, after you have written it out, you do not get back the same object. You get back a different object with identical values in the data fields.

There are some commonly used terms for serializing an object. Writing it to disk is called *pickling* or *preserving* the object. People also talk about marshalling and unmarshalling an object when it is being sent somewhere. I prefer the term lyophilize (pronounced "laff-alize") as it is a better description. When you pickle something you add brine to it.

Lyophilize is a term from chemistry meaning "freeze-dry." When you freeze dry something you take the water out and just leave the dry stuff. When you lyophilize an object you remove the code and just save the data.

Serialization Code Example

We should note at this point that the example is based on the alpha 2 version of RMI, released in July 1996. Some changes can be expected as the design proceeds to final form. Be sure to look at the Javasoft site http://java.sun.com to get the latest update, which will be released with JDK 1.1 in any event.

```
import java.io.*;
public class writeobj {

    public static void main(String arg[]) {
        Integer I = new Integer(65);
        try {
           FileOutputStream fos = new FileOutputStream("plum.dat");
           ObjectOutputStream oos = new ObjectOutputStream(fos);
           oos.writeObject(I);
        } catch(Exception e) {System.out.println(e);}

        try {
           FileInputStream fis = new FileInputStream("plum.dat");
           ObjectInputStream ois = new ObjectInputStream(fis);
           Object o = ois.readObject();
           I = (Integer) o;
           int i = I.intValue();
           System.out.println("i="+i);
        } catch(Exception e) {System.out.println(e);}
    }
}
```

This little program creates a FileOutputStream then pushes an ObjectOutput-Stream on it, to write an Integer object to the file "plum.dat." It then reads it in again. Notice that you just read in a raw object, and need to cast it back to its original type. You need to have some way of remembering what that type is, such as only writing one kind of object in a given file.

Java and Databases: JDBC

Right at the beginning it was realized that getting information into and out of databases would be a really useful ability to give Java. Large enterprises stand or fall by the quality of their corporate databases, and Java has a bright future in enterprise computing. So the very first library that Sun provided after the Java Development Kit was the Java DataBase Connectivity (JDBC). Sun designed the JDBC to allow access to any ANSI SQL-2 standard database.

We'll describe the JDBC in full here, and show a working example that you can copy and try. To get the most out of this section, you really need to understand database terms and techniques (like "SQL"). We'll sketch out some of these, but the topic really requires a complete book of its own. A good one is recommended at the end of this chapter.

About SQL and Relational Databases

Extracting information from a database and writing it back is done in Structured Query Language. SQL has been refined over more than two decades, and is the language used to access essentially all modern databases.

Years ago, there used to be several fundamentally different architectures for databases: there were hierarchical databases (like IBM's IMS), network databases (like the Codasyl model), and relational databases. It is now almost universally accepted that the relational design is superior to the other alternatives. We're also starting to see early use of object-oriented databases, some of which are accessed in a relational fashion. The collision between *object-oriented* and *relational-databases* is an area of emerging technology.

The database gurus have their own terminology of relations, tuples and N'th normal form, but (in plain words) the central idea to a relational database is that data appears to be kept in tables. The database can contain several tables. In a way, a table in a relational database is like an enormous spreadsheet. It might have millions of rows and hundreds of columns. Each column contains only one kind of data. A row in a table corresponds to a record. A programmer will use SQL statements to merge tables and extract data from them. There is a whole arithmetic or algebra, based on set theory, for merging and extracting from tables.

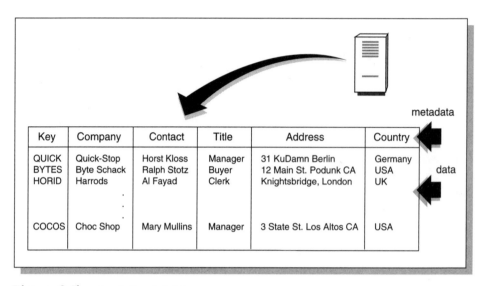

Figure 8-5: A relational database

At first every database vendor had its own special database query language. Users eventually got fed up enough to create an industry standard around IBM's SQL. There was the SQL'89 standard, followed by the SQL'92 standard, both created under the ANSI umbrella. But SQL is still fragmented into many subtly-different slightly incompatible dialects.

The JDBC classes do their work in terms of SQL, so it takes an understanding of SQL to describe what these are. SQL is a pretty elaborate programming language in its own right, customized to handle tables, rows and columns. Describing SQL would take more room than is available here. Suffice it to say that SQL has statements like SELECT, INSERT, DELETE, and UPDATE. Interested readers are referred to the further reading. SQL operates on tables; merging, matching and extracting from them and it provides its result sets in the form of further tables. We don't want Java to replace SQL; we just want Java to be able to bundle up SQL queries, direct them to the right database, and listen for the answers. The package that holds the Java code for the JDBC is called java.sql.

The JDBC API defines Java classes to represent database connections, SQL statements, result sets, database metadata (data about data), etc. It allows a Java programmer to issue SQL statements to read/write a database. The JDBC itself is written entirely in Java, will run anywhere and (from JDK 1.1 on) can be downloaded as part of an applet. JDBC access does not currently work in Internet Explorer. More software than just the JDBC may be needed to talk to a database, so the security model needs careful consideration if you want to use applets (i.e. can you connect to native code?).

The JDBC consists of an API (the specification of a library or application programmer's interface), and a package containing about 20 Java classes to implement the application program side of the API. Some of the classes are interfaces, and the code that implements them must be provided by an additional database-specific piece of software called a driver.

Java programs call methods in the JDBC package to connect with databases through their drivers, then retrieve, process, and write information. See Figure 8-5. The package that holds the Java code for the JDBC is called java.sql. We'll be saying more about SQL later. For now, just note that it is a specialized programming language used to access just about all databases. We don't want to make Java replace SQL, we just want Java to be able to bundle up SQL queries, direct them to the right database, and listen for the answers.

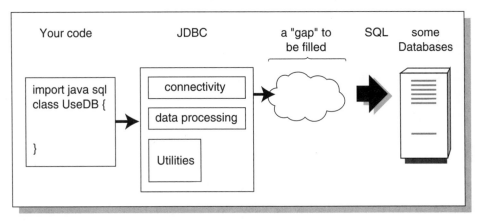

Figure 8-6: Where the JDBC fits

Note that we are not saying what kind of database is upstream from the JDBC. Your Java code knows very little about this. What your program does know is that by talking to the JDBC it can indirectly talk to a database, just as by talking to a broker you can accomplish a transaction (sell a house, shop for a new car, buy a diamond) through a third party you might never meet directly. This approach was pioneered by Borland with the Borland Database Engine and its IDAPI protocol. It was also one of the virtues claimed for ODBC.

Vendor independence is one of the reasons that the large commercial database users are excited by the Java-DBMS integration. These companies see great value in front-end software that doesn't lock them in to one particular database supplier. The network distributed feature of Java is an additional boost, making it almost trivial to build true distributed data processing systems.

The JDBC-ODBC Bridge

In the early 1990s there was a further development in the SQL world. Microsoft got involved in the process and used its monopoly leverage, just the way IBM used to, to impose the *Open DataBase Connectivity* (ODBC) standard on the industry. ODBC is an Application Programmer Interface that allows C programs to make calls into an SQL server and get back results. ODBC provided a unified way for Microsoft applications such as Access, Excel, FoxPro, and Btrieve to talk to IBM, Oracle, Paradox and other back end database systems.

Every database vendor was then pretty much obliged to provide not just a driver for their own dialect of SQL, but also a driver that would allow ODBC to communicate with their protocols. If they didn't support ODBC they would be locked out of the high volume PC desktop market.

Most of the ANSI SQL-2 databases out there now have ODBC drivers. So in order to provide instant Java connectivity to lots of products, Sun joined with Intersolv to create the jdbc.odbc package that implements the java.sql package for ODBC databases. This was a brilliant move as it leveraged (some would say "finessed") Microsoft's earlier work.

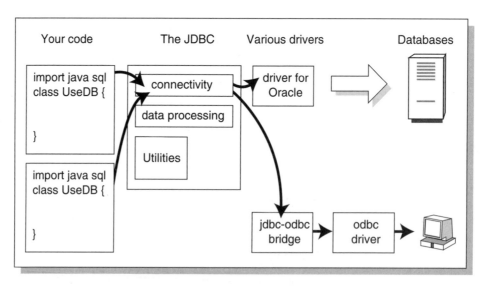

Figure 8-7: The JDBC-ODBC bridge

By creating an open standard for its desktop applications to connect to anybody's database, Microsoft also inadvertently provided a way for Java to connect to their standard, and thence to anybody's database. The JDBC-ODBC bridge implements the JDBC by making the appropriate calls to the ODBC Standard C API.

The JDBC-ODBC bridge is a little inefficient perhaps, using a driver to talk to a driver, but it provides instant connectivity to all popular databases. ODBC is a C language interface so the bridge needs to take Java types, and unhand them into C types on the way over to ODBC, and re-hand them on the way back. The JDBC-ODBC bridge is a separate C library that needs to be accessible to your code. There's a Java part that is a driver manager for the bridge, and a native code part that's the driver. Since it's native code, there are separate versions of the bridge driver for Windows and for Solaris.

People also talk about *tiers* of database access. This has nothing to do with how many drivers and driver managers are in the chain between the application and the database. It has to do with how the application code is partitioned. Before client/server, you had to connect directly to the system with the database and run your program on it. Such a mainframe might have hundreds or even thousands of terminals like the IBM 3270 attached to it. This was a one-tier solution.

In the early days of client/server, there was a simple split between code on the client and data on the server. That was the so-called "fat client" or two-tiered approach with no middleware. Now the model has become more refined: often the client only has code for the GUI, and there is separate application logic on a server, which the client accesses (often by browsing an applet on a Web page). The application logic in turn may talk to a database server on another system. The client never talks directly to the database. This is the three-tiered approach.

JDBC drivers have been classified by JavaSoft into four categories:

- type 1: JDBC-ODBC bridge. The cheapest alternative, as it is built on a PC standard. It requires some native code on the client side.

- type 2: Java-to-native API. The easiest driver for a vendor to implement. It converts JDBC calls into calls on the client API for a given database. It requires some native code on the client side.

- type 3: net protocol all-Java driver. This is the most flexible type as it connects to database vendor-neutral middleware.

- type 4: native-protocol all-Java driver: This gives the highest performance. Because it involves knowledge of the vendor-specific database access protocol, the database vendors will supply these kind of drivers.

The Classes in the JDBC

The JDBC Application Programmer Interface is implemented by about 20 Java classes, in the java.sql package. In Table 8-2, the 20-odd classes are divided into three groups concerned with connectivity, data processing, and utility functions.

Table 8-2: JDBClasses can be divided into three groups

Class	Purpose
Connectivity java.sql.DriverManager java.sql.Driver java.sql.DriverPropertyInfo java.sql.Connection	Manages the drivers that are registered with it Handles one specific type of database Gets and sets Connection properties Represents a session with a specific database. SQL statements are executed and results are returned for an individual connection
Data Processing java.sql.DatabaseMetaData java.sql.Statement java.sql.CallableStatement java.sql.PreparedStatement java.sql.ResultSet java.sql.ResultSetMetaData	Provide information on the database as a whole. Sends over an SQL statement. A variant on Statement (used to execute an SQL stored procedure). Another variant on Statement (holds a static pre-compiled SQL statement). These are often more efficient to execute. Holds the result of executing an SQL statement. Provides information on the types and properties of a ResultSet
Support java.sql.Types java.sql.Numeric java.sql.Date java.sql.Time java.sql.Timestamp java.sql.SQLException java.sql.SQLWarning java.sql.DataTruncation	Constants used by SQL Supports arbitrary precision numbers Supports dates Supports times Supports a combined date/time A database access exception class with more information added about the error A subclass of SQLException A subclass of SQLWarning relating to a data value being unexpectedly cut short.

The source for these classes and interfaces is provided, too.

Using the JDBC

There are four steps that all Java programs follow to talk to a database using the JDBC.

1. Load any drivers you are going to need.

2. Tell the JDBC what database you want to use.

3. Connect to that database.

4. SQL statements across the connection, and get results back.

Step 1: Load any drivers you are going to need

This is a system-specific step that depends on how exactly you will connect to the database. The drivers are the software component that "fill the gap" in Figure 9-5. There are several possibilities for how the gap may be filled. In Java, you will simply invoke the static method Class.forName("drivername"); using the actual name of the driver. The forName() method gets the runtime class descriptor, and has the side effect of loading the associated library or class into your Java runtime.

All databases have a driver at their end to accept queries, feed them into the database's internal form and deliver results. As Figure 8-8 shows, the driver for Oracle is specific to Oracle, the driver for Sybase is specific to Sybase and so on. Although just about all databases speak SQL in theory, they all actually have slightly incompatible local dialects of SQL.

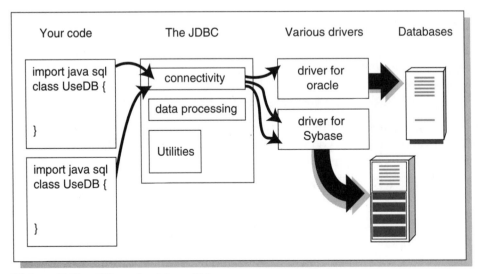

Figure 8-8: Where the drivers fit in

What's needed is a driver or a pipeline of drivers that speak to the JDBC at one end, and can speak the database dialect at the other end. Right here is where you can start to get into trouble, because there are no drivers supplied with the JDBC. You have to obtain them from the database vendors or from the third party tools companies. These companies are flourishing filling this need and will usually let you download an evaluation copy of a driver for a limited use period.

Although these driver components are essential to use the JDBC, this is a "batteries not included" kind of deal. If you want to run a Java program that accesses a database, you need to additionally procure both the database and its drivers. The drivers could be in the form of a Java program, or (more likely at this point) a dynamically linked library of native code, which must be loaded into your running Java system.

The slickest kind of driver implements the JDBC interfaces and talks directly to the database server with no other intervening code. It's a big programming job to get the proprietary and usually unpublished database protocols working, and it must be rewritten for each kind of database. It offers the best performance however.

Another implementation possibility is a bit simpler: provide some code that talks to the JDBC at one end, and can speak the language expected by an existing database driver at the other. This code in the middle is, of course, termed *middleware*. Such a driver would be a bridge between JDBC and the database driver at the back end. We'll say more about this later.

Step 2: Specify what database you want to use

There can be several programs active on one system and talking to different databases at one time. You need to tell the JDBC which one will be used by this program. Rather than giving a file name (which doesn't scale across different machines very well), you tell the JDBC what database you want to use in the form of a URL. An example URL might be like the one shown in Figure 8-9.

As you might guess, the form and content of the URL is very specific to individual databases and the drivers you will use for access. Whether or not the port number is necessary, or even required, is a driver-dependent feature, as are the parameters in the URL after the subprotocol (odbc, here). You just have to read the documentation that comes with the driver.

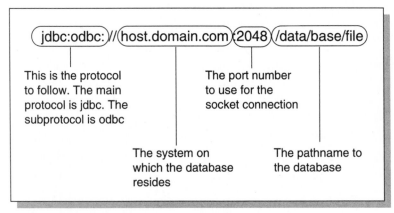

Figure 8-9: A URL tells the JDBC what database to use

Step 3: Connect to that database

This is the point where your code registers with the JDBC. You will use the connectivity classes to connect to the database of interest. Your program can be talking to several different databases at once. For this reason, the JDBC package is sometimes called a *driver manager*, which can be anything that controls multiple drivers. However, the JDBC does a lot more than just manage a few drivers.

Your application program needs to tell the driver manager to open a connection to the URL you put together in Step 2. Making the connection is an iterative process: the JDBC driver manager will load all the drivers it can find and ask each in turn to try to process the URL. The driver manager looks up a property called "jdbc.drivers" in the system properties table. This should contain a list of class names for driver classes, separated by colons. You can set these in a ~/.hotjava/ properties file, which might contain a property key/value pair like:

```
jdbc.drivers=foo.bah.Driver:wombat.sql.Driver:some.other.ourDriver
```

The DriverManager class will attempt to load each of these driver classes. If you have all the right software "glue" in place, then one of them will be able to connect to that URL successfully. The rest will fail silently, without throwing an exception. Typically there will only be a handful of drivers on any given system, so the connection is established very quickly.

Step 4: Send SQL statements across the connection and get results back

Once you have a connection open to your database, you will start sending SQL statements across and getting back result sets. Some database APIs have special mechanisms to support asynchronous querying, but this is not needed by Java. You simply create a new thread for any SQL statement that might take a long time. Be careful to ensure that you only use the java.sql classes in a "thread-safe" manner. That is, you are responsible for providing synchronization and avoiding data races where necessary.

Queries and updates are sent across to the database in the form of SQL statements, which are just Strings containing the SQL text. The results usually come back as something called a "Result Set." Some SQL statements just return an integer, while one SQL statement (DDL) returns nothing. If you refer back to the list of classes in the JDBC, you'll notice there is one called ResultSet that has many methods for retrieving the result of executing an SQL statement.

The result will usually be in the form of a table (several rows each of several columns of data). There are methods to access individual rows by index and to get the data back as a String or some other type. There is also a class ResultSetMeta-Data. *Meta* is a Greek word meaning "I will try to impress you by using Greek words." In computer science it means "information about," so the meta-data of a result set is merely the information about the data in a result set (the number of columns and rows, their names and sizes, and so on). The ResultSet lets you look at the values you got back. The ResultSetMetaData lets you look at the types.

When you have finished all the processing, close everything down in an orderly manner.

Code Example of Database Access

This section presents a step-by-step example of the actual set-up and code for an access to a database using Java. This is a one tiered access because everything is on one system: the application, the JDBC, the bridge, and the database. On the other hand we are stringing all these components together in just the way you need to for a multi-tiered approach. There is a large number of different databases, access methods, and host platforms, so the example I have chosen to present is the one that can be tried at least cost for most people. It uses a small scale database MS-Access on Windows 95, rather than an industrial-strength database like Oracle, Sybase or Informix on an enterprise server system. The principle remains the same however.

The example has a Java application that talks to the JDBC, and then a bridge from JDBC to ODBC, ending up at an ODBC database. This example shows how to configure everything if you are going in across the bridge. But, bear in mind that the JDBC-ODBC bridge is really just an interim solution while we wait for vendors to provide direct access drivers. You don't have to use the bridge and if you have a more direct driver, you wouldn't. Before a direct driver is available, developers can use the ODBC drivers to begin development, and later switch to a JDBC driver and avoid two layers of driver software.

The JDBC-ODBC bridge (which also contains a driver to interface to the ODBC driver) translates JDBC calls into ODBC calls. Thus, it allows the JDBC to talk to an ODBC driver front ending a database. It's a bridge in the sense that it allows you to pass over a rocky chasm separating two different protocols. The standard Java JDBC-ODBC bridge does not currently work if you are using a Microsoft Java compiler. This is because Microsoft has not yet implemented the standard Java Native Interface.

This example describes how your Java application can use the JDBC to process a Microsoft Access database running under Windows 95. Frankly, the process depends on a long chain of actions, each of which must be done exactly right, to avoid mysterious failures. You should read through all these steps before trying it for yourself. And with that warning in mind, here goes.

Step 1. Make sure you have MS-Access for Windows 95, version 7.00 or later running on your Windows 95 system.

Typical error: Trying to use MS Access version 2.0. The 16-bit Windows 3.1 version of MS Access cannot be used as JDBC uses the 32-bit ODBC which Microsoft only supplies in Access for Windows 95/NT. The downrev version of Access will result in the following error in Step 7:

```
Unable to load dll "JdbcOdbc.dll" (errcode = 45a)
*** SQLException caught ***

SQLState: 08001
Message:  No suitable driver
Vendow:   0
```

The message indicates that you do not have the 32-bit ODBC driver for the database you are trying to access.

Step 2. The "typical installation" option of MS Access for Windows 95 does not include the ODBC drivers you require. If necessary, go back and reinstall everything in MS Access to get the ODBC drivers on your system. This will make a "32-bit ODBC" icon appear on your control panel.

The 32-bit MS-Access driver for ODBC comes with Access 95 / Office Pro. It is not a standard part of Windows 95.

Typical error: Mistaking the "ODBC" icon on your Windows 95 control panel for the required "32bit ODBC" icon.

Step 3. Set up a Data Source Name for the sample database. Open the "32-bit ODBC" icon on your Control Panel to bring up the "Data Sources" panel then press "add" to bring up "Add Data Source" and highlight "Microsoft Access Driver (*.mdb)" and press "OK."

This brings up a panel labeled "ODBC Microsoft Access 7.0 Setup" in which you enter a Data Source Name. Use "myDSN." Also enter the description "bananas." Then press Database: "Select," which brings up a file chooser panel.

Choose the pathname C:\Access\Samples\Northwind.mdb, which is one of the sample databases that comes with Access, assuming you installed in C:\Access. If you installed in a different place, use that path to the Northwind.mdb file instead.

Press "OK" and get back to the "Data Sources" panel, where you should now see the entry "myDSN." You have successfully associated the Data Source Name and 32bit ODBC with the Access database.

Step 4. Set up the Java side to match this DSN. Make certain that the Java program names the right database. The program is on the CD and is called simple.java. It contains:

```java
import java.sql.*;
class simple {

  public static void main (String args[]) {

            String url   = "jdbc:odbc:myDSN";
            String query = "SELECT * FROM Customers "
                           + "WHERE CustomerID = 'QUICK'";
    try {
      // Load the jdbc-odbc bridge driver
      Class.forName ("sun.jdbc.odbc.JdbcOdbcDriver");

      // Attempt to connect to a driver.
      Connection con = DriverManager.getConnection (
                                   url, "", "" );

      // Create a Statement object so we can submit
      // SQL statements to the driver
      Statement stmt = con.createStatement ();

      // Submit a query, creating a ResultSet object
                ResultSet rs = stmt.executeQuery (query);

      // Display all columns and rows from the result set
                printResultSet (rs);

      rs.close();
      stmt.close();
      con.close();
    }
    catch (SQLException ex) {
        while (ex != null) {
      System.out.println ("SQL Exception:   " +
              ex.getMessage ());
            ex = ex.getNextException ();
        }
      }
      catch (java.lang.Exception ex) {
        ex.printStackTrace ();
      }
    }

  private static void printResultSet (ResultSet rs)
        throws SQLException
  {
    int numCols = rs.getMetaData().getColumnCount ();

    while ( rs.next() ) {
      for (int i=1; i<=numCols; i++) {
        System.out.print(rs.getString(i) + " | " );
          }
      System.out.println();
    }
  }
 }
}
```

The SQL statement in this program retrieves the record for the customer key "QUICK." There are two declarations right at the beginning of the main routine, URL and query. When you have this working, you can try changing

```
String url = "jdbc:odbc:myDSN";
```

to point to another database. You could also change query to:

```
String query = "SELECT * FROM Customers";
```

This would make it retrieve every customer record. Half a dozen lines down, the connection line is:

```
Connection con = DriverManager.getConnection(
                    url, "", "" );
```

The two null strings are for user-id and password. The program source is set up correctly as it is, but these are some things to try experimenting with.

Step 5. Compile the Java program

```
javac Simple.java
```

Fix any compilation errors that show up (typically problems caused by not setting classpath correctly).

Step 6. Run the Java program

```
java Simple
```

You should see one entry in the Customers table print out.

```
QUICK | QUICK-Stop | Horst Kloss | Accounting Manager | ....
```

You can look at this table using Access, and confirm that the record is correct.

Review of Classes

This section takes a closer look at some of the important classes used in the preceding program and in the JDBC generally. It highlights some of the important methods of each.

Connectivity classes

`java.sql.DriverManager` manages the drivers that are registered with it.

```
public static synchronized Connection getConnection(String url)
        throws SQLException;
// try to establish a connection to the given database URL

public static Driver getDriver(String url)
        throws SQLException;

// try to find a driver that understands this URL.

public static synchronized void registerDriver(java.sql.Driver driver)
        throws SQLException;
// how a newly loaded driver tells the driver manager about itself

public static void setLoginTimeout(int seconds) {
// maximum time a database login can take before failing.

public static void setLogStream(java.io.PrintStream out) {
// Set the logging/tracing PrintStream
```

`java.sql.Driver` handles one specific type of database. This class is an interface.

```
Connection connect(String url, java.util.Properties info)
            throws SQLException;
// try to connect to the database at the given URL

boolean acceptsURL(String url) throws SQLException;
// return true if the driver thinks it can process url.
```

`java.sql.Connection` represents a session with a specific database. SQL statements are executed and results are returned for an individual connection. This class is an interface.

```
Statement createStatement() throws SQLException;
// a statement is an SQL string to send to the database.

void setAutoCommit(boolean autoCommit) throws SQLException;
// By default the Connection automatically commits
// changes after executing each statement. If auto commit has been
// disabled an explicit commit must be done or database changes
// will not be saved.

DatabaseMetaData getMetaData() throws SQLException;;
// get the metadata.

void commit() throws SQLException;
// makes all changes since the previous commit/rollback

void rollback() throws SQLException;
// drops all changes made since previous commit/rollback
```

There are other, more advanced methods in this interface, too.

Data processing classes

`java.sql.Statement` sends over an SQL statement. This class is an interface.

```
ResultSet executeQuery(String sql) throws SQLException;
// Execute a SQL statement that returns a single ResultSet

int executeUpdate(String sql) throws SQLException;
// Execute a SQL DDL, INSERT, UPDATE or DELETE statement

void close() throws SQLException;
// close the database

void cancel() throws SQLException;
// can be used by one thread to cancel a statement being
// executed by another thread.

SQLWarning getWarnings() throws SQLException;
// executing a statement clears the old value of Warnings
// and possibly creates a list of new warnings.
```

`java.sql.ResultSet` holds the result of executing an SQL statement. This class is an interface. A ResultSet provides access to a table of data generated by executing a Statement. The table rows are retrieved in sequence. Within a row its column values can be accessed in any order.

```
String getString(int columnIndex) throws SQLException;
// Get the value of a column in the current row as a String

boolean getBoolean(int columnIndex) throws SQLException;
// ... as a boolean
// there are also corresponding methods to get value of the
// entry in that column as any kind of Java primitive type,
// and as an SQL.Numeric, a byte array, a Time, Date, or Timestamp,
// ASCII stream, Unicode Stream, a binaryStream, or an Object!
// if you can put it into a database, Java can pull it out.

SQLWarning getWarnings() throws SQLException;
// get warning messages

void clearWarnings() throws SQLException;
// clear warning messages

ResultSetMetaData getMetaData() throws SQLException;
// get metadata describing the number, types and properties of
// a ResultSet's columns. The first column number is 1, not 0.

boolean next() throws SQLException;
// true if the current row is valid. False when no more rows.
```

`java.sql.ResultSetMetaData` provides information on the types and properties of a ResultSet.

```
int getColumnCount() throws SQLException;
// the number of columns in this result set

boolean isCaseSensitive(int column) throws SQLException;
// does upper/lower case matter in this column?

boolean isSearchable(int column) throws SQLException;
// can this column be used in a 'WHERE' clause?

boolean isCurrency(int column) throws SQLException;
// is this column a cash value?

int isNullable(int column) throws SQLException;
// can you store null in this column

String getColumnLabel(int column) throws SQLException;
// what is the full name of the column?

String getColumnName(int column) throws SQLException;
// what is the column known as internally?

String getSchemaName(int column) throws SQLException;
// get the schema (loosely "plan") name for the table that
// this column came from.

boolean isReadOnly(int column) throws SQLException;
// is this column definitely not writeable?
```

Useful URLs

You will find more information about Java database connectivity at the following URLs:

http://www.xdb.com/home.htm

http://www.weblogic.com

http://www.microsoft.com/vfoxpro/vfinfo/vfpodbc.htm

http://dataramp.com/

http://splash.javasoft.com/jdbc/

http://www.vincent.se/

These URLs are for companies that are producing commercial JDBC (or jdbc-odbc) drivers and tools.

If you are on a tight budget, then consider the Postgres95 software. It can be downloaded for free, and it has a Java class library available. Further details are at URL: http://www.ki.net/postgres95/

Some Light Relief

Those Messy Messages

How many times have you encountered some kind of software failure, and ended up with an error message that told you precisely nothing? If you've been programming for any length of time at all, you'll recognize this as an all-too-familiar source of frustration.

The all time classic used to be the Unix "bus error-core dumped" but that has been replaced in recent years by the infamous Microsoft Windows "GPF." What are systems programmers thinking of when they design error messages like that? Are they deliberately trying to confuse and annoy applications programmers?

Well, no. We hardly ever try to do that deliberately. The problem arises because at the point where the problem is detected in the operating system kernel, there is no application-specific knowledge to report the problem in terms meaningful to the user. Let me give you an example of what I mean.

Inside Sun's operating system development group, there is a special interest committee known as the Ease-of-Use group. I was a co-founder and ardent supporter of this free-ranging think tank some years ago, and was for a long period the representative from kernel software development.

One day the Ease-of-Use committee decided to study kernel messages and see if there were any candidates for improvement. The person who did the study was an experienced technical writer, skilled in the art of communication, and she found many kernel error messages to complain of, including these ones:

Bad terminal owner

bread error, fatstart

Error walking tree %s.

FAT size error

Flushing job

Hit BOTTOM

lpExec confused.

object exists in wastebasket

Out of register space (ugh) allocator

POSSIBLE ATTACK from %s: newline in string "%s"

That must be tomorrow

real error

repeated leap second moment

runt packet

Bogus wildcard from %s

I read through this list, and the first thing that jumped out at me was that these were all reasonable error messages, so what was the problem? Then I read the list again, and thought about it a bit longer and the reason became clear: Every one of these messages was ambiguous. If you didn't have programming experience, you would only see the English meaning. If you did have programming experience, in this context you would only see the programming meaning. Table 8-3 explains this more clearly.

Table 8-3: Interpreting error messages

Error	English Meaning	Programming Meaning
Bad terminal owner device.	The person who bought the system has been naughty.	The system has lost track of the process that controls this device.
bread error, fatstart.	Something to do with putting on weight if you eat too much bread.	There was an error when we tried to read one of the blocks near the beginning of the File Allocation Table.
Error walking tree.	Something went wrong when we were trying to take a tree for a walk.	An invalid pointer was found as we were traversing the data structure known as a "tree."
Hit BOTTOM	User needs spanking.	Unexpectedly encountered the end of a table
Flushing job.	More toilet humor.	This process is being completely removed from the queue of the shell.
real error	As opposed to a fake one?	An error in a real (floating-point) number calculation.
repeated leap second moment	What? We have leap years and leap days, but surely we don't have leap seconds?	Actually we do, perhaps James Gosling was right after all to comment on it at length in the Date.java class.
object exists in wastebasket	How can the computer possibly know how untidy my office is?	The wastebasket icon on the window desktop has a discarded object in it.
Out of register space (ugh) allocator.	What is "ugh" supposed to add to this?	I'm tempted to pretend that "ugh" is the Universal Graphic Hash code, but actually it conveys that a distasteful and irrecoverable error situation has occurred in the code generator. It has encountered an expression so complex that it has bedeviled the compiler.
That must be tomorrow	Too whimsical?	This message is the response from shutdown when you give an invalid time.

. . . and so on. The point is that both parties have merit here. The programmer has chosen brief messages that describe the situation well—to other programmers. The Ease-of-Use fan has demonstrated that the messages are surprisingly easy to misinterpret. Neither party has understood the perspective of the other. It's clearly a mistake to demand that users have a programming background. On the other hand we can't expect every diagnostic message from the kernel to be meaningful to the lay person, but neither should it be ambiguous.

The moral is clear: As systems programmers we must avoid ambiguous messages. We must spell out the full name of data structures where possible. We don't necessarily have to make a message meaningful to the end user, but at least it must be incapable of misinterpretation. Don't tell users "hit bottom" when "item not found in table" will do just as well. Whenever you write an error message that will be seen by the user, take an extra minute to phrase it with care.

I'll finish by presenting one final example. I like this because it reveals a programmer who's trying hard, but can't quite let go of the techno-babble:

```
Printer out of media (paper).
```

That error used to be in PrintTool, but we have since sent the programmer to a re-education camp, and it has now been changed to

```
Printer out of paper (media).
```

Hey, even small improvements count.

Further Reading

Java Database Programming with JDBC

by Pratik Patel
published by Coriolis, 1996.

CHAPTER
9

- How the Java Abstract Window Toolkit Works

- Services Provided by the AWT

- All About Event Handling

- All About AWT Controls

- All About Containers

- Layout in a Container

- Tying Up Loose Ends

The Abstract
Window Toolkit

"Mach is the biggest intellectual fraud of the last decade."
"Really, not X-Windows?"
"I said 'intellectual.'"

—overheard in Silicon Valley

The Java Abstract Window Toolkit (AWT) continues the portability goals of the language. It provides a common user interface on systems with wildly-different native window systems. The Java AWT interface does this in a clever way: It offers the functions that are common to all window systems. The AWT code then uses the underlying native (or "peer") window system to actually render the screen images and manipulate GUI objects. The AWT thus consists of a series of abstract interfaces along with Java code to map them into the actual native code on each system. This is why it is an *abstract* window toolkit; it is not tailored for a specific computer but offers the same API on all.

Supporting a Java interface to the underlying native window system has the benefit of making Java GUI programs highly portable, but it comes at the cost of a little inefficiency: peer events must be translated into Java events before they can be handled by Java code. An additional characteristic, which can be a plus or a minus, depending on your view, is that Java programs have the look and feel of the native window system on each platform. A Java program on the Mac looks like a regular Mac program. The exact same Java executable run on Windows 95 takes on the Windows look and feel.

Some users have expressed a preference instead for one universal Java look and feel with the same appearance on all platforms. The Java Foundation Classes fulfill this need. At the April 1997 JavaOne conference, Sun announced a set of Java Foundation Classes (JFC) that essentially merge the AWT with similar work from Netscape. The JFC is being worked on by Sun, Apple, IBM, and Netscape. It will be shipped as part of the JDK 1.2 release and will add to the components described here. A preview of some early components of JFC is given in Chapter 11.

Sun has hinted that peer classes will go away for JDK 1.2. This is perfectly feasible technically and, if done right, will not have any impact on programmers or their programs, except to make things run more reliably. Incompatible peer behavior is a big source of headaches for everyone.

How the Java Abstract Window Toolkit Works

The AWT currently requires the native window system to be running on the platform because it uses the native window system to support windows within Java. Figure 9-1 shows how the Java AWT interacts with the native window system.

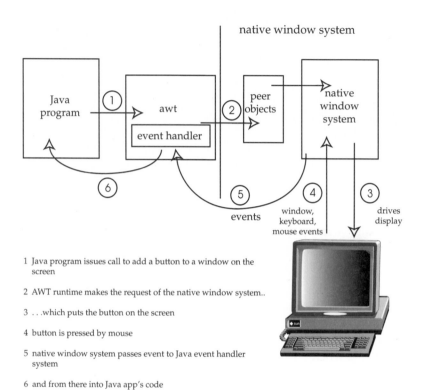

1 Java program issues call to add a button to a window on the screen

2 AWT runtime makes the request of the native window system..

3 . . .which puts the button on the screen

4 button is pressed by mouse

5 native window system passes event to Java event handler system

6 and from there into Java app's code

Figure 9-1:   How the Java abstract window toolkit works

Mnemonic: Peer objects let your Java runtime "peer" at the underlying window implementation. They are only of interest to people porting the Java Development Kit. To a Java applications programmer, all window system code is written in Java.

The policy of supporting the "highest common factor" of all the supported native window toolkits works well. The windowing operations that are common to all toolkits tend to be the most useful ones. Highest-common-factor GUI toolkits are not a new idea. It is a new idea to support a highest-common-factor toolkit as a class library that is highly integrated with its own general-purpose programming language.

How the AWT Smooths Over Hardware Differences

Where there are big differences in window tookits, Java adopts conventions that smooth over the differences. For example,

> Macs have one button on the mouse
> PCs have two buttons on the mouse
> Unix systems have three buttons on the mouse (left, right, and center).

Java deals with this hardware difference by adopting the convention that mice have three buttons. If the GUI invites a user to "click on the right button," a one-button mouse user can simulate it by holding down the META key while clicking. There is sample code for this later in the chapter.

It would be possible to approach the GUI with a different philosophy and have the Java AWT support on every platform every operation that is supported by one native toolkit. This would require a huge amount of extra implementation and maintenance effort for a small increase in functionality. It would be completely the wrong direction.

Window systems have become too complicated and overblown in recent years. When there are 1,000-page manuals explaining the Microsoft Windows API, when you are pretty much obliged to use a development environment for MS Windows programming, and when it takes hundreds of lines of code to put a window on the screen (using X Windows), you know that it's time for something simpler and better. Supporting only the window operations that are common to all toolkits means that programmers have an easier job learning the window toolkit. Java software gets written faster and is less buggy. Sure, it may not feature "balloon help," but you can have it now and it works.

You can write Java windowing programs with one specific platform in mind, but you get code that runs on all the other platforms for free. Application software companies no longer have to produce different versions of their software for each supported platform. As soon as these companies transition their products to Java, on which they are working flat out, we will no longer see "123 for Windows 3.x," "123 for Windows 95," "123 for Solaris." There will just be "123 for Java."

Platform portability, even for GUI programs, is a huge and compelling reason to program in Java. Even people who run on only one kind of computer and don't care about making their own programs portable should be interested in portability. Platform portability means that we can all choose from a much greater variety of application software products. Software vendors have a potential market of the 240 million Java-capable computer systems, rather than only the 20 million Macs or the 40 million MS-DOS systems or the 7 million Unix systems.

Services Provided by the AWT

The Abstract Window Toolkit provides five services to the programmer.

- A set of the usual GUI components (controls or widgets): buttons, menus, choices, checkboxes, scrollbars, text input fields, and so on

- An event handling system that notices when the user adjusts one of the controls and conveys that information to the program

- The concept of containers—objects that form a backdrop and to which you can add controls

- Some layout managers that provide help in automatically positioning where a control goes when you add it to a container

- Simple support for graphics operations: draw an arc, fill a polygon, clip a rectangle, etc.

In this chapter, I use the PC term *control* to mean the group of all the GUI things that users can press, scroll, choose between, type into, draw on, etc. In the Unix world, a control is called a *widget*. Neither control nor widget is a Java term, and in reality there is no control class. However, it's so useful to be able to say "control" instead of "GUI thing that the user interacts with" or "Components plus menus" that we use the term here wherever convenient. Because each control is a subclass of Component, each control (button, etc.) also inherits all the methods and data fields of Component.

The important top-level classes that make up the AWT are shown in Figure 9-2.

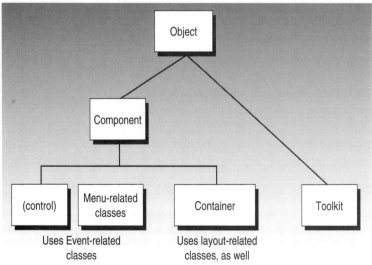

Figure 9-2:   The most important of the AWT classes

The basic idea is that you:

- Declare controls. You can subclass them to add to the behavior, but this is often not necessary.

- Add the controls to a container. Again, subclassing is possible but frequently not necessary.

- Implement an interface to get the event handler that responds to control activity.

It's a little challenging to explain all this because the first three topics (controls, events, and containers) fit together closely, so that you have to understand a bit of all of them before you can fully understand any of them. To tackle that thorny problem, I will briefly outline Component and the two main other classes—controls and containers—and then describe event handling in full. Next, we will look at all the dozen or so individual controls in depth. This amounts to quite a few pages, so I recommend you read one or two in depth, then just look at the screen dumps to see what each does. Return to the appropriate section in the chapter as you need actual code examples. Finally, we will revisit containers and related material. The topic of graphics programming forms a separate chapter following this one. The graphics material is (thankfully) simple, but there is a lot of it.

Overview of Component

Object-oriented programming fits well with window systems. The concept of making new controls by subclassing existing ones and overriding part of their behavior saves time and effort. Another philosophical similarity is the way that controls have to handle events just as objects handle messages. (Method calls are equivalent to sending a message).

As you can see in Figure 9-2, there is a parent class called Component that is the parent class for most of the things that can appear on screen. The basic ingredients of a GUI (buttons, text fields, scrollbars, lists, and so on) are all subclasses of the class called Component. Menu is an exception—it's an on-screen thing that isn't a subclass of Component. That exception was made for practical implementation reasons, but menu is philosophically a control like any other.

Component is the class that holds information about the visible appearance of an on-screen object:

- Location

- Size (current, preferred, minimum, and maximum)

- Color

- Current font

- What the cursor looks like on this component at this moment

- Locale

- Whether is currently visible or invisible on the screen

- Ability to accept input (enabled or disabled)

- The "toolkit," which has useful information and methods about the screen this component is painted onto

- Validity, i.e., whether it needs to be laid out (repositioned) again

- A paint() routine that will render it on the screen

Component has methods to get and set many of these attributes. You can and should review all the methods by running

```
javap java.awt.Component
```

Controls, Containers, Components . . . Where Will It All End?	
Here's the way to tell these three similar-sounding names apart!	
Control	Not a Java term. This is the PC term for what is called a widget in the Unix world. It's a software thingie on the screen (a button, scroll bar, etc).
Container	These are screen windows that physically contain groups of controls or other containers. You can move or hide or show a Container and all its contents in one operation.
Component	A collective name for Controls and Containers. They have some common operations so Component is their common parent class.

There are essentially two kinds of Component: controls and containers. These correspond to "things that interact with the user" and "backdrops to put them on," respectively.

> ### What are Peerless or Lightweight Components?
>
> Peerless components, also called lightweight components, were formally introduced at JavaOne in April 1997. They are the basis for the Java Foundation Classes implementation. They are components or controls that do not rely on a native implementations but instead are solely based upon existing AWT components.
>
> Lightweight components are transparent; you can see the background of their container through them. A lightweight component is typically created by extending Component and overriding paint().

Overview of Controls

The controls are: Button, Canvas, Checkbox, Choice, Label, List, Scrollbar, TextField, TextArea, and the variations on Menu. Each control has methods appropriate to what it does. The Scrollbar control has methods to set the width, orientation, and height of scrollbars, for instance. We'll examine each individual control in depth later in the chapter. One obvious control that is missing is a control into which you can write HTML and have it automatically formatted. More controls will be added with the Java Foundation Classes, adopted from Netscape's Internet Foundation Classes. This has been announced for the JDK 1.2 release.

Overview of Containers

The AWT class called Container is the kind of component whose purpose is to hold several controls. An example is the container called Window, which may hold, for example, a scrollbar, text field, and a button. A Container is essentially a rectangular portion of the screen that allows you to treat several individual controls as a group. You don't display a control directly; you add it to a Container, and it is the container that gets displayed. Container is the class that holds information about:

- The number of components in it; a container can contain nested containers as well as controls

- The way to lay out its control contents on the screen

- The size of the border, or "insets," around the edge

- A paint() routine that will render it on the screen

Container also has methods to get and set many of these attributes and to add and remove Components from itself. Because Container is a subclass of Component, it also inherits all the methods and data fields of Component, like getting and setting the cursor. Containers must have their initial size set before they will show up on the screen. Set their size by using

```
public void setSize(int width, int height)
```

or

```
public void setBounds(int x, int y, int width, int height).
```

The units are pixels (dots on the screen).

The various subclasses of Container have small differences between them. A Window is a basic free-floating window that can be moved around the screen. A Panel is a Container that is nested in some larger Container and cannot be moved independently. A Frame is a subclass of Window that adds a title string and a menu bar on which you can add several menus, each with a number of menu items.

Let's take a look at the simplest example of putting a Container on the screen. In earlier chapters, we have already seen the code to pop up a window for an applet (since all applets run in a panel, having an applet means that we have already implicitly used a container). The most frequently used kind of Container is a subclass of Window, known as a Frame. Here is the code to put up a Frame from an application.

```
import java.awt.*;
    public class cherry {
        static Frame f = new Frame("cherry");

        public static void main(String[] a) {
            f.setSize(300,100);
            f.show();
    }
}
```

Compiling and executing this program will cause a Frame like that shown in Figure 9-3 to appear on the screen. Pretty simple, yes?

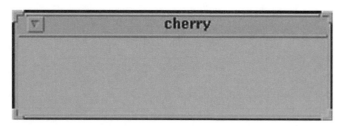

Figure 9-3:   The Frame Is a Subclass of Container.

A `Frame` is a window with a title bar. Here, we just gave it the title on the title bar of "cherry." Almost everything that you can see on the screen from Java is ultimately taking place in a `Frame` or a `Panel`. These are the "corkboards" or containers to which we attach scrollbars, text fields, menu items, etc., etc.

At this point we now have enough background knowledge of the various GUI elements to present an in-depth treatment of how they talk to your code. Read on for the fascinating details!

All About Event Handling

We'll start with a few words of explanation about the programming model for window systems. Unlike procedural programs in which things happen sequentially from beginning to end, windowing programs are asynchronous. You cannot predict at any given instance which of the on-screen buttons, menus, frames, etc., the user will touch. Accordingly, a model known as *event-driven programming* is used.

In event-driven programming, the logic of your code is inverted. Instead of one flow of control from beginning to end, the window system sits in a "window main loop" simply waiting for user input. When the user touches something on screen with the mouse pointer, the window system catches that event and passes it on to a handler that you earlier supplied. This is known as a callback, and your handler is a *callback routine* because the window system calls back to it when the event happens. Your handler will deal with the graphics event and the action that is associated with it. If a button says "press here to read the file," then your button handler must handle the button event and also read the file in. Handling a button event just means noticing that it occurred and doing the associated action, but other events may involve some drawing on the screen. Dragging something with the mouse is just repeatedly drawing it under the mouse coordinates as it moves, for instance.

The "event model" is the name we give to the framework that turns a GUI interaction (mouse click, menu selection, button press, etc.) into a call to your code that processes it. The event model can also be used for something unrelated to the GUI, like a timer going off. In other words, the event model is the design for connecting arbitrary actions, termed *events*, with your code to handle them. Obviously the runtime system can't just directly call your event handling routines because the runtime library doesn't even see your code until it is asked to run it. So, the event model can't know in advance which Components you will be using and which of your routines are there to handle their events. It has to be told somehow.

Summary of AWT Event Handling: JDK1.0 vs JDK 1.1

Event handling changed completely in JDK 1.1 mostly in order to better accommodate JavaBeans. In the JDK 1.0.2, the event handling callbacks were based on inheritance. Your event handling code had to be subclassed from Component so it would override the Component's handleEvent() or action() method. You may see this code when you maintain older Java programs, so a description of it appears in Appendix A of this book.

In the JDK 1.1, the callbacks are based on delegation: there is an interface for listening to each kind of event (mouse event, button event, scrollbar event, etc.). When an event occurs, the window system calls a method of a class that implements the specific listener interface. You create a class of your own that implements the appropriate interface, and register it with the window system. When that event occurs, the method that you have delegated (appointed) will be called back by the window system.

JDK 1.1 event handling is a big improvement on the former model, and as Java programmers we should always use it and try to help it become universally adopted. The problem is that there are a lot of browsers still in use that support only JDK 1.0. Until the whole world has upgraded to JDK 1.1, there will be an issue with older browsers not being able to run applets with the newer event handling. So, you need to carefully consider who will try to run your applets and what browsers they might use. My advice and practice is to give people an incentive to upgrade by using the new event model exclusively, but that might not be the right answer for all organizations and programmers.

Never use a mixture of the two event models in the same program. That is not supported and will lead to bugs that can only be solved by a rewrite.

JDK 1.0 Event Model

We summarize the old JDK 1.0 model here because you might see it in old code or have to maintain programs that use it. If you'd rather not confuse matters by learning something outdated, just skip to the next section.

The original event model as implemented in all releases of the JDK up to JDK 1.0.2 was based on inheritance. The AWT class Component is the parent class of most screen controls (scrollbar, button, check box, etc.). Component has a method called handleEvent() that the runtime system calls whenever the user does something like click the mouse or press a button. The 1.0 programmer could provide his/her own version of handleEvent() to override the default Component handleEvent() and actually handle the event.

In an application (in contrast to an applet), the programmer usually needs to subclass the various screen controls in order to insert the overriding version of handleEvent. It is easier in an Applet because Applet extends Panel which extends `Container` which extends `Component`. Thus, providing a routine called `handleEvent()` inside an applet automatically makes it part of the right inheritance hierarchy to receive events (without subclassing any Components). The default routine `handleEvent()` looks at the incoming event and splits off mouse-related events, keypress-related events, and action (control-generated) events into further methods which could alternatively be overridden.

The JDK 1.0 Event model had a number of problems. It worked tolerably for small, low-volume programs, but because all events got passed up the inheritance hierarchy (whether the consumer wanted them or not), it didn't scale well. It had performance problems for high frequency events like mouse motions. Worst of all, it didn't adapt well to the needs of Java beans (software components).

JDK 1.1 Event Model

JDK 1.1 introduced a new event handling model, called the *delegation-based* model. A better name would be "registration based" event handling. You don't subclass; instead, your code tells the window system "send those events of yours to these methods of mine." It is a bit simpler than the inheritance-based model, and because it doesn't rely on overriding methods that are inherited by `Applet`, the code is the same in both applets and applications. Your code has a number of controls that can fire events (mouse clicks, button presses, etc.), and your code has a number of methods that handle events. *Firing* an event just means causing or generating it. You connect an event handler with an event generator by registering a callback with it, as shown in Figure 9-4.

You can now get all varieties of events from all varieties of components, which was not true under the old model. If you want to handle mouse clicks from a button, this is now possible. If you have registered listeners for both mouse clicks and button pushes, the same, one event will be fired to both listeners (which is good). Under the old model, a mouse click over a button was always interpreted as pressing the button.

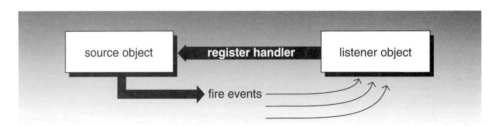

Figure 9-4: How Events are passed in JDK 1.1

If you are not 100% clear on callbacks, go back and read the section at the end of Chapter 4 on "Using Interfaces Dynamically." It is essential that you understand callbacks fully because they form the basis of the new event handling model. 🍒

The event information that gets fired, or passed, from the source to the listener is simply an object that has several data fields holding information about where on the screen the event took place, what the event is, how many mouse clicks, or the state of a checkbox, and so on. There is a general `java.util.EventObject` type, and all AWT events are children of that, as shown in Figure 9-5.

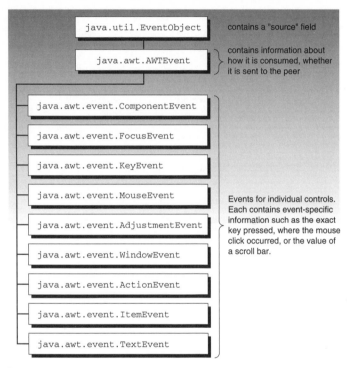

Figure 9-5:   The hierarchy of Event Objects in JDK 1.1

In the new JDK 1.1 event handling model, in an applet the button is declared as before.

```
public class myClass extends Applet {

    Button plum = new Button("press me");

    public void init() {
        add(plum);   // add the button to the applet

        plum.addActionListener(myButtonHandlerObj);
```

The callback for a button press is registered by calling the method `addActionLis-tener`. This is a method in `Button` that takes as a parameter an interface called `ActionListener`. Your applet will need to declare an instance of the class that implements the `ActionListener` interface and that you intend to be the event handler for this button.

```
MyButtonHandlerClass myButtonHandlerObj = new MyButtonHandlerClass();
```

The `ActionListener` interface (like all the XxxListener interfaces) is declared in the `java.awt.event` package. That interface simply promises that there will be a method called `actionPerformed()`. Your method `actionPerformed()` will be called whenever the Button apple is pressed. The final step is to write the class that implements the interface and provides the promised method. The class can be in a separate file or the same one.

```
MyButtonHandlerClass implements ActionListener {
    public void actionPerformed(ActionEvent e) {
       // this gets called when button pressed...
    }
}
```

The `actionPerformed()` method of class `MyButtonHandlerClass` will be called whenever the button is pressed. The good news is that the new way is far simpler for all but the most minimal case. It has better performance because events are sent only to objects that have asked for them. Another advantage of this framework is that the GUI-related code is easily separated from the application logic code. Finally, the framework can be used for Java beans as well as the AWT.

Putting the whole thing together, the code is:

```
//<applet code=f.class height=100 width=200> </applet>
    import java.applet.*;
    import java.awt.*;
    import java.awt.event.*;

    public class f extends Applet {

        Button apple = new Button("press me");
        MyBHClass myButtonHandler = new MyBHClass();

      public void init() {
            add(apple);
            apple.addActionListener(myButtonHandler);
        }
    }

class MyBHClass implements java.awt.event.ActionListener {
    int i=1;
```

```
public void actionPerformed(ActionEvent e) {
// this gets called when button pressed...
System.out.println("button pressed "+ i++ +" times");

}
}
```

and this results in a display like that in Figure 9-6 (try it).

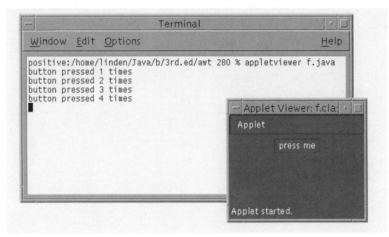

Figure 9-6:   Handling Action events from a button

The Observer/Observable design pattern was also considered for the new event model, but it was decided against. The Observer/Observable paradigm of two unrelated objects, one of which must be informed of state changes in the other, matches what is happening here. The reason for not using the Observer/Observable design pattern was because Observable is a class, not an interface. Any class that uses the Observable paradigm must be a subclass of Observable. Hence, the class cannot be a subclass of anything else (since Java permits no more than one parent class). It would be an unacceptable restriction on the window system classes to make them use up their one opportunity to inherit by becoming Observables. Making Observable a class instead of an interface (or possibly an interface and a class that implements it, too) is a mistake in the original conception of Observable.

Inner Classes and Anonymous Classes

One of the criticisms that people sometimes (rightfully) make of OOP is that everything has to be a class. In particular, even if you just want a single function for something like an event handler, you still have to create a class and instantiate an object of that class and invoke a method on that instance. The code for that class might have to be pages and pages away from the place in the source file where you do the addXxxListener. It's a bit heavyweight if your event handler is just a few lines of code. The 1.1 release of Java introduces two related new features, inner classes and anonymous classes, that improve the situation.

An *inner class* is just a nested class. JDK 1.1 supports one class being declared within another class, just as a method or data field can be declared within a class. Just as any method in a class can see any other method in the same class, the scope of the inner class is the entire parent in which it is directly nested. That is, the inner class can see anything in its parent, (and its parent's parent and so on, if you are unlucky enough to have to maintain code that someone has misused this way). The parent can see any immediate inner classes that it has, declare instances of them, invoke the inner class methods on those instances, assign to data fields (including private ones), and so on. Nothing outside a class can see an inner class. Inner classes are intended for event handlers. They allow you to put the event handling class and method right next to the place where you declare the control or register the callback listener. Figure 9-7 button described in the preceding code with the button listener rewritten as an inner class.

```java
//<applet code=f.class height=100 width=200> </applet>
import java.applet.*;
import java.awt.*;
import java.awt.event.*;

public class f extends Applet {
                                                    Inner Class
    Button apple = new Button ("press me");
    public void init() {

        class MyinnerBHClass implements java.awt.event.ActionListener {
            int i=1;
            public void actionPerformed (ActionEvent e) {
            // this gets called when button pressed . . .
            System.out.println ("button pressed" + i++ +" times");
            }
        }

        add (apple);
        apple.addActionListener (new MyinnerBHClass () );

    }

}
```

The inner class can be placed wherever any declaration can go, including inside the init ( ) method.

Figure 9-7:   An inner class

Here is the same code as in Figure 9-7, but without the shaded boxes.

```
//<applet code=f.class height=100 width=200> </applet>
    import java.applet.*;
    import java.awt.*;
    import java.awt.event.*;

public class f extends Applet {
        Button apple = new Button("press me");

        public void init() {

        class MyinnerBHClass implements java.awt.event.ActionListener {
            int i=1;
            public void actionPerformed(ActionEvent e) {
            // this gets called when button pressed...
            System.out.println("button pressed "+ i++ +" times");
            }
        }

        add(apple);
        apple.addActionListener( new MyinnerBHClass() );
        }

}
```

The inner class can be placed wherever any declaration can go, including inside the init() method.

It's not that stunningly different in a small example like this, but it does make the code slightly more readable by allowing two things that belong together to appear together. You might be interested to learn that inner classes are defined in terms of a source transformation to the corresponding free-standing class and that this is how the Sun compiler implements them. An inner class "pips" like this

```
public class orange {
    int i=0;
    void foo() {   }

    class pips {
        int seeds=2;
        void bar() { }
    }
}
```

is defined to be transformed into JDK 1.0 compatible code like this. First, separate out the inner class and prepend the containing class to its name.

```
public class orange {
    int i=0;
    void foo() {  }
}
class orange$pips {
    int seeds=2;
    void bar() { }
}
```

Then, give the inner class a private field that keeps a reference to the object in which it appears. Also, make sure all the constructors initialize this field.

```
class orange$pips {
    private orange this$0;    // saved copy of orange.this

    orange$pips(orange o) {   // constructor
        this$0 = o;
    }
    int seeds=2;
    void bar() { }
}
```

The manufactured field `this$0` allows the inner class to access any fields of its containing class, even private fields (which could not otherwise be accessed). If you try compiling this example, you will note that the compiler produces class files with names like `orange$pips.class`. Having a consistent explicit policy for naming inner classes allows everyone's tools (debugger, linker, etc.) to work the same way.

One restriction on inner classes is that they can't access variables of the method in which they are embedded. The reason is clear if you think it through: the source transformation shown above lets an inner class get back to its outer class, but the scoping rules don't give it anyway to see the local variables of a method in that class. If you break this rule, as in the code below, the compiler will give the error message like the one shown:

```
public void init() {
    int i = 20;
            ... // lines omitted
    s.addAdjustmentListener(
        new AdjustmentListener() {
            public void adjustmentValueChanged(AdjustmentEvent ae) {
                    something.setSize( i, ae.getValue()  );
^  Attempt to use a non-final variable i from a different method.
From enclosing blocks, only final local variables are available.
```

The simplest fix is to make the variable final if possible. A constant (final) variable can be used because the compiler will pass a copy of it to the inner class constructor, as an extra argument. Since it is final, that value won't later change to something else.

Anonymous Classes

It's possible to go one step further from an inner class, to something called an anonymous class. Again, this feature was introduced with JDK 1.1. Anonymous classes are a refinement of inner classes, allowing you to combine the definition of the class with the instance allocation. Instead of just nesting the class like any other field, you go to the new ... () statement where an object is instantiated and put the entire class there in brackets, as shown in Figure 9-8

```
//<applet code=f.class height=100 width=200> </applet>
import java.applet.*;
import java.awt.*;
import java.awt.event.*;

public class f extends Applet {

        Button apple = new Button("press me");

        public void init() {
                add(apple);
                apple.addActionListener(
                        new ActionListener ()

        {
                        public void actionPerformed(ActionEvent e) {
                        System.out.println ( e.paramString () +" pressed");
                }
        } // end anon class

        ); // end method call
    }
}
```

what kind of class or interface implementor it is

Anonymous Class

Figure 9-8: An anonymous class

Here is the same code as in Figure 9-8, but without the explanatory decorations.

```
//<applet code=f.class height=100 width=200> </applet>
import java.applet.*;
import java.awt.*;
import java.awt.event.*;

public class f extends Applet {

   Button apple = new Button("press me");

   public void init() {
     add(apple);
     apple.addActionListener(
        new ActionListener()
        {
          public void actionPerformed(ActionEvent e) {
             System.out.println( e.paramString() + " pressed");
          }
        } // end anon class
      ); // end method call
   }
}
```

This example compiles and runs, and you should try it. Your `f.java` file will generate class files called `f.class` and `f$1.class`. The second of these represents the anonymous `ActionListener` inner class. You should only use inner classes and anonymous classes where the event handler is just a few lines long. If the event handler is more than a screenful of text, it should be in a named top-level class. However, we have to admit that the notational convenience for smaller cases is considerable. Just don't get carried away with it.

Inner Class Thread

One Java expert on the HotJava team pointed out that you can write:

```
(new Thread() {
     public void run() {
          // 2 or 3 lines to do in the background
     }
} ).start();
```

to create and start a background thread close to the place where it's relevant. That's true, but for goodness sake, don't make your programs impossible to maintain by putting more than two or three lines in an inner class. In theory, you can nest an inner class in an inner class, but don't let me catch you doing it. 🍎

A lot of people feel strongly that inner classes take away more from the simplicity and purity of model than they provide. So, don't make the problem worse by using them for large classes.

Different Kinds of an Event

We have seen a specific example of handling the event generated by pressing a button. We saw that you write a class that implements the `ActionListener` interface, and you add an instance of that class to the `Button`. It can be written a little more compactly if you write it as an inner class or even as an anonymous class. There are several different kinds of events for the different controls: a button generates one kind of event, a scrollbar another, and so on. So, to impose a little order and split them up a bit according to what they do, there are a dozen or so individual Listener interfaces shown in Table 9-1. They all work the same way: You write a handler class that implements the interface and register it with the control. When the control fires an event, the method in your handler object is called.

Table 9-1 Which event is handled by implementing which interface

General category	Events that it generates	Interface that the Event handler will implement
mouse	dragging, moving mouse causes a MouseEvent	MouseMotionListener
	clicking, selecting, releasing, causes a MouseEvent	MouseListener
keyboard	key press, or key release causes a KeyEvent	KeyListener
selection— when an item is selected (from a list, checkbox, etc)	when item is selected causes an ItemEvent	ItemListener
text input controls	when newline is entered causes a TextEvent	TextListener
scrolling controls	when a scrollbar slider is moved causes an AdjustmentEvent	AdjustmentListener

Table 9-1 Which event is handled by implementing which interface *(continued)*

General category	Events that it generates	Interface that the Event handler will implement
other controls (button, menu, etc.)	when pressed, etc. causes an ActionEvent	ActionListener
window changes	open, close, iconify, etc. causes a WindowEvent	WindowListener
keyboard focus changes	tabbing to next field or requesting focus causes a FocusEvent. A component must have the focus to generate key events	FocusListener
Component change	Resizing, hiding, revealing, or moving a component causes a ComponentEvent	ComponentListener
Container change	Adding or removing a component to a container causes a ContainerEvent	ContainerListener

As you can see, GUI handling became quite a bit more sophisticated in JDK 1.1! The key points to note are:

- Each interface XxxListener has one or more methods that are invoked when the corresponding XxxEvent occurs.

- Your handler code will implement the XxxListener interface and will have methods with signatures that duplicate those in the interface.

- Each control will have a method called something like addXxxListener(). The addXxxlistener() method takes a single argument: an object that fulfills the XxxListener interface.

- You call addXxxListener(), using an instance of your handler class as the parameter. This registers your object as the handler for that kind of event for that control.

You can register several handlers to receive the same, one event if you wish. You can dynamically (at runtime) remove an event handler from a control or add a different one.

The XxxEvent class is a subclass of class AWTEvent and stores all the information about what just happened, where, and when. An object of the XxxEvent class is passed to the method in the XxxListener interface. It sounds more complicated than it actually is. The design pattern is shown in Figure 9-9.

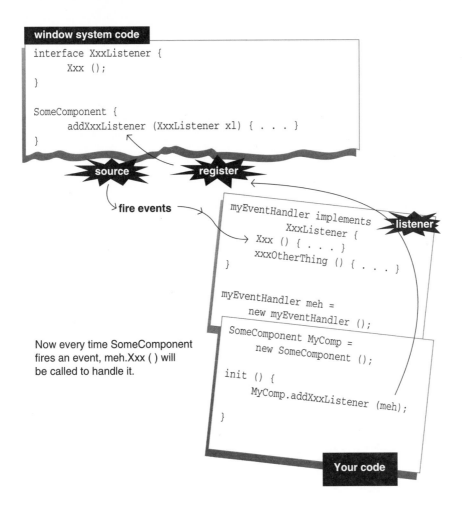

Figure 9-9: Design pattern of JDK 1.1 event handling

We won't show all the dozen or so XxxEvent classes and XxxListener interfaces here. You can and should look at them by typing, e.g.,

```
javap java.awt.event.MouseEvent
```

Compiled from `MouseEvent.java`

```
public synchronized class java.awt.event.MouseEvent
        extends java.awt.event.InputEvent
{
    public static final int MOUSE_FIRST;
    public static final int MOUSE_LAST;
    public static final int MOUSE_CLICKED;
    public static final int MOUSE_PRESSED;
    public static final int MOUSE_RELEASED;
    public static final int MOUSE_MOVED;
    public static final int MOUSE_ENTERED;
    public static final int MOUSE_EXITED;
    public static final int MOUSE_DRAGGED;
    int x;
    int y;
    int clickCount;
    boolean popupTrigger;
    public int getX();
    public int getY();
    public java.awt.Point getPoint();
    public synchronized void translatePoint(int, int);
    public int getClickCount();
    public boolean isPopupTrigger();
    public java.lang.String paramString();
    // constructor
    public java.awt.event.MouseEvent(java.awt.Component,
        int,long,int,int,int,int,boolean);
}
```

Similarly, the interface that will be implemented by your handler is:

```
javap java.awt.event.MouseListener
```

Compiled from `MouseListener.java`

```
public interface java.awt.event.MouseListener extends
        java.lang.Object implements java.util.EventListener {
    public void mouseClicked(java.awt.event.MouseEvent);
    public void mousePressed(java.awt.event.MouseEvent);
    public void mouseReleased(java.awt.event.MouseEvent);
    public void mouseEntered(java.awt.event.MouseEvent);
    public void mouseExited(java.awt.event.MouseEvent);
}
```

You should use `javap` to look at the public fields and methods of all the other Events and Listeners. A full list of the events and listeners is given (Table 9-2) at the end of the chapter.

How to Simulate Multibutton Mice

Here, as a further example, is the code to show which mouse button has been pressed. This applet will run on Macs, MS Windows, and Unix (1-, 2-, and 3-button mice systems, respectively). It will allow you to generate events from button 2 and button 3, even on single-button mice.

```java
//<applet code=exmouse.class height=100 width=200> </applet>
import java.applet.*;
import java.awt.*;
import java.awt.event.*;

public class exmouse extends Applet {

    public void init() {
        addMouseListener( new MouseAdapter() {
        public void mouseClicked(MouseEvent e) {
           if ((e.getModifiers() & InputEvent.BUTTON1_MASK) != 0)
                  System.out.println( "button1 pressed" );
           if ((e.getModifiers() & InputEvent.BUTTON2_MASK) != 0)
                  System.out.println( "button2 pressed" );
           if ((e.getModifiers() & InputEvent.BUTTON3_MASK) != 0)
                  System.out.println( "button3 pressed" );

           if ((e.getModifiers() & InputEvent.ALT_MASK) != 0)
                  System.out.println( "alt held down" );
           if ((e.getModifiers() & InputEvent.META_MASK) != 0)
                  System.out.println( "meta held down" );
        }
      } // end anon class
      ); // end method call
    }
}
```

Under JDK 1.1.1, if you hold down the ALT key while you click button one, you will get a mouse button two event. If you hold down the META key while you click button one on the mouse, you will get a mouse button three event.

On a 2-button mouse system, clicking the left button will result in the output:

```
button1 pressed
```

Holding down the ALT key while clicking the same left mouse button will result in the output:

```
button2 pressed
alt held down
```

How do you know which is the ALT key and which is the META key? Often one or both of these is marked on the keyboard. Equally frequently, the META key is not marked or is marked something else. Use a bit of intelligent experimentation, and get a better keyboard.

Note that I am using an adapter class here to minimize the amount of code in the example. An adapter class in the AWT is a class that implements an interface by providing null bodies for all of the methods. This allows you to later extend the adapter class and just provide an overriding body for the method(s) of interest. Here I provide an anonymous subclass of MouseAdapter, which has only one method, and that method overrides mouseClicked () in MouseAdapter. There is a fuller explanation of adapter classes later on.

There are a lot of new ideas in this eventhandling stuff, so don't worry if it doesn't all make sense now. Sleep on it, re-read it, try the sample programs, and it will all come together. Get the event-handling down straight before going on.

All About AWT Controls (Components)

We now have enough knowledge to start looking at individual controls in detail
and to describe the kinds of event they can generate. Almost the whole of window
programming is learning about the different objects that you can put on the screen
(windows, scrollbars, buttons, etc.) and how to drive them. This section (at last)
describes the individual controls. It explains how to register for and process the
events (input) that you get back from controls. A control isn't a free-standing
thing; it is always added to a `Container` such as an `Applet`, `Frame`, `Panel`, or `Win-
dow`, with a method call like `MyContainer.add(myComponent)`. The controls
that we will cover here are buttons, text fields, scrollbars, mouse events, and so
on. The class hierarchy is quite flat. The controls shown in Figure 9-10 are all subclasses of the general class `Component` that we have already seen.

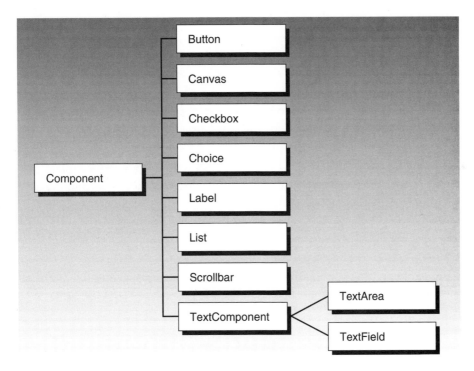

Figure 9-10: The controls (visible AWT objects) of Java

These classes are the controls or building blocks from which you will create your
GUI. What you do with all these components is:

1. Add them to a container (usually `Frame` or `Applet`), then display the
    container with the `show()` method.

2. Register your event handler, using the `addXxxListener()` method of the control. This will tell the window system which routine of yours should be called when the user presses buttons, makes selections, etc., to process the event.

Fortunately, both of these activities are quite straightforward, and we'll cover them here in source code, words, and pictures. The `add` method can be applied to a `Frame` in an application, like this:

```
Frame f = new Frame();
        . . .
f.add( something );
```

Or, it can be applied to the `Applet`'s panel in an applet, like so:

```
public static void init () {
    this.add( something );
```

Or, more simply:

```
public static void init () {
    add( something );
```

Recall the `Applet` life cycle described in an earlier chapter. That discussion made clear that there is an `init()` method which each `Applet` should override. It will be called when the Applet is loaded, and it is a good place to place the code that creates these GUI objects. We will use `init()` for that purpose.

Whenever a user operates a `Component` (presses a button, clicks on a choice), an event is generated. The `XxxEvent` argument is a class that can be seen in the `awt/event` directory. It contains much information about the coordinates of the event, the time it occurred, and the kind of event that it was. If the event was a keypress, it has the value of the key. If the event was a selection from a list, it has the string chosen.

Having explained the general theory of controls and control events, let's take a look at how they appear on the screen and the typical code to handle them.

Button

What it is:

This is a GUI button. You can program the action that takes place when the button is pressed

What it looks like on screen:

The code to create it:

```
Button b = new Button("peach");
add(b);
```

The code to retrieve user input from it:

```
MyBHClass myButtonHandler = new MyBHClass();

public void init() {
    add(apple);
    apple.addActionListener(myButtonHandler);
}
}

class MyBHClass implements java.awt.event.ActionListener {
    int i=1;

    public void actionPerformed(ActionEvent e) {
        // this gets called when button pressed...
            String s = e.paramString(); // gets the button label
    }
}
```

An event handler this small would typically be written using an inner class, and we will use inner classes for the rest of the examples.

In an applet, you will typically override the init() method and, inside it, call the add() method to add these objects to your Applet's panel. In an application, there is no predetermined convention, and you can set the objects where you like. (Note: in future examples in this section, we won't bother repeating the context that this is part of the init() method in an applet).

Program an "Alice in Wonderland" applet: a panel with two buttons, one of which makes the panel grow larger, the other smaller. The Component method

```
                setSize(int, int)
```

will resize a Panel or other Container. (Easy—about 20 lines of code).

Canvas

What it is:

A Canvas is a screen area that you can use for drawing graphics or receiving user input. A Canvas usually is subclassed to add the behavior you need, especially when you use it to display a GIF or JPEG image. A Canvas contains almost no methods. All its functionality is either inherited from Component (setting font, color, size) or from functionality you add when you extend the class.

To draw on a canvas, you supply your own version of the paint(Graphics g) method. To do that, you need to extend the class and override the paint() method for this Canvas. A more descriptive name for the paint() method would be do_this_to_draw_me(). That gives you a Graphics context (the argument to paint()), which is used in all drawing operations. The many methods of Graphics let you render (the fancy graphics word for "draw") lines, shapes, text, etc., on the screen. These methods are described later.

What it looks like on screen:

The screen dump is not very exciting, merely showing a rectangular area that has been highlighted with a different color to make it visible (see code below). Canvases are relatively inert until you extend them and use them to display images or do other graphics programming.

The code to create it:

This code gives the Canvas a red color, so you can distinguish it from the Panel (as long as your *Applet* panel isn't red to begin with, of course). The code then gives the Canvas a size of 80 pixels wide by 40 pixels high and adds it to the Applet.

```
Canvas n = new Canvas();
n.setBackground(Color.red);
n.setSize(80,40);
add(n);
```

Note that you cannot draw on objects of class Canvas. You must extend Canvas and override the paint() method and do your drawing in that routine. The paint() method needs to contain all the statements to draw everything that you want to see in the canvas at that time. Here is how you would extend Canvas to provide a surface that you can draw on:

```
// <applet code=can.class width=250 height=100>  </applet>
import java.awt.*;
import java.applet.*;
public class can extends Applet {
    myCanvas c = new myCanvas();

    public void init() {
        c.setSize(200,50);
        add(c);
    }
}

class myCanvas extends Canvas{
    public void paint(Graphics g) {
        g.drawString("don't go in the basement", 10,25);
        g.drawLine(10,35, 165,35);
    }
}
```

You can compile and execute this by typing

```
javac can.java appletviewer can.java
```

A window like this is displayed on the screen:

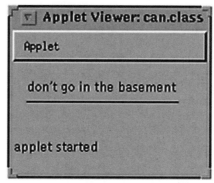

A Canvas is similar to a Panel, in that you can draw on it, render images, and accept events. A Canvas is not a container, however, so you cannot add other components to it. Here is how you would accept mouse events on a Canvas.

```java
//   <applet code=can.class width=250 height=100> </applet>
import java.awt.*;
import java.awt.event.*;
import java.applet.*;
public class can extends Applet {
    Canvas c = new Canvas();

    public void init() {
       c.setSize(200,50);
       c.setEnabled(true);
       c.setBackground(Color.blue);
       c.addMouseListener ( new MouseListener() {
          public void mouseEntered(java.awt.event.MouseEvent e)
             {System.out.println(e.toString() );}
          public void mouseClicked(java.awt.event.MouseEvent e) {}
          public void mousePressed(java.awt.event.MouseEvent e) {}
          public void mouseReleased(java.awt.event.MouseEvent e) {}
          public void mouseExited(java.awt.event.MouseEvent e) {}
          });
       add(c);
    }
}
```

The preceding code handles the event fired when the mouse enters the blue canvas. If you run it, you'll see something like this.

```
% appletviewer can.java
java.awt.event.MouseEvent[MOUSE_ENTERED,(131,49),mods=0,clickCount
    =0]  on canvas0
```

Adapter Classes

Even though we were only interested in the mouseEntered event, we had to supply null bodies for all the methods in the MouseListener interface. To make things a little more convenient, a concept called *adapter classes* can be used. An adapter is one specific example of a design pattern. An adapter is the design pattern that converts the API of some class into a different, more convenient, API.

In Java AWT event handling, for some of the Listener interfaces (such as WindowListener), you might want to implement only one or two functions to handle the one or two events of interest, but the XxxListener interface may specify half a dozen methods. The language rules are such that you must implement all the functions in an interface even if you just give them empty bodies, as in the MouseListener above.

So, the package java.awt.event provides these adapters that help with the situation, by allowing you to override only one method:

- ComponentAdapter.java

- MouseMotionAdapter.java

- WindowAdapter.java

- ContainerAdapter.java

- MouseAdapter.java

- FocusAdapter.java

- KeyAdapter.java

These adapters are classes that provide empty bodies for all of the methods in the corresponding XxxListener interface. You can declare your event handler as a child class of one of these adapters and provide only the one or two methods that you are interested in, instead of needing to implement all the methods in the interface. Another way of doing this would have been to have one Adapter class that implemented all the Listener classes and all the methods in them.

Here is an example showing how the MouseAdapter class is used when all we are interested in is the mouse entering the Canvas.

```
//   <applet code=can.class width=250 height=100>   </applet>
import java.awt.*;
import java.awt.event.*;
import java.applet.*;
public class can extends Applet {
    Canvas c = new Canvas();

    public void init() {
        c.setSize(200,50);
        c.setEnabled(true);
        c.setBackground(Color.blue);
        c.addMouseListener ( new MouseAdapter() {
            public void mouseEntered(java.awt.event.MouseEvent e)
                {System.out.println(e.toString() );}
            });
        add(c);
    }
}
```

Here is an example of how a game program might capture individual key presses, in an applet as they are made. Note that the output is to System.out, which isn't displayed in a browser unless you bring up the right window. This example is best run in the applet viewer.

```
// <applet code=game.class height=200 width=300> </applet>
import java.awt.*;
import java.awt.event.*;
import java.applet.*;
public class game   extends Applet {

    public void init() {
        requestFocus(); // a component must have the focus to get
                        //key events
        addKeyListener(
            new KeyAdapter() {
                public void keyPressed(java.awt.event.KeyEvent e)
                { System.out.println("got "+e.getKeyChar()); }
            } // end anon class
        ); // end method call
    }
}
```

The requestFocus() call is a Component method to ask that keyboard input be directed to this control. Having to explicitly ask for the focus is a change from JDK 1.0.2. The Component must be visible on the screen for the requestFocus() to succeed. A FocusGained event will then be delivered if there's a listener for it.

What could be simpler than an adapter? Well, it turns out there is a major pitfall with adapter classes, and it's one of those awful problems that takes you an hour of swearing at the keyboard the first time you encounter it. Thereafter, you'll know to check for it, but the first time is a little frustrating.

When you create an inner class for an adapter class, you simply supply the one or two methods that you wish to override, like this:

```
new KeyAdapter() {
    public void keyPressed(java.awt.event.KeyEvent e)
    { System.out.println("got "+e.getKeyChar()); }
} // end anon class
```

However, you may make a small spelling or letter case error in supplying your method, like this:

```
new KeyAdapter() {
    public void KeyPressed(java.awt.event.KeyEvent e)
    // Notice capital "K" in "KeyPressed" WRONG!
    { System.out.println("got "+e.getKeyChar()); }
} // end anon class
```

Such a spelling mistake means that your method will not override the intended method in the adapter class. Instead, you will have added a new method that never gets invoked. The empty body of the correctly spelled method in the adapter class will be invoked instead, and it will do nothing. If your event handler seems to do nothing and you used an adapter, your first check should be that the method name and signature exactly matches something in the adapter class. ❦

Let's continue with our description of the individual controls.

Checkbox

What it is:

A checkbox screen object that represents a boolean choice: "pressed" or "not pressed" or "on" or "off." Usually some text explains the choice. For example, "Press for fries" would have a Checkbox "button" allowing yes or no.

What it looks like on screen:

The code to create it:

```
Checkbox cb  = new Checkbox("small");
add(cb);
```

The code to retrieve user input from it:

Checkbox generates `ItemEvent`. The code to register an `ItemListener` looks like

```
//   <applet code=excheck.class width=250 height=100>   </applet>
import java.awt.*;
import java.awt.event.*;
import java.applet.*;
public class excheck extends Applet {
    Checkbox c1 = new Checkbox("small");

    public void init() {
       c1.addItemListener ( new ItemListener() {
          public void itemStateChanged(java.awt.event.ItemEvent ie)
          { System.out.println(ie.paramString() );}
    });
       add(c1);
    }
}
```

In this example, as in most of them, we simply print out a String representation of the event that has occurred. Running the applet and clicking the checkbox will cause this output in the system console:

```
appletviewer excheck.java
ITEM_STATE_CHANGED,item=small,stateChange=SELECTED
ITEM_STATE_CHANGED,item=small,stateChange=DESELECTED
```

Handlers in real programs will do more useful actions: assign values, create objects, etc., as necessary. The ItemEvent contains fields and methods that specify which object generated the event and whether it was selected or deselected.

CheckboxGroup

What it is:

There is a way to group a series of checkboxes to create a CheckboxGroup of *radio buttons*. The term "radio buttons" arises from the old manual station selection buttons in car radios. When you pressed in one of the buttons, all the others would pop out and be deselected. CheckboxGroups work the same way.

What it looks like on screen:

On Windows 95, mutually-exclusive checkboxes are round, while multiple-selection checkboxes are square. This is one of those "look and feel" differences that vary between window systems.

The code to create it:

You first instantiate a CheckboxGroup object, then use that in each Checkbox constructor, along with a parameter saying whether it is selected or not. This ensures that only one of those Checkbox buttons will be allowed to be on at a time.

```java
//   <applet code=excheck2.class width=250 height=100>  </applet>
import java.awt.*;
import java.awt.event.*;
import java.applet.*;
public class excheck2 extends Applet {
    CheckboxGroup cbg = new CheckboxGroup();

    Checkbox c1 = new Checkbox("small", false,  cbg);
    Checkbox c2 = new Checkbox("medium", false, cbg);
    Checkbox c3 = new Checkbox("large",  true,  cbg);

    ItemListener ie = new ItemListener () {
        public void itemStateChanged(java.awt.event.ItemEvent ie)
            { System.out.println(ie.toString());}
        };
    public void init() {
        c1.addItemListener ( ie );
        c2.addItemListener ( ie );
        c3.addItemListener ( ie );
        add(c1);
        add(c2);
        add(c3);
    }
}
```

Note here that we are using the same, one instance of an inner class as the handler for events from all three of these Checkboxes. It is common to have one handler for several related objects, and let the handler decode which of them actually caused the event. We couldn't do this if we had created an anonymous class, because we would not have kept a reference to use in the later `addItemListener()` calls.

Choice

What it is:

This is a pop-up list, akin to a pull-down menu, which allows a selection from several text strings. When you hold down the mouse button on the choice, a list of all the other choices appears and you can move the mouse over the one you want.

What it looks like on screen:

Choices are very similar to the List control. Lists look a little more like text; Choices look a little more like buttons and menus. When you click the mouse on a Choice, it pops up the full range of choices, looking like this:

The code to create it:

```
<applet code=exchoice.class width=250 height=100>  </applet>
import java.awt.*;
import java.awt.event.*;
import java.applet.*;
public class exchoice extends Applet {
    Choice c = new Choice();

    public void init() {
        add(c);
        c.addItem("lemon");
        c.addItem("orange");
        c.addItem("lime");
    ItemListener il = new ItemListener () {
        public void itemStateChanged(java.awt.event.ItemEvent ie)
            { System.out.println(ie.getItem()); }
        };

        c.addItemListener ( il );
    }
}
```

Note that it is perfectly feasible to build the items in a Choice list dynamically. If you wanted to, you could build at runtime a `Choice` representing every file in a directory. A control called `FileDialog` does this for you, however.

Label

What it is:

This is a very simple component. It is just a string of text that appears on screen. The text can be left, right, or center aligned according to an argument to the constructor. The default is left aligned.

What it looks like on screen:

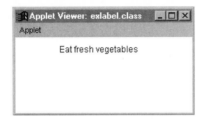

The code to create it:

```
//  <applet code=exlabel.class width=250 height=100>  </applet>
import java.awt.*;
import java.awt.event.*;
import java.applet.*;
public class exlabel extends Applet {
    String s = "Eat fresh vegetables";
    Label l = new Label(s);

    public void init() {
        add(l);
    }
}
```

Labels do not generate any events in and of themselves. However, it is possible to change the text of a label (perhaps in response to an event from a different component).

Labels are typically used as a cheap, fast way to get some text on the screen and to label other controls with descriptions or instructions. People often want to know how to get a multiline label (or a multiline button). There is no direct way. You will have to program the functionality in for yourself, by extending the class Canvas or Component to do what you want.

List

What it is:

Lists are very similar to Choices, in that you can select from several text alternatives. With a Choice, only the top selection is visible until you click the mouse on it to bring them all up. With a List, many or all of the selections are visible on the screen with no mousing needed.

A List also allows the user to select one or several entries (single or multiple selection is configurable). A Choice only allows one entry at a time to be chosen.

What it looks like on screen:

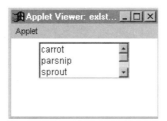

The code to create it:

This creates a scrolling list with three items visible initially and does not allow multiple selections at the same time (multiple selections is false).

```
//<applet code=exlist.class width=200 height=100> </applet>
import java.awt.*;
import java.awt.event.*;
import java.applet.*;

public class exlist extends Applet {
   List l = new List(3,false);

   public void init() {
     add(l);
     l.addItem("carrot");
     l.addItem("parsnip");
     l.addItem("sprout");
     l.addItem("cabbage");
     l.addItem("turnip");
     ItemListener il = new ItemListener () {
        public void itemStateChanged(java.awt.event.ItemEvent ie)
       { System.out.println(ie.getItem() ); }
        };
     l.addItemListener ( il );
   }
}
```

The code to retrieve user input from it:

The `ItemListener` is called when the selection is made by clicking on the list entry. Unlike a Choice, which returns the text string representing the selection, a `List` selection event returns an integer in the range 0 to N, representing the selection of the zeroth to Nth item.

The `List` class (not the `ItemEvent` class) has methods to turn that list index into a String and to get an array containing the indexes of all currently selected elements.

```
public String getItem(int index);
public synchronized int[] getSelectedIndexes();
```

Scrollbar

What it is:

A scrollbar is a box that can be dragged between two end points. Dragging the box, or clicking on an end point, will generate events that say how far along the range the box is.

You don't have to use Scrollbar much, as scrollbars are given to you automatically on several controls (TextArea, Choice, and ScrollPane). When you do use one, it is typically related by your code to some other control. When the user moves the scrollbar, your program reads the incoming event and makes a related change in the other control. Often, that involves changing the visual appearance, but it doesn't have to. A scrollbar could be used to input numeric values between two end points.

What it looks like on screen:

The code to create it:

```java
public void init() {
    Scrollbar s = new Scrollbar(Scrollbar.VERTICAL,20,10,5,35);
    add(s);
```

The arguments are:

- whether the bar should go up Scrollbar.VERTICAL or along Scrollbar.HORIZONTAL

- the initial setting for the bar (here, 20), which should be a value between the high and low ends of the scale

- the length of the slider box (here, 10)

- the value at the low end of the scale (here, 5)

- the value at the high end of the scale (here, 35)

The code to retrieve user input from it:

Scrollbars have various methods for getting and setting the values, but the method you'll use most is `public int getValue()`. There is a method of this name in both the `Scrollbar` class and the `AdjustmentEvent` class. When you call it, it returns the current value of the `Scrollbar` or (when you invoke it on the `AdjustmentEvent` object), the value that it had when this event was generated.

Here is an example of using `Scrollbar` to input a numeric value. It draws a simple bar graph by resizing a canvas according to the scroll value.

```
// <applet code=A.class height=200 width=300> </applet>

import java.awt.*;
import java.awt.event.*;
import java.applet.*;
public class A   extends Applet {

   public void init() {
      resize(250,200);

      final Canvas n      = new Canvas();
      n.setBackground(Color.red);
      n.setSize(20,20);
      add(n);

      Scrollbar s  = new Scrollbar(Scrollbar.VERTICAL,10,20,1,75);
      add(s);
      s.addAdjustmentListener(
        new AdjustmentListener() {
          public void adjustmentValueChanged(AdjustmentEvent ae) {
            System.out.println("ae="+ae);
            n.setSize( 20, ae.getValue() *5 );
            repaint();
          }
        }
      );
   }
}
```

Now that JDK 1.1 has introduced the `ScrollPane` container type, scrollbars don't need to be programmed explicitly nearly so much.

TextField

What it is:

A TextField is a field into which the user can type a single line of characters. The number of characters displayed is configurable. A TextField can also be given an initial value of characters. Changing the field is called editing it, and editing can be enabled or disabled.

The TextField component sets its background color differently, depending on whether the TextField is editable, or not. If the Textfield can be edited, the background is set to backgroundColor.brighter(); if it is not editable, the whole text field is set to the same color as the background color.

What it looks like on screen:

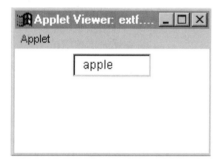

The code to create it:

This code creates a TextField with eight characters showing, and initialized to with the characters "apple". You can type different characters in there and more than eight, but only eight will show at a time.

```
TextField tf = new TextField("apple",8);
add(tf);
```

The code to retrieve user input from it:

A `TextField` causes an event when a Return is entered in the field. At that point, the `ActionEvent` method `getActionCommand()` will retrieve the text.

```
//<applet code=extf.class height=100 width=200> </applet>
import java.applet.*;
import java.awt.*;
import java.awt.event.*;

public class extf extends Applet {
    TextField tf = new TextField("apple",8);
    public void init() {
        add(tf);
        tf.addActionListener(
            new ActionListener()
            {
                public void actionPerformed(ActionEvent e) {
                    System.out.println("field is"
                        +e.getActionCommand());
                }
            } // end anon class
        ); // end method call
    }
}
```

Remember that any component can register to receive any kind of event. A useful thing you might want to do is register a `KeyListener` for the text field. You could use this to filter incoming keystrokes, perhaps validating them. The code below will make the text field beep if you type any non-numeric input.

```
//<applet code=extf2.class height=100 width=200> </applet>
import java.applet.*;
import java.awt.*;
import java.awt.event.*;

public class extf2 extends Applet {

    TextField tf = new TextField("numbers only",14);

    public void init() {
        add(tf);

        tf.addKeyListener( new KeyAdapter() {
            public void keyPressed(KeyEvent e) {
                char k = e.getKeyChar();
                if (k<'0' || k>'9'){
                    tf.getToolkit().beep();
                    e.setKeyChar('0');
```

```
                }
            }
        } // end anon class
    ); // end method call
    tf.addActionListener( new ActionListener() {
        public void actionPerformed(ActionEvent e) {
            System.out.println("got "+e.getActionCommand());
        }
    } // end anon class
    ); // end method call
    }
}
```

A KeyListener is registered with the text field. As keystrokes come in, it examines them and converts any non-numerics to the character "0", effectively forcing the field to be numeric. An ActionListener is registered with the text field too. The ActionListener retrieves the entire numeric string when the user presses Return. Note: A bug in the Windows 95 version of JDK 1.1.1 prevents the setKeyChar() method from changing the character to zero.

A better approach would be to allow the character to be typed, and then use the getText() and setText() methods of the TextComponent parent class to remove the non-numeric characters.

Finally, note the setFont() method, which will use a different font in the component. A typical call looks like this:

```
myTextArea.setFont(
new Font("FONTNAME", FONTSTYLE, FONTSIZE) );
```

Where FONTNAME is the name of the font (e.g., Dialog, TimesRoman) as a String. FONTSTYLE is Font.PLAIN, Font.ITALIC, Font.BOLD or any additive combination (e.g., Font.ITALIC+Font.BOLD). FONTSIZE is an int representing the size of the font, (e.g., 12 means 12 point).

TextArea

What it is:

A TextField that is several lines long. It can be set to allow editing or read-only modes.

What it looks like on screen:

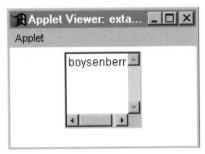

The code to create it:

```
TextArea t = new TextArea("boysenberry", 4, 9);
add(t);
```

This creates a text area of 4 lines, each showing 9 characters. The first line shows the first nine characters of the string "boysenberry." You can place text on the next line in the initializer by embedding a '\n' character in the string.

TextAreas automatically come with scrollbars, so you can type an unbounded amount of text.

```
//<applet code=exta.class height=100 width=200> </applet>
import java.applet.*;
import java.awt.*;
import java.awt.event.*;

public class exta extends Applet {

    TextArea ta = new TextArea("boysenberry", 4, 9);

    public void init() {
        add(ta);

        ta.addTextListener(  new TextListener()
          {
            public void textValueChanged(java.awt.event.TextEvent e)
              { System.out.println("got "+ta.getText()); }
            } // end anon class
          ); // end method call
    }
}
```

Like all of these controls, TextAreas use the underlying native window system control and are subject to the same limitations of the underlying window system. Under Microsoft Windows, TextAreas can only hold 32 Kbytes of characters, less a few Kb for overhead. A big benefit of moving to peerless, pure Java components is to lose platform-specific limitations.

Unlike a TextField, a TextArea might have embedded newlines, so a newline can't be used to cause the event that says "I am ready to give up my value." The same solution is used as with a multiple-selection list. Use another control, say, a button or checkbox, to signal that the text is ready to be picked up. Alternatively, as in this example, you simply can pull in the text for the whole area as each new character comes in.

Menus: Design

In an eccentric design choice, menus are not Components—they are an on-screen thing that isn't a subclass of Component. This inconsistency was originally perpetrated to reflect the same design limitation in Microsoft Windows, namely, menus in Win32 are not first-class controls. Some books claim that menus are not a subclass of Component because you cannot do many of the things with menus that you can with other components. In technical terms, that claim is just a crock of frog brains, as it is also true for all components: you can't paint a Label, you can't draw on a Scrollbar. For the new "Swing" set of AWT components coming with JDK 1.2, menus will be first-class components and implemented 100 percent in Java. Swing is the project name for the first delivery of the Java Foundation Classes. It includes some exciting new components: TreeView, ListView, and TabbedFolder, all written in pure Java.

The terminology of menus is shown in Figure 9-11.

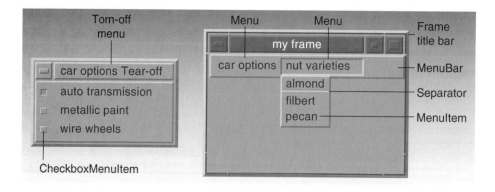

Figure 9-11:   The terminology of menus

The Menu-related classes match the terminology shown in Figure 9-11. We have a MenuBar class on which menus can be placed. Each menu can have zero or more MenuItems. Because menus aren't Components, we have two additional classes: MenuComponent and MenuContainer.

Menu: Class

What it is:

A Frame can hold a MenuBar, which can have several pull-down menus. The MenuBar has its top edge on the top edge of the Frame, so if you add anything to (0,0) on the Frame, the MenuBar will obscure it. The MenuBar holds the names of each Menu that has been added to it. Each pull-down menu has selectable Menu-Items on it, each identified by a String. You can populate a menu with menu items and also with other menus. The second case is a multilevel menu.

What it looks like on screen:

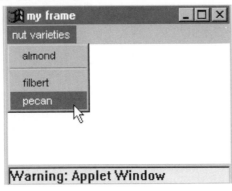

The code to create it :

```
//<applet code=exmenu.class height=100 width=200> </applet>
import java.applet.*;
import java.awt.*;
import java.awt.event.*;

public class exmenu extends Applet {

    Frame f = new Frame("my frame");
    MenuBar mb = new MenuBar();
    Menu nuts = new Menu("nut varieties", /*tearoff=*/ true);

    public void init() {
        nuts.add(new MenuItem("almond"));
        nuts.add(new MenuItem("-") );    // a separator in the menu
        nuts.add(new MenuItem("filbert"));
        nuts.add(new MenuItem("pecan"));

        mb.add(nuts);
        f.setSize(500,100);
        f.setMenuBar(mb);
        f.show();
```

The code to retrieve user input from it

MenuItems can be handled by registering an Event with the Menu, like this:

```
nuts.addActionListener(
    new ActionListener()
    {
        public void actionPerformed(ActionEvent e) {
            System.out.println("field is "+e.getActionCommand());
        }
    } // end anon class
); // end method call
```

A *tear-off* menu is one that remains visible even after you take your finger off the mouse button and click elsewhere. Not all window systems support tear-off menus, and the boolean is simply ignored in that case. Under CDE (the Unix window system), a tear-off menu is indicated by a dotted line across the top of the menu.

CheckboxMenuItem

An alternative kind of `MenuItem` is a `CheckboxMenuItem`. This variety of `Menu-Item` allows on/off selection/deselection, possibly several at once. It looks like the `Checkbox` control that we saw earlier.

What it looks like on screen:

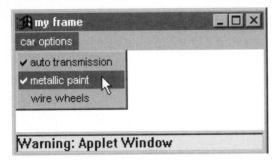

As the name suggests, this is a menu item that can be checked off or selected (like a checkbox). You receive ItemEvents from this kind of control, to say whether it is currently selected or not. Other than that, it works like a `MenuItem`, because it is a subclass of `MenuItem`.

With all these `Menu` gadgets, there are more methods than are shown here. A menu item can be disabled so it can't be selected, then later it can be enabled again.

There are menu item shortcuts, which are single-character keyboard accelerators that cause a menu event when you type them, just as if you had selected a menu item. A menu item shortcut can be set and changed with methods in the `MenuItem` class.

```
MenuItem myItem = new MenuItem("Open...");
myMenu.add(myItem);
myItem.setShortcut(new MenuShortcut((int)'O', false);
```

Note that under Windows, the standard controls parse their text names for special characters that indicate a letter in the control's text should be underlined (indicating a shortcut). For OS/2, the special character is ~; for Win32, it is &. Java does not support this feature.

The code to create it:

```
//<applet code=exmenu2.class height=100 width=200> </applet>
import java.applet.*;
import java.awt.*;
import java.awt.event.*;

public class exmenu2 extends Applet {

    Frame f = new Frame("my frame");
    MenuBar mb = new MenuBar();
    Menu car = new Menu("car options", /*tearoff=*/ true);

    public void init() {
        CheckboxMenuItem cbm1 = new CheckboxMenuItem(
                                    "auto transmission");
        CheckboxMenuItem cbm2 = new CheckboxMenuItem(
                                    "metallic paint");
        CheckboxMenuItem cbm3 = new CheckboxMenuItem(
                                    "wire wheels");

        options action = new options();
        cbm1.addItemListener(action);
        cbm2.addItemListener(action);
        cbm3.addItemListener(action);

        car.add(cbm1); car.add(cbm2); car.add(cbm3);
```

```
            mb.add(car);
            f.setSize(500,100);
            f.setMenuBar(mb);
            f.show();
        }
    }

class options implements ItemListener {
    public void itemStateChanged(ItemEvent e) {
        System.out.println("field is "+e.toString());
    }
}
```

Pop-up Menus

As well as pull-down menus, most modern systems have pop-up menus, which are menus that are not attached to a menu bar on a Frame. Pop-up menus are usually triggered by clicking or holding down a mouse button over a Container. One of the mouse event methods is `PopupTrigger()`, allowing you to check on this eventuality and if so display the pop-up menu at the (x,y) coordinates of the mouse. On Unix, the right mouse button is the trigger for a pop-up.

Pop-up menus, introduced in JDK 1.1, made menus much more useful in applets. Until then, people had tended not to use menus in applets, because the top-level container is a `Panel` (not a `Frame`) and so can't have a `MenuBar` added to it. You can create Frames in applets, but they are independent windows, floating free on the desktop.

What it looks like on screen:

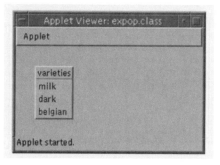

The code to create it:

```
//<applet code=expop.class height=100 width=200> </applet>
import java.applet.*;
import java.awt.*;
import java.awt.event.*;

public class expop extends Applet {

    PopupMenu choc = new PopupMenu("varieties");

    public void init() {
      choc.add(new MenuItem("milk"));
      choc.add(new MenuItem("dark"));
      choc.add(new MenuItem("belgian"));

      add(choc);

      final Applet app = this;
      addMouseListener( new MouseAdapter() {
        public void mousePressed(MouseEvent e) {
           if (e.isPopupTrigger())
              choc.show(app,30,30);
      } } );
      choc.addActionListener(
        new ActionListener()
        {
           public void actionPerformed(ActionEvent e) {
              System.out.println("field is "+e.getActionCommand());
           }
        }
        // end anon class
); // end method call
    }
}
```

A bug in the Windows 95 implementation prevents pop-up menus appearing when you are using JDK 1.1.1.

All About Containers

The previous section describes all the controls of JDK 1.1, now let's take a look at the Containers that hold them. To refresh our memories, the class hierarchy for containers is as shown in Figure 9-12.

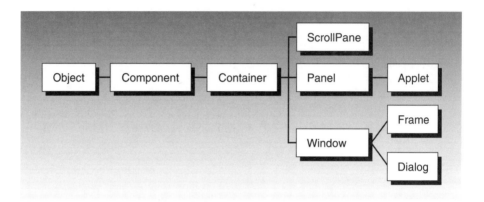

Figure 9-12: Class hierarchy of containers

On the following pages, we will outline each of these containers, suggest typical uses, and show code examples. Container is the class that groups together a number of controls and provides a framework for how they will be positioned on the screen. Container has fields and methods to deal with:

- The layout manager used to automatically position controls

- Forcing the layout to be done

- Refreshing the appearance on screen

- Adding a ContainerListener for ContainerEvents

- Adding, removing, and getting a list of any of the controls

- Size (current, preferred, minimum, and maximum)

- Requesting the window focus

- A paint() routine that will render it on the screen

`Container` has methods to get and set many of these attributes. Since a `Container` is a subclass of `Component`. It also has all the `Component` fields. You can and should review the `Container` methods by running

```
javap java.awt.Container
```

On the following pages we will review the different kinds (subclasses) of `Container` in the AWT. Containers are for holding, positioning, and displaying all the controls you add to them. When you have finished adding or changing the components in a Container, you typically call these three methods on the Container:

```
myContainer.invalidate();   // tell AWT it needs laying out
myContainer.validate();     // ask AWT to lay it out
myContainer.show();         // make it visible
```

These methods aren't needed if you are just adding to an applet, but you will need to use them in your more complicated programs.

ScrollPane

What it is:

ScrollPane is a Container that implements automatic horizontal and/or vertical scrolling for a single child component. You will create a ScrollPane, call set-Size() on it to give it a size, then add some other control to it. The control you add will often be a canvas with an image, though it can be any single component (such as a panel full of buttons).

You can ask for scrollbars never, as needed, or always. Note the inconsistent use of capitals; we have a Scrollbar but a ScrollPane.

What it looks like on screen:

The code to create it:

```java
//<applet code=exsp.class width=150 height=130 > </applet>
import java.awt.*;
import java.applet.*;
import java.awt.event.*;
public class exsp extends Applet  {
    public void init() {
        Image i = getImage(getDocumentBase(),"puppy.jpg");
        myCanvas mc = new myCanvas(i);

        ScrollPane sp = new ScrollPane();
        sp.setSize(120,100);
        sp.add(mc);
        sp.add(mc);

        add(sp);
    }
}

class myCanvas extends Canvas {
    Image si;
    public myCanvas(Image i) { this.setSize(200,200); si=i;}
    public void paint(Graphics g) { g.drawImage(si,0,0,this);}
}
```

Don't worry about the way we brought in a JPEG file to display. That will be described in the next chapter.

Window

What it is:

This Container is a totally blank window. It doesn't even have a border. You can display messages by putting Labels on it. Typically you don't use Window directly but use its more useful subclasses (Frame and Dialog).

Windows can be modal, meaning they prevent all other windows from responding until they are dealt with (usually with a checkbox). Window has a few methods to do with bringing it to the front or back, packing (resizing to preferred size,) or showing (making it visible).

What it looks like on screen:

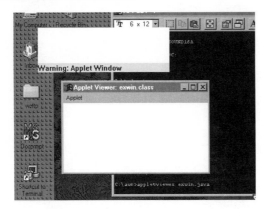

The code to create it:

```
//<applet code=exwin.class width=275 height=125 > </applet>
import java.awt.*;
import java.applet.*;
import java.awt.event.*;
public class exwin extends Applet  {

    public void init() {

    Component c = this.getParent();
    while (c!=null && !(c instanceof Frame)) c=c.getParent();

    Window w = new Window( (Frame)c);
    w.setBounds(50,50,250,100);
    w.show();
    }
}
```

The public constructor of `Window` needs to know the `Frame` that it belongs to, so we walk up the parent tree until we find it. This repeated `getParent()` code is a Java idiom you will see in AWT code from time to time.

For security purposes, the browser will typically make sure any `Window` or subclass of `Window` popped up from an untrusted applet will contain a line of text warning that it is an "untrusted window" or an "applet window." This message ensures the user of an applet will never be in any doubt about the origin of the window. Without this clear label, it would be too easy to pop up a window that looked like it came from the OS and ask for confidential information to send back to the applet server. It is not possible for an applet to prevent this security label from being shown.

Frame

What it is:

A Frame is a window that also has a title bar, a menu bar, a border (known as the inset), and that can be closed to an icon. In JDK 1.0.2, the cursor could be set for a Frame (only). In JDK 1.1, this restriction was lifted, and the cursor can now be set for each individual Component.

The origin of a Frame is its top left corner. You can draw on a Frame just as you can on a Canvas. When you create a Frame, it is not physically displayed inside the applet or other Container but is a separate free-floating window on the monitor.

What it looks like on screen:

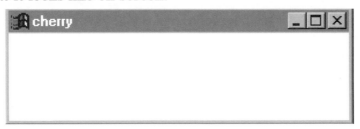

The code to create it:

```
import java.awt.*;
public class exfr {
    static Frame f = new Frame("cherry");

    public static void main(String[] a) {
        f.setBounds(100,50,300,100);
        f.show();
    }
}
```

Note that this is an application, but frames can equally be displayed from an applet, as in the code below.

```
//<applet code=exfr2.class width=275 height=125 > </applet>
import java.awt.*;
import java.applet.*;
import java.awt.event.*;
public class exfr2 extends Applet {

    public void init() {
        Frame f = new Frame("Frame of an Applet");
        f.setBounds(100,50,300,100);
        f.show();
    }
}
```

What it looks like on screen:

Here is how you associate a file containing an icon with a Frame, so that when you close the Frame, it collapses to the icon.

```
// load the image from a file Toolkit
t = MyFrame.getToolkit();
Image FrameIcon = t.getImage(filename);
if (FrameIcon != null) {
    // change the icon
    MyFrame.setIconImage(FrameIcon);
}
```

The file name should point to a GIF or JPEG file that is the icon you want to use. Typically, this image will be thumbnail-sized, 32 x 32 pixels or so.

Panel

What it is:

A `Panel` is a generic container that is always in some other container. It does not float loose on the desktop, as `Window` and `Frame` do. A panel is used when you want to group several controls inside your GUI. For example, you might have several buttons that go together, as shown in the screen dump below (Figure 9-13). Adding them all to a Panel allows them to be treated as one unit, all displayed together, and laid out on the screen under the same set of rules (more about this later!) .

What it looks like on screen:

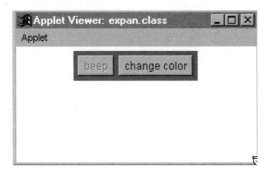

Figure 9-13: A Panel with a couple of buttons on it.

The code to create it:

```
//<applet code=expan.class width=275 height=125 > </applet>
import java.awt.*;
import java.applet.*;
import java.awt.event.*;

public class expan extends Applet  {

  public void init() {

    final Panel p = new Panel();
    add(p);
    invalidate();
    validate();

    final Button b1 = new Button("beep");
    b1.addActionListener( new ActionListener() {
      public void actionPerformed(ActionEvent e) {
      b1.getToolkit().beep(); } } // end anon class
    ); // end method call
```

```
    Button b2 = new Button("change color");
    b2.addActionListener( new ActionListener() {
        public void actionPerformed(ActionEvent e) {
        Color c = p.getBackground()==Color.red? Color.white:
            Color.red;
        p.setBackground( c );
        b1.setEnabled(false);  } } // end anon class
    ); // end method call
    p.add(b1);  p.add(b2);
  }
}
```

This code displays two buttons, one of which beeps, and the other of which changes the panel color. Once the panel color has been changed, the beeping button is disabled. Note how that changes its appearance on the screen.

Applet

Applet is a subclass of Panel. The major thing this says is that applets come readymade with some GUI stuff in place. We've seen applets many times now. Figure 9-14 is another example screendump of one.

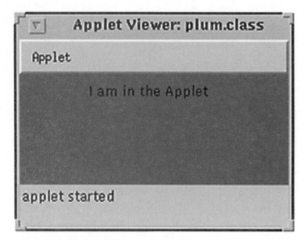

Figure 9-14: Just another applet

Here is the code that created that applet:

```
import java.awt.*;
import java.applet.*;

public class plum extends Applet {

    public void init() {
        setBackground(Color.green);
        resize(250,100);
    }

    public void paint(Graphics g) {
        g.drawString("I am in the Applet", 35,15);
    }

}
```

One advantage of an applet over an application for a GUI program is that you can start adding components and displaying them without needing to create an underlying backdrop, as one already exists.

Here are some popular methods of Applet:

```
public URL getDocumentBase() //the URL of the page
                                    containing the applet
public URL getCodeBase() //the URL of the applet code

public String getParameter(String name)
public void resize(int width, int height)

public void showStatus(String msg)
public Image getImage(URL url) //bring in an image
public Image getImage(URL url, String name)

public AudioClip getAudioClip(URL url) //bring in a sound file
public void play(URL url)
```

These four methods are for the stages in the applet life cycle:

```
public void init()
public void start()
public void stop()
public void destroy()
```

As you can see, Applet has several methods that deal with sounds and pictures. For both of these, it uses a URL (the "Uniform Resource Locator" that we met in Chapter 1) to pinpoint the file containing the goodies. You do not have to do anything special to make an Applet retrieve an image from its server over the Internet—it is a built-in method for you. A URL can locate something that is local to your system, or anywhere remote on Internet. Some people like to imagine that is why it is a "Universal" resource locator. It will look anywhere in the Universe.

The DocumentBase referred to in the first method, is simply the directory containing the HTML page that you are currently visiting. Similarly, the CodeBase is the directory that contains the applet you are currently executing. Often these two directories will be the same. Since the codebase is a URL, it can be anywhere on the Internet though.

Applet has other methods too. The source can be seen in

```
$JAVAHOME/src/java/applet/Applet.java
```

You will usually want to put in the three or four lines of code that deal with a window being quit or destroyed (when the user has finished with it—this is usually a standard choice on the frame menu bar). The code looks like:

```
class wl extends WindowAdapter {
    Window w;
    public wl(Window w) {
        this.w=w;
    }
    public void windowClosed(WindowEvent e) {
        w.setVisible(false);
        w=null;
    }
}
```

You could also exit the application. That would be appropriate when the user quits from the top-level window. For a lower-level window, the right thing to do may be to hide the window and release the resource for garbage collection by removing any pointers to it.

Dialog

What it is:

A Dialog is a top-level, free-floating window like Frame. Dialog lacks the menu bar and iconification of Frame. A Dialog is the way you show a line of text to the user, often relating to the most recent action, such as "really overwrite the file? Y/N."

According to a boolean mode parameter in the constructor, a Dialog can be modal or modeless. Modal Dialogs disable all other AWT windows until the modal Dialog is no longer on the screen.

What it looks like on screen:

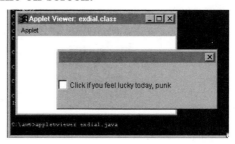

The code to create it:

```
//<applet code=exdial.class width=275 height=125 > </applet>
import java.awt.*;
import java.applet.*;
import java.awt.event.*;

public class exdial extends Applet  {

  public void init() {

    Component c = this.getParent();
    while (c!=null && !(c instanceof Frame)) c=c.getParent();

    final Dialog d = new Dialog((Frame)c);
    Checkbox c1 = new Checkbox("Click if you feel lucky today, punk");
    c1.addItemListener ( new ItemListener() {
      public void itemStateChanged(java.awt.event.ItemEvent ie)
          { d.setVisible(false); }
      });
    d.add(c1);
    d.setBounds(50,50, 280,100);
    d.show();
  }
}
```

FileDialog

What it is:

FileDialog is a Container, but you are not supposed to add anything to it. It is a Container by virtue of being a subclass of Window. FileDialog brings up the native "file selection" control, allowing you to choose a file in the file system. A list of files in the current directory is displayed, optionally filtered by some criteria such as "only include files that end in .gif."

A FileDialog can be either a Load dialog, allowing you to select a file for input, or a Save dialog, allowing you to specify a file for output.

What it looks like on screen:

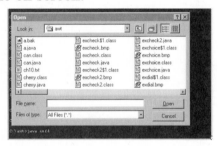

The code to create it:

```java
import java.awt.*;
import java.awt.event.*;
import java.io.*;
public class exfd {

    public static void main(String args[]) {

        Frame f = new Frame("myFrame");
        final FileDialog fd = new FileDialog(f,"get a GIF file");

        fd.show();
        fd.setFilenameFilter(new myFilter());

        System.out.println("Filter is " + fd.getFilenameFilter() );

        String s = fd.getFile();
        System.out.println("You chose file "+ s );
    }
}
class myFilter implements FilenameFilter {

    public boolean accept(File dir, String name) {
        return( name.endsWith(".gif") );
    }
}
```

The FileDialog control is only of use in applications and trusted applets because you cannot usually see the client file system in an untrusted applet running in a browser. A bug in JDK 1.1.1 meant the accept() method was never called at all. The workaround is to use the method myFileDialog.setFile("*.gif") before you run show() on it. Don't forget that most operating systems have case sensitive file names, so foo.gif is different from foo.GIF.

Layout in a Container

Here is an applet to which we have added several controls. As you can see, they are positioned automatically.

Figure 9-15 is the applet that consists of the widgets described above, placed in the Applet panel.

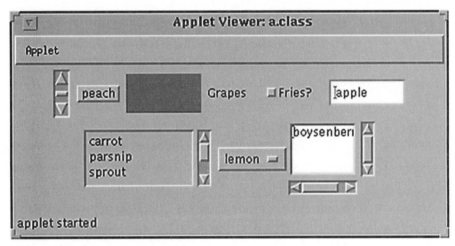

Figure 9-15:   One big happy family of widgets

The code for this is on the CD in the directory containing all the other AWT programming material.

Rewrite the above program so that it is an application not an applet. Create a Frame, add all the components to it, and then "show()" the Frame. (Easy)

Note that there is a significant GUI difference between applications and applets. Applets display their components as soon as they are added to the panel, but in an Application you must call "show()" to display the Frame and widgets you created. E.g. one way to do it would be:

```
Frame f = new Frame("Even more Fruit");
    ... lots of widget adding ...
f.show()
```

You may be wondering how the Applet knows where to put the individual elements that have been added to it. The answer is Layouts. Layout Managers are classes that specify how components should be placed in a Container. You choose a layout manager for a Container with a call like this:

```
setLayout( new FlowLayout() );
```

Flow Layout

Figure 9-16 is an Applet full of buttons laid out with FlowLayout (the default for all Panels).

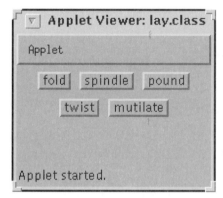

Figure 9-16:   In this applet, buttons are laid out left to right and centered

A flow layout means that Components are added left to right keeping them centered in the Container, and starting a new line whenever necessary. When you resize the applet components might move to a new line. There are possible "left" and "right" arguments to the constructor to make the components be left or right justified instead of centered, as shown here:

```
setLayout (new FlowLayout (FlowLayout.RIGHT));
```

Most of the layouts allow you to specify the gap in pixels between adjacent components, by specifing the values to the constructor. One FlowLayout constructor looks like this:

```
public FlowLayout(int align, int hgap, int vgap);
```

Grid Layout

Figure 9-17 is the same applet with a one-line change to give it a grid layout.

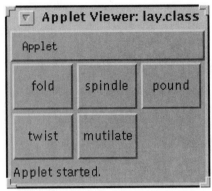

Figure 9-17: A grid layout puts things in equal sized boxes starting from top, left

In the constructor you specify the number of rows and columns, like this:

```
setLayout( new GridLayout(2,3) );
```

That creates a two-row grid, with three boxes in each row. Grid layouts are simple and somewhat rigid. One thing that always surprises and annoys programmers is the way the widgets change in size to match the grid size. To avoid this, add a button to a panel, and add the panel to the container with the grid layout.

BorderLayout

The third popular type of layout is BorderLayout. As the name suggests you can put four components around the four edges of the Frame, with a fifth component taking any remaining space in the middle. The default layout for a Frame or Window is BorderLayout. You can set it in another kind of Container with a line like:

```
setLayout( new BorderLayout() );
```

Then you add up to five widgets, specifying whether they go at the North (top), East (right) and so on. Actually, for consistency, you can specify this for the other layout managers, too. The same applet with a one-line change to use BorderLayout looks like that shown in Figure 9-18.

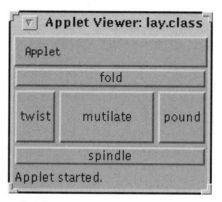

Figure 9-18: Grid setup using BorderLayout

Here is the code used to generate the three preceding examples.

```
// <applet code=lay.class    height=100 width=200>  </applet>

import java.awt.*;
import java.applet.*;

public class lay  extends Applet {
    public void init(){
    Button b1      = new Button("fold");
    Button b2      = new Button("spindle");
    Button b3      = new Button("pound");
    Button b4      = new Button("twist");
    Button b5      = new Button("mutilate");

    // setLayout( new FlowLayout() );
    // setLayout( new GridLayout(2, 5) );
    setLayout( new BorderLayout() );

    add("North",b1);
    add("South",b2);
    add("East",b3);
    add("West",b4);
    add("Center",b5);
    show();

    }

}
```

Two important points to watch with BorderLayout: First, you have to set BorderLayout before adding components otherwise you mysteriously see nothing (however, this isn't true for the other two layout managers). Second, letter case is significant when setting the position (you can't use "north" instead of "North").

CardLayout

A fourth kind of Layout Manager is CardLayout, named with a deck of playing cards in mind. You can only see one card at a time, but you can shuffle through the deck and pull another card to the top to display at any time. You use this when you have several alternative screens to present in succession. Perhaps a button on each screen leads you to the next. Each "card" in the CardLayout will typically be a Panel with its own layout manager, as shown in Figure 9-19.

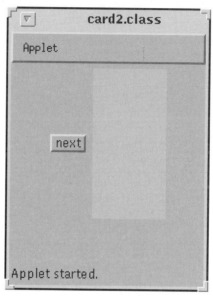

Figure 9-19: A screen shot using CardLayout

The code to generate this card layout is:

```
// <applet code=card2.class    height=200 width=200>  </applet>

import java.awt.*;
import java.applet.*;

public class card2   extends Applet {
    Button b1      = new Button("next");
    Panel p = new Panel();
    CardLayout c = new CardLayout();

    public void init(){
       p.resize(100,100);
       p.setLayout( c );

       myCanvas mc1 = new myCanvas( Color.green );
       myCanvas mc2 = new myCanvas( Color.red );
       myCanvas mc3 = new myCanvas( Color.blue );

       add(b1);
       add(p);
       p.add("starter", mc1);
       p.add("middle", mc2);
       p.add("finish",  mc3);
    }

    public boolean handleEvent(Event e) {
        if (e.target instanceof Button){
                c.next(p);
                System.out.println("button press");
                return true;
        }
    return false;
    }

}


class myCanvas extends Canvas {
 // this simply sets up a colored canvas, so you
 // can see when a new one is brought to the front.
    public myCanvas(Color c) {
        setBackground(c);
        resize(75,150);
    }

}
```

The card layout code above creates three canvases of different colors and adds them to a panel P using a card layout. We've used canvases in the example so that the container that had the card layout (here a Panel) was a different type to the individual cards (here, canvases) to minimize confusion.

The example code also creates a button. When the button is pressed, the next card is brought to the front, and you will see the color change as a different canvas comes up to the front. Unlike the other layout managers, you need to keep a reference to this one. That is, you cannot write:

```
setLayout( new CardLayout() );
```

you must write

```
CardLayout c = new CardLayout();
something.setLayout( c );
```

This is because you need to reference the first(), last(), next(), and previous() or show() methods of the card layout manager to flip through the cards. You also need to pass the container that is card-laid-out as an argument. Here are two examples:

```
c.next( p );
```

or

```
c.show(p, "middle");
```

The second example will bring up the card with the name "middle."

GridBagLayout

The final kind of Layout Manager is GridBagLayout, which is a variation of GridLayout. It doesn't force you to fit components one per grid position, but allows you to let a component take up the space of several adjacent grid positions. It uses a series of constraints and weights to work out what goes where.

Frankly, GridBagLayout is excessively complicated, and I'm not recommending it to anyone. Its value lies in demonstrating that ordinary programmers can write new implementations of the public interface LayoutManager. GridBagLayout was written by a public-spirited programmer outside Sun and donated out of a desire to advance the Java effort. If you really want to spend time on GridBagLayout there is a tutorial about it online at:

```
http://www.javasoft.com/nav/read/Tutorial/ui/layout/gridbag.html
```

GridBagLayout will be replaced by SpringLayout to be introduced in JDK 1.2. GridBagLayout won't be removed, but it will probably be deprecated. In the meantime, nest components on panels and then layout the panels using the first four layout managers.

Layouts are funky. You probably won't find any one layout that does exactly what you want. The solution is to divide your Panels and Frames into sub-panels, and use a different layout manager (as appropriate) for each panel. Then display the different panels together in a single frame.

Some layout managers adjust their components to fit the container, and some layout managers just lay out components unchanged. The `BorderLayout` tells its enclosing container the size to allow for each control by invoking the `preferredSize()` methods of each control. Other layout managers (`GridBagLayout` and `GridLayout`) force the components to adjust their size according to the actual dimensions of the container. `FlowLayout` doesn't change the sizes of contained components at all.

Finally, you always have the option of setting a null layout manager and positioning controls at absolute coordinates, using `public void setLocation(int x, int y)`. In general, it is better to use a layout manager than to use absolute positions. It's less work for you, and the GUI will look better when run on different platforms. An absolute layout that looks good on one platform can look terrible on another platform.

Tying Up the Loose Ends

At this point, we have dealt with events, components, and containers both in summary and in depth. There are just three minor topics to cover to conclude the chapter. The three topics are applet/application differences, cursors, and the toolkit.

The Difference Between an Applet and an Application and How to Convert Between Them.

Many programmers are unduly worried about the differences between applets and applications. People often post questions on the Java newsgroups complaining that the book they are reading focuses on one of these and they are interested in the other. The truth is that 95 percent of the information carries over between applets and applications. All the GUI information is common.

In fact, apart from the security restrictions (on file I/O, etc.) on untrusted applets each kind of execution framework can easily be transformed into the other. All the examples here can be rewritten as an applet or an application.

To Turn an Applet into an Application

This is the simpler direction because the security restrictions are relaxed. The basic process is to provide the same kind of execution context that an applet provides. Then, call explicitly the methods that are called automatically in an applet. Follow these steps.

1. Make your top-level class extend `Frame`, not `Applet`. Since the default layout in a `Panel` (and hence its subclasses like `Applet`) is `FlowLayout`, explicitly set that layout manager on the `Frame`.

2. Add a `main` routine in the class.

3. The `main` routine should read its arguments, and you should arrange to pass it the same arguments as were passed to the applet as params in HTML.

4. The `main` routine should instantiate an object of the class. The constructor should call `start()`, and then `init()`.

5. Add a menu with an Exit item or an exit button; otherwise, there may be no internal way to exit.

The JDK demo directory has a class in file `$JAVAHOME/demo/GraphicsTest/AppletFrame.java` that provides the surrounding framework to run an applet as an application. `AppletFrame` actually lets your program run either as an applet or an application. In application mode, it creates a frame and puts the applet inside. You could use this class as the basis for your code. This doesn't quite take you all the way, as you still need to take care of applications that need applet services like `appletContext()`, but it does 99 percent of what you need.

To Turn an Application into an Applet

It's more common to want to turn an application into an applet because this gives you the ability to invoke the program just by browsing the web page that contains it. This direction is a little tougher because of the security restrictions on applets. You need to remove file and network I/O, except that permitted by the applet framework. The simplest approach is to sign your applet to make it trusted. Then follow these steps.

1. Create the HTML that will invoke the applet. We put it here in the source file because that is quick and dirty. That's not the right place for it in a production program.

2. The top-level class should extend `Applet`, rather than `Frame`, which is the starting point for most application GUIs. Give the `Applet` the `BorderLayout` that the `Frame` has by default.

3. Replace the class constructor with a method called `init()` to do the one time setup.

4. Move any initialization statements from `main()` into `init()`. Other statements that do "revisit page" setup will need to be put in a method called `start()`.

5. Fix up any code that may not be done in an `Applet`, such as setting the title bar, adding menus to the Frame bar, calling native routines, I/O, or OS commands.

6. Don't forget to put the "leaving a page" cleanup in `stop()`.

It is also possible to have a program that contains all the elements of both an application and an applet and which can be run as either, according to convenience.

Changing Cursor Appearance

The cursor is the little graphic icon that moves about the screen tracking the mouse movements. There are 14 different cursor icons namely,

Appearance	Name
8 different directions for resizing	Cursor.SW_RESIZE_CURSOR, etc.
1 default cursor	Cursor.DEFAULT_CURSOR
1 crosshair cursor	Cursor.CROSSHAIR_CURSOR
1 text cursor	Cursor.TEXT_CURSOR
1 busy waiting cursor	Cursor.WAIT_CURSOR
1 hand cursor	Cursor.HAND_CURSOR
1 move cursor	Cursor.MOVE_CURSOR

Some of these are shown in the figure below.

Arrow	Busy	Resize	SizeEast	Text	CrossHair
⬉	⧗	✥	↔	I	+

Figure 9-20:   Just some of the many cursor icons

The cursor appearance can be set for any component with the method

```
public synchronized void setCursor(Cursor cursor)
```

For example,

```
this.setCursor(new Cursor(Cursor.HAND_CURSOR) );
```

There is a getCursor() method, too. There is no way in JDK 1.1 to supply your own bitmap for a custom cursor, though obviously this is a reasonable thing to want to do.

The Toolkit

A Component method called get Toolkit() returns a reference to the toolkit. The name "toolkit" just means "bunch of generally useful window-related things" and is the "T" in AWT. Once you have a Toolkit, you can call any of its methods, which can do things like:

- Set things up for printing the screen

- Get information about the screen size and resolution

- Beep the keyboard

- Get information about the color model in use

- Get information about font size

- Transfer data to/from the system clipboard

- Set the icon image of the Frame

For example, `java.awt.Toolkit.getDefaultToolkit().getScreenSize()`
returns a `java.awt.Dimension` object, which has ints representing height and
width. As usual, you can view all the methods by typing

```
javap java.awt.Toolkit
```

Transfering data to/from the system clipboard is expected to be introduced with
JDK 1.2.

Printing the Screen

Printing is one of the services provided by the window toolkit. JDK 1.1 introduced
the ability to print the screen from an applet. JDK 1.1.1 took it away again, at least
for untrusted applets. To prevent a rogue applet from spawning large or offensive
print jobs behind your back, an untrusted applet cannot directly start a print job.
The printing support just pops up the native "print this" dialog box, allowing the
user to review the job and initiate it.

Setting up a print job is a little elaborate.

- First, you get the Toolkit.

- From the Toolkit, you get a `PrintJob`.

- From the `PrintJob`, you get a `Graphics` object, called, say, go.
  Since this a regular graphics object, you can do all the things with it
  that you can do with any graphics object, including drawing in it
  directly, with the kinds of statements that you typically use inside
  `paint()`, like `drawString()`.

- Then, you call `printAll(go)`. This method will pop up the native
  printing dialog. Every component has a `print()` method which by
  default just calls its `paint()` routine. You can override these as needed
  for special effects.

- Finally, invoke dispose on the go, and invoke `end()` on the PrintJob.

Yes, I know. This all seems to have been designed with the "principle of most astonishment" in mind. The code looks like this:

```
import java.awt.*;
import java.awt.event.*;

public class exprint extends Frame {

    Image si;
    public exprint(Image i) { this.setSize(200,200); si=i;}
    public void paint(Graphics g) { g.drawImage(si,0,0,this);}

    public static void main(String args[]) {

        Image i = Toolkit.getDefaultToolkit().getImage("puppy.jpg");
        exprint f = new exprint(i);
        f.show();
        f.printMe();
    }

    public void printMe() {
        Toolkit t = getToolkit();
        PrintJob pj = t.getPrintJob(this, "my printing", null);
        Graphics pg = pj.getGraphics();
        printAll(pg);
        pg.dispose();
        pj.end();
    }
}
```

The third argument to `getPrintJob` is a property table that can be used to specify the printer, etc., to use. A null reference works here.

The standard print properties are shown in Table 9-2.

Table 9-2 Print properties

Print property	Description or Effect
awt.print.destination	can be "printer" or "file"
awt.print.printer	print command
awt.print.fileName	name of the file to print
awt.print.numCopies	number of copies to print
awt.print.options	options to pass to the print command
awt.print.orientation	can be "portrait" or "landscape"
awt.print.paperSize	can be "letter," "legal,""executive" or "a4"

The defaults are destination=printer, orientation=portrait, paperSize=letter, and numCopies=1.

Running the code will pop up a print dialog like this:

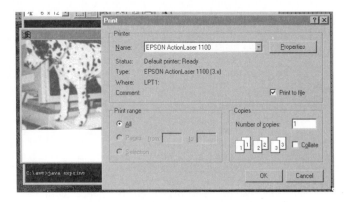

Some Light Relief

The Domestic Obfuscated Java Code Non-Competition

Readers of my book "Expert C Programming" will be aware of the International Obfuscated C Code Competition (IOCCC). It's an annual contest run over Usenet since 1984 to find the most horrible and unreadable C programs of the year. Not horrible in the sense of badly written, but the much subtler concept of horrible to figure out what they do and how they work.

The IOCCC accepts entries in the winter, they are judged over spring, and the winners are announced at the summer Usenix conference. It is a great honor to be one of the dozen or so category winners at the IOCCC, as many very good programmers turn their talents to the dark side of the force for this event. If you know C pretty well you might be interested in figuring out what this IOCCC past winner does:

```
main() {printf(&unix["\021%six\012\0"], (unix)["have"]+"fun"-0x60);}
```

Hint: it doesn't print "have fun."

Here, in the spirit of the IOCCC are two Java programs that I wrote for April Fool's Day. You should be pretty good at reading Java code at this point so I won't spoil your fun. This program is on the CD in directory justjava/ch10/h.java. It looks like one big comment, so it should compile without problems. When you run it, it greets you! But how?

```
/*   Just Java
     Peter van der Linden
     April 1, 1996.

\u0050\u0076\u0064\u004c\u0020\u0031\u0020\u0041\u0070\u0072\u0039\u0036
 \u002a\u002f\u0020\u0063\u006c\u0061\u0073\u0073\u0020\u0068\u0020\u007b
  \u0020\u0020\u0070\u0075\u0062\u006c\u0069\u0063\u0020\u0020\u0020\u0020
   \u0073\u0074\u0061\u0074\u0069\u0063\u0020\u0020\u0076\u006f\u0069\u0064
    \u006d\u0061\u0069\u006e\u0028\u0020\u0053\u0074\u0072\u0069\u006e\u0067
     \u005b\u005d\u0061\u0029\u0020\u007b\u0053\u0079\u0073\u0074\u0065\u006d
      \u002e\u006f\u0075\u0074\u002e\u0070\u0072\u0069\u006e\u0074\u006c\u006e
       \u0028\u0022\u0048\u0069\u0021\u0022\u0029\u003b\u007d\u007d\u002f\u002a

   */
```

Computer consultant Mike Morton suggested to me that these *should* be an Obfuscated *Java* competition, just so we could name it the "OJ trial."

The second program is my attempt to greatly improve program portability. This one source file can be compiled by an ANSI C compiler, and executed. The same code can also be compiled by a Java compiler, and executed. And by a C++ compiler! Am I having a great day or what. True source portability! Every program should do as well. This program is on the CD.

```
/*  Peter van der Linden,    "Just Java"
    April 1, 1996
    Real portability: this is both a Java program and a C program.

    Compile and run this Java program with:  javac b.java    java b
    Compile and run this C program with:     cc    b.c       a.out
    \u002a\u002f\u002f*/

#define String char*
#define t struct
#include <stdio.h>
t{t{int(*print)(const char*,...);}out;}
System={{printf}};/*\u002a\u002f

public class b {
                              public static void
/* The main routine                          */     main (
/* The number of arguments \u002a\u002f\u002f*/          int     argc,
/* The array of argument strings             */         String argv[] )
                        {
                              System.out.print("Hi!\n");
                        }


/*\u002a\u002f}/**/
```

How does this tri-lingual program work?

Please don't suggest an International Obfuscated Java Code Competition! It works for C because there are so many opportunities to abuse the preprocessor, the expression semantics, the library calls, and so on. Java doesn't offer half so many opportunities to unscrew the unscrutable, so let's keep things that way, OK?

Table 9-3 Public fields and methods of Events and Listeners.

Component that generates this kind of Event	Interface that your event-handling code will implement	Method(s) that the interface promises
Button, List MenuItem TextField	`ActionListener`	`public void actionPerformed(ActionEvent e);`
ScrollPane Scrollbar	`AdjustmentListener`	`public void adjustmentValueChanged(AdjustmentEvent e);`

	`ComponentListener`	`public void componentResized(ComponentEvent);`
		`public void componentMoved(ComponentEvent);`
		`public void componentShown(ComponentEvent);`
		`public void componentHidden(ComponentEvent);`

	`ContainerListener`	`public void componentAdded(ContainerEvent);` `public void componentRemoved(ContainerEvent);`
Component	`FocusListener`	`public void focusGained(FocusEvent e);` `public void focusLost(FocusEvent e);`
Checkbox Checkbox- MenuItem Choice List	`ItemListener`	`public void itemStateChanged(ItemEvent e);`

Component	`KeyListener`	`public void keyTyped(KeyEvent e);`
		`public void keyPressed(KeyEvent e);`
		`public void keyReleased(KeyEvent e);`

Component	`MouseListener`	`public void mouseClicked(MouseEvent e);`
		`public void mousePressed(MouseEvent e);`
		`public void mouseReleased(MouseEvent e);`
		`public void mouseEntered(MouseEvent e);`
		`public void mouseExited(MouseEvent e);`

Component	`MouseMotionListener`	`public void mouseDragged(MouseEvent e);` `public void mouseMoved(MouseEvent e);`
Text- Component	`TextListener`	`public void textValueChanged(TextEvent e);`
	`WindowListener`	`public void windowOpened(WindowEvent e);`

Dialog Frame Window		`public void windowClosing(WindowEvent e);`
		`public void windowClosed(WindowEvent e);`
		`public void windowIconified(WindowEvent e);`
		`public void windowDeiconified(WindowEvent e):`
		`public void windowActivated(WindowEvent e);`
		`public void WindowDeactivated (WindowEvent e);`

CHAPTER
10

Graphics
Programming

"A disciple of the temple once asked a Zen master "What is Risk?" The master patiently explained, "It is that which has caused men to venture everything in its pursuit. It is associated with intense speed, and it is prominent in the overlapping flow of events. It embraces the simplest and most consistent of designs in life."

"I see," said the disciple, "so that is peril, hazard, chance, or risk." "Risk?" said the master, "I thought you said RISC."

-Anonymous

This chapter covers the more advanced features of window programming, namely those associated with graphics rather than window widgets. In this chapter we will cover color, fonts, and how to draw shapes on a Canvas or Panel. We will then look at Images and some Image Processing. We'll finish up with an explanation and some sample programs showing Java's support for audio output. Table 10-1 lists the methods that cause the screen to be displayed.

Table 10-1: Common Graphics methods

Method	Description
void repaint()	You may call this to request that the window be refreshed. Typically, you would call it if you have changed the appearance of something, and you want to see it on the screen. It calls update()
void update(Graphics g)	This routine exists to let you participate in painting the window. It defaults to clearing the area then painting it, but you can conceivably override it to do something additional. However, most of your programs will not override this, and will not call this.
void paint(Graphics g)	Will be called by the window system when the component needs to be redisplayed. You will not call this. You will override this if you dynamically change the appearance of the screen, and want to see it appear.

Colors

Naturally, Java allows you to put colors on the screen and there is a class called Color in the java.awt package. The basic color model used by Java is a common one in the computer industry. Colors are made up of a red, a green, and a blue component, each of which is described by a byte value saying how vivid that color is, ranging from 0 (darkest shade) to 255 (lightest shade). This is known as the RGB model. The actual color used in rendering will be the best match in the color space available for a given output device. Images (like JPEG files) also have an "alpha" component that describes how transparent a pixel[1] is.

Again this is stored in a byte, so it takes 32 bits just to store a single pixel on the screen. This is why some graphics programs can swamp your system. For large images, megabytes of data need to be moved around. The "alpha" comes in later with images, it isn't part of the Color class.

You need to experiment with this a little to get a feel for it. Figure 10-1 shows an applet that allows you to set the R, G, and B values and see the resulting color mix.

---

1. A Pixel is a "Picture Element." It is a dot on a computer screen. When people say screens are 1024 by 768 (or whatever) they are referring to the number of pixels it can display. A pixel is like a grain of sand. By itself it is almost unnoticeable, nothing happens until you have thousands of them.

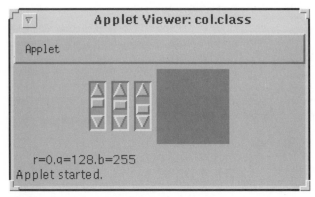

Figure 10-1:   The RGB can be set like this

To get these results, type in the following 30-line program (or copy it off the CD in file ch10/col.java):

```java
// <applet code=col.class   height=100 width=300>  </applet>
//
//  An applet to show how colors are made up of three values,
//   0-255 representing each of red, green, and blue.
//  Uses the JDK 1.1 event model

import java.awt.*;
import java.awt.event.*;
import java.applet.*;
public class col extends Applet {

    Scrollbar s1 = new Scrollbar(Scrollbar.VERTICAL,0,50,0,255);
    Scrollbar s2 = new Scrollbar(Scrollbar.VERTICAL,0,50,0,255);
    Scrollbar s3 = new Scrollbar(Scrollbar.VERTICAL,0,50,0,255);
    Canvas c = new Canvas();

    int r,g,b;
    public void init () {
        s1.setUnitIncrement(10); s1.setBlockIncrement(25);
        s2.setUnitIncrement(10); s2.setBlockIncrement(25);
        s3.setUnitIncrement(10); s3.setBlockIncrement(25);
        add(s1); add(s2); add(s3); add(c);
        ScrAdj sa = new ScrAdj();
        s1.addAdjustmentListener(sa);
        s2.addAdjustmentListener(sa);
        s3.addAdjustmentListener(sa);
        c.setSize(75,75);
    }
```

```
public void paint(Graphics gr) {
    c.setBackground(new Color(r,g,b) );
    gr.drawString("r="+r+ ",g="+g+ ",b="+b, 20,100);
}


class ScrAdj implements AdjustmentListener {
  public void adjustmentValueChanged(AdjustmentEvent ae) {
    System.out.println("ae="+ae);
    Scrollbar s = (Scrollbar) ae.getAdjustable();
        if (s==s1) r=ae.getValue();
    else if (s==s2) g=ae.getValue();
    else            b=ae.getValue();
    repaint();
  }
}

}
```

We've already seen how you can use a Color object to set the color of a component. Here's an example of how that might be done in practice.

```
Frame f = new Frame("my frame");
f.setForeground( Color.white );

f.setBackground( new Color(255,175,175) ); //pink
```

The class Color has the following methods and constants, among others:

```
public final class Color {

  public final static Color white = new Color(255, 255, 255);
  public final static Color gray = new Color(128, 128, 128);
  public final static Color black = new Color(0, 0, 0);
  public final static Color red = new Color(255, 0, 0);
  public final static Color pink = new Color(255, 175, 175);
  public final static Color orange = new Color(255, 200, 0);
  public final static Color yellow = new Color(255, 255, 0);
  public final static Color green = new Color(0, 255, 0);
  public final static Color magenta= new Color(255, 0, 255);
  public final static Color cyan = new Color(0, 255, 255);
  public final static Color blue = new Color(0, 0, 255);

  public Color(int r, int g, int b);
  public Color(int rgb);
  public Color(float r, float g, float b);

  public int getRed();
  public int getGreen();
  public int getBlue();
  public int getRGB();

  public Color brighter();
  public Color darker();

  public static int HSBtoRGB(float hue, float saturation, float brightness);
  public static float[] RGBtoHSB(int r, int g, int b, float[] hsbvals);
  public static Color getHSBColor(float h, float s, float b);
}
```

There's an alternative color model, known as HSB, meaning *Hue Saturation and Brightness*. Java doesn't use this, but it allows easy translations using the methods just described.

So when will I use the `paint()`, `repaint()`, **or** `update()` **methods?**

If you just use the static display typical of a GUI, you might never need to override any of the three above methods. You can often just hide() and show() Components as needed. Let's explain when you use paint().

Normally the window system keeps track of what you have put on the screen. If you obscure it with other windows and then bring it to the front, the window system is responsible for restoring the state.

If, however, you wish to *change* what you have put on the screen (say you have displayed a GIF that you now want to replace with something else), this would be accomplished by overriding paint(). Code in init() can get something on the screen to begin with. Code in paint() can change the screen and get something different up there. You call repaint() to signal to the window system that it needs to update the screen. The window system will then call your paint() method to put the new image on the screen. It's done this way because paint takes an argument (a Graphics context) that you don't normally have (or need to have) access to. Repaint() doesn't need any arguments.

Repaint() calls update() which calls clear() and then paint(). You might override update() if you are doing some advanced graphics work, and you know that you only need a small portion of the screen to be changed (e.g. in an animation). Update gives you the opportunity to achieve this, by providing a point where you can insert your own code between repaint() and paint(). In addition,

```
repaint(x,y,w,h);
```

will repaint just the stated size rectangle at the given coordinates. Paint may be called by the runtime independent of update.

Summary: You never call paint() yourself. You may override it, but the understanding is always that it will be called for you at the times the window system thinks it needs to update the screen. If you want to force the window system to think that, then call "repaint()."

Repaint() simply lodges a request to update the screen, and returns immediately. Its effect is asynchronous, and if there are several paint requests outstanding it is possible that only the last `paint()` will be done. ☙

Fonts and Font Metrics

Fonts and information about font size are encapsulated into two classes: Font and FontMetrics. Just as with Colors, whatever font is current will be used in all text drawing operations in the AWT. However, it will not be used in operations like System.out.println. Think about it: those are Stream operations that merely push data in and out of files, and not to the screen. Only the window system cares about the physical appearance of that data.

Notice in the following example that the "foo" text will appear in the current font.

```
paint(Graphics g) {
  g.drawString("foo",10,10);
}
```

You're given a default font to start you off, then you can change any of the characteristics, or construct a new font and set it as the font to use.

> Try modifying the "mobile button" program q.java, so that the button has a background color of red, a foreground color of white, and is labeled in italic courier size 18 point. The source is on the CD. Setting colors on buttons is buggy in JDK 1.0.2.

You can construct a new font with:

```
Font loud = new Font  ("TimesRoman", Font.BOLD, 18);
```

You can make that the current font for any Component (any Button, Label, MenuItem, Canvas) or Graphics object, with:

```
this.setFont(loud);
```

The constructor for a Font is simply:

```
public Font( String name, int style, int size);
```

You can set the font (courier, helvetica, etc.), the style (PLAIN, **BOLD**, *ITALIC*, or combinations of the three), and the size (8 point, 10 point, 12 point etc.) any way you like.

Different computer systems will have fonts that are similar but have different names. The reason font names vary is that owners of the font can charge for using its name. For example, the closest thing available to the Windows WingDings font on Unix is called Zapf Dingbats (really). It's a screwy font, so everyone gives it a screwy name. Java copes with this by mapping your font request to the closest font, size and style that is on the underlying system. These five font names can be taken for granted:

- TimesRoman

- `Courier`

- Helvetica

- Σψμβολ (Symbol. The font will be different on different systems)

- Dialog

Fonts are very straightforward. The FontMetric class allows you to compute the exact position of Strings, namely how wide and high they are in terms of pixels. This will allow you to lay out strings exactly centered or to mix Strings of different styles and get the spacing right. You might do this if you were writing a word processor in Java, but it's a bit fussy for everyday use. Figure 10.2 shows how the terms relate to typeface measurements.

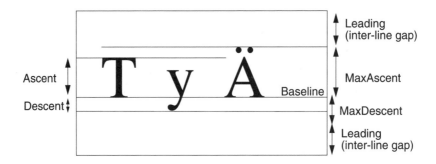

FontMetrics

getLeading()   is the standard line spacing for the font. This is the amount of space between the max descent of one line and the maximum ascent of the next line.

getAscent()   is the distance from the baseline to the top of most characters in the font.

getMaxAscent() is the distance from the baseline to the highest pixel painted of any character in the font. This may be the same as the ascent.

Figure 10-2:   FontMetrics terms as they relate to typeface measurements

FontMetrics has these methods, which return values in units of a pixel (a dot on the screen).

```
public abstract class FontMetrics {
    public Font getFont() {

    public int getLeading(); // print term for line spacing
    public int getAscent();
    public int getDescent();
    public int getHeight() // leading + ascent + descent

    public int getMaxAscent() {
    public int getMaxDescent() {

    // For backward compatibility only.
    public int getMaxDecent() // some programmers can't spell...

    public int charWidth(char ch);
    public int stringWidth(String str);
}
```

The font metrics give you the real measurements of the font that is actually in use on your system, not the theoretical measurements of the font you asked for. The two may well be different.

The Graphics Context

A Graphics object is what you ultimately draw lines, shapes and text on. It is also called a "graphics context" in some window systems because it bundles together information about a drawable area, plus font, color, clipping region, and other situational factors. If you look at the code in $JAVAHOME/src/java/awt/Graphics.java, you will see that it is an abstract class:

```
public abstract class Graphics { ...
```

Therefore it cannot be instantiated directly, and you will never see code like:

```
Graphics gr = new Graphics(); // NO!
```

The most common way to obtain a Graphics object is as the argument to a paint() routine in a Canvas or Panel. (You'll actually get some concrete subclass of graphics, the details of which you never need worry about). Less commonly, you can explicitly ask for the Graphics object belonging to any Component or any Image with the call:

```
myComponent mc ...

Graphics mg = mc.getGraphics();
```

When you call getGraphics() it is usually for an Image, Panel or Canvas. It's unlikely you'll want to get the Graphics object for anything else, such as a button. There is too much peer behavior associated with it for you to be able to add to it sensibly. When you have a Graphics object, you can draw on it, and later paint it to the screen. You can clip it (shrink the drawing area). You can modify the colors and fonts. A common reason for explicitly getting the Graphics context of an Image is to do double-buffering, or to draw over an Image you have read in. All these techniques are explained in this chapter. If you do explicitly call:

```
Graphics g = myPanel.getGraphics();
```

make sure you also call this when you are done with it:

```
g.dispose();
```

Graphics objects take up operating system resources (more than just memory), and a window system may have a limited number of them. When you clean them up explicitly without waiting for garbage collection to kick in, your system will usually tick along more smoothly.

Drawing Text, Lines, and Shapes

These are the methods of Graphics that draw text, lines, and shapes. Most of these come in two varieties: a drawXXX and a fillXXX. The first puts an empty outline on the screen, the second puts the outline and fills the interior with a solid color. In both cases the foreground color is used. A graphics object has the method `setColor(Color c)` to change the foreground color, but it doesn't have any direct way to change the background color. The underlying panel (or whatever) must do that, as shown in the following cases.

```
public void drawString(String str, int x, int y);
```

Here, the string is placed at location x,y on this component. For example:

```
public void paint(Graphics g) {
    g.drawString("The dentist whined incessantly", 10, 15);
}
```

A common pitfall with this method and the next two is drawing with y coordinate zero. That makes the characters disappear as they will be almost completely off the top of the canvas.

```
public void drawChars(char data[], int offset, int length, int x, int y)
public void drawBytes(byte data[], int offset, int length, int x, int y)
```

These two methods place characters or bytes from the array data[offset] to data[offset+length-1] on the component starting at location (x,y).

```
public void drawLine(int x1, int y1, int x2, int y2);
```

A line one pixel wide is drawn from (x1,y1) to (x2,y2). There is no support for drawing lines thicker than one pixel. The workaround is to use the fillPolygon described later. Like all of these methods, the rendering is done in whatever you have set the color to. The default foreground color is black.

```
public void drawRect(int x, int y, int width, int height);
public void fillRect(int x, int y, int width, int height);
```

A rectangle of the stated width and height is drawn with its top left corner at (x,y). There is also a `void clearRect(x,y,w,h)` that gets rid of a rectangle.

```
public void draw3DRect(int x, int y, int width, int height, boolean raised);
public void fill3DRect(int x, int y, int width, int height, boolean raised);
```

A rectangle of the stated width and height is drawn with its top left corner at (x,y). The rectangle is artfully shaded on two sides to make it appear to be standing out (raised=true) or to be impressed (raised=false). A raised rectangle is shaded with brighter color, and a non-raised one with a darker color. Figure 10-3 shows some 3D rectangles.

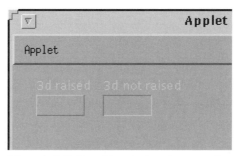

Figure 10-3:   3D raised and unraised

Here is the code that generated the screen shot:

```
// <applet code=graf.class height=300 width=500> </applet>
import java.awt.*;
import java.applet.*;
public class graf  extends Applet {

    public void paint(Graphics g) {
        g.setColor(Color.cyan);
        g.drawString("3d raised", 25,25);
        g.draw3DRect(25,30,50,20,true);
        g.drawString("3d not raised", 95,25);
        g.draw3DRect(95,30,50,20,false);
    }
}
```

Here are two more ways to draw a rectangle

```
public void drawRoundRect(int x, int y, int width, int height, int
  arcWidth, int arcHeight);
public void fillRoundRect(int x, int y, int width, int height, int
  arcWidth, int arcHeight);
```

There are Like drawRect and fillRect, only these rectangles have rounded corners.

You control the diameter of the rounded corners by setting the width and height of the curved portion in pixels. If you use values that are comparable to the width and height of the rectangle, you end up with an oval not a rectangle, as shown in Figure 10-4. Rule of thumb: use arc width and height that are 15-25% of the rectangle width and height

Figure 10-4: A rounded rectangle

Here is the code that generated the diagram:

```
// <applet code=graf.class    height=300 width=500> </applet>
import java.awt.*;
import java.applet.*;
public class graf  extends Applet {

    public void paint(Graphics g) {
        g.setColor(Color.cyan);
        g.drawString("round", 25,25);
        g.fillRoundRect(25,30,  50,100,15,25);
    }
}
```

```
public void drawOval(int x, int y, int width, int height);
public void fillOval(int x, int y, int width, int height);
```

These two methods draw ovals. The arguments are easy to understand if you compare the methods to drawRect(). The oval that is drawn is one that fits exactly in the rectangle of that width and height. The imaginary rectangle's top left corner is at the (x,y) location (see Figure 10-5).

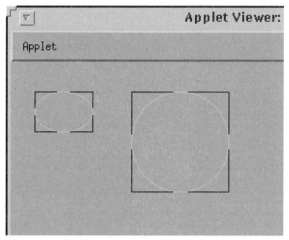

Figure 10-5: Two ovals, and their bounding rectangles

Here is the code that generated the diagram:

```
// <applet code=graf.class height=300 width=500> </applet>
import java.awt.*;
import java.applet.*;
public class graf  extends Applet {

    public void paint(Graphics g) {
        g.drawRect(25,30, 60,40);
        g.drawRect(125,30, 100,100);

        g.setColor(Color.cyan);
        g.drawOval(25,30, 60,40);
        g.drawOval(125,30, 100,100);
    }
}
```

As can be seen, an oval with the width=height is a circle.

```
public void drawArc(int x, int y, int width, int height,
            int startAngle, int arcAngle);
public void fillArc(int x, int y, int width, int height,
            int startAngle, int arcAngle);
```

Again, the starting point for understanding these two methods is the rectangle located at (x,y). Then imagine dividing the rectangle into four quadrants. This x axis from the origin of the quadrants represents 0 degrees. The starting point for the arc is the offset from this line: 90 is straight up (along the y axis), 270 is straight down.

Finally, the arcAngle is how many degrees to sweep from that starting point. See Figure 10-6. Note that it is *not* the end angle as many people assume. A negative arcAngle sweeps clockwise, and a positive one counter clockwise. You never need use a negative angle because an arc sweeping 40 degrees forward from 90 degrees is the same as an arc sweeping 40 degrees back from 50 degrees.

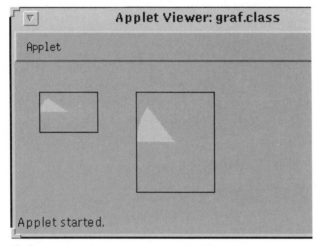

Figure 10-6:   An arc has the same concept of bounding box as an oval

Here is the code that generated the diagram:

```
import java.awt.*;
import java.applet.*;
public class graf  extends Applet {

    public void paint(Graphics g) {
        g.drawRect(25,30,  60,40);
        g.drawRect(125,30,  80,100);
        g.setColor(Color.cyan);
        g.fillArc(25,30,  60,40,  135,45);
        g.fillArc(125,30,  80,100,  135,45);
    }
}
```

```
public void drawPolygon(int xPoints[], int yPoints[], int nPoints);
public void fillPolygon(int xPoints[], int yPoints[], int nPoints);
```

Polygons are shapes with an arbitrary number of straight sides. To draw or fill one using these methods, you provide an array of x coordinates, and an array of corresponding y coordinates, along with the total number of points.

If you want the polygon to be drawn closed you have to duplicate the starting point at the end of the arrays. Figure 10-7 is an example of polygons:

Figure 10-7: A filled polygon connects its endpoints automatically as it fills

Here is the code that generated the diagram:

```
// <applet    code=graf.class height=300 width=500> </applet>
import java.awt.*;
import java.applet.*;
public class graf   extends Applet {

    public void paint(Graphics g) {
        g.setColor(Color.cyan);
        int x_vals[] = {75,45,15,45,45 };
        int y_vals[] = {40,70,40,10,40 };

        g.drawPolygon(x_vals, y_vals, x_vals.length);

        for (int i=0;i<5;i++) x_vals[i]+=80;
        g.fillPolygon(x_vals, y_vals, x_vals.length);
    }
}
```

```
public void drawPolygon(Polygon p);
public void fillPolygon(Polygon p);
```

These two overloaded methods draw or fill a Polygon object. A Polygon object is constructed from the same arrays of (x,y) pairs as used previously:

```
Polygon(int xPoints[], int yPoints[], int nPoints);
```

You pass in the number of points if you only want the first N elements of the array to form the polygon. However, you can also add new points to a polygon, simply by calling this method with an (x,y) pair:

```
pol.addPoint(10,20);
```

A Polygon also knows what its bounding box is.

That concludes most of the important routines for drawing text, lines and shapes. The next section covers the topic of loading images into memory and rendering (drawing) them onto a graphics context.

Loading and Drawing Images

An Image, as the name suggests holds a picture in memory. Originally, a picture will have been scanned in and stored in a file in GIF, JPEG, raster, postscript or other format. Java can currently only process the GIF and JPEG format.

A GIF is a file format for storing pictures. GIF stands for Graphic Interchange Format, and it was originally developed by CompuServe to be a system-independent way to store images. GIFs only store 8 bits of color information per pixel. Just adequate for run-of-the-mill PCs that only allow 256 different colors on screen at once, it is rapidly heading for technical obsolescence. Only use GIFs for cartoons and line drawings. GIF includes compression based on the Lempel-Ziv-Welch (LZW) algorithm, so the files are smaller than they would otherwise be. LZW compression is protected by a software patent filed by Unisys a few years ago. A copy of the public record for this patent is on the CD in just-java/ch1. If you've never seen a software patent before, take a look at this example, for some incredible claims about what has been "invented."

A JPEG is a newer and superior file format for compressing images. It's an acronym for Joint Photographic Experts Group (the committee that wrote the standard). An image in JPEG format can take much less storage space than the same picture in GIF format. However, the JPEG format also allows you to trade off image quality against storage needs—more requires more. When you save an image in JPEG format, you can specify a percentage for the image quality. JPEG stores full color information: 24 bits per pixel.

Before you can draw an Image onto a Graphics object, you must have an Image to draw. The most common way of getting one is to load it from a file. Another way of getting an Image is to call createImage() for a particular Component. We'll start by dealing with an image in GIF or JPEG format in a file. An image can be displayed in either an applet or an application. The two alternatives vary slightly.

Loading an Image File in an Application

Here is some code to display a file in an application. We create a Frame, read in the image file from our URL, instantiate a canvas, and off we go.

The only novelty about this is the way we get the image. We have to use something called the "default toolkit" which is available in the AWT. It provides a getImage() method for applications. Note that you can get an Image from a URL (i.e. anywhere) as well as from a local file specified by a pathname as shown here.

```java
import java.awt.*;
import java.net.*;
public class display {

    static public void main(String a[]) {
        Image i = Toolkit.getDefaultToolkit().getImage("dickens.jpg");
        Frame f = new Frame("my frame");

        myCanvas mc = new myCanvas(i);
        f.resize(350,200);
        f.add(mc);
        f.show();
    }
}

class myCanvas extends Canvas {
    Image saved_i;
    public myCanvas(Image i) {
        this.resize(300,200);
        saved_i = i;
    }

    public void paint(Graphics g){
        g.drawImage(saved_i, 10, 10, this);
    }
}
```

There are plenty of pitfalls to avoid when you type in this code. If you get one of these wrong, your image will not appear and you will not get any kind of helpful error message either. Here are some potential problems:

- You must resize the frame in order to see it!

- If you provide a file name which doesn't exist or can't be accessed, it will fail silently. The same if you use the URL alternative for getImage.

- If you don't resize the canvas, it won't show up.

If you get all this correct, Figure 10-8 will appear.

Figure 10-8: See Dickens lay down —on the Internet sometimes they *do* know you're a dog.

Loading an Image File in an Applet

To load an image file in an Applet, we simply reference its URL. File access is usually restricted in an Applet, so there is no getImage that takes a pathname as an argument. However, recall that a URL can point to a resource anywhere on the Internet, so if the file is local to your system it can find it (if your security manager allows your applet to read local files). The Applet method is:

```
public Image getImage(URL url);
```

It allows you to specify a complete absolute URL to the image file. Some examples would be:

```
URL u1 = new URL("http://sparcs/images/ball.jpg");     //remote
URL u2 = new URL("file:///home/linden/puppy.jpg"); // local
```

The other alternative lets you specify a URL and an image filename that is relative to where the URL points.

```
public Image getImage(URL url, String name);
```

This is more common in an applet because the images files are usually stored in the same directory as the HTML document or the class files. For these cases you can use

```
getDocumentBase() // the URL of the document containing the applet
getCodeBase() // the URL of the applet class file
```

So an example would be:

```
Image i;
  ...
i=getImage( getDocumentBase(), "puppy.jpg");
```

Note there is a pitfall here! A very common mistake is to try to call getImage() to initialize the image as you declare it, like this:

```
Image i1 = getImage(getDocumentBase(), "spot.jpg");
```

That compiles without a problem, but (if the Image is declared outside any method, as normal) it fails at runtime like this:

```
java.lang.NullPointerException
      at java.applet.Applet.getDocumentBase(Applet.java:59)
      at jpg.<init>(jpg.java:7)
      at sun.applet.AppletPanel.runLoader(AppletPanel.java:386)
```

The reason is that before the init() method of an Applet is called there isn't enough structure in place for calls to other methods of Applet to succeed. You can't do much with an Applet until its init() method has been called, which is the right place to put this getImage() call.

If you can't remember which methods belong to Applet, just use the following rule of thumb: In an applet don't call any methods to initialize data fields in their declaration. Instead declare them, then initialize them separately in the init() method.

A related pitfall concerns the createImage() method. Many people want to create an Image in the constructor of, for example, a Canvas.

```
public class MyCanvas extends Canvas{
   Image myImage;
   Graphics myGraphics;

   public MyCanvas(){
      myImage=this.createImage(100,50); //  this returns Null.
      myGraphics=myImage.getGraphics(); // so this throws NullPtrExcptn.
   }
```

The createImage() method does not work until *after* the Canvas has been added to a Container. So in general you can't create the Image in the constructor. One workaround is to also add the Canvas to its Container in the constructor. This is because a peer for the Canvas component must have been created before we can get its image. But we are still in the class constructor, so unless we force peer creation by doing an add(), createImage here will always fail and return a null pointer. These limitations are defects in the design of this Java library.

The code using getImage () brings the image into memory, and holds it in the Image object. The next step is to render it on the screen.

How do you get a Java applet to load an HTML page into the browser?

The method `this.getAppletContext().showDocument(URL)` will make the browser load the page from the specified URL. There is also a version that takes a String argument:

```
public abstract void showDocument(URL url, String target)
```

The string says where to show it:

- "`_self`" (bring the URL up in the current frame)
- "`_parent`" (bring it up in the parent frame)
- "`_top`" (show it in the top-most frame)
- "`_blank`" (show it in a new unnamed frame)

Similarly,

```
this.getAppletContext().showStatus("Get out in the fresh air more.");
```

will put the message on the browser status line. ❦

Drawing an Image Onto a Graphics Object

The Graphics object has four variations of the drawImage() method:

- ```
  public boolean drawImage(Image img, int x, int y,
        ImageObserver observer);
  ```

  This draws the specified image at the specified coordinates (x, y). The image is cut off as necessary if it is larger than the area it is being drawn onto.

- ```
  public boolean drawImage(Image img, int x, int y,
        int width, int height,
        ImageObserver observer);
  ```

  This scales the image as needed to fit within the width and height specified as it draws it. Depending on the values you supply, that might change the proportions of the picture, stretching or shrinking it in one direction.

- ```
  public boolean drawImage(Image img, int x, int y,
       Color bgcolor,
       ImageObserver observer);
  ```

- ```
  public boolean drawImage(Image img, int x, int y,
       int width, int height,
       Color bgcolor,
       ImageObserver observer);.
  ```

These last two methods are just variations on the first, with the addition of providing a solid background color behind the image being drawn.

At this point, you are probably asking yourself what is that final parameter called "ImageObserver." If you have a good memory, you might recall that we described it in Chapter 6. We will review it again shortly, but for now let's note that an Applet is an example of an ImageObserver, so wherever one is required, we can just provide the "this" of an Applet. The entire code to load and display a file in an Applet is thus just this:

```java
// <applet code=jpg.class height=250  width=300> </applet>
import java.awt.*;
import java.applet.*;

public class jpg extends Applet {

    Image i;

    public void init() {
        i=getImage( getDocumentBase(), "puppy.jpg");
    }

    public void paint(Graphics g) {
        boolean b = g.drawImage(i,25,25, this);
    }
}
```

Running this code results in Figure 10-9 appearing on the screen.

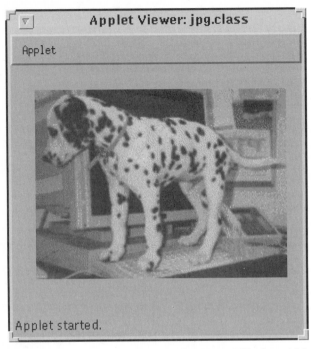

Figure 10-9: See Young Dickens do the "Type-5 Keyboard Macarena"

The ImageObserver Argument

Let's get back to the ImageObserver argument used in drawImage. When you call getImage() to bring an image file into memory, the method returns at once, and in the background at some point a separate thread starts reading the file off disk somewhere on the Internet. That incoming image data is said to be an observable event. And you can specify who or what is going to observe it.

As a matter of fact, Component implements the ImageObserver interface. Every button, frame, canvas, panel, label etc is an ImageObserver and able to register its interest in observing incoming images. An applet being a subclass of Panel is also therefore an ImageObserver. We normally just put "this" down as the argument and the right thing happens by default. As the image comes in gradually, more and more of it is painted onto the screen.

Why have an ImageObserver? Why not just use Observer/Observable? Through an oversight or by design, Observable is a class, not an interface. Any class wishing to be observable must use up its one chance to inherit. In the case of Image it was felt better to provide the specialized interface ImageObserver.

Why bother with an Observer at all, though? The reason it's done this way, instead of the obvious implementation of making getImage() stall until the bytes are loaded, is twofold:

1. The human factors of waiting for an image file to load are truly horrible. In other words, few things make users angrier than being forced to sit idle while some hideous GIF loads scanline by scanline, so

2. Everyone would end up writing every getImage() as a separate thread. This way, your applet is decoupled from the slow net for free.

Better yet, as pieces of the image are gradually loaded into memory, there will be a number of times when there is enough information to call ImageObserver.imageupdate(). It may be called when the image file header has been read, when we have decoded enough to know the height of the image, when we know the width, and when the entire transfer has been completed.

The Component class contains an imageUpdate() method. When it is called, it schedules a repaint, allowing a little more of the image to be drawn without interfering at all with your thread of control. There are a couple of properties in Table 10-2 that affect this.

Table 10-2: System Properties

Property	Effect
"awt.image.incrementaldraw"	True: (default) draw parts of an image as it arrives. False: don't draw until all the image is loaded.
"awt.image.redrawrate"	The default value is 100. It is the minimum period in milliseconds between calls to repaint for images. This property only applies if the first one is true.

JDK1.0 doesn't support setting an individual property. You change a property by instantiating a new property table based on the system one, then appending your modifications.

The code below updates the entire system properties table. If you just want to add one or two properties, you can't do it directly, but you can do it indirectly as shown in Chapter 6. You create a new properties table, supplying the system properties table to the constructor. You add properties one by one to your new table. When you search, if a property isn't found in your new table, the program will proceed to look in the system properties table. Clumsy but it works.

```
import java.io.*;
import java.util.*;

public class read {

  public static void main(String args[]) {
    try {

        // get the standard system properties into a property table
        Properties MyProps = new Properties(System.getProperties());

        // add my new properties to that table
        MyProps.put( "awt.image.incrementaldraw", "true" );
        MyProps.put( "awt.image.redrawrate", "50" );

        // set that table as the system property table.
        System.setProperties(MyProps);

        // list all properties
        System.getProperties().list(System.out);

    } catch (Exception e) {e.printStackTrace();}

  }
}
```

When you change a property, the change only lasts for as long as your program runs. If you want to permanently change a property you need to write the property file out to disk (with your change) and read it back in at the start of each program.

You can save a property table to a file with

```
// save a property table to a file
FileOutputStream fos = new FileOutputStream("banana.txt");
MyProps.save(fos, "my own properties");
fos.close();
```

You can read a property table back from a file with

```
// read in a property table from a file
FileInputStream fis = new FileInputStream("banana.txt");
MyProps.load(fis);
fis.close();
```

Image Update

If you want to retain really tight control over an incoming image you can overload imageUpdate() in your applet that will override the regular version in the Component parent class. Whenever there is more information available, your imageUpdate() will be called repeatedly until you return a value of false to indicate that you've got enough information. The following code example will clarify how this works:

```java
import java.applet.*;
import java.awt.*;

public class iu extends Applet {
    Image    i;
        int times=0,  flags=0,x=0,y=0,w=0,h=0;

    public void init() {
        i = getImage(getDocumentBase(), "spots.jpeg" );
        w = i.getWidth(this);   System.err.println("INIT:w="+w);
        h = i.getHeight(this);  System.err.println("INIT:h="+h);
    }

    public boolean imageUpdate(Image i, int flags,
                        int x, int y, int w, int h) {
                if (times++<5)
                    System.err.println("my IMAGEUPDATE: flags="
                                    +flags+ " w="+w+ " h="+h);
                return true;
    }

    public void paint (Graphics g) {
        g.drawImage(i,50,50, this);

    }

}
```

This clearly shows how imageUpdate is a callback routine. Experiment with this example (invoke with the usual html file), including removing the limitation of 5 prints in the middle of imageUpdate (done so that the information doesn't scroll off the screen the first time you try it).

The Media Tracker

The ImageObserver interface is good for really low-level control of loading media files. But for some purposes it's a bit too low-level. If you just want to wait till a file is loaded completely, and you don't care to hear about the 57 intermediate stages of loading it, then the MediaTracker class is for you.

MediaTracker is actually built using ImageObserver, and it allows you to track the status of a number of media objects. Media objects could include audio clips, though currently only images are supported.

To use MediaTracker, simply create an instance and then call addImage() for each image to be tracked. Each image can be assigned a unique ID for indentification purposes. The IDs control the priority order in which the images are fetched as well as identifying unique subsets of the images that can be waited on independently. You then waitForID(n), which will suspend the thread until the image is completely loaded. The methods isErrorAny() and isErrorID(i) let you know if everything went OK for all the images or for a particular ID group.

Here is an example of the MediaTracker in use:

```
public void init() {
    MediaTracker t = new MediaTracker (this);
    Image i = getImage (getDocumentBase "spots.gif");
    t.addImage (i,1);
    try    {t.waitForID(1);}
    catch  (InterruptedException ie) {return;}
    //Image is now in memory, ready to draw
}
```

Image Processing

By putting together the basic classes that have already been described, and sprinkling a couple of new ones in, some pretty sophisticated image processing can be achieved. This section will describe the standard techniques for getting smoother animation by overriding update and double buffering. Start with this brief applet. The code and JPEG image files are on the CD in directory justjava/ch10.

```java
//<applet  code=pin.class   width=600 height=350>  </applet>
import java.awt.*;
import java.awt.event.*;
import java.awt.image.*;

public class pin extends java.applet.Applet {
    Image spirit, rolls;
    int new_x=550;
    int new_y=100;

    public void init () {
        spirit = getImage(getDocumentBase(), "spirit.jpg");
        rolls = getImage(getDocumentBase(), "rolls.jpg");
        addMouseMotionListener( new MouseMotionListener () {
          public void mouseDragged(MouseEvent e){
              System.out.println("what a drag");
              new_x=e.getX();
              new_y=e.getY();
              repaint();
          }
          public void mouseMoved(MouseEvent e){}
      } );
    }


    public void paint (Graphics g) {
        g.setColor(Color.gray);
        g.fillRect(0,0,getSize().width, getSize().height );
        g.drawImage (rolls,5, 5, this);
        g.drawImage (spirit, new_x-25, new_y-25, this);
    }

}
```

The code implements a simple "Pin the tail on the donkey" game. In other words, you can use the mouse to drag the image of the Spirit of Ecstasy over to its place on the Rolls Royce radiator. Incidentally, the Spirit of Ecstasy was modeled on a real person: Eleanor Thornton. She was the paramour of early motoring pioneer, the second Lord Montagu. He artfully suggested to his pals on the Rolls-Royce board in 1911 that their cars would be enhanced by a graceful radiator mascot, and he "just happened to know a good one." Sadly, Eleanor Thornton perished in a tragic torpedo mishap in 1915, (Lord Montagu on the same boat was wearing an inflatable cork waistcoat and he made it back to England in time to read his obituary in *The Times*). Thornton's spirit lives on, immortalized on the bonnet of every Rolls-Royce motor car for the last 85 years. But I digress. The applet screen looks like that in Figure 10-10.

Figure 10-10: A moment of silence for Eleanor Thornton

When you run the code you will notice that the applet flickers annoyingly as you drag the mouse. The flickering problem is a well known artifact of imaging programs in all languages. To fix this, there are some Java-specific things to try and some algorithmic things to try. The first and easiest improvement is to look at the default implementation of one of the utility routines, update().

As we drag the mouse, each event causes the new_x and new_y coordinates to be noted, then a request to repaint() is made. Repaint will call Component.update, which looks like this:

```
public void update(Graphics g) {
    g.setColor(getBackground());
    g.fillRect(0, 0, width, height);
    g.setColor(getForeground());
    paint(g);
}
```

It sets the color to the background color, then fills the whole Graphics context with it (in other words erases whatever image is currently there). It then sets the foreground color, and calls paint.

However, we are already painting the whole background in our paint routine. So, repaint calls update which paints the whole panel, then calls paint, which again paints the whole panel. Voila: a flicker or flash is seen as an unnecessary paint is done. We could remove the fillRect() in paint, for it was put there precisely to demonstrate this flicker as a teaching example (and it represents some more general background painting that you may do). A better solution is to override update(), and provide your own version that doesn't clear the applet panel.

```
public void update(Graphics g) {
    paint(g);
}
```

You can (and should) do this whenever your paint routine updates the entire component. If your paint didn't update the entire component, then you couldn't override update in this manner. You'd get pieces of the old image left in place as you dragged it to a new location. Overriding update with a more sensible version reduces flashing considerably, but doesn't eliminate it. For that we'll use a technique called double buffering or offscreen imaging (they mean the same thing).

Double Buffering

Double buffering, or *offscreen imaging* (a more accurate description), is the process of doing all your (slow) drawing to a graphics area in memory. When the entire image is complete, it zaps it up onto the screen in one (fast) operation. The overall time is slightly longer because of the overhead, but the overall effect is stunning because the new graphics context appears instantly.

Here is the code to make the image rendering be double buffered.

```
//<applet  code=pin2.class   width=600 height=350>  </applet>
// same as pin, but uses double buffered output.
// PvdL.
import java.awt.*;
import java.awt.event.*;
import java.awt.image.*;

public class pin2 extends java.applet.Applet {
    Image spirit, rolls;
    Image myOffScreenImage;
    Graphics myOffScreenGraphics;
    int new_x=550;
    int new_y=100;

    public void init () {
        spirit = getImage(getDocumentBase(), "spirit.jpg");
        rolls = getImage(getDocumentBase(), "rolls.jpg");
        myOffScreenImage= createImage(
                getSize().width, getSize().height );
        myOffScreenGraphics = myOffScreenImage.getGraphics();
        addMouseMotionListener( new MouseMotionListener () {
            public void mouseDragged(MouseEvent e){
                System.out.println("what a drag");
                new_x=e.getX();
                new_y=e.getY();
                repaint();
            }
            public void mouseMoved(MouseEvent e){}
        } );
    }

    public void paint (Graphics g) {
        g.setColor(Color.gray);
        g.fillRect(0,0,getSize().width, getSize().height );
        g.drawImage (rolls,5, 5, this);
        g.drawImage (spirit, new_x-25, new_y-25, this);
    }

    public void update(Graphics g) {
        paint(myOffScreenGraphics);     // draws on the db
        // draws the double buffer onto applet
        g.drawImage(myOffScreenImage,0,0, this);
    }

}
```

We don't change paint() at all. Paint will still do its rendering thing onto whatever Graphics context you give it. Here's where the magic comes in. We have added two off-screen objects:

```
Image myOffScreenImage;
Graphics myOffScreenGraphics;
```

In init() these two are initialized. We create an Image the same size of the applet. Then we get a graphics context for it. Now the clever part. We modify update so *first* it paints the offscreen image myOffScreenGraphics. It simply uses the regular call to paint, with myOffScreenGraphics as the argument. That painting won't appear on the screen, as it would if the AWT had called paint with the Graphics object for the applet. Instead it goes to myOffScreenGraphics object. (Sorry to belabor the point, but it is important to understand this thoroughly).

Finally, instead of update() only calling paint() as it did in the previous version, we now do a very quick g.drawImage() to get the just-painted myOffScreenImage onto the Applet's graphics context! Drawing a single pre-constructed image onto the screen is a lot faster than building up a screenful of images one at a time. And that is double buffering.

Clipping Rectangles

The final possible optimization is to use a clipping rectangle to only draw where the image has changed. Clipping is a standard graphics technique to optimize the amount of (slow) drawing that takes place. When you clip, you are telling the paint routine "I know that the only changes in this image are inside this rectangle, so you only need paint inside the rectangle. Everything else remains unchanged."

The clipRect method of Graphics, namely

```
public void clipRect(int x, int y, int width, int height);
```

cuts down the size of the area that is painted to just the *intersection* of what it was and the new rectangle specified by the arguments. This is an optimization used in animations and other graphics programming to speed up output and make it smoother. Many people have complained about the way the clipping rectangle can only be reduced in size. So JDK1.1 added a method

```
setClip(int x, int y, int width, int height)
```

to set the current clip to the specified rectangle. Rendering doesn't take place outside this area.

Depending on how much can be clipped and how long it takes to calculate the overall image, clipping can save a lot of time and effort. Clipping works best on big images where only a little changes at a time. It's tailor-made for animations.

Taking Images Apart: java.awt.image

Java features some pretty substantial support for pulling Images apart to get at individual pixels. It also has a class that takes bytes from memory and assembles them into an Image. One problem with mastering this area of Java is that there is a lot of classes, generality, and infrastructure. As with the stream I/O classes, the profusion of abstractions creates a learning barrier for programmers.

We'll look at two concrete classes in java.awt.image that allow you to have absolute control over your screen images, namely:

- PixelGrabber (implements the abstract class ImageConsumer)

- MemoryImageSource (implements the abstract class ImageProducer).

As the names suggest, ImageConsumer takes an Image away from you (giving you something else you'd rather have, like an array of pixels), while ImageProducer takes something and gives you back the Image that it created from it.

Here's how PixelGrabber works:

1. You construct a new instance of the class supplying the image (or ImageProducer) and lots of sizes and an int array as arguments:

   ```
   PixelGrabber pg = new PixelGrabber ( .... );
   ```

2. You call grabPixels(), which fills the int array with the pixels from the image:

   ```
   pg.grabPixels();
   ```

3. You check the status to see if all bits were grabbed without problems:

   ```
   if (pg.status() & ImageObserver.ALLBITS) != 0)
           // we grabbed all the bits OK
   ```

The two constructors of PixelGrabber are:

```
public PixelGrabber(Image img, int x, int y, int w, int h,  int[]
pix, int off, int scansize);

public PixelGrabber(ImageProducer ip, int x, int y, int w, int h,
int[] pix, int off, int scansize);
```

As you can see, the second constructor has an ImageProducer as its first parameter, but the other arguments (defined here) are the same.

- img is the image to retrieve pixels from

- x is the x coordinate of the upper left corner of the rectangle of pixels to retrieve from the image, relative to the default (unscaled) size of the image

- y is the y coordinate of the upper left corner of the rectangle of pixels to retrieve from the image

- w is the width of the rectangle of pixels to retrieve

- h is the height of the rectangle of pixels to retrieve

- pix is the array of integers which are to be used to hold the RGB pixels retrieved from the image

- off is the offset into the array of where to store the first pixel

- scansize is the distance from one row of pixels to the next in the array

Here's how MemoryImageSource works. It is essentially the complement of Pixel-Grabber. It reads an int array of pixels and gives you back the corresponding image. First, you construct a new instance of the class MemoryImageSource supplying arguments of the int array, and lots of sizes (height, width, scanline size, etc). That will get you a MemoryImageSource object, which implements ImageProducer, and hence can be fed into the Component.createImage() method to obtain a real renderable Image.

There are six constructors for MemoryImageSource. The simplest one is:

```
public MemoryImageSource(int w, int h, int pix[],
                             int off, int scan)
```

This instantiates a w-by-h MemoryImageSource starting from the pix[off] element in the array of pixels, and with scan pixels in each line. The other five constructors allow various combinations of with and without HashTables and ColorModels.

Transparent Backgrounds

We are going to use these two classes on our image of the Spirit of Ecstasy. We are going to grab the pixels, and turn all the pink ones transparent, by setting the alpha byte to zero. If the alpha value of a pixel is 0 it is totally invisible. If the alpha value is 255 it is totally solid color. Values in between allow for varying degrees of translucence or opacity. Since the background is mostly pink, this will turn it transparent, and allow Eleanor Thornton to be seamlessly reunited with her pedestal.

How do I turn the background of my image transparent?

In general, there is no way to say "filter this image, and give it a transparent background." You need a way to identify what is a background pixel and what is a foreground pixel. Here we are using color to identify the background. If the foreground is a regular shape you could use (x,y) position. For more on this, read on.

I touched up these images in Adobe Photoshop beforehand to give them a uniform pink background and sharper edges. If your company won't spring for Adobe Photoshop so you can play around with stuff like this, use the shareware "xv" software that can do many of the same things.

To minimize the learning curve here, let's highlight the new code by making this class extend the class pin2 above. Notice what we are doing here. We already have a class pin2 that does most of what we want. Instead of copying all that code into a new file, and starting hacking from scratch, we just create a new class that *extends* pin2. Then in our new class we place new versions of the methods that we want to replace in pin2. Our new methods will override the corresponding methods in pin2. We have reused pin2 by extending it and adding the changed functionality. The compiler has done most of the work for us. We only have to test the features that have changed. (Isn't Object-Oriented Programming wonderful?)

```
//<applet  code=transp.class   width=600 height=350>  </applet>
// double buffered
// transparent image
// Peter van der Linden, Sept 1996, Silicon Valley, Calif.
import java.awt.*;
import java.awt.image.*;

public class transp extends pin2 {

  public void init () {
   spirit = getImage(getDocumentBase(), "spirit.jpg");
   rolls = getImage(getDocumentBase(), "rolls.jpg");
   myOffScreenImage= createImage(size().width, size().height );
   myOffScreenGraphics = myOffScreenImage.getGraphics();

   spirit = getRidOfPink(spirit);    // filter the image

  }


  int  width=475, height=265;

  public Image getRidOfPink(Image im) {
   try {
 // grab the pixels from the image
    int[] pgPixels = new int [width*height];
    PixelGrabber pg = new PixelGrabber (im, 0, 0,
     width, height, pgPixels, 0, width);

  if (pg.grabPixels() && ((pg.status() & ImageObserver.ALLBITS) != 0))
{
  // Now change some of the bits
   for (int y=0;y<height;y++) {
    for (int x=0;x<width;x++) {
    int i = y*width+x;
    int a = (pgPixels[i] & 0xff000000)>>24;
    int r = (pgPixels[i] & 0x00ff0000)>>16;
    int g = (pgPixels[i] & 0x0000ff00)>>8;
    int b = pgPixels[i] & 0x000000ff;
    // turn the pink-ish pixels transparent.
    if (r>200 && g>100&&g<200&&b>100&&b<200) {
     a=0;
     pgPixels[i] =  a  | (r<<16) | (g<<8) | b;
     }
    }
   }
   im = createImage (new MemoryImageSource (width, height, pgPixels, 0, width));
   }
   } catch (InterruptedException e) { e.printStackTrace (); }
      return im;
  }
}
```

We have overriden init() to add the filtering statement:

```
spirit = getRidOfPink(spirit);   // filter the image
```

And we have added the routine getRidOfPink(). That routine looks fearsome at first, but it quickly breaks down into four simple stages:

1. Grab the pixels

2. Look at each individual pixel. You may be wondering why the pixel array isn't two dimensional, just as an image is. The reason is to keep it closer to the model the hardware uses. Frame buffer (graphics adapter) and CPU memory is one dimensional.

3. If the RGB values are within the range of "generally pink" then make the pixel transparent by setting its alpha value to 0.

4. Reassemble the pixel array into an image with MemoryImageSource.

It's as simple as that. When you run this, you'll see a picture like that in Figure 10-11.

Figure 10-11:   Eleanor transparently on her pedestal

Comparing this image with Figure 10-10, you'll see that the ugly pink background has disappeared.

Note that it is a very expensive operation to grab pixels and look at them. To help your program performance you should do this as sparingly as possible, and look at as few pixels as you can. Don't grab pixels from the whole image if you don't need to. On a SPARCStation 5 desktop computer, this applet took about five seconds to initialize. On an Intel Pentium 66Mhz system, it took about twice as long.

How do I save to a file an Image I have created on the screen?

The beauty of pixel grabbing is that it turns a picture into an array of ints. You can do anything you like with that array of ints including process it, send it down a socket, or write it out to a file. If you write it out to a file, you have saved your image to disk. It will not be in a recognized standard format like GIF or JPEG, and you will not get the benefit of compression. But it does let you save an image to a file. ☙

The final point is that the java.awt.image package has a couple of other specialized classes for filtering RGB values and for chaining ImageProducers together so you can do multiple filtering.

> *Exercise:* Try filtering an image by adapting the code above. Turn the black Rolls-Royce into a pink one.

Animation

Animation is the last major Image Processing topic we are going to cover, and it is thankfully simple. In fact if you already know how to get an image on the screen, you already know how to animate. Just as in cartoon movies, Java animation consists of showing several images (known as "frames") in quick succession. The human eye has a quality called *persistence* that means a series of slightly different frames fools us into thinking we see movement. When we change the entire image it is called "frame animation." When we just change a small area of the image, that area is called a "sprite" and we do "sprite animation."

So all we do for animation is bring all our frames in memory and display them one after the other. If we need to we will also use double buffering and clipping to make things appear smoother. There is a cheesy example of Animation that comes with the JDK in directory $JAVAHOME/demo/Animator. If you go to that directory, you can run the following to see some jumping beans.

```
appletviewer  example4.html
```

The CD that comes with this book has a Java program to save images to disk in GIF and JPEG format in the goodies directory.

You can also review the Animator.java source code. As an example here, let's make Dickens the Dalmatian wag his tail in Figure 10-12.

Figure 10-12:   See Dickens wag his tail

Before we show the code, let's look at the Java idiom for starting a thread in an Applet. You don't need a user thread in an applet if all you do is respond to GUI events. You *do* need one if you are animating, though.

A regular applet has the framework shown in Figure 10-13

```
public class foo extends java.applet.Applet {

    public void init() { ... }

    public void start() { ... }

    public void stop() { ... }

    public void paint (Graphics g) { ... }

}
```

Figure 10-13:   Framework of a normal applet

To give yourself a thread, the idiom is that you do these five things:

- Make your applet class implement Runnable.

- Add the run() method of the thread. Inside here will be the statements to do all the work that your thread must do.

- Declare a Thread object: Thread t;

- Inside start(), instantiate the thread with the Applet:

      t = new Thread(this);

  the thread running:

      t.start();

- Inside stop(), stop the thread running by

      t.stop();
      t=null; // so it can be garbage collected.

So the applet framework with a thread looks like Figure 10-14.

```
public class foo extends java.applet.Applet
implements Runnable{

    Thread t;

    public void run()   { ...}

    public void init() { ... }

    public void start() {
        t = new Thread(this);
        t.start();    }

    public void stop() {
        t.stop();
        t=null;        }

    public void paint (Graphics g) { ... }

}
```

Figure 10-14: Threaded applet

Here is the code to animate the tail. It closely follows the preceeding framework. Again, by making this extend the "transp" class of the previous example, we can present the minimum new code. It's not too surprising that we can use the framework of the "pin the silver lady on the Rolls" code as the basis of the "animate the dog's tail" program. They both involve putting images on the screen and moving them about. All animation programs will have the same general form.

```
//<applet   code=wag.class    width=280 height=200>  </applet>
// double buffered, transparent image, animation
import java.awt.*;
import java.awt.image.*;
import java.awt.event.*;

public class wag extends transp implements Runnable {
    Image dal, appendage, tail1, tail2;
    Font f;

    public void init () {
        tail1 = getImage(getDocumentBase(), "tail.jpg");
        tail2 = getImage(getDocumentBase(), "tail2.jpg");
        dal = getImage(getDocumentBase(), "dickens.jpg");
        dal = getRidOfPink(dal);
        tail1 = getRidOfPink(tail1);
        tail2 = getRidOfPink(tail2);
        appendage=tail2;

        addMouseMotionListener( new MouseMotionListener () {
            public void mouseDragged(MouseEvent e){
                System.out.println("what a drag");
                new_x=e.getX();
                new_y=e.getY();
                repaint();
            }
            public void mouseMoved(MouseEvent e){}
        } );

        f = new Font("Helvetica", Font.BOLD, 18);

        myOffScreenImage = createImage(getSize().width, getSize().height );
        myOffScreenGraphics = myOffScreenImage.getGraphics();

    }

    public void paint (Graphics g) {
        g.setColor(Color.lightGray);
        g.fillRect(0,0,getSize().width, getSize().height );
        g.setColor(Color.yellow);
        g.setFont(f);
        g.drawString("Dickens is a happy dog",10,20);
        g.drawImage (appendage, 10, 50, this);
        appendage= (appendage==tail2?tail1:tail2); // swap frames
        g.drawImage (dal, 35, 65, this);
    }

        public void run() {
        while (true) {
            try{Thread.sleep( 100 ); }
            catch(InterruptedException ie){}
            repaint();
            }
        }

        Thread t;

        public void start() {
            t = new Thread(this);
            t.start();
        }
        public void stop() {
            t.stop();
            t = null;
        }
}
```

The init() method brings in an extra image, tail2.jpg, which looks similar to tail, but is slightly displaced. All the images are filtered to give them a transparent background.

The two tails look like those shown in Figures 10-15 and 10-16.

Figure 10-15:   Dickens tail can look like this . . .

Figure 10-16:   . . . or this

I created Figure 10-15 from Figure 10-14 by rotating it 10 degrees in Adobe Photoshop (image rotation is one of the features that xv doesn't offer). If you don't have Photoshop, it doesn't matter—you now know enough Java to whip up a special purpose program to do any image processing you want!

In the paint method, I added some text at the top just for fun. The only other change is we now draw an "appendage" instead of a tail. The appendage just holds a reference to either tail1 or tail2. Immediately after we have drawn the appendage, this line:

```
appendage= (appendage==tail2?tail1:tail2); // swap frames
```

swaps it over to point to the other one. In this way, when paint is called, it alternates between Figure 10-15 and Figure 10-16. Another way to accomplish this is to change what appendage refers to in the run() routine. It doesn't have to alternate between two images; you may have dozens in your animation.

The run routine just spins in an infinite loop, sleeping for a tenth of a second, then issuing a repaint request. About 24 frames per second is all you need to fool the eye into seeing continuous motion. Here we're running at 10 frames per second.

The start() instantiates and kicks the thread off. The stop() is equally important. It's very poor programming to leave a thread running after the user leaves a page, so you kill the thread in the stop routine. And that is image animation. Finally, putting the whole thing together, so you can see all the code in one place, here is the program written without inheritance:

```
//<applet  code=fullwag.class    width=280 height=200>  </applet>
// double buffered
// transparent image
// animated tail
// Peter van der Linden

import java.awt.*;
import java.awt.image.*;
import java.awt.event.*;
import java.applet.*;

public class fullwag extends Applet implements Runnable {
    Image dal, appendage, tail1, tail2;
    Image myOffScreenImage;
    Font f;
    Graphics myOffScreenGraphics;

    public void update(Graphics g) {
        paint(myOffScreenGraphics);     // draws on double buffer
     // draws the db onto applet
        g.drawImage(myOffScreenImage,0,0, this);
}
    int  width=475, height=265;

    public Image getRidOfPink(Image im) {
        try {
     // grab the pixels from the image
            int[] pgPixels = new int [width*height];
            PixelGrabber pg = new PixelGrabber (im, 0, 0,
                    width, height, pgPixels, 0, width);

        if (pg.grabPixels() &&
           ((pg.status() & ImageObserver.ALLBITS) != 0)) {
        // Now change some of the bits
           for (int y=0;y<height;y++) {
               for (int x=0;x<width;x++) {
                    int i = y*width+x;
                    int a = (pgPixels[i] & 0xff000000)>>24;
                    int r = (pgPixels[i] & 0x00ff0000)>>16;
                    int g = (pgPixels[i] & 0x0000ff00)>>8;
                    int b = pgPixels[i] & 0x000000ff;
                    // turn the pink-ish pixels transparent.
                    if (r>200 && g>100&&g<200&&b>100&&b<200) {
                       a=0;
                       pgPixels[i] =  a  | (r<<16) | (g<<8) | b;
                    }
                }
            }
        }
```

```
        im = createImage (new MemoryImageSource (width, height,
                                        pgPixels, 0, width));
    }
  } catch (InterruptedException e) { e.printStackTrace (); }
  return im;
}

public void init () {
    tail1 = getImage(getDocumentBase(), "tail.jpg");
    tail2 = getImage(getDocumentBase(), "tail2.jpg");
    dal = getImage(getDocumentBase(), "dickens.jpg");
    dal = getRidOfPink(dal);
    tail1 = getRidOfPink(tail1);
    tail2 = getRidOfPink(tail2);
    appendage=tail2;
    f = new Font("Helvetica", Font.BOLD, 18);
    myOffScreenImage = createImage(getSize().width,
                                    getSize().height );
    myOffScreenGraphics = myOffScreenImage.getGraphics();
}

public void paint (Graphics g) {
    g.setColor(Color.lightGray);
    g.fillRect(0,0,getSize().width, getSize().height );
    g.setColor(Color.yellow);
    g.setFont(f);
    g.drawString("Dickens is a happy dog",10,20);
    g.drawImage (appendage, 10, 50, this);
    appendage= (appendage==tail2?tail1:tail2); // swap frames
    g.drawImage (dal, 35, 65, this);
}

    public void run() {
    while (true) {
        try{Thread.sleep( 100 ); }
        catch(InterruptedException ie){}
        repaint();
        }
    }
    Thread t;
    public void start() {
        t = new Thread(this);
        t.start();
    }
    public void stop() {
        t.stop();
        t = null;
    }
}
```

Table 10-3: Image Utilities

Here are some Image Processing utilities:	
Windows	The windows equiv to xv is Lview pro, downloadable from http://www.lview.com
	Other people like Paint Shop Pro from Jasc, downloadable from http://www.zdnet.com
Solaris	xv is an interactive image manipulation program for X windows (i.e. Unix). It understands all popular formats and can be downloaded for free from ftp.cis.upenn.edu in directory pub/xv.
Mac	Mac image processing software can be downloaded from: ftp://rever.nmsu.edu/pub/macfaq/JPEGView.* ftp://rever.nmsu.edu/pub/macfaq/GIF_Converter.sit.bin

Now try these exercises:

1. Add to the filtering, to turn Dickens into a black lab, by turning all his white fur black.

2. Change the animation so the "tail wags the dog."

Sounds

Applets have some simple methods to play sound files. The 1.1 release can deal with sounds in the .au format, but support for more formats (including the PC standard .wav wave format) is coming in the Java Media Format to be introduced with JDK 1.2 estimated for December 1997. There are a number of sound files on the CD that comes with this book, in the top level "noises" directory. You can use these as datafiles to experiment with. You can search at http://www.yahoo.com on ".au" to find dozens and dozens more sites and soundfiles.

You can also browse the site   http://cuiwww.unige.ch/OSG/AudioFormats

which describes the implementation of all the popular sound file formats including:

.WAV   **Windows**

.au   **Sun and NeXT.**

.AIF   **Mac and SGI**

There are 4 kinds of information making up a Digital Audio stream. The man (manual) page explains that digital audio data represents a quantized approximation of an analog audio signal waveform. In the simplest case, these quantized numbers represent the amplitude of the input waveform at particular sampling intervals. I hate it when man pages (the UNIX online documentation) read like dictionary entries instead of making a reasonable attempt at explaining something.

Sample Rate

This says how many times per second we sample (take a reading from) our noise source. Java currently supports only 8000 Hz.

Encoding

The encoding says how the audio data is represented. Java uses μ-law encoding (pronounced mew-law) which is the standard CCITT G.711 for voice data used by telephone companies in the United States, Canada, and Japan.

There is an alternative A-law encoding (also part of G.711) which is the standard encoding for telephony elsewhere in the world. A-law and μ-law audio data are sampled at a rate of 8000 samples per second with 12-bit precision, with the data compressed to 8-bit samples. The resulting audio data quality is equivalent to that of standard analog telephone service, i.e. in technical terms, pretty crappy.

Precision

Precision indicates the number of bits used to store each audio sample. For instance, μ-law and A-law data are stored with 8-bit precision. 16-bit precision is common elsewhere but not used in Java.

Channels

This says whether the audio is mono or multi-channel. Since it is basically telephone audio, Java is mono (single channel).

For a standard audio CD the audio is sampled at 44.1KHz which means that for every second of music (or silence, or the conductor coughing) the CD has to take 44,100 16bit samples for each of the two stereo channels.

To summarize JDk 1.1 supports sounds encoded as:

> mono (1 channel)
> 8 bit (as opposed to 16)
> μ-law (not A-law or CD quality)

The whole is stored in .au files (not .wav or .aif).

One minute of monaural audio recorded in μ-law format at 8 KHz requires about 0.5 megabytes of storage, while the standard Compact Disc audio format (stereo 16-bit linear PCM data sampled at 44.1 KHz) requires approximately 10 megabytes per minute.

Table 10-4: Sound Utilities

Here are some sound utilities:	
Windows	One sound utility that works is is SOund eXchange or SOX, available at http://www.spies.com/Sox. There are many others that work, and also a few that don't. Q: How do I use it? A: sox file.wav -r 8012 -U -b file.au

Table 10-4: Sound Utilities *(continued)*

Here are some sound utilities:	
Solaris	One Solaris Unix sound utility that works is /usr/demo/SOUND/bin/soundtool. Another is audiotool. All modern desktop SPARCs with the exception of the SS4 come with the audio hardware and software needed to record input from line-in or headphone jack. I recorded my message on the CD in the goodies directory using the little microphone that came with my SS5. It plugs into a port on the back. You can also use audiorecord to record the incoming audio data in any format supported by the audio device. For example, use /bin/audiorecord -p line -c 2 -s 44.1k -e linear -t 15 foo.au to record 15 seconds of cd quality sound to file foo.au. Use /bin/audiorecord -p line -t 15 foo.au to record 15 seconds of 8 Khz ulaw data (default) to file foo.au. You can use audiotool to edit the resulting file if needed.
Mac	One Mac sound utility that works is ConvertMachine at http://www.anutech.com.au/tprogman/ SoundMachine_WWW

Here is a minimal applet to play a sound effect:

```
import java.applet.*;
public class noise extends Applet {
    public void init() {
        play( getCodeBase(), "danger.au");
    }
}
```

The file "danger.au" is on the CD. It makes a noise like a drumstick rattling on the side of a tin cup. The program would be invoked from the usual html file:

```
<applet code=noise.class  width = 150 height =100> </applet>
```

The applet directory $JAVAHOME/src/java/applet contains several other useful methods:

```
public AudioClip getAudioClip(URL url)
```

Once you have retrieved an AudioClip from a URL, you can play it once, play it in a loop continuously, or cease playing it with these methods:

```
play()
loop()
stop()
```

If you play it continuously, make sure that you stop playing it in the stop() method, called when the applet's Panel is no longer on the screen. Otherwise the noise will continue longer than you probably want.

Write an applet that plays a sound file, and evaluates it for hidden Satanic messages. There is an easy way to do this and a hard way. The easy way is to play the sound file, and then conclude:

```
println("That contained 0 Satanic messages \n");
```

The hard way would actually involve some analysis of the sound waveforms, but it would probably produce exactly the same result. 🐛

In the first edition of this book I threw down the challenge to readers inviting them to submit code to play a sound file backwards. It would be a non-trivial task to figure out the .au format and do that, but alert programmer Manfred Thole from Germany realized that the task would be considerably simplified by using one of the vendor-specific classes that turns a FileInputStream into an AudioStream. This was a clever piece of programming to get the job done more simply.

```java
import java.io.*;
import sun.audio.*;


/**
 *
 * This application plays audio files backwards!
 * Only applicable for "8-bit u-law 8kHz mono" encoded audio files.
 * Usage: BackwardAudio audio-file-to-play-backwards
 */



public class BackwardAudio {

  static void swap(byte [] b) {
    int l = b.length;
    int i;
    byte tmp;

    for (i = 0; i < l/2; i++) {
      tmp = b[i];
      b[i] = b[l-i-1];
      b[l-i-1] = tmp;
    }
  }
```

```
public static void main(String[] args) {

    AudioPlayer ap = AudioPlayer.player;
    AudioStream as = null;
    byte [] ad = null;

    if ( args.length != 1 ) {
      System.err.println("Usage: BackwardAudio audio-file-to-play-backwards");
       return;
    }
    try {
      as = new AudioStream(new FileInputStream(args[0]));
      // Some files give strange results...
      // Maybe they have an incorrect file header.
      if ( as.getLength() < 1 ) {
        System.err.println("Length: "+as.getLength()+"!");
        return;
      }
      ad = new byte[as.getLength()];
      as.read(ad, 0, as.getLength()-1);
      swap(ad);
      //ap.start(new ByteArrayInputStream(ad));
      ap.start(new AudioDataStream(new AudioData(ad)));
      // We have to wait for the ap daemon thread to play the sound!
      Thread.sleep(as.getLength()/8+100);
    }
    catch (FileNotFoundException fne) {
      System.err.println(fne);

    }
    catch (IOException ioe) {
      System.err.println(ioe);
    }
    catch (InterruptedException ie) {
      System.err.println(ie);
    }
  }
}
```

As well as the java.*.* hierarchy of packages, Java vendors can supply vendor-specific packages under <vendor>.* Sun has a large number of sun.* packages that it does not tell you about explicitly. . . . Good programmers will find them because good programmers tend to investigate on their own.

The classes are in the $JAVAHOME/lib/classes.zip file. Copy this file somewhere safe, and unzip it. By the way, this is the file that the JDK README warns you not to unzip. I think they are trying to use reverse psychology on you.

You'll see all the standard java.*.* classes in there, and several dozen interesting looking Sun ones, too, including these:

```
Extracting: sun/misc/Ref.class
Extracting: sun/misc/MessageUtils.class
Extracting: sun/misc/CEStreamExhausted.class
Extracting: sun/misc/UUEncoder.class
Extracting: sun/misc/CharacterEncoder.class
Extracting: sun/misc/HexDumpEncoder.class
Extracting: sun/misc/UUDecoder.class
Extracting: sun/misc/BASE64Encoder.class
Extracting: sun/misc/UCDecoder.class
Extracting: sun/misc/CacheEnumerator.class
Extracting: sun/misc/Timeable.class
Extracting: sun/misc/TimerThread.class
Extracting: sun/misc/UCEncoder.class
Extracting: sun/misc/CRC16.class
Extracting: sun/misc/ConditionLock.class
Extracting: sun/misc/BASE64Decoder.class
Extracting: sun/misc/CacheEntry.class
Extracting: sun/misc/CEFormatException.class
Extracting: sun/misc/Timer.class
Extracting: sun/misc/TimerTickThread.class
Extracting: sun/misc/Lock.class
Extracting: sun/misc/CharacterDecoder.class
Extracting: sun/misc/Cache.class
  Creating: sun/audio/
Extracting: sun/audio/AudioStream.class
Extracting: sun/audio/InvalidAudioFormatException.class
Extracting: sun/audio/AudioStreamSequence.class
Extracting: sun/audio/ContinuousAudioDataStream.class
Extracting: sun/audio/AudioDevice.class
Extracting: sun/audio/AudioPlayer.class
Extracting: sun/audio/AudioData.class
Extracting: sun/audio/AudioTranslatorStream.class
Extracting: sun/audio/NativeAudioStream.class
Extracting: sun/audio/AudioDataStream.class
```

That gives you the package name. Of course, you remember that you can use javap to look at any of the methods of these!

```
    % javap sun.audio.AudioStream
Compiled from AudioStream.java
public class sun.audio.AudioStream extends
java.io.FilterInputStream {
    sun.audio.NativeAudioStream audioIn;
    public sun.audio.AudioStream(java.io.InputStream);
    public int read(byte [],int,int);
    public sun.audio.AudioData getData();
    public int getLength();
}
```

Fuller documentation on these Sun classes has been put together by some Swedish programmers and is available at: http://www.cdt.luth.se/java/doc/sun.

Note that Sun's position is that the classes in the vendor-specific hierarchy are intended solely for Sun's use to implement the public APIs in the JDK. So Sun might change these classes around without notice. Use these at your own risk, they may change, and they make programs nonportable. Other Java vendors have other policies—Microsoft really wants you to use its vendor classes to lock you into its platforms.

Some Light Relief

Satan: oscillate my metallic sonatas

Some people claim that "backwards masking" conceals satanic messages in popular music. They believe that if you play the music backwards (like reading the phrase above backwards) a hidden message will be revealed.

You can easily play a piece of music backwards by recording it onto a cassette tape. Then take the cassette apart by unscrewing the little screws, and swap the reels left to right (don't flip them upside down). You will have to thread the tape a little differently onto one spool.

You've done it correctly if the feed and take-up spools revolve in opposite directions to each other when you hit "play." Rewind once to remove this anomaly, and away you go with your backwards masking. This experiment is so much fun, you should drop whatever you're doing (you're probably reading a book) and go and try this *right now.*

For advanced students: overdub a tape to produce a gimmicked version on which you have added some suitable wording ("Sacrifice homework. Cthulu is our thesis advisor. Wear leather and stay out late on Fridays. Stack dirty dishes in the sink, and cut in line at supermarkets"). Leave the tape out for a suitable colleague to "discover" your backwards masked work.

Finally, I urge you to try running the Backward audio class on the file yenrab.au on the CD: `java BackwardAudio yenrab.au`

If that sound file isn't evidence of demonic possession, I don't know what is.

CHAPTER
11

- Java Foundation Classes

- SwingSet

- Component Previews

- Some Light Relief

Java Foundation
Classes (JFC)
Preview (Swingset)

"All wiyht. Rho sritched mg kegtops awound?"

— traditional Apr 1 programmer's lament.

As you read through the chapter on the Abstract Window
Toolkit, you may have been thinking (if you have done a lot of GUI programming) *this is nice, but it is rather a basic toolkit*, and you'd be right. As this book
was in the final stages of preparation, Sun announced more details of the Java
Foundation Classes (JFC) which provide support for all the advanced GUI features programmers have come to know and love.

This chapter provides a preview of some of the Swing components of the Java
Foundation Classes in the form of screendumps showing their early appearance.
The Java roadmap shows that JFC will ship with JDK 1.2 at the end of 1997. In the
meantime, Sun is making an early version of JFC available for public feedback. We
don't show the API for these classes because it is still changing, based on the feedback.

The Java Foundation Classes are squarely aimed at programmers who want to
build enterprise-ready software, every bit as good as software built with non-Java
native GUI classes. The JFC has the additional advantages of being available from

multiple vendors, and running on all systems, too. JFC had its genesis in IFC—Netscape's Internet Foundation Classes. These were such a good idea that everyone recognized the value in making them available to the industry as a whole. Netscape and JavaSoft cooperated to find licensing terms acceptable to both. Netscape really does have some of the best programmers in the world, and their pace of development and release is breathtaking.

The final content of JFC was put together by an industrywide advisory council with members from more than 50 companies. The code was developed by a team that included some of the best programmers from JavaSoft, Netscape, IBM, and Apple. In other words, as with all Java standards, JFC was developed by an open process involving all members of the computer industry, and not by a closed process intended to benefit a single company. The JFC stuff is very new and exciting, so I wanted to show it to you, even though the final form may change.

Contents of the JFC

JFC introduces many innovations and new components. One of the biggest innovations is that the AWT gets a pluggable look and feel. A pluggable look-and-feel means that end users can chose at runtime the style of their applications. If users want an application to look and behave like a typical Windows application, they can have that. If users want a Mac® GUI look and feel, they can switch to that without even restarting the program. Some users will prefer a consistent Java look and feel, different from Windows, Motif®, or the Mac, that is the same on all platforms; this is a third possibility. Finally, a pluggable look and feel will make it easy to support basic windowing on low resolution PDAs. Any complicated widgets like scrollbars can be changed to a simplified form by the runtime library, without changing the program at all.

The Java Foundation Classes contain these features:

- Pluggable look and feel
  Users argue vehemently over how closely GUI applications should look like native applications. The truth is, people should be allowed to choose and switch at runtime.

- Support for people with disabilities
  A new Accessibility API provides help for people with visual disabilities. The JFC will be able to interoperate with software such as screen readers, screen magnifiers, and speech recognition.

- The 2-dimensional API
  The 2D API supports sophisticated drawing and shading operations on a two dimensional surface.

- Drag and Drop
  This API will allow Java programs to drag and drop icons between Java and non-Java applications.

- The Swing Components
  This is the set of new lightweight (peerless) components previewed in the rest of this chapter. Because the components are peerless, it's easy to base their appearance on a property that can be changed dynamically. This feature supports the pluggable look and feel.
  "Swing" is the project internal code name. It was invented by team member Georges Saab while working on the JavaOne music demo. For the musically uninitiated (like myself), swing music is currently enjoying great popularity. The Swing components are designed to add some world-class components to the AWT and are not a layer which covers up the AWT.

How the Swing Components Look

The first thing to note about the Swing Components is there are a lot of them! Here we preview the appearance of Tree, Menu with image, Toolbar, ToolTip, Label with image, TabbedPane, Table, and Springs and Struts.

In addition, other components include progress bar, titled pane, combo box, split panel, spinner, standard dialog boxes, and several choosers (font, color, file, date/ time, money). Some of these were not available for previewing at press time.

The preview version of Swing allowed the user to choose either a Windows 95 style or a Rose style (named after the graphics designer). The Rose style is just used as a quick example and is not the Java standard look and feel. A third choice, the Mac style, was not yet available at the time of preview. Since the Mac style wasn't available and the Rose style is just a proof of concept, I'm only going to show the Windows 95 style of the Swing components that we preview here.

Tree

This component displays hierarchical data in an easy-to-read form that positions children under and to the right of their parents. Tree is probably the most frequently requested component of all because it is so convenient for looking at directories and files on disk.

The version of this component in Windows 95 style has this appearance.

Figure 11-1: A tree

Menu with image

This component offers the ability to put images in menus, so users can choose from pictures as well as text.

The version of this component in Windows 95 style has this appearance.

Figure 11-2:   Menu with image

Toolbar

This component offers a row (or rows) of icons which can be pressed like buttons.

The version of this component in Windows 95 style has this appearance.

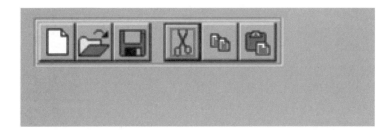

Figure 11-3:   A toolbar

Toolbars demand excellence in inventing little icons to represent actions. All too frequently, toolbars leave new users scratching their heads and wondering "Well, I suppose the scissors might be cut and paste, and the diskette might mean 'save file.' But what are the things that look like salt and pepper shakers next to the scissors? And what if that diskette icon really means 'reformat all my disks'?"

ToolTip

This component offers a delayed pop-up, pop-down advice string when you let the mouse linger over button, toolbar, or other selectable area.

The version of this component in Windows 95 style has this appearance.

Figure 11-4:   ToolTip

The cursor was lingering over the left button in this screen shot.

Label with Image

This component offers the ability to add a picture to a label, as well as just text. Labels are just a quick and easy way of getting some text on the screen. Now you have the ability to do the same with images.

The version of this component in Windows 95 style has this appearance.

Figure 11-5:   Label with Image

TabbedPane

This component lets the user switch between a group of components by clicking on a thumb-tab. TabbedPanes are a very useful way of organizing a large amount of information, without overwhelming the user with too many choices on one screen.

The version of this component in Windows 95 style has this appearance.

Figure 11-6: TabbedPane

Table

This component offers the display of textual data in rows and columns. Table elements can contain checkboxes as well as text.

The version of this component in Windows 95 style has this appearance.

First Name	Last Name	Favorite Color	Favorite Number	Vegetarian
Tim	Prinzing	Blue	22	☐
Chester	Rose	Black	0	☐
Ray	Ryan	Gray	77	☐
Georges	Saab	Red	4	☐
Kathy	Walrath	Blue	8	☐
Arnaud	Weber	Green	44	☐

Figure 11-7:   A table

Although this component looks like a spreadsheet, that is not its primary purpose.

Springs and Struts

This component is the long-awaited layout manager to replace the yukky Grid-BagLayout! (I like to throw words like "yukky" and "bodacious" into my books occasionally, as it results in interesting e-mail from translators in Japan, Brazil, and Germany.) SpringLayout lets you choose which components should change size when their container is resized. Each component has a height and width, and a left, right, top, and bottom margin. All of these are candidates for growth or shrinkage on resizing.

The way you indicate the directions for movement is by naming each of these dimensions as either a spring or a strut. Springs change size, struts prefer not to.

In the screendump below, five buttons are laid out on a panel similar to the BorderLayout. The top and right buttons are struts (they do not want to change in size). For this example, the strut is illustrated as a dark line in the middle of the button. The left, bottom, and center buttons are configured as springs. They can expand as needed.

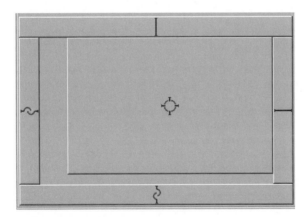

Figure 11-8: Springs and Struts

 The top and right struts are "rigid." They hold the center button against themselves. Now notice what happens if the right button is changed to a spring, and the panel is relaid out, as shown in the following screendump.

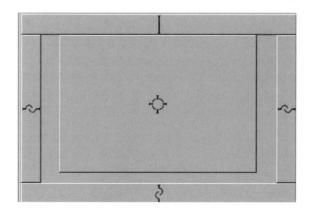

Figure 11-9: Springs and Struts

The center component is now not rigidly held on the right side, and, being pulled from the spring on the left, it moves left until it reaches equilibrium in the center.

I should emphasize that the "springs and struts" are only a mental model to explain how this works. Components don't actually vibrate back and forth on springs when being laid out. The little bars and hooks glyphs on the buttons aren't there on real components. They are shown here so you can clearly see what's what. SpringLayout at last brings sanity to the business of laying out complicated components.

Download the JFC

If you want to download the latest version of the JFC for yourself, visit the Java-Soft website at `http://java.sun.com` and search for JFC download.

Some Light Relief —Programmer's Cake Pie Pudding

Here's a recipe that has long been a theoretical favorite of mine, and if you make it, I'd be interested to hear how it actually turns out in practice. My buddy Charlie Springer invented Programmer's Cake Pie Pudding. What is the connection with programming, I hear you ask? Well, Charlie is a computer programmer, of course. He taught me to count in binary on my fingers, and you can count up to 1023 that way. Plus, I either put in this story, or the story about the time my dog hurled up all over the software marketing manager. Which would you rather read? Oh, really? Well, isn't that just typical.

Maybe I'll put the barf story on the CD, and if enough people send me e-mail to say they found it amusing, I'll put it in the next book.

Programmer's Cake Pie Pudding

1. Get a chocolate cake mix (e.g., Betty Crocker® Devil's Food Cake). Feed the frosting to the dog, and bake the cake.

2. The next day, get a "no baking needed" cheesecake mix. Feed the graham cracker base to the dog.

3. Make the cheesecake mix and crumble in the chocolate cake from the day before. If your mom is out, use the mixer on it. There should be no pieces larger than an ant. Put in tea cups or something for individual servings, and stick in the fridge to set.

4. While you're waiting for it to set, check if the dog likes whipped cream from a spray can. If he does, spray a little into his mouth, and slowly draw back while continuing to spray.
    See how far back you can get while still spraying. My brother Paul got clear out of the kitchen and halfway down the hall before the dog had enough whipped cream. The cream that gets on the floor, he'll lick up after he's finished being sick.

5. If there's any whipped cream left, dump it on the cake pie pudding. Let it set in the fridge.

Eat. Enjoy. Rinse. Blather. Repeat. Stand clear of any marketing managers that my dog is approaching.

CHAPTER 12

File I/O

*"As part of the conversion, computer specialists rewrote
1,500 programs—a process that traditionally requires some debugging."*

—those masters of understatement at **USA Today**

It is not completely fair to remark, as some have, that support for I/O in Java is "bone headed." Support for I/O in Java does make loose sense eventually, once you understand the whole panorama.

I/O in Java is highly modular: there are lots of classes that each do one specialized kind of I/O, and it is very easy to connect objects of these classes (like a pipe of several connected OS commands) so that as the data flows through, it is modified or filtered in the way you need. The key to understanding I/O in Java is getting comfortable with connecting different file processing objects. But, frankly, I/O is not one of the better-designed APIs. There are three major criticisms of the current Java I/O model.

The first issue is that in computing it should be simple to do simple things. Reading a number from the keyboard is a simple thing, and there should be a core library function that does this simply and elegantly. But there is not.

The second issue is that the JDK 1.1 release did not cleanly fix up the JDK 1.0 release that got I/O wrong. JDK 1.0 built everything off 8-bit streams, which did not properly support the 16-bit character streams needed for internationalization. Accordingly, the I/O package virtually doubled in size in JDK 1.1, with a whole set of new 16-bit Reader/Writer classes added to the old 8-bit Stream classes. But the changeover was not completed: the old classes were left around, and keyboard I/O was still based on 8-bit streams. Programmers are supposed to use the Reader and Writer classes when coding character I/O, but the Stream classes are still used for binary I/O—except that interactive character I/O is still based on the Stream classes.

The third issue is that, in striving for generality, the I/O classes have become too numerous and too general. The excessive generality is a problem that is becoming worse, not better. In JDK 1.0, there was a class called `PushbackInputStream` that provided the ability to "unread" or push back a single byte. Pushing back the last character read is a rare operation, mostly used by those writing `LALR(1)` parsers for a compiler. It should not have been set up as a class of its own; the function should have been made part of an existing class, probably `DataInput`. In JDK 1.1, `PushbackInputStream` was augmented by `PushbackReader`, which can push back an arbitrary number of Unicode characters into the input stream, not just a single 8-bit byte onto a Stream.

The reason for the unhappy I/O situation is that designers of programming languages and runtime libraries form a very different community from application programmers. They get close to their work and lose the perspective of someone seeing it for the first time. What appears clear and obvious to the designer can be obscure to someone else. Hence, all software should be approved by a human interface engineer before release. Well, enough of the gripes. Let's take a look at what services the `java.io` API offers.

Formats, Encodings, and I/O

The place to start is with a brief review of the formats that you are able to process with I/O. Table 12-1 describes the bit-level appearance of data in the different formats. Do not confuse what I am calling a "format" with a "type." I may want to output a character, an integer, a boolean, or any of the primitive types. The type defines the range of admissible values, e.g., "A to z" or "`false`, `true`." The format (also known as an *encoding*) defines how those values will be represented in terms of bits.

Table 12-1:   The Different Formats for Data

- Format: **ASCII**
  Size: 1 byte   Example Description: letter "A"
  Binary value: 0x41   Printable Representation: A

  The American Standard Code for Information Interchange is an 8-bit code in which most of the characters are human readable. There are also a few dozen control characters. ASCII is essentially a 7-bit subset of the 8-bit ISO 8859_1 encoding, shown in the appendix at the end of this book.

- Format: **Unicode**
  Size: 2 bytes   Example Description: capital letter "E acute"
  Binary value: 0x00C9   Printable Representation: É

  The problem with 8859_1 is that it can represent only 256 distinct characters. That's barely enough for all the accented and diacritical characters used in Western Europe, let alone the many alphabets used around the rest of the world. Unicode is a 16-bit character set developed to solve this problem by allowing for 65,536 different characters. A String in Java holds adjacent Unicode characters.

- Format: **UCS**
  Size: 2 or 4 bytes   Example Description: capital letter "E acute"
  Binary value: 0x00C9   Printable Representation: É

  UCS is the Universal Character Set. There are two forms: UCS-2 and UCS-4. UCS-2 is a 2-byte encoding, UCS-4 is a 4-byte encoding. The ISO/IEC standard 10646 provides for a full 4-bytes-per-character encoding, called UCS-4. Fortunately, this enormous encoding space is divided into 64K "planes" of 64K characters each. The ISO people want everyone to think of Unicode as just a shorthand way of referring to Plane Zero of the complete 4-byte ISO/IEC 10646 encoding space. UCS-2, in other words, is a subset of the full UCS-4. They call this the "Basic Multilingual Plane" or BMP. Personally, I think they all need a good talking to for taking a very simple concept and dressing it up with a lot of confusing terminology. I have never seen UCS or Unicode simply explained in plain language anywhere. Since Unicode is essentially just UCS-2, you may also hear people say (correctly) Java uses UCS-2 as its internal encoding.

- Format: **UTF**
  Size: 1-3 bytes   Example Description: letter "A"
  Binary value: 0x41   Printable Representation: A

  UCS Transformation Format is an interim code that allows systems to operate with both ASCII and Unicode. In UTF, a character is either 1, 2, or 3 bytes long. ASCII values less than 0x7F are written as one byte. Unicode values less than 0x7FF are written as two bytes. Other Unicode values are written as three bytes.

Table 12-1: The Different Formats for Data (Continued)

The initial bits of a UTF character identify how long it is. If the first bit of a value is 0, it is a 1-byte ASCII value. If the first bits are 110, it is the first byte of a 2-byte sequence. If the first bits are 1110, it is the first byte of a 3-byte sequence. The second and third bytes of a multibyte sequence start with the bits set to 10.

UTF is a hack best avoided if possible. It complicates code quite a bit when you can no longer rely on all characters being the same size. However, UTF offers the benefit of backward compatibility with existing ASCII-based data, and forward compatibility with Unicode data.

- Format: **binary**
  Size: 1-8 bytes
  Binary value: 0x41

  Example Description: value 65 (decimal byte)
  Printable Representation: A

Java has the ability to do I/O on binary values. Binary output makes a big difference when you are using numbers. Just as an int representation of a number is very different from the String representation, binary I/O is very different from Unicode I/O. In fact, binary I/O is simply transferring the data as an int (or long, float, etc.) to or from disk. The binary value of a character is the same as the Unicode or ASCII value of the character, which occasionally leaves room for confusion. The binary value of an int is different from the Unicode or ASCII value of the int. A binary byte holding a single ASCII digit is (of course) 1 byte long, whereas a binary double-precision floating-point number is 8 bytes long.

A very common mistake in Java is to use binary I/O where Unicode or ASCII I/O was intended. The numeric values transferred will not necessarily be human readable, and you'll usually get a different length of data and different value of data than you were expecting. The character values transferred will be fine because an ASCII character has the same bit representation whether it was written using an ASCII method or a binary method.

- Format: **objects**
  Size: varies

Java allows objects to be written out, and read back in, in a process known as serialization/deserialization. It's quite powerful to be able to do I/O on an entire object in one go.

Table 12-2 shows the code sets or "encodings" that various popular operating systems support:

Table 12-2: Encodings supported by some operating systems

OS	Encoding
Solaris (Sun Unix)	ASCII, ISO 8859_1, and UTF
Apple Macintosh	A nonstandard character set in which the first 128 characters are ASCII and the rest are Apple's own invention.
Windows 95	MS-Windows (using code page 1252) normally uses the first 256 characters of Unicode, which is (for all practical purposes) equivalent to ISO 8859-1. Can also convert to UCS2 as needed.
Windows NT	Uses Unicode internally. Can also cope with ASCII, UCS, and other encodings.

Characters are always 16-bit Unicode internally in Java. Characters may be represented as Unicode, ASCII, UTF or something else entirely on a particular operating system. Therefore, I/O routines must translate the native character set into Unicode. The actual scheme that is used is called the *encoding*. An encoding is a protocol for translating characters to bit patterns.

The Reader/Writer Unicode stream classes should be used instead of the old JDK 1.0 InputStream/OutputStream classes because the Reader/Writer classes make it easy to write code that can be internationalized. Specifically, the Reader/Writer classes process Unicode internally. At the lowest level, they also provide the "hooks" for getting between Unicode and characters in a different protocol, such as ASCII or UTF. Many of today's popular operating systems use ASCII or UTF as their native codeset. All operating systems of the future will likely use Unicode as their native codeset.

The two rules of character I/O are:

- If you want to do character input, all the classes you use should have names that end in `Reader` (not in `InputStream`).
- If you want to do character output, all the classes you use should have names that end in `Writer` (not in `OutputStream`).

These rules don't apply to the predefined `System` objects for interactive I/O.

Files and Streams

The way that an operating system stores data is by putting it in a file. The way that Java puts data in a file is by connecting a stream to the file. Files have path names that identify where they are stored and also what they are called. Files have many other attributes such as whether they are readable, what directory they live in, and when they were last modified. A Java class called `File` allows you to look at these attributes of a file.

The `File` Class

The class called `File` does not let you do any I/O. `File` just has methods to look at and modify file-related information (the so-called meta-data), not file contents. The methods of `File` allow you to:

- Return a `File` object, given a String containing a path name

- Test whether a `File` object exists, can be read/written,

- Test whether a `File` object is a file or a directory

- Say how many bytes are in the file or when it was last modified

- Delete the file

- Get various forms of the file path name

- Create a directory

As always, running

```
javap java.io.File
```

will reveal the method signatures.

A number of methods are available in the class File to provide information about a file or a directory. Here are the methods:

```
public class File {

    constructors:
        public File(String path)
        public File(String path, String name)
        public File(File dir, String name)

    deleting a file:
        public boolean delete()

    to do with file name:
        public String getName()
        public String getPath()
        public String getAbsolutePath()
        public String getParent()
        public boolean renameTo(File dest)

    getting the attributes of a file:
        public boolean exists()
        public boolean canWrite()
        public boolean canRead()
        public boolean isFile()
        public boolean isDirectory()
        public native boolean isAbsolute()
        public long lastModified()
        public long length()
        public boolean equals(Object obj)

    to do with the directory:
        public boolean mkdir()
        public boolean mkdirs()
        public String[] list()
        public String[] list(FilenameFilter filter)

    miscellaneous:
        public static final char pathSeparatorChar
        public int hashCode()
        public String toString()
```

Typically, you will only bother instantiating a `File` object if one of those operations is of interest to you. If you simply want to do I/O, you will use a different class.

Although you can use the `File` class to create and delete files and directories, there is currently no method that allows you to change the current working directory of the program. You always stay in whatever directory you were in when you started the program.

Is it possible to lock a file with Java?

Java does not currently feature an API to lock a file or regions within a file for exclusive use by one thread or process but the feature seems like an obvious thing to add. Meanwhile, code that needs to do file locking must take one of three approaches:

1. Implement an advisory locking scheme using features that Java does have (synchronized methods). This approach allows you to lock files against use by other Java code running in the same JVM.

2. Use an atomic operation like "file delete" and have all processes (Java and non-Java) follow the same protocol: if the file was deleted by you, you have the lock, and you create the file again to give up the lock. File creation is not atomic (if two threads try to create the same file, only one will actually create it, but they will both return success), so can't be used for the synchronization.

3. Make calls to native code to issue the locking calls. This approach is not portable but gives you a shot at having your locks respected by other programs that also use standard locking calls outside Java.

Streams of Data

A file is but one possible source for data. We may equally acquire data from sources that are not files, such as the keyboard, a socket on the network, consecutive elements of an array, and so on. Accordingly, Java has another, higher abstraction called a *Stream*.

A stream in real life could be supplied by a lake, by another stream, by a spring, by a pumping station, and so on. Similarly a Stream in Java could be getting its bytes from (or sending them to) a file, a String, a socket on the net, an array, the keyboard, and so on. A Stream is a flow of data, never mind where it comes from or goes to. A Stream lets you put or take data as it goes by.

In JDK 1.0, Streams were a flow of 8-bit bytes, but this was not adequate for the conversion between different external codesets and Unicode. Proper internationalization relies on this conversion, so JDK 1.1 introduced Readers (input streams of Unicode characters) and Writers (output streams of Unicode characters). Readers and Writers should now be used everywhere you want to do character I/O. Readers and Writers are 16-bit character streams that also know how to properly convert those characters into the native codeset.

`PrintWriter.println()` now emits an end-of-line marker that matches the conventions of the platform it is on. On Windows 95, it outputs \r\n, on Unix, it outputs \n, and on Macs, it outputs \r. The old `PrintStream` class just used \n on all systems.

The Essentials of Java I/O

If you do not memorize anything else about Java I/O, memorize this:

- All I/O in Java is done using a stream.
- There are two kinds of stream: 8-bit streams and 16-bit streams.
- The 8-bit streams are known as InputStreams or OutputStreams. The 16-bit streams are known as Readers (input) or Writers (output).
- Because the class name has Reader, Writer, InputStream, or OutputStream in it, it's easy to know which set of services you are using.
- Each stream offers just one kind of service (e.g., character I/O, binary I/O, I/O to a byte array, to a file). You are supposed to connect several streams to get the exact processing you want.
- I/O streams are connected by passing one stream as an argument to the constructor of another.

I/O in Java is a little harder to grasp than in other languages because it has forsaken simplicity in the basic case, for generality of all cases. It remains to be seen if that was a wise course, but it is the way things are, so we must all deal with it.

The old JDK 1.0 `Stream` classes are 8-bit byte streams and are still used for binary I/O (and interactive I/O). When you hear the term "stream," make sure you are clear about whether you're dealing with a byte stream or a Unicode stream.

Predefined Streams

Three predefined Streams are already open and ready to use in every program. These Streams are declared in the `java.lang.System` class, and they are all byte streams.

- `System.in`—InputStream used to read bytes from the keyboard.

- `System.out`—PrintStream used to write bytes to the screen.

- `System.err`—PrintStream used to report errors. `System.out` can also be used to report errors, but having a separate channel for errors makes it easier to notice errors when program output has been redirected to a file.

Why Standard I/O Still Uses 8-bit Streams

The predefined objects `System.in`, `System.out`, and `System.err` are built on the now-deprecated 8-bit byte streams left over from JDK 1.0. Beta versions of JDK 1.1 replaced these three streams by Unicode streams, but many people complained that the change was incompatible with their existing code. So, to minimize transition costs Sun left `in`, `out`, and `err` as 8-bit streams, placed a "deprecated" tag on the constructors, and provided an adapter class to accept an 8-bit stream and give back a 16-bit Reader stream. This adapter class is called `InputStreamReader`.

Deprecating the constructors rather than the entire class allows existing uses of `System.out` and `System.err` to be compiled without generating deprecation warnings. It generates the warning when the runtime library is built, but application programmers never do that. Programmers writing code that explicitly constructs an InputStream or a PrintStream will get a deprecation warning when that code is compiled. Programmers just using `System.err.println` calls for debugging purposes will not be bothered by deprecated warnings.

Although these streams are intended for interactive I/O, you can redirect them to a file. This can be done on the command line, using the OS feature for I/O redirection, or in the program. The method `System.setOut(PrintStream)` will redirect `System.out` after checking with the SecurityManager. There are also methods `System.setErr()` and `System.setIn()`.

If you do create a new PrintStream and reset `System.out` or `System.err`, you will get the deprecation warning when you compile. Javasoft's (somewhat unfortunate) position is that standard in, out, and error are only for debugging or low-volume I/O, and programmers must live with it.

Converting from an 8-bit stream to a 16-bit reader/writer.

Two new adapters can be connected to an 8-bit stream to give you a 16-bit stream.

The `InputStreamReader` class can be layered onto an input stream to give you a Reader.

```
InputStreamReader isr = new InputStreamReader( System.in );
```

The `java.io.OutputStreamWriter` class connects a Writer to an OutputStream.

```
PrintWriter pw = new PrintWriter(
  new OutputStreamWriter(conn.getOutputStream()));
```

Often, you then layer a BufferedReader or BufferedWriter on top of that, to get the best performance or to be able to read or write a line at a time. Connecting a PrintWriter will let you output printable characters to the stream.

JDK 1.1 Input

Let's focus on input only to begin with. Output works in a similar way, and we'll look at it later. In this section on input, we will cover the following topics

- Character input

- Reading characters from the keyboard

- Reading characters from a file

- Reading binary data from a file

- Reading numbers and other types from the keyboard

We use different classes to read the different I/O formats, as shown in Table 12-3.

Table 12-3: Classes to use for different I/O formats

If you have a value in this format...	Use this class, or one of its sub-classes to read it
character	FileReader (if it's in a file) InputStreamReader (if it's in a byte stream)
binary (including chars) data	DataInputStream
persistent object	ObjectInputStream

Character Input

Character input is done by using one (or more) of the Reader classes. There is a different Reader subclass for each different source of characters (file, String, array, etc.). You are expected to call the constructor with the character source as an argument. It will hand you back a Reader, which means from that point on you never have to worry about lower-level details like how an array differs from the keyboard. The Reader class hides or encapsulates all the implementation details from you. A Reader is a class that works on a Unicode character stream.

Reader is abstract, so you will always be dealing with one of its concrete subclasses. Reader has the following public methods, along with others: Making the class abstract forces the subclasses to have a method of the given name and to implement it in its own way.

```
int read() throws IOException
 // returns Unicode value, or -1 if end of stream

int read(char cbuf[]) throws IOException
 // fills the array with chars, and returns the
 // number of chars read, or -1 if end of stream

int read(char cbuf[], int off, int len) throws IOException
 // puts up to len chars in the array starting at element off,
 // and returns the number of chars read,
 // or -1 if end of stream

long skip(long n) throws IOException
 // tries to advance over n chars and
 // return the number actually skipped

boolean markSupported()
 // tells whether this stream supports the mark() operation

void mark(int);
 // marks the present position in the stream.
 // if you read more than int more characters, you are
 // allowed to forget the marked place.

void reset();
 // goes back to the point previously marked.

void close();
 // closes the stream. Throws IOException if further reads
 // are attempted.
```

These are the same method names that InputStream has, but the Reader methods convert to native codesets properly. The read routine returns an int rather than a char because it has to allow for every possible legal 16-bit value, plus an additional value to say that end of stream was hit. If a character was successfully read, the return value is the Unicode value of that character in the range 0 to 0xFFFF. If a character was not successfully read, read() returns the value 0xFFFFFFFF (minus one). Note that this class does not throw the EOFException (end of file exception), but returns an out-of-range value to indicate EOF.

The read() method will read one "chunk" from the stream and convert it into a Unicode character by following the default encoding conversion that is in effect. On an ASCII system, it will read one byte and promote it to a Unicode character. On a system with Unicode in effect, it will read two bytes and no conversion is needed. Where the encoding has been set to UTF, the method will read one to three bytes and assemble them into a Unicode character. You cannot currently change the encoding that is in effect for a file, as the InputStreamReader constructor that does this is marked private.

Reading Characters from the Keyboard

System.in is an InputStream (actually a BufferedInputStream) that just offers three methods for getting data: read a byte, read enough to fill my array of bytes, and read enough to fill a specified range within my array of bytes. A code example looks like this:

```
import java.io.*;

public class exreadin {

    public static void main(String f[]) {
        int i=0;
        char c;

        try {
          while ( i != -1 ) {
            i = System.in.read();
            c = (char) i;
            System.out.println( "read: " + c
                        + " hex value: "+Integer.toString(i,16));
          }
        } catch (IOException ioe) {
            System.out.println( "IO error:" + ioe );
        }

    }

}
```

Running the program and typing some input will look like this:

```
java exreadin
def 123
read: d hex value: 64
read: e hex value: 65
read: f hex value: 66
read: hex value: 20
read: 1 hex value: 31
read: 2 hex value: 32
read: 3 hex value: 33
read:
hex value: a
read:? hex value: -1
```

When we type the end of file indicator (Ctrl-Z on PCs, Ctrl-D on Unix) the program stops reading from `System.in` and returns –1.

Good Java programmers will want to make sure that incoming characters are correctly converted to Unicode by reading through a Reader rather than a Stream. The way to get Unicode characters from an InputStream (like `System.in`) is to layer an InputStreamReader on top of it.

`InputStreamReader` is an adapter from a byte stream to a character Reader. You pass the constructor one of the old-style JDK 1.0 8-bit byte input streams, and it gives you back a Reader. The input bytes are translated into characters according to a default character encoding (e.g., ISO 8859_1, ASCII, Unicode). It assumes sensible defaults.

The other methods of `InputStreamReader` are just the methods of `Reader` that we saw above. So, this is how to read characters (not bytes) from the keyboard.

• Wrap an InputStreamReader around `System.in`

```
InputStreamReader isr = new InputStreamReader( System.in );
```

• Read a character or (a portion of) a character array at a time from the InputStreamReader object.

Why does this seem so hard? Because it caters for the general case of fully internationalized software, not the simple case of I/O in the USA. You want to sell your software to the French, don't you?

Notice that so far we just have character-by-character input. Ideally, we would like to read numeric values, such as 123, and have them handed back to us as an int without us having to program it in detail. We'll get to that.

Reading Characters from a File

`Reader` is an abstract class, so it is subclassed by other classes in the `java.io` package before it is used in practice. Here are four popular subclasses of `Reader`, corresponding to four possible sources for the data.

`FileReader`—Translates bytes from a file into a character stream

`InputStreamReader`—Fetch characters from a byte stream

`StringReader`—Gets characters from a String

`CharArrayReader`—Gets characters from a char array

All of these subclasses offer the Reader methods just outlined above. Here is an example program that uses `FileReader` to access and count the number of bytes in a file. It compares the total to the `File.length()` value. They should be equal.

```
import java.io.*;

public class exfileread {

    public static void main(String args[]){
        int i=0;
        int bytesRead=0;

        try {
            FileReader fr = new FileReader( "animals.txt" );
            while ( i != -1 ) {
                i = fr.read();
                if (i!=-1) bytesRead++;
            }
        } catch (IOException ioe) {
            System.out.println( "IO error:" + ioe );
        }
        System.out.println("bytes read from file: "+bytesRead);

        File f = new File("animals.txt");
        System.out.println("bytes in File.length(): "+f.length() );
    }
}
```

If you create a text file called `animals.txt` with the names of a few animals in it, and run the program, you will see:

```
java exfileread
bytes read from file: 27
bytes in File.length(): 27
```

`FileReader` offers several constructors: it can take a path name as an argument, as in the example above. Another constructor takes a `File` object as an argument. A third constructor takes a `FileDescriptor` as an argument. Application programmers don't use file descriptors, but one may be constructed on your behalf to represent an open file or open socket.

Notice that there is no concept of a separate `open()` step as occurs in C. You just instantiate the stream object and if it didn't throw an exception, you are ready to do I/O immediately. And there is no concept of "I am opening this file for ASCII/binary data" as occurs on the PC. You read the data in different formats by using different methods. However, don't be fooled—although there is no `open()`, there is a `close()`! You should always explicitly use `close()` to close your output streams to ensure that the last few bytes are flushed into the system.

Reading or writing is synchronous. You don't return from the call until you have passed the bytes to the operating system. Depending on the implementation, I/O may block all threads in a program until it has completed. Watch out for this. The best implementations will block only the thread making the I/O call.

Reading Binary Data From a File

So far, so good, but what if you don't want to read characters? What if you want to read binary numbers? Table 12-3 showed that binary data is read with `DataInputStream`. `DataInputStream` has these public methods, along with others:

```
boolean readBoolean()
byte readByte()
int readUnsignedByte()
short readShort()
int readUnsignedShort()
int readInt()
long readLong()
float readFloat()
double readDouble()
```

Each method either reads in a binary representation of the value of the stated type or throws an `EOFException` or other `IOException`. The EOF exception would be thrown when you order (say) a four-byte value to be read, but fewer bytes are available before the end of the input stream.

When you have binary data in a stream, `DataInputStream` can be used to read it into your program. DataInputStream would really have been better named BinaryInputStream, as that might have prevented the confusion that arises when people wrongly use it on a character stream. The question of conversion between character sets does not arise for binary data, although the question of conversion between endians may. A number like 0xFF00 takes two bytes to store, and those two bytes might be stored in the order FF then 00 (known as big endian, because the big end comes first), or the other way around, with 00 then FF (known as little endian). Java stores everything as big endian. If a computer system is little endian (as PCs are), some care must be taken to convert values to big endian on input, if the file was not written by Java.

Layering Streams on Top of Each Other

If you run `javap` on `java.io.DataInputStream`, you'll see that it has only one constructor, which looks like this:

```
public java.io.DataInputStream(java.io.InputStream);
```

How, then, can I get a `DataInputStream` that operates on a file? The answer is to layer one stream on top of another.

Many of the Java I/O classes have constructors that take one kind of stream as an argument and return a different kind of stream. You are supposed to connect several streams to get the exact processing you need (see Figure 12-1), just the way you might connect a garden spigot to a hose, and the hose to a lawn sprinkler.

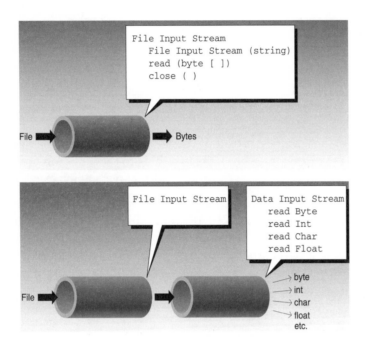

Figure 12-1: Connecting streams to get the exact processing you want

In this case, just construct a `FileInputStream` with the path name of your file (passed in as an argument to the program in the example below). Then, construct a `DataInputStream` from the `FileInputStream`. The code looks like this:

```
import java.io.*;
public class exreaddata {
    public static void main(String f[]) {
        FileInputStream fis;
        DataInputStream dis;
        try {
            fis = new FileInputStream(f[0]);
            dis = new DataInputStream( fis );
            System.out.println( "file: " + f[0] );
            int i;
            while ( true ) {
            i = dis.readInt();
            System.out.println( "read: " + i );
        }
    } catch (EOFException eof)
        {System.out.println( "EOF reached " ); }
    catch (IOException ioe)
        {System.out.println( "IO error: " + ioe ); }
    }
}
```

If you run this program on a data file with characters in it, the characters will be interpreted as binary data. It's all bits inside a processor, and it just does what you tell it. If the data file contained the ASCII characters "1 CAT," that would be 0x31 0x20 0x43 0x41 0x54.

If you (mistakenly) called readInt on a DataInputStream connected to this file, you would get the first four bytes (0x31204341) and interpret them as one int, giving a result of 824197953 in decimal. If the file actually does contain binary data, you'll get those values instead. If you are trying to read small values and you find you are getting huge ones, the first thing to check is "Am I reading binary values instead of character values?" It is a very common error.

In all cases, you need to know what the data was written as, in order to read it in successfully. This is true for most programming languages because data is just a collection of arbitrary bits on the media. The same bits can be interpreted equally well as an integer, a floating-point number, or four bytes from the 8859-1 encoding. If you're expecting an int at that point in the input stream, use readInt(). If you're expecting a boolean, use readBoolean(). If you don't know what to expect, whatever wrote the file needs to be redesigned.

Reading Numbers and Other Types from the Keyboard

Now that we are comfortable with the concept of pushing streams on top of streams to get the methods we need, let's go back to `system.in` and see how we can assemble numbers out of the characters we know how to read in. This book comes with an easy keyboard input class called `EasyIn`. Before describing that, we'll describe how you must read values from the keyboard if you don't want to use `EasyIn`.

In all cases, we have to know in advance what type we are reading in. We need to know what to expect because the methods for reading a boolean, an int, a floating-point number, and so on, are all different. Follow this process:

1. Layer an `InputStreamReader` on `System.in`. This gives us a `Reader` class, on which we can layer other Readers.

2. Layer a `BufferedReader` on the `InputStreamReader`. This gives us a method that reads an entire line, allowing us to get all the text as a String when the user presses Return.

3. Layer a `java.util.StringTokenizer` on the String just read in. Call the `nextToken()` method to extract just the nonspace characters. This makes the input format a little more forgiving by removing trailing and leading whitespace.

4. Use the `parseXxx` method of the primitive types wrapper classes to extract the expected value.

The exact combination of features to read from the keyboard is painful, to say the least. It is a major wart on Java's mostly reasonable claim to simplicity. Table 12-4 shows how to read values from the keyboard and get them into a primitive type in your program.

Table 12-4: How to read from the keyboard

Preliminary declarations
| ```
import java.io.*;
import java.util.*;
...

InputStreamReader is = new InputStreamReader( System.in );
BufferedReader br = new BufferedReader( is );
  ...
String s = br.readLine();
StringTokenizer st = new StringTokenizer(s);
``` |

Note: An exception handler is also needed. Wrap a `try...catch` around the input statements.

Primitive type	Code to read it from `System.in`
| char | ```
int i = is.read(); // -1 denotes EOF
char c = (char) i;
``` |
| String | `String s = br.readLine();` |
| boolean | ```
boolean bo = new
Boolean(st.nextToken()).booleanValue();
``` |
| int | `int i = Integer.parseInt(st.nextToken());` |
| byte | `byte by = Byte.parseByte(st.nextToken());` |
| short | ```
short sh =
Short.parseShort(st.nextToken());
``` |
| long | `long lo = Long.parseLong(st.nextToken());` |
| float | ```
float fl = new
Float(st.nextToken()).floatValue();
``` |
| double | ```
double db = new
Double(st.nextToken()).doubleValue();
``` |
| Note: each statement or group of statements must have an exception handler wrapped around it, as shown in the column opposite. Or the method must declare that it throws an IOException. | ```
try {
   // put I/O statement here
} catch(IOException ioe)
   { ioe.printStackTrace(); }
``` |
```

For the sake of completeness, here is the full code to prompt for and read an int value.

```
import java.io.*;
import java.util.*;

public class exreadin2 {

    public static void main(String f[]) {
        int i=0;
        char c;
        InputStreamReader is = new InputStreamReader( System.in );
        BufferedReader br = new BufferedReader( is );
        StringTokenizer st;

        try {
                System.out.print( "int: " );    System.out.flush();
                String myline = br.readLine();
                st = new StringTokenizer(myline);
                i = Integer.parseInt(st.nextToken());
                System.out.println( "got: " + i );
        } catch (IOException ioe) {
                System.out.println( "IO error:" + ioe );
        }

    }

}
```

Most programmers would agree that this is excessively complicated for a simple thing like interactive I/O. When Java 1.0 came out, I filed a bug against the I/O library on this topic and included in the bug report my suggested fix: the code for a new class that supported simple keyboard I/O.

Easy Keyboard Input

Alas, my efforts were in vain, for matters did not improve with JDK 1.1; indeed, they became worse. The I/O classes changed between JDK 1.0 and JDK 1.1, such that many existing programs with I/O became deprecated. However, the new features introduced did not address the basic problem that the common, simple cases of I/O were complicated and involved to program. Drat!

The code that I included in the bug report collected the keyboard input methods in a class called `EasyIn`, which is on the CD. The class `EasyIn` has these methods:

```
public class EasyIn {
    boolean readBoolean();
       byte readByte();
      short readShort();
        int readInt();
       long readLong();
      float readFloat();
     double readDouble();
       char readChar();
     String readString();
}
```

You are welcome to copy this source file from the CD and use it without restriction in your programs. It supports easy keyboard input for the basic types. You would compile it with your code and use it like this:

```
EasyIn easy = new EasyIn();

int i = easy.readInt(); // gets an int from System.in
boolean b = easy.readBoolean(); // gets a boolean from System.in
```

`EasyIn` is not part of the JDK but is a utility I put together to provide the missing functionality. I didn't make it work with any arbitrary stream because I wanted it to be customized for simplicity in the most frequent case: use with `System.in`.

JDK 1.1 Output

At this point we have seen how to read both character and binary data from the keyboard and from files. Now it is time to look at the corresponding output classes. In this section on output, we will cover the following topics

- Character output

- Writing characters to the console

- Writing characters to a file

- Formatted character output

- Writing binary data to a file

Again, there are different classes according to the format that you wish to output. Table 12-5 lists them.

Table 12-5:   Classes to use for different output formats

If you have a value in this format...	Use this class, or one of its subclasses to write it
character	`FileWriter` (if it's to a file) `OutputStreamWriter` (if it's to a byte stream)
binary data (including chars)	`DataOutputStream`
persistent object	`ObjectOutputStream`

Character Output

Character output is done using one or more of the `Writer` classes. There is a different Writer subclass for each different destination of characters (file, String, array, etc.). You are expected to call the constructor with the character destination as an argument. It will hand you back a Writer, which means from that point on you never have to worry about lower-level details like how an array differs from the keyboard or how the Unicode is converted into the native codeset. The `Writer` class hides or encapsulates all the implementation details from you.

Writer has these public methods, along with others:

```
void write(java.lang.String);
    // Write out a String

void write(java.lang.String, int, int);
    // Write out a portion of a String

void write(int);
    // The single char to be written out. The low 16 bits of
    // the int are output, and the high 16 bits are ignored.

void write(char[]);
    // The array of chars to be written out.

abstract void write(char[], int, int);
    // Write a portion of an array of characters

abstract void flush();
    // Flush internal buffers for this stream

abstract void close();
    // Close this stream (no further processing)
```

As with the Reader classes, `Writer` is abstract, so you will always be dealing with one of its concrete subclasses.

Programmers writing applications frequently ask how they can access the RS232 serial port (or modem, etc.) on a system. There's a hard way and an easy way.

The hard way is to use a native method (a method written in C or some other non-Java language) and link that into your code.

The easy way can only be done if your operating system makes devices appear like files in the file system. For instance, on Unix systems, the serial port typically has a name like `/dev/ttya`, and under Windows, the serial port may be called COM2:.

If you can get at the serial port through the file system, then you can open it just as a regular file and have at it. The problem is that the file system doesn't provide any way to set the characteristics of the port: parity, line speed, etc. Setting these parameters currently requires jumping outside Java into C or assembler.

Writing Characters to the Console

We have seen code like

```
System.out.println("send more beer");
```

frequently enough to be confident about writing to the console. The line of code breaks down like this. System is a class in the java.lang package. It roughly corresponds to the AppletContext or Toolkit classes. It contains a number of useful objects and methods for the program, *not* for the system as the name suggests.

out is an object declaration within System. The declaration is

```
public final static PrintStream out = nullPrintStream();
```

PrintStream is marked as final, but that just means Java can't change it. PrintStream is actually given an initial value in a native code method in System in the Sun JDK. This code is called from an initializer that can be seen in file $JAVAHOME/src/java/lang/System.java.

```
FileOutputStream fdOut = new FileOutputStream(FileDescriptor.out);
setOut0(new PrintStream(new BufferedOutputStream(fdOut, 128), true));
```

The PrintStream class has "Stream" in the name, so we know it deals with 8-bit byte streams. It has methods like this

```
public void print(int);
public void print(byte);
public void print(float);
public void print(double);
public void print(String);
```

to print a value of every primitive type, and for Strings and Objects too. It also has a println() method for each of these that will print the value and then print a new line. When you invoke print() on an object it calls the toString() method of that object, and prints the resulting string.

Writing Characters to a File

Let's take a look at how to write characters to a file. This is a place where you may need to know about the underlying encoding or codeset of the operating system. There will be a default encoding in place, and if you want something different, you must change it (not supported in JDK 1.1.1).

`Writer` is an abstract class, so it is subclassed by other classes in the `java.io` package before it is used in practice. Here are four popular subclasses of `Writer`, corresponding to four possible destinations for the data.

- `FileWriter`—Writes a character stream into a file

- `InputStreamWriter`—Writes characters into a byte stream

- `StringWriter`—Writes characters into a String

- `CharArrayWriter`—Writes characters into a char array

All of these subclasses offer the `Writer` methods outlined above. Here is an example program that uses `FileWriter` to write whatever you type into a file. Provide the file name as a command-line argument.

```java
import java.io.*;

public class exfilewrite {
    public static void main(String f[]) {
        FileWriter fw;
        int i;
        try {
          fw = new FileWriter( f[0] );

            while ( (i=System.in.read()) != -1 ) {
                fw.write( (char) i );
            }
            fw.close();
        } catch (IOException ioe) {
                System.out.println( "IO error:" + ioe );
        }
    }

}
```

The file can be compiled and run on Windows 95 like this:

```
c:\> javac exfilewrite.java

c:\> java exfilewrite cars.txt
jaguar
ford chevy rolls
^Z

c:\> type cars.txt
jaguar
ford chevy rolls
```

So far, so good. But that just shows you how to write characters as characters. How can we write binary values as character data so it will be human readable? Say we have an int that we want to write into a file as a series of characters. We have already seen that the System.out object can do exactly that, so perhaps there is some way to construct an object of class PrintStream from a FileOutputStream.

Indeed there is, but it is now deprecated. The code looks like this:

```java
import java.io.*;
// write binary data as characters (deprecated)
public class exfilewrite2 {
    public static void main(String f[]) {
        try {
            FileOutputStream fos = new FileOutputStream("foo.txt");
            PrintStream ps = new PrintStream(fos);

            boolean b=true;
            int i=27;
            double d=432.5;

            ps.print( b );
            ps.print( i );
            ps.print( d );

            ps.close();
        } catch (IOException ioe) {
            System.out.println( "IO error:" + ioe );
        }
    }
}
```

Compiling it gives you this warning message:

```
% javac exfilewrite2.java

Note: exfilewrite2.java uses a deprecated API.
        Recompile with "-deprecation" for details.
1 warning


% javac -deprecation exfilewrite2.java
exfilewrite2.java:7:
Note: The constructor java.io.PrintStream(java.io.OutputStream)
        has been deprecated.
            PrintStream ps = new PrintStream(fos);
                                       ^
Note: exfilewrite2.java uses a deprecated API.
        Please consult the documentation for a better alternative.
2 warnings
```

That was the way we would have written binary data to a file as characters in
JDK1.0. If you run this program and look inside foo.txt, you'll see it contains
human-readable characters. Notice this breaks the character I/O rules at the
beginning of the chapter. We are trying to do character output, but the name of the
class does not end in Writer.

The new approved way is to use a PrintWriter, as shown in the example below.

```java
import java.io.*;
// write binary data as characters (new way)
public class exfilewrite3 {
    public static void main(String f[]) {
        try {
            FileWriter fw = new FileWriter("foo.txt");
            PrintWriter pw = new PrintWriter(fw);

            boolean b=true;
            int i=27;
            double d=432.5;

            pw.print( b );
            pw.print( i );
            pw.print( d );

            pw.close();
        } catch (IOException ioe) {
                System.out.println( "IO error:" + ioe );
        }
    }

}
```

Quick and dirty ways to fake out untrusted client-side I/O

For security reasons, untrusted applets are not allowed to write to the client's local disk. One quick and dirty approach to saving information permanently is for the applet to open a socket connection back to the server's SMTP port and e-mail the data to the client. The user at the client can then decide if he or she wishes to save the e-mail into a file. The chapter on networking explains how to connect to a mail server port and gives an example program.

If you want to do clientside I/O, you should simply use a signed (trusted) applet. That's not possible if you only have JDK 1.0-level browsers. So here's an ingenious approach that works.

The steps are:

1. Install a CGI script on the server, which simply stashes all its input into a temporary file.

2. Have your applet write the data to the URL of this CGI script, as shown in the networking chapter. Use Java strings to GET or POST the data to the CGI program.

3. The CGI program should give the file a MIME type which ensures the browser won't try to display it as HTML when you try to browse the file. Giving the temporary file an extension of ".zip" acomplishes this.

4. Finally, in your applet, open a URL to this temporary .zip file on the server, and do a showDocument () command on it, like this:

```
URL data = new URL(getDocumentBase(), "write/tmp.zip");

getAppletContext().showDocument(data);
```

The MIME type will cause Netscape to put up a dialog box, asking if the user wants to save the document (your file) to local disk. Just say yes. (This workaround was put together by my colleague Robert Lynch. All the scripts and classes that Robert generated are on the CD at `goodies/saveit`.)

If you have permission to install perl scripts on your applet server, these scripts give your applet users the ability to save files locally on their system. Note that this does not subvert system security—users must still explicitly choose whether or not to allow the file to be written to their system. 🦃

Formatted Character Output

Being able to write binary data as characters leads directly to the next requirement? How do we control the format of the character output? How do I specify that I want exactly two decimal places for my floating-point number? "Format" in this section means "appearance on the printed page," not character encoding.

The support for formatted output was introduced with JDK 1.1, and it uses the classes in the new package `java.text`. The package contains classes to help with collation (sorting order), formatting numbers and dates, and messaging. The JDK code for `java.text` was licensed from Taligent, the ill-fated Apple-IBM joint venture, to which Java has given a new lease on life.

Formatting a number allows localization to Western, Arabic, or Indic numbers, as well as specifying such things as the number of decimal places. A class called `java.text.DecimalFormat` has a constructor that takes a string which is a template for the format you want. You call the `format()` method, passing in your number. (The method is overloaded for doubles and longs, so you can call it with any kind of primitive type number.)

The format string you pass to the constructor will be made up of the symbols shown in Table 12-6 to indicate the significant digits, where to put the sign, and how positive numbers differ from negative numbers.

Table 12-6: Some characters that can be used in a format string

Symbol	Meaning
0	A digit
#	A digit; zero shows as absent (not space)
.	Placeholder for decimal separator
,	Placeholder for grouping separator
;	Separates positive and negative formats
-	Default negative prefix
%	Divide by 100 and show as percentage

You can put two of these formats together, separated by a semicolon. The first format will then be used for positive and zero numbers, and the second format will be applied to negative numbers. Some useful complete format strings are shown in Table 12-7.

Table 12-7: Some typical format strings

Format String	Meaning	Value	Output String
`"##0.00"`	At least one digit before the decimal point, and two after.	1234.567 .256	1234.56 0.25
`"#.000"`	Possibly no digits before the point, three after.	1234.567 .256	1234.567 .256
`",###"`	Use thousands separator and no decimal places	1234.567 .256	1,234 0
`"0.00;0.00-"`	Show negative numbers with sign on the right	–27.5	27.5–

The class `java.text.DecimalFormat` is designed for common uses; for very large or small numbers, instead use a format that can express exponential values. Here is an example of using the number format class to get numbers printed with two decimal places. Notice that if rounding is needed, we have to do it ourselves. The format just truncates, though it would be a good idea to add a format character that says "round this digit in that direction."

```
import java.io.*;
import java.text.*;
// write binary data as formatted characters

public class exformat {
    public static void main(String f[]) {

        double db[] = { -1.1, 2.2, -3.33, 4.444, -5.5555, 6.66666};

        DecimalFormat df = new DecimalFormat( "#0.00;#0.00CR" );

        for (int i=0; i<db.length; i++) {
            System.out.println( df.format( db[i]) );
        }

    }

}
```

Running this code gives the output shown below. The symbol CR (credit) used for negative numbers is a common business usage.

```
% java exformat
1.10CR
2.20
3.33CR
4.44
5.55CR
6.66
```

A comment in the `DecimalFormat` class warns that the normal use is to get a proper format string for a specific locale, using one of the factory methods such as `getInstance()`. You may then modify it from there (after testing to make sure it is a `DecimalFormat`). They are suggesting that the proper usage is something like this:

```
NumberFormat nf = NumberFormat.getInstance();
System.out.println( nf.format( mydouble ));
```

Finally, note that the format in which a number is printed can depend on the locale (geographical region). In some parts of Europe, a decimal point is a "." and in other parts it is a "," so formatting a number is bound up with internationalization and localization (a topic that deserves a book in its own right).

Here is how you can get a list of locales known to your system:

```java
import java.io.*;
import java.util.Locale;
import java.text.*;

public class exlocales {
    public static void main(String f[]) {

        java.util.Locale[] locales =
                java.text.NumberFormat.getAvailableLocales();

        System.out.println("The locales on this system are:");

        for (int i = 0; i < locales.length; ++i) {
            if (locales[i].getCountry().length() == 0) {
                // skip locales with no country
                continue;
            }
            System.out.println(locales[i].getDisplayName());
        }
    }
}
```

Running this program on a Unix system and on a PC produced exactly the same
result:

```
C:\> java exlocales
The locales on this system are:
German (Austria)
German (Switzerland)
English (Canada)
English (United Kingdom)
English (Ireland)
English (United States)
French (Belgium)
French (Canada)
French (Switzerland)
Italian (Switzerland)
Dutch (Belgium)
Norwegian (Nynorsk) (Norway,NY)
Chinese (ROC)
```

The Java Language Specification says that when you output a double or float as a
character string, by default it should print as many decimal places as are necessary to ensure that the number can be read back in without loss of precision:

> *How many digits must be printed for the fractional part of m or a? There
> must be at least one digit to represent the fractional part, and beyond that as
> many, but only as many, more digits as are needed to uniquely distinguish
> the argument value from adjacent values of type double.*

> *Java Language Specification, Section 20.10.15.*

> http://www.javasoft.com/doc/language_specification/index.html

Before JDK 1.1, the floating-point output routines output at most six decimal
places. From JDK 1.1 on, you get floating-point output that ensures exactly that
value can be read back in again, which sometimes leads to what looks like an
excessive number of decimal places being printed. When you use a NumberFor-
mat class, you get neater output, but you lose the ability to read the number back
in with the same exact value it had when output.

Writing Binary Data to a File

Finally, what if you want to write binary data to a file? Binary data cannot be read directly by people, but it is faster for computers to read in, and the values are of a fixed length. Table 12-5 showed that binary data written with DataOutput-Stream. DataOutputStream has these public methods, along with others:

```
public java.io.DataOutputStream(java.io.OutputStream);
public synchronized void write(int);
public synchronized void write(byte[], int, int);
public void flush();
public final void writeBoolean(boolean);
public final void writeByte(int);
public final void writeShort(int);
public final void writeChar(int);
public final void writeInt(int);
public final void writeLong(long);
public final void writeFloat(float);
public final void writeDouble(double);
public final void writeBytes(java.lang.String);
public final void writeChars(java.lang.String);
public final void writeUTF(java.lang.String);
public final int size();
```

Each method writes a binary representation of the value of the stated type or throws an IOException. DataOutputStream is guaranteed to be able to read anything that DataInputStream wrote because they both use network byte order (big endian format). DataOutputStream might not be able to read data that you have written using a program in a different language or on a system with a different byte order. The Intel® x86™ architecture uses the reverse order to standard network byte order. So, to read binary integers written by a C program on an Intel machine, read byte by byte and manually assemble into integers, using bit shifting.

DataOutputStream would really have been better named BinaryOutputStream as that accurately describes what it does. Here is an example of writing ints to a file, using a DataOutputStream. As before, we just construct a FileOutput-Stream with the path name of your file (passed in as an argument to the program in the example that follows). Then, construct a DataOutputStream from the FileOutputStream. The code looks like this:

```
import java.io.*;

public class exwritedata {
    public static void main(String f[]) {
        FileOutputStream fos;
        DataOutputStream ds;
        try {
          fos = new FileOutputStream(f[0]);
          ds = new DataOutputStream( fos );

          int a[] = {0,1,2,3,4,5,6,7,8,9};

          for (int i=0; i<a.length; i++) {
              ds.writeInt(a[i]);
          }

        } catch (IOException ioe) {
                System.out.println( "IO error: " + ioe );
        }

    }

}
```

If you run this program, you will find that the data file it creates can be read perfectly by the exreaddata program given earlier in the chapter. Running this program, followed by the read program looks like this:

% java exwritedata myfile.dat

% java exreaddata myfile.dat
```
file: myfile.dat
read: 0
read: 1
read: 2
read: 3
read: 4
read: 5
read: 6
read: 7
read: 8
read: 9
EOF reached
```

Random Access File and Appending

The class `RandomAccessFile` allows the file pointer to be moved to arbitrary positions in the file prior to reading or writing. This allows you to "jump around" in the file, reading and writing data with random (nonsequential) access. You provide a mode string when you open the file, specifying whether you are opening it for read access only `r`, or read and update access `rw`.

Here is an example of how you would append to a file, using the `RandomAccessFile` class. Create a file called `animals.txt` with the names of a few animals in it. We will write a few more animals on the end of the `animals.txt` file, using `RandomAccessFile`.

```
import java.io.RandomAccessFile;
class exraf {

    static public void main(String a[]) {
        RandomAccessFile rf;
        try {
            rf = new RandomAccessFile("animals.txt", "rw");

            rf.seek( rf.length() );

            rf.writeBytes("ant bee\ncat dog\n");

            rf.close();

        } catch (Exception e) {
            System.out.println("file snafu");
            System.exit(0);
        }
    }
}
```

This example will extend the `animals.txt` file by appending the string on the end.

Note that you cannot jump to a specific line number in the file. `RandomAccessFile` only keeps track of the number of bytes in the file, not the interpretation of those bytes as line endings. Also note that the class `Reader` has `mark()` and `reset()` methods, allowing you to jump back to a file position you have already visited once. `RandomAccessFile` allows you to jump to an offset in the file without having previously passed it.

JDK 1.1 introduced a new constructor for `FileOutputStream` that lets you open a file in append mode, like this:

```
FileOutputStream fos = new FileOutputStream ("animals.txt, true);
```

There is a similar constructor in `FileWriter`:

```
public FileWriter(String fileName, boolean append)
                throws IOException;
```

Platform-Specific I/O

Since file I/O results in something that has an existence outside a program, we should (alas) expect some visible differences between the different platforms. There are several such differences, as listed in Table 12-8.

Table 12-8:   Platform differences relating to I/O

Property	Usual value		
	Unix	**Windows**	**Macintosh**
`file.separator`	/	\	:
`line.separator`	\n	\r\n	\r
`path.separator`	:	;	:

The file separator is the character used to separate components in a path name (e.g., in `c:\windows\bin\foo.exe` the character "\" is the file separator). Remember "\" is also the escape character, so you must double it up when you use it in strings, e.g., "c:\\windows\\bin\\foo.exe". The path separator is an OS concept, used when you want to specify several path names as starting points for searching for a command or library. Path separators are used when you set, for example, `CLASSPATH`.

On Unix, a newline is just a linefeed character. On Windows, a newline is usually represented by two characters, carriage return followed by linefeed. On the Mac, a newline is represented by a carriage return. The standard I/O streams are capable of coping with any of these manifestations.

On the other hand, you can use "/" to separate the components in a file name in Windows, just as in Unix. The Windows file system calls all use it internally anyway, and only `COMMAND.COM` (the shell) can't handle it. This is an interesting artifact of history, dating from the origins of DOS as an unofficial port (known as QDOS) of CP/M with a few trivial changes.

Reading/Writing Objects

It is perfectly possible to input and output entire objects. If an object can be written to a stream, it can also be sent through a socket, backed up onto a file, and later read back in again and reconstituted.

To make an object serializable, all you need do is make its class implement the Serializable or Externalizable interface. If you are happy with the default methods for writing its fields out, implement `java.io.Serializable`. If you want your own `writeExternal()` method to participate in writing the object out, then implement `java.io.Externalizable`. There is a corresponding `readExternal`, too.

Making an object serializable only requires implementing an interface. It is not turned on by default because there are certain classes that should not be serialized for security reasons. It is more secure to allow serialization by explicitly saying so than to allow it by default. Reading and writing objects is thankfully very simple. It is extensively used in Remote Method Invocation, and the chapter describing RMI walks through a practical example.

More Examples of Layering Streams

A significant Java idiom is the use of streams to connect one stream to another. The result is also a stream that can be further connected. Each Stream in a chain has the chance to modify the data as it goes by, and it can also offer a selection of more sophisticated methods to operate on the stream.

> **Really Important:** *Streams can be "pushed" or layered on top of each other to provide filtered processing.*

Let's show how this works in practice. Suppose that I have two or three data files, each containing the names of some animals. I want to read each of the files one after the other and do the same processing on each, let us say, print out the contents. And I also want to read the files buffered, meaning that I want the runtime system to read great chunks of the file at a time and dole out individual characters to me as I ask for them. Buffered I/O often provides a big performance speed-up because one large read from a (slow) disk is faster than many small reads.

The best way to write the specified program is as follows:

- Create a `FileInputStream` for each input file.

- Group all the `FileInputStreams` together as a single `Sequence-InputStream`. This class makes two streams look like one long concatenated stream.

- Convert the stream to a reader by using InputStreamReader.

- Layer a BufferedReader on the InputStreamReader.

- Read from the BufferedReader.

The code is remarkably compact and looks like this.

```
import java.io.*;
public class exlayer {

    public static void main(String args[]) {
      try {
        FileInputStream fr1 = new FileInputStream( "mammals.txt" );
        FileInputStream fr2 = new FileInputStream( "reptiles.txt" );

        SequenceInputStream sis = new SequenceInputStream( fr1, fr2 );
        InputStreamReader isr = new InputStreamReader(sis);
        BufferedReader br = new BufferedReader( isr );

        int i=0;
        while( (i=br.read() )!= -1 ) {
          System.out.print( (char) i);
        }
      } catch(FileNotFoundException fnf){System.out.println(fnf); }
        catch(IOException ioe) {ioe.printStackTrace(); }
    }
}
```

This little program does a lot of layered processing, using the built-in classes. If you had to program all this functionality from scratch (stream aggregation and so on), it would take hundreds of lines. I wrote and tested this program in about fifteen minutes, and so can you after you become familiar with the classes in `java.io`.

There is another class that is sometimes layered on top of others. The class Line-NumberReader counts the lines as you read from the stream and, at any time, can tell you how many lines it has seen. Programmers can also implement their own classes that extend `Reader` or `Writer` to filter the characters as they flow through the stream.

Piped I/O for Threads

A pipe forms a shared buffer between two threads. One thread writes into the pipe, and the other reads from it. This forms a producer/consumer buffer, ready-programmed for you. There are two stream classes that we always use together in a matched consumer/producer pair:

- `PipedInputStream`—Gets bytes from a pipe (think "hosepipe"; it's just a data structure that squirts bytes at you)

- `PipedOutputStream`—Puts bytes into a pipe (think "drainpipe"; it's just a data structure that drinks down bytes that you pour into it).

An object of one of these classes is connected to an object of the other class, providing a safe way (without data race conditions) for one thread to send a stream of data to another thread.

As an example of the use of piped streams, the program below reimplements the Producer/Consumer problem, but uses piped streams instead of `wait`/`notify`. The version using `wait`/`notify` was shown in Chapter 5, and if you compare the two versions, you'll see that this one is considerably simpler. There is no explicit shared buffer—the pipe stream between the two threads carries out that job.

This example shows one thread sending longs to another. You can also send Strings, using the classes `PipedWriter` and `PipedReader`.

```java
import java.io.*;
public class expipes {

  public static void main(String args[]) {
      Producer p = new Producer();
      p.start();

      Consumer c = new Consumer(p);
      c.start();
  }
}


///// This class writes into the pipe until it is full, at which
///// point it is blocked until the consumer takes something out.

class Producer extends Thread {
    protected PipedOutputStream po = new PipedOutputStream();
    private DataOutputStream dos = new DataOutputStream(po);

    public void run() {
        // just keep producing numbers that represent the
        // amount of millisecs program has been running.
        for(;;) produce();
    }

    private final long start = System.currentTimeMillis();
    private final long banana() {
        return (System.currentTimeMillis() - start);
    }

    void produce() {
       long t = banana();
       System.out.println("produced " + t);
       try {dos.writeLong( t );}
       catch (IOException ie) { System.out.println(ie); }
    }

}
```

```
///// This class consumes everything sent over the pipe.
///// The pipe does the synchronization.  When the pipe is full,
///// this thread's read from the pipe is blocked.

class Consumer extends Thread {
    private PipedInputStream pip;
    private DataInputStream d;

    // java constructor idiom, save argument.
    Consumer(Producer who) {
        try {
            pip = new PipedInputStream(who.po);
            d = new DataInputStream( pip );
        } catch (IOException ie) {
            System.out.println(ie);
        }
    }

    long get(){
        long i=0;
        try {   i= d.readLong();  // read from pipe.
        } catch (IOException ie) {System.out.println(ie);}
        return i;
    }

    public void run() {
        java.util.Random r = new java.util.Random();
        for(;;) {
            long result = get();
            System.out.println("consumed: "+result);
            // next lines are just to make things asynchronous
            int randomtime = r.nextInt() % 1250;
            try{sleep(randomtime);} catch(Exception e){}
        }
    }
}
```

The output of this program is a list of numbers that represent the number of milliseconds the program has been running. The numbers are passed in a buffer in a thread-safe way from the producer thread to the consumer thread. The piped streams allow for real simplification in interthread communication.

A Word About IOExceptions

Let's say a few words on the subject of IOExceptions. If you look at the runtime source, you'll see that there are 16 I/O-related exceptions. The basic I/O related exceptions are:

```
CharConversionException

StreamCorruptedException

WriteAbortedException

FileNotFoundException

InterruptedIOException

UTFDataFormatError

EOFException
```

These names are self-explanatory, except for the last one. The name EOFException suggests that it is thrown whenever EOF (end of file) is encountered, and that therefore this exception might be used as the condition to break out of a loop.

That's not what happens, and no, it can't always be used that way. The `EOFException` would be better named UnexpectedEOFException, as it is only raised when the programmer has asked for a fixed definite amount of input, and the end of file is reached before all the requested amount of data has been obtained. `EOFException` is raised in only three classes: `DataInputStream`, `ObjectInputStream`, and `RandomAccessFile`, (and their subclasses, of course). It is never raised when the normal end of file is reached.

Other than in the classes mentioned, the usual way to detect EOF is to check for the –1 return value from a byte read, not try to catch `EOFexception`.

How to Execute a Program from Java

This section explains how to execute a program from Java and read the output of that program back into your application. Just as a reminder, untrusted applets cannot do this.

Executing a program from your Java program has four general steps.

1. Get the object representing the current runtime environment. A call in class `java.lang.Runtime` does this.

2. Call the `exec` method in the runtime object with your command as an argument. This call creates a `Process` object. Give the full path name to the executable, and make sure the executable really exists on the system.

3. Connect the output of the `Process` (which will be coming to you as an input stream) to an input stream reader in your program.

4. You can either read individual characters from the input stream or layer a `BufferedReader` on it and read a line at a time, as in the code below.

```
import java.io.*;
   public class exwho {

       public static void main(String args[]) {
          try {
              Runtime rt = Runtime.getRuntime();           // step 1

              Process prcs = rt.exec("/bin/who");          // step 2

              InputStreamReader isr =                       // step 3
                 new InputStreamReader( prcs.getInputStream() );

              BufferedReader br = new BufferedReader(  // step 4.
                                    isr );
              String line;
              while  ((line = br.readLine()) != null)
                    System.out.println(line);
          } catch(IOException ioe) { System.out.println(ioe); }
       }

   }
```

This code program uses a class inside `System` called `Runtime` which does a couple of runtime-related things. The main use is to provide a way to execute other programs, but it can also force garbage collection or finalization and tell you how much total memory and free memory is available. It also uses the class `Process` that allows you to get in, out, err streams, and to destroy, or to wait for a process.

Several books use the example of listing files in a directory, but there is already a Java method to do that in class `File`. The code

```
File f = new File(".");

String lst[] = f.list();
```

will return an array of Strings, one string for each file name in the directory. The file with the magic name of "." is used on many operating systems to refer to the current working directory.

The program `/bin/who` is a Unix program that lists the users on a system. Compiling and running the program above gives this output.

```
% javac exwho.java
% java exwho
pvdl      console      Aug 17 12:29
pvdl      pts/1        Aug 17 12:30
pvdl      pts/2        Aug 17 12:30
pvdl      pts/3        Aug 17 12:30
```

Here, it shows that I logged on to my workstation in four different windows at the stated times.

Watch out for these common errors when executing a program from your Java code:

- Remember that an untrusted applet does not have permission to run executables.

- You must provide the complete path name for the command. The `exec` method does not use a shell, so does not have the ability to look for executables in the search path that your shell (or command interpreter) knows about.

- Note that this also means you cannot use commands that are built into a shell unless you explicitly call a shell as the program you wish to run (see upcoming tip).

- Remember to instantiate an input stream to read the output from running the command. You will only be able to communicate with programs that use standard in, out, and err. Some programs like `xterm` open a new tty, so can't be used as you would wish.

How to execute an MS-DOS® batch file from a Java application

As previously mentioned, the Java exec method does not use a shell, so you can't directly use it to execute shell-supported features. In MS-DOS, the DIR and DEL commands are not programs, but are internal commands which are processed by the command interpreter (COMMAND.COM).

To execute one of these internal commands or to run a batch file (another feature of the shell), you make the shell itself be the command you execute, and you give the appropriate parameters to it. To run the batch file c:\foo\mybatch.bat, you would change step 2 on page 531 in the code above to say:

```
Process prcs = rt.exec("command.com /c c:\\foo\\mybatch.bat");
```

The name command.com is the shell under Windows 95. Note that early versions of the JDK had a bug in Windows which made the Java process hang after running the command. ❦

ZIP Files and Streams

ZIP is a multifile archive format popularized by the PC but available on almost all systems now. The ZIP format offers two principal benefits: it can bundle several files into one file, and it can compress the data as it writes it to the ZIP archive. It's more convenient to pass around one file than twenty separate files. Compressed files are faster and cheaper to download or e-mail than their uncompressed versions. Java Archives (.jar) files are in ZIP format.

JDK 1.1 introduced several new utilities in the package java.util. It collected some classes that can read and write ZIP and gzip archives. gzip, an alternative to ZIP, uses a different format for the data. To conserve programmer sanity, most people writing compression and archiving utilities make sure that their software can deal with both .zip files and .gz files. ZIP traditionally uses the file extension .zip, and gzip uses .gz for its files. The gzip program was written by the GNU folks, and it compresses its input by using the Lempel-Ziv coding.

Another difference between the two programs is that many files can be put into a .zip archive, but only one file at a time can be compressed with gzip. JDK 1.1 included both utilities because ZIP is something of a standard on PCs, while gzip (and the OS commands gzip, gunzip) is found most often on Unix systems. There is more information about gzip at

```
http://www.sdsu.edu/doc/texi/gzip_toc.html
```

You should be comfortable with the idea of connecting streams to each other now, and it's no surprise that the ZIP utilities just work this way. Here is a program that creates a `.zip` file of its own source (you could easily change it to pass the file name in as an argument).

```java
import java.io.*;
import java.util.zip.*;
public class exzip {

    public static void main(String args[]) {
      try {
          FileInputStream fis = new FileInputStream("exzip.java");

          FileOutputStream fos = new
           FileOutputStream("output.zip");
          ZipOutputStream z = new ZipOutputStream(fos);

          z.putNextEntry( new ZipEntry("myfile.java") );
          int i;
          while  ((i = fis.read()) != -1)
                z.write((byte)i);

          z.close();

      } catch(IOException ioe) { System.out.println(ioe); }
    }

}
```

The line

```java
    z.putNextEntry( new ZipEntry("myfile.java") );
```

tells the ZIP archive what name to give this file when it is extracted. We are putting only one file in the archive in this example. We use a different name (`myfile.zip`) than the name of the original source file because we want to have both of them together for this example, so we can compare them.

Compiling and running this program gives:

```
% javac exzip.java

% java exzip

% ls -l *.zip
-rw-rw-r--   1 linden    staff            415 May   6 12:09 output.zip

% ls -l exzip.java
-rw-rw-r--   1 linden    staff            557 May   6 12:06 exzip.java

% unzip output.zip
  Inflating: myfile.java

% diff myfile.java exzip.java
  (no differences found)
```

The ls command lists the files in a directory in Unix. The diff command compares two files for any differences. You don't need to write ZIP streams to a file. You can equally send them through a socket, put them in a String or byte array for later retrieval, or send them through a pipe to another thread.

The class ZipOutputStream has these methods:

```
public java.util.zip.ZipOutputStream(java.io.OutputStream);

public void setComment(java.lang.String);
public void setMethod(int);
public void setLevel(int);

public void putNextEntry(java.util.zip.ZipEntry);
public void closeEntry();
public synchronized void write(byte[], int, int);
public void finish();
public void close();
```

The method setLevel() sets the compression level, 0–9. A higher level of compression takes longer to zip and unzip but potentially yields more space saving. Some kinds of data, such as human-readable characters, compress better than others. The default compression level is set to 8.

Light Relief—Crossing the Chasm

If you've read my book, *Expert C Programming*, you'll have seen the appendix that describes how to conduct yourself in a Silicon Valley programmer job interview (don't critique the interviewer with your imaginary friend while you are actually interviewing, etc.). I also described some of the puzzles that are used in job interviews. Some companies interview programmers by posing a few logic puzzles to them and seeing how they handle it. Microsoft is famous for interviewing programmers this way. It's great if you can solve the puzzle, but even if you can't, you're supposed to make intelligent remarks and look as though you care.

Here is a puzzle that Microsoft has been using in recent job interviews. There are four men who want to cross a bridge at night, by the light of a flashlight that one of them has. They all begin on the same side, and the bridge can only hold two of them at once. They all walk at different speeds and take different amounts of time to cross the bridge, namely, 1, 2, 5, and 10 minutes. Whenever two are on the bridge together they walk at the pace of the slower person. Any party who crosses the bridge must carry the flashlight, and the flashlight must be walked back to the other side to bring over any remaining people. The flashlight cannot be thrown, sent by Federal Express, etc.

For example, if the 1 minute man and the 10 minute man walk across first, 10 minutes have elapsed when they get to the far side of the bridge. If the 1 minute man then crosses back with the flashlight, a total of 11 minutes has passed and there are still three people on the wrong side of the bridge. Describe how everyone can get across in 17 minutes.

Before reading on, take a little while to try this problem. Stop reading now. Don't read any further. Hey! I said stop. What, can't you read? OK, you asked for it. The "obvious" solution is to have the fastest people travel with the slowest, so men 10 and 1 go over (10 minutes), 1 returns (total 11 minutes), 2 and 5 go over (16 minutes), 2 returns (18 minutes, and you've blown the mission), 2 and 1 go over for a total of 20 minutes.

How can it be done in less time? The answer is that this is one of those puzzles where your intuition is just plain wrong! You need to drop the preconceived idea about what works best and explore other alternatives. The insight to move you to the correct answer is to view the problem from the point of view of your slowest walkers instead of your fastest. If you make your two slowest walkers go over together, they will only take 10 minutes, instead of the 15 minutes taken if they go separately. But if they go over together, you need to have someone quick on the other side ready to bring the light back. Hence, 1 and 2 should go first. So, one answer is men 1 and 2 go over (2 minutes), 1 returns (3 minutes), men 10 and 5 go over (13 minutes), men 2 returns (15 minutes), men 1 and 2 go over (17 minutes).

Well, it's just a puzzle, but as I mentioned, Microsoft has been using it lately in their interviews. I was reminded of this when I called the Microsoft telephone support line. The support line was my last resort. My problem was that when I upgraded from Windows 3.1 to Windows 95, some pieces of networking stopped working. The problem had nothing to do with Java, except that it meant many Java applets would not run.

At first I could see only the symptoms, and I did not know what the problem was. I worked hard to gather more information about the problem and was soon able to conclude that my Netscape browser could not resolve domain names. Domain Name Service (DNS) is the Internet protocol for mapping between computer names (like ds.internic.net) and computer IP addresses (like 198.49.45.10). When a domain name needs to be resolved (translated into the other form), a DNS server (anyone's DNS server) first goes to the central Network Information Center (NIC) to ask where to go to resolve the domain name. The NIC itself cannot resolve domains, but it tells DNS server where to go to get that service for that name. The DNS server then goes to the specified remote site to resolve the domain name, which typically belongs to the site that owns the domain name in question. The remote site replies with the answer, which the local DNS server caches for future reference, and returns to the original requester.

But DNS names weren't being resolved for me. To cut a long story short, I invested many hours over a period of months to solve this problem. It seemed that DNS worked for everyone else at my Internet Service Provider. I followed cookbooks, I reconfigured the software, I reinstalled Windows 95 several times. Nothing solved the problem, but it worked for everyone else at the ISP. Eventually, I made an appointment with the top troubleshooter at the ISP and physically took my system into their premises, where we hooked it up to a phone line, dialed in, and brought up Netscape. The problem was right there still. I could access a site via its IP address but not by name.

The top troubleshooter quickly went to work and was quickly able to demonstrate that the problem was nothing to do with Netscape or my configuration. The Windows 95 ftp command failed the same way. Under his eye, I reinstalled Windows 95 from scratch, and DNS resolution still failed. Aha! This was a Windows 95 bug!

Later that day, at home, I browsed the Microsoft web site looking for a patch to fix the problem. There were many patches, but none seemed to address the problem I was seeing. After months of troubleshooting, it looked like I had to call the Microsoft support line. I carefully set up everything I would need: two phone lines (one for the support line, one for the PC to my ISP), manuals, invoices, notes of things I had tried, notes of configurations and versions, and so on.

As everyone in the computer industry knows, 90 percent of all calls to support lines are made by novices and can be solved by checking the basics like "Is your computer plugged in?" and "Did you remove the old floppy disk from the drive before inserting the new one?" Front-line support staff usually deal with trivial problems, so I made sure I was ready with a clear, full description of the bug. The conversation went like this:

> **me:** "Hi, I'm having a network software problem with Windows 95.

> **Microsoft support guy** (enthusiastically): "OK! Is your system powered on?"

> **me:** "Yes, the system is on and running.
> The problem is that DNS name resolution doesn't work, so programs can't turn fully qualified domain names into network IP addresses. I'd like to know if there's a patch for it."

> **Microsoft support guy:** "Oh. We recommend you contact your ISP to fix any networking problems at their end."

> **me:** "I have taken the system in to the ISP's office, and we have eliminated any problems in their configuration or mine. I have reinstalled Windows 95 multiple times, including immediately before this call.

> The problem has been traced down to the Windows 95 networking library not successfully using DNS to resolve symbolic domain names into their equivalent IP addresses. We know this because even the basic Window tcp commands like ping and ftp fail.

> I want to know if failure to do DNS resolution is a known bug and if there's a Windows 95 patch for it."

> **Microsoft support guy** (goes very quiet for several seconds, then asks in a small voice): "... Could you hold the line for few minutes? I'm going to get some help."

A few minutes pass while I hold the line. Then the Microsoft support guy comes back.

> **Microsoft support guy** (still in a small voice): "Um. I'm still waiting to hear from the network group. In the meantime, have you heard this one? There are four fellows with a flashlight who want to cross a bridge,..."

me: "Send the two fastest guys over together, bring back the light, and send the two slowest over together. Call me when you get an answer."

I never did hear back from them. I found a workaround and have been living with it ever since. Giving and getting telephone support for computer software is tough!

List of I/O Classes

There are now 71 classes in the `java.io` package. Here is a list of some of the classes, grouped into categories by function.

Input Streams (for 8-bit input)

```
BufferedInputStream
ByteArrayInputStream
DataInputStream
FileInputStream
FilterInputStream
InputStream
InputStreamReader
LineNumberInputStream
ObjectInputStream
PipedInputStream
PushbackInputStream
SequenceInputStream
StringBufferInputStream
```

Readers (for 16-bit character input)

```
BufferedReader
CharArrayReader
FileReader
FilterReader
InputStreamReader
LineNumberReader
PipedReader
PushbackReader
Reader
StringReader
```

Output Streams (8-bit output)

```
OutputStream
DataOutputStream
FileOutputStream
PipedOutputStream
ObjectOutputStream
FilterOutputStream
BufferedOutputStream
ByteArrayOutputStresm
OutputStreamWriter
```

Writers (for 16-bit character output)

```
BufferedWriter
CharArrayWriter
FileWriter
FilterWriter
OutputStreamWriter
PipedWriter
PrinterWriter
StringWrtier
Writer
```

Answer To Programming Challenge

Here is a Java program that creates a subdirectory, and a file in it.

```java
// create a subdirectory Fruit
// then create a file called yam in that directory
import java.io.*;
class files {
    public static final PrintStream o = System.out;

    public static void main(String a[]) throws IOException {
        File d = new File("Fruit");
        checkDirectory(d);
        checkFile("Fruit/yam");
    }

    static void checkFile(String s) {
        File f = new File(s);
        if (!f.exists() ) {
            o.println("File " + f.getName() + " doesn't exist");
            FileOutputStream fos;
            try { fos = new FileOutputStream(f);
                    fos.write(' ');
            } catch (IOException ioe) {
                    o.println("IO Exception!");
            }
        } else {
            o.println("File " + f.getName() + " already exists");
        }
    }

    static void checkDirectory(File d) throws IOException {
        boolean success;
        if (!d.exists() ) {
            o.println("Directory "
                + d.getName() + " doesn't exist");
            if (success=d.mkdir())
                o.println("Have created directory " + d.getName());
            else
                o.println("Failed to create directory "
                    + d.getName());
        } else {
            o.println( d.getName() + " exists already");
            if (d.isDirectory()) {
                o.println( "and is a directory.");
            } else {
                o.println( "and is a file.");
                throw new IOException();
            }
        }
    }
}
```

Answer To Programming Challenge

This program uses a SequenceInputStream to jam two different sources of data seamlessly together. It pushes a LineNumberInputStream on top of that, to keep track of line numbers.

```
// shows the use of various input streams
import java.io.*;
public class test7c {
    static String s=new String("aardvark butterfly\n" +
        "carp dalmatian\n" +
            "eagle fish\ngopher hippo\ninyala jackal\nkyloe " +
            "lamb\nmoose nanny-goat\nopossum pandora\n" );

    static StringBufferInputStream sbis=
        new StringBufferInputStream(s);

    public static void main (String a[])
        throws FileNotFoundException {
         int c;
         FileInputStream fis = new FileInputStream("animals.txt");

         SequenceInputStream sis =
             new SequenceInputStream( sbis, fis );

         LineNumberInputStream lsis =
        new LineNumberInputStream( sis );

         try {
             while ((c=lsis.read())!= -1) {

                 System.out.print((char)c);
                 if (c=='\n') {
                     System.out.print("that finishes input line "
                             + lsis.getLineNumber() + "\n\n");
                 }

             }
        } catch (IOException ioe) {
                 System.out.println("Exception reading stream");
                 ioe.printStackTrace();
                 System.exit(0);
         }
    }
}
```

CHAPTER
13

- TCP and IP basics

- Client/server sockets

- Sending e-mail in Java

- Reading data from URLs

- A network client/server application

- A threaded server

Networking in Java

"If a packet hits a pocket on a socket on a port,
and the bus is interrupted and the interrupt's not caught,
then the socket packet pocket has an error to report.

—*Programmer's traditional nursery rhyme*

The biggest difficulty most people face in understanding the Java networking features lies in understanding the network part rather than the Java part. If you learn French, it doesn't mean that you can translate an article from a French medical journal. Similarly if you learn Java, you need to have an understanding of the network services and terminology before you can blithely write Internet code. This section provides a solid review, followed by a description of the Java support.

Everything You Need To Know about TCP/IP But Failed to Learn in Kindergarten

Networking at heart is all about shifting bits from point A to point B. Usually we bundle the data bits into a packet with some more bits that say where they are to go. That, in a nutshell, is the Internet Protocol or IP. If we want to send more bits than will fit into a single packet, we can divide the bits into groups and send them in several successive packets. These are called "User Datagrams."

User Datagrams can be sent across the Internet using the User Datagram Protocol (UDP), which relies on the Internet Protocol for addressing and routing. UDP is like going to the post office, sticking on a stamp, and dropping off the packet. IP is what the mail carrier does to route and deliver the packet. Two common applications that use the UDP are: SNMP, the Simple Network Management Protocol, and TFTP, the Trivial File Transfer Protocol.

Just as when we send several pieces of postal mail to the same address, the packages might arrive in any order. Some of them might even be delayed, or even on occasion lost altogether. This is true for UDP too; you wave good-bye to the bits as they leave your workstation, and you have no idea when they will arrive where you sent them, or even if they did.

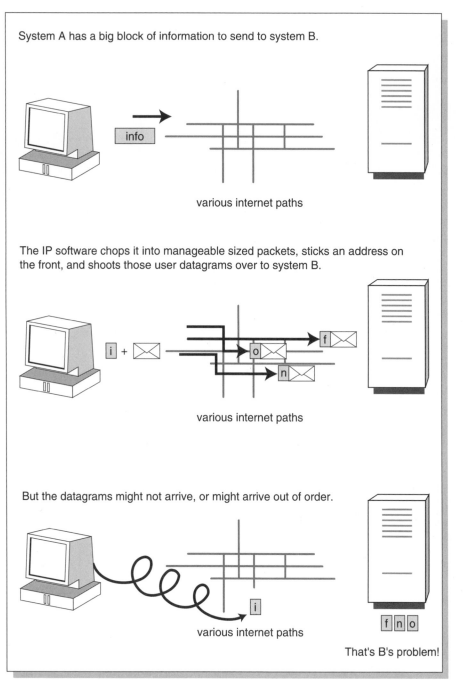

System A has a big block of information to send to system B.

info

various internet paths

The IP software chops it into manageable sized packets, sticks an address on the front, and shoots those user datagrams over to system B.

i +

various internet paths

But the datagrams might not arrive, or might arrive out of order.

i

various internet paths

That's B's problem!

Figure 13-1: IP and UDP (Datagram sockets)

Uncertain delivery is equally undesirable for postal mail and for network bit streams. We deal with the problem in the postal mail world (when the importance warrants the cost) by paying an extra fee to register the mail and have the mail carrier collect and bring back a signature acknowledging delivery. A similar protocol is used in the network work to guarantee reliable delivery in the order in which the packets were sent. This protocol is known as Transmission Control Protocol or "TCP." Two applications that run on top of, or use, TCP are: FTP, the File Transfer Protocol, and Telnet.

TCP uses IP as its underlying protocol (just as UDP does) for routing and delivering the bits to the correct address. However, TCP is more like a phone call than a registered mail delivery, in that a real end-to-end connection is held open for the duration of the transmission session. It takes a while to set up this stream connection, and it costs more to assure reliable sequenced delivery, but often the cost is justified. See Figure 12-2.

The access device at each end-point of a phone conversation is a telephone. The access object at each end-point of a TCP/IP session is a socket. Sockets started life as a way for two processes on the same Unix system to talk to each other, but some smart programmers realized that they could be generalized into connection end-points between processes on different machines connected by a TCP/IP network.

Sockets can deliver fast and dirty using UDP (this is a datagram socket), or slower, fussier, and reliably using TCP (this is termed a stream socket). Socket connections generally have a client end and a server end. Generally the server end just keeps listening for incoming requests ("operators are standing by" kind of thing). The client end initiates a connection, and then passes or requests information from the server.

Note that the number of socket writes is not at all synchronized with the number of socket reads. A packet may be broken into smaller packets as it is sent across the network, so your code should never assume that a read will get the same number of bytes that were just written into the socket.

There! Now you know everything you need to use the Java networking features.

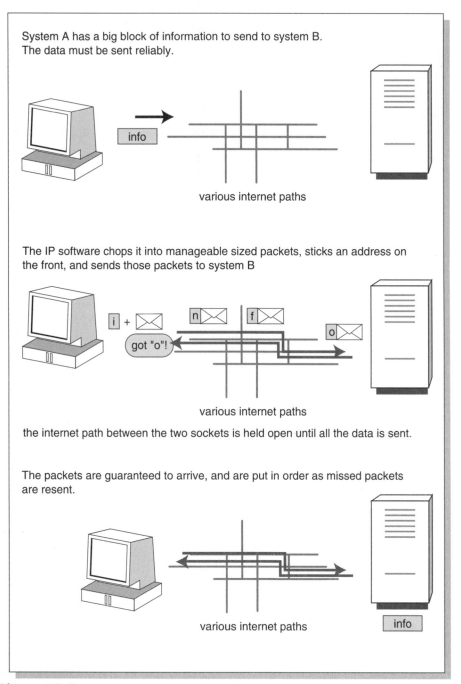

Figure 13-2:   TCP/IP (Stream sockets)

What's in the Networking Library?

If you browse the network library source in $JAVAHOME/src/java/net, you'll find these classes:

InetAddress	The class that represents IP addresses and the operations on them.
DatagramPacket	A class that represents a datagram packet containing packet data, packet length, internet addresses and port. Packets can be sent and received.
DatagramSocket	This class allows datagrams to be sent and received using the UDP.
ServerSocket	The server Socket class. It uses a SocketImpl to implement the actual socket operations. It is done this way so that you can change socket implementations depending on the kind of firewall that is used.
Socket	The client Socket class. It uses a SocketImpl class to implement the actual socket operations. Again, this permits you to change socket implementations depending on the kind of firewall that is used.
URL	The class represents a Uniform Resource Locator—a reference to an object on the Web. You can open a URL and retrieve the contents, or write to it.

There are a few other classes too, but these are the key ones.

TCP/IP Client Server Model

Before we look at actual Java code, a diagram is in order showing how a client and server typically communicate over a TCP/IP network connection. Figure 12-3 shows the way the processes contact each other is by knowing the IP address (which identifies a unique computer on the Internet) and a port number (which is a simple software convention the OS maintains, allowing an incoming network connection to be routed to a specific process).

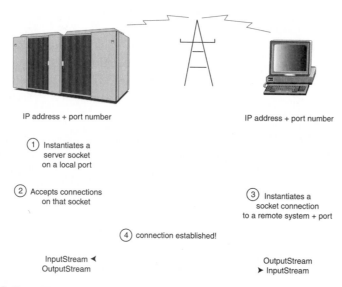

Figure 13-3: Client and server communication using a TCP/IP connection

An IP address is like a telephone number, and a port number is like an extension at that number. Together they specify a unique destination. As a matter of fact, a socket is defined as an IP address and a port number.

The client and server must agree on the same port number. The port numbers under 1024 are reserved for system software use. For simplicity, network socket connections are made to look like streams. You simply read and write data using the usual stream methods, and it automagically appears at the other end. Unlike a stream, a socket supports two-way communication. There is a method to get the input stream of a socket, and another method to get the output stream. This allows the client and server to talk back and forth.

Many Internet programs work as client/server pairs. The server is on a host system somewhere in cyberspace, and the client is a program running on your local system. When the client wants an Internet service (such as retrieving a Web page from an HTTP server), it issues a request, usually to a symbolic address such as www.sun.com rather than an IP address.

There will be a Domain Name Server locally (usually one per subnet, per campus, or per company) that resolves the symbolic name into an Internet address.

The bits forming the request are assembled into a *datagram*, and routed to the server. The server reads the incoming packets, notes what the request is, where it came from, and then tries to respond to it by providing either the service (web page, shell account, file contents, etc.) or a sensible error message. The response is sent back across the Internet to the client.

Almost all the standard Internet utilities (telnet, rdist, ftp, ping, rcp, and so on) operate in client/server mode connected by a TCP socket or by UDP. Programs that send mail don't really know how to send mail—they just know how to take it to the Post Office. In this case, mail has a socket connection, and talks to a daemon at the other end with a fairly simple protocol. The standard mail *daemon* knows how to accept text and addresses from clients and transmit it for delivery. If you can talk to the mail daemon, you can send mail. There is little else to it.

Many of the Internet services are actually quite simple. But often considerable frustration comes in doing the socket programming in C and in learning the correct protocol. The socket programming API presented to C is quite low-level, and all too easy to screw up. Needless to say, errors are poorly handled and diagnosed. As a result many programmers naturally conclude that sockets are brittle and error-prone.

The C code to establish a socket connection is:

```
int set_up_socket(u_short port) {
    char    myname[MAXHOSTNAME+1];
    int     s;
    struct sockaddr_in sa;
    struct hostent *he;

    bzero(&sa,sizeof(struct sockaddr_in));  /* clear the address */
    gethostname(myname,MAXHOSTNAME);        /* establish identity */
    he= gethostbyname(myname);              /* get our address   */
    if (he == NULL)                         /* if addr not found... */
        return(-1);
    sa.sin_family= he->h_addrtype;          /* host address */
    sa.sin_port= htons(port);               /* port number */

    if ((s= socket(AF_INET,SOCK_STREAM,0)) <0)  /* finally, create socket */
        return(-1);
    if (bind(s, &sa, sizeof(sa), 0) < 0) {
        close(s);
        return(-1);                         /* bind address to socket */
    }

    listen(s, 3);                           /* max queued connections */
    return(s);
}
```

By way of contrast, the Java code is:

```
ServerSocket servsock = new ServerSocket(port, 3);
```

That's it! Just one line of code to do all the things the C code does.

The good news is that Java handles that complexity "under the covers" for you. It doesn't expose the full range of socket possibilities, which lets the novice socketeer choose contradictory options. So, some sockety things cannot be done in Java. You cannot create a raw socket in JDK 1.0, and hence cannot write the ping program that relies on raw sockets. The benefit is overwhelming however: you can open sockets and start writing to another system just as easily as you open a file and start writing to hard disk.

Every computer system on the Internet has a unique IP address consisting of four groups of digits separated by periods, like this: 204.156.141.229

They are currently revising and increasing the IP address specification so that there will be enough new IP addresses to give one to every conceivable embedded processor on earth, and a few nearby friendly planets.

One special IP address is: 127.0.0.1

This is the "loopback" address used in testing and debugging. If a computer sends a packet to this address, it is routed out and back in again, without actually leaving the system. Thus this special address can be used to run Internet software even if you are not connected to the Internet. Set your system up so that the Internet services it will be requesting are all at the loopback address. Make sure your system is actually running the daemons corresponding to the services you want to use.

The special hostname associated with the loopback address is "localhost," if you are requesting services by name rather than IP address. On any system, you should be able to enter the command "ping localhost" and have it echo a reply from the loopback IP address. If you can't do this, it indicates that your TCP/IP stack is not set up properly.

Sending E-mail by Java

As our first example, let's write a Java program to send some e-mail. As we hinted above, e-mail is sent by socketed communication with port 25 on a computer system.

All we are going to do is open a socket connected to port 25 on some system, and speak "mail protocol" to the daemon at the other end. In an applet, open a socket back to the server. In an application, you can open a socket on the same system. If we speak the mail protocol correctly, it will listen to what we say, and send the e-mail for us.

Note that this program requires an Internet standard mail (SMTP) program running on the server. If your server has some non-standard proprietary mail program on it, you're out of luck. You can check which program you have by telnetting to port 25 on the server, and seeing if you get a mail server to talk to you.

The code to send e-mail is:

```java
import java.io.*;
import java.net.*;
public class email {

    public static void main(String args[]) throws IOException {
        Socket sock;
        DataInputStream dis;
        PrintStream ps;

        sock = new Socket("localhost", 25);
        dis = new DataInputStream( sock.getInputStream());
        ps = new PrintStream( sock.getOutputStream());

        ps.println("mail from: trelford");
        System.out.println( dis.readLine() );

        String Addressee= "linden";
        ps.println("rcpt to: " + Addressee );
        System.out.println( dis.readLine() );

        ps.println("data");
        System.out.println( dis.readLine() );

        ps.println("This is the message\n that Java sent");
        ps.println(".");
        System.out.println( dis.readLine() );

        ps.flush();
        sock.close();
    }
}
```

Many of the Internet services are like this one. You set up a socket connection, and talk a simple protocol to tell the server at the other end what you want.

Note that the main() routine has been declared as throwing an Exception. This is a shortcut, permissible in development, to save the necessity of handling any exceptions that might be raised. It only works because exceptions are not considered part of the signature of a method. In production code, it is crucial to catch and handle any exceptions.

 You can find all the Internet Protocols described in documents *Request For Comments* (RFCs), the format in which they were originally issued, available online at: http://www.internic.net/std. The mail RFC is RFC821.txt.

You can find all the WWW protocols described in documents linked to from this URL: http://www.w3.org/pub/WWW/Protocols/.

A careful study of some of these documents will often answer any protocol questions you have. ❦

HTTP and Web-Browsing: Retrieving HTTP Pages

Here is an example of using the HTTP daemon to retrieve a Web page from a system on the network. The http daemon sits on port 80 by convention. It understands a dozen or so requests, including "GET" followed by a path name. The argument "sparcs" is the name of a Web-server system on my subnet inside Sun Microsystems in Menlo Park, California, so change that to the name of your local Web server.

```java
import java.io.*;
import java.net.*;
public class http {

    public static void main(String args[]) throws IOException {
        String webserver = "sparcs";
        int http_port = 80;
        Socket sock;
        DataInputStream dis;
        PrintStream ps;

        sock = new Socket(webserver, http_port);
        dis = new DataInputStream( sock.getInputStream() );
        ps = new PrintStream( sock.getOutputStream() );

        ps.println("GET /index.html");
        String s=null;
        while ( (s=dis.readLine())!=null)
                System.out.println( s );

        sock.close();
    }
}
```

Note : If you are not on a network, before you run this code, start the http server daemon on your local system and use the local host address. If you are on a local network, your firewall will probably limit the visibility of outside systems, so pick a local server system that is running httpd as your test case.

The program prints out everything the http daemon sends back to it. In this case, running the program yields:

```
<Html>
<Head>
<Title>SPARCS</Title>
<!-- Author: Susan P. Motorcycles -->
</Head>
<Body>

<h2>Resources</h2>
<p>
<hr>Go to
<a HREF="estar/public_html/index.html"><u>Estar Homepage</u>
</a></p>
```

This is indeed the page at http://sparcs.eng/index.html inside Sun. As may be expected, Java has some awareness of various net protocols. In particular it can deal with a URL directly, and not require the programmer to descend into the underlying netherworld of sockets. So in practice, if we wanted to look at the contents of a URL, we would use the URL class, like this:

```
import java.net.*;
import java.io.*;
public class page {

  public static void main(String a[]) {
    DataInputStream dis;
    try {
      URL u  = new URL( "http://sparcs.eng/index.html" );
      dis = new DataInputStream(
                    u.openConnection().getInputStream() );

      String s ;
      while ( (s=dis.readLine())!=null ) {
        System.out.println( s );
      }
    } catch (Exception e) { System.out.println( e ); }
  }

}
```

A URL can pose a security risk, since you can pass along information even by reading a URL. For instance, you could request "http://www.spies.com/cgi-bin/cgi.exe/secretinfo", and "secretinfo" would be passed along to the CGI script. Since requesting a URL can send out information just as a Socket can, requesting a URL has the same security model as access to Sockets.

Coding the program this way is not only shorter, but allows us to interrogate certain other URL properties, such as the protocol that is being used, and the host system (these methods are of use when you don't use literal values as in this example).

Putting the following lines in the above program

```
System.out.println("    file: "+ u.getFile() );
System.out.println("    host: "+ u.getHost() );
System.out.println("     ref: "+ u.getRef() );
System.out.println("protocol:" + u.getProtocol() );
```

gives the result

```
    file: /index.html
    host: sparcs.eng
     ref: null
protocol:http
```

The "ref" is the reference or label that you can put in the middle of an html file to take you there instead of starting at the beginning. The ref part of a URL isn't much used.

What if there is a GIF at that URL—won't we print out image information as though it were text? Yes, the program would. You need to build just a little more intelligence into it so it recognizes file types, and handles them appropriately. This is what the content handler/protocol handler guff is about. If a browser doesn't recognize a media type, it should be able to download the code to process it from the same place it got the file. If they ever get this working, it will be (as flaxen-coiffured domestic harpie Martha Stewart likes to say) "a good thing."

If you modify the basic program above so that it transmits the other 10 or 11 http commands and give it a GUI front-end to display the formatted http text, you will have written a Web browser! A Web browser is at heart a fairly simple program. The prototype HotJava Web browser, at that time called "Webrunner," was written in just one week according to Patrick Naughton (who was there and worked on it).

Both this example, and the mailer program, are client applications. The server end of the http protocol is not much more complicated. A basic http daemon can be implemented in a few hundred lines of code.

Drawing by P. Steiner; ©1993 The New Yorker Magazine, Inc.

"On the Internet, nobody knows you're a dog."

On the Internet, No One Knows You're a Dog . . .

Let's make a brief digression at this point, and recall the phenomenon in which the Internet entered the public consciousness in a big way. One of the early indicators of this was a 1993 cartoon in the New Yorker Magazine, with the punchline "On the Internet nobody knows you're a dog!" This cartoon was cut out and displayed in every network programmer's office from Albuquerque to Zimbabwe. Mainstream recognition! On the Internet, nobody knows you're a dog.

Our code example is a Canine Turing Test—a Java program to distinguish whether the communicating party is a dog or not. People greet each other by shaking hands, while dogs sniff each other. Dogs are loyal companions, and part of their loyalty is absolute truthfulness. To tell if a dog is at the other end of a socket, just ask the question "If you met me, would you shake my hand, or sniff it?" Depending on the answer that the client sends back over the socket to the server, the server will know if the client is a dog or a human.

Obviously this program is only going to work if you are using a computer that has an IP address and a connection to a TCP/IP network. Or if you run it all on one system, and you have socket support working. On a Unix workstation TCP/IP support is a standard basic part of the operation system. On a PC you'll need to have the TCP/IP "protocol stack" installed. Calling this software a "protocol stack" is a bit of a misnomer, as it has nothing to do with LIFO stacks. "TCP/IP software" would be a more accurate name.

Under Windows 95 the TCP/IP protocol stack (wsock32.dll) is present on the system, but needs to be configured to work. You configure it by clicking on "My Computer" -> "Control Panel" -> "Network" -> "Network." Where the window shows a list reading "The following network components are installed," make sure you have at least "Dial-Up adapter" and "TCP/IP" in the list.

Click on "TCP/IP" to highlight it, and activate the "Properties" button underneath the network component list. Press the button to bring up TCP/IP properties. There are six tabbed entries here, and they all need to be set up correctly for your networking code to work correctly. Your Internet Service Provider should supply full instructions.

Under Windows 3.1 there is no standard support for TCP/IP. Every vendor supplies their own custom library, creating a morass of truly hideous software complexity. If you have dial-up access to the Internet, your service provider should provide instructions on how to configure the TCP/IP software.

The code comes in two parts: a server that listens for clients and asks them the question, and clients that connect to the server. The server is going to detect whether clients are dogs or not. The heart of this server code just creates a server socket and then, in a loop, accepts connections to it and handles them. When a connection is accepted, it returns a new socket over which the client and server can talk without affecting new incoming connection requests. First the server code, which looks like this:

```java
/**
 *  a network server that detects presence of dogs on the Internet
 *
 *  @author     Peter van der Linden
 *  @author     From the book "Just Java"
 */
import java.io.*;
import java.net.*;

class server {
    public static void main(String a[]) throws IOException {
        int q_len = 6;
        int port = 4444;
        Socket sock;
        String query = "If you met me would you shake my hand, "
                        + "or sniff it?";

        ServerSocket servsock =
            new ServerSocket(port, q_len);

    while (true) {
        // wait for the next client connection
            sock=servsock.accept();

        // Get I/O streams from the socket
          PrintStream out =
           new PrintStream( sock.getOutputStream() );
          DataInputStream in  =
          new DataInputStream( sock.getInputStream() );

        // Send our query
        out.println(query);
        out.flush();

        // get the reply
        String reply = in.readLine();
        if (reply.indexOf("sniff") > -1)
            System.out.println(
             "On the Internet I know this is a DOG!");
            else System.out.println(
             "Probably a person or an AI experiment");

        // Close this connection, (not overall server socket)
          sock.close();
      }
   }
}
```

Now the client end of the socket, which looks like this:

```java
// On the Internet no one knows you're a dog...
// unless you tell them.

import java.io.*;
import java.net.*;

class dog {

    public static void main(String a[]) throws IOException {
        Socket sock;
        DataInputStream dis;
        PrintStream dat;

        // Open our connection to positive, at port 4444
        sock = new Socket("positive",4444);

        // Get I/O streams from the socket
        dis = new DataInputStream( sock.getInputStream() );
        dat = new PrintStream( sock.getOutputStream() );

        String fromServer = dis.readLine();

        System.out.println("Got this from server:" + fromServer);

        dat.println("I would sniff you");
        dat.flush();

        sock.close();
    }
}
```

When you try running this program, make sure that you change the client socket connect to refer not to "positive" (my workstation) but to a system where you intend to run the server code. You can identify this system by using either the name (as long as the name will uniquely locate it on your net), or the IP address. (If in doubt, just use the IP address).

Here's how to run the example:

1. Put the server program on the system that you want to be the server. Compile the server program, and start it:

    ```
    javac server.java
    java server
    ```

2. Put the client program on the system that you want to be the client. Change the client program so it references your server machine, not machine "positive." Then compile it.

    ```
    javac dog.java
    ```

3. When you execute the client program, on the client system you will see the output:

    ```
    java dog
    ```

    Got this from server: If you met me would you shake my hand, or sniff it?

4. On the server machine, you will see the output.

    ```
    On the Internet I know this is a DOG!
    ```

Make sure the server is running before you execute the client, otherwise it will have no one to talk to.

 Write a second client program that would reply with the "shake hands" typical of a person. Run this from the same or another client system. (Easy). 🐾

There's one improvement that is customary in servers, and we will make it here. For all but the smallest of servers, it is usual to spawn a new thread to handle each request. This has three big advantages:

-   The program source is less cluttered, as the server processing is written in a different class

-   By handling each request in a new thread, clients do not have to wait for every request ahead of them to be served

-   Finally, it makes the server scalable: It can accept new requests independent of its speed in handling them (of course you better buy a server that has the mippage to keep up with requests).

The following code demonstrates how we would rewrite the Internet dog detector using a new thread for each client request.

```java
/**
 *   a network server that detects presence of dogs on the Internet
 *   and which spawns a new thread for each client request.
 *   @author    Peter van der Linden
 *
 */
import java.io.*;
import java.net.*;

class Worker extends Thread {
 Socket sock;
 Worker(Socket s) { sock =s; }
 public void run(){
 System.out.println("Thread running:"+currentThread() );
 // Get I/O streams from the socket
   PrintStream out = null;
   DataInputStream in  = null;
 try {
   out = new PrintStream( sock.getOutputStream() );
   in  = new DataInputStream( sock.getInputStream() );
 // Send our query
 String query = "If you met me would you shake my hand, or sniff it?";
 out.println(query);
 out.flush();

 // get the reply
 String reply = in.readLine();
 if (reply.indexOf("sniff") > -1)
   System.out.println("On the Internet I know this is a DOG!");
 else System.out.println("Probably a person or an AI experiment");

   // Close this connection, (not the overall server socket)

   sock.close();
 } catch(IOException ioe){System.out.println(ioe); }
 }
}

public class server2 {
 public static void main(String a[]) throws IOException {
 int q_len = 6;
 int port = 4444;
 Socket sock;

 ServerSocket servsock = new ServerSocket(port, q_len);

 while (true) {
 // wait for the next client connection
   sock=servsock.accept();
 new Worker( sock ).start();
  }
 }
}
```

Page Counters in Web Pages

Finally, lets answer a question that many people have, namely: "How do I use Java to implement a counter on my web page?" It seems like this should be trivial to do—there's probably even a class to increment a count every time a web page is accessed and display the new value on the page.

Well it turns out that this can be done in Java, but it's a little more work than just calling a method. The problem is that an applet can't write files on the server. Only the server can write files on the server, although you can set up a daemon on the server to listen to and act on "write this file" requests from applets. An ftp server already does this. An ingenious programmer could write code to talk to the ftp daemon on port 21, and do file I/O that way.

Here are the obvious steps to set up a page counter in Java:

1. Keep the "page access count" in a file on the server, which is referred to by an HTML document.

2. When the page is accessed, an applet in the page executes on the client.

3. Send a message to a daemon running on the server to say "add one to the number in the page access count file."

4. The daemon on the server reads and updates the file.

People always want to be able to do this totally from the applet, but that is not possible. The cooperation of the server is required. This kind of communication was traditionally done with CGI scripts, with the following new steps replacing previous steps 3 and 4, respectively.

- A CGI GET request can be made, and the output can be read by code like this:

```
try { URL u=new URL ("http:// ... some URL" + "... some query
    string");
// read results back
DataInputStream dis = new DataInputStream (u.openStream());
string firstline = dis.readLine ();
```
Open a socket and write an http GET or POST request to the server. GET requests encode their arguments to the CGI script as the last part of the URL. POST requests send the arguments along so the CGI script can read them from standard input. In either case, the argument must be encoded according to the standard CGI rules: parameter name/value fields are separated by "=", pairs of these are separated by ampersands "&", and non-alphanumerics are converted to percent escape form "%nnn". You have to code this yourself.

- The http request will start up the CGI script. The output of the script (with a MIME header stripped off) will be sent back down the socket to the applet.

However, Java now offers the Java Web Server framework for servers . The JWS API for "servlets" is intended to replace work formerly done by CGI scripts.

More information on JWS, including a white paper is available at the JavaSoft website http://java.sun.com/.

JWS allows you to program everything in Java, and leave the CGI muddle alone. You get the benefit of doing everything in one language plus Java's security.

How to Find the IP Address Given a Machine Name

This code will be able to find the IP address of all computers that it knows about. That may mean all systems that have an entry in the local hosts table, or (if it is served by a name server) the domain of the name server, which could be as extensive as a large subnet or the entire organization.

```java
import java.io.*;
import java.net.*;

class who {

    public static void main(String a[]) throws IOException {

        InetAddress InetAddr =
            InetAddress.getByName (a[0]);
        System.out.println(
            "inet address is " + InetAddr.toString() );

    }
}
```

Some Notes on Protocol and Content Handlers

Some of the Java documentation makes a big production about the extensibility of the HotJava browser. If it is asked to browse some data whose type it doesn't recognize, it can simply download the code for the appropriate handler based on the name of the datetype, and use that to grok the data. Or so the theory runs. It hasn't yet been proved in practice.

A prime opportunity to showcase dynamic handlers arose when the Java Development Kit was switching over from the Alpha to Beta versions in late 1995. There were significant applet incompatibilities between the two. It provided a fine opportunity to use dynamic content handling. The browser source (which worked exclusively with Alpha applets) was widely available for the asking. No beta-capable version of the alpha Browser has appeared to date. The general wonderfulness of dynamic handlers in the browser has still to be proven in practice.

The theory of the handlers is this. There are two kinds of handler that you can write: protocol handlers and content handlers.

A **protocol handler** talks to other programs. Both ends follow the same protocol in order to communicate ("After you.", "No, I insist, after you.") If you wrote an Oracle database protocol handler, it would deal with SQL queries to pull data out of an Oracle database.

A **content handler** knows how to decode the contents of a file. It handles data (think of it as the contents of something pointed to by a URL). It gets the bytes and assembles them into an object. If you wrote an MPEG content handler, then it would be able to play MPEG movies in your browser, once you had brought the data over there. Bringing MPEG data to your browser could be done using the FTP protocol, or you might wish to write your own high performance protocol handler.

By the way, the reason that MPEG and video shows so poorly on even top-end PC's is the heavy bandwidth it consumes. The back-of-the-envelope calculations are:

```
Frame size          = NTSC screensize  * size of index to color table
                    = (768 * 486)      * 3 bits
                    = 1.1 Megabits
Data transfer rate  = Frame size       * rate
                    = 1.1 Megabits     * 24 frames per second
                    = 268 Megabits
```

So a proper quality moving digital image on your monitor requires 26.8 Mbits (3.3 Mbytes) minimum, sustained bandwidth from the source to your display card (graphics adapter, framebuffer, whatever you want to call it). This is not possible in the current generation of PC's, and to even think of putting this kind of load on the network is absurd.

Content handlers and protocol handlers may be particularly convenient for web browsers, and they may also be useful in stand-alone applications. There is not a lot of practical experience with these handlers yet, so it is hard to offer definitive advice about their use. Some people predict they are going to be very important for decoding file formats of arbitrary wackiness, while other people are ready to be convinced by an existence proof.

Some Light Relief

The Nerd Detection System

Most people are familiar with the little security decals that electronic and other high-value stores use to deter shoplifters. The sticker contains a metallic strip. Unless deactivated by a store cashier, the sticker sets off an alarm when carried past a detector at the store doors.

These security stickers are actually a form of antenna. The sticker detector sends out a weak RF signal between two posts through which shoppers will pass. It looks for a return signal at a specific frequency, which indicates that one of the stickers has entered the field between the posts.

All this theory was obvious to a couple of California Institute of Technology students Dwight Berg and Tom Capellari, who decided to test the system in practice. Naturally, they selected a freshman to (unknowingly) participate in the trials. At preregistration, after the unlucky frosh's picture was taken, but before it was laminated into his I.D. card, Dwight and Tom fixed a couple of active security decals from local stores onto the back of the photo.

The gimmicked card was then laminated together hiding the McGuffin, and the two conspirators awaited further developments. A couple of months later they caught up with their victim as he was entering one of the stores. He was carrying his wallet above his head. In response to a comment that this was an unusual posture, the frosh replied that something in his wallet, probably his bank card, seemed to set off store alarms. He had been conditioned to carry his wallet above his head after several weeks of setting off the alarms while entering and leaving many of the local stores.

The frosh seemed unimpressed with Dwight and Tom's suggestion that perhaps the local merchants had installed some new type of nerd detection system. Apparently the comment got the frosh thinking though, because the next occasion he met Dwight, he put Dwight in a headlock until he confessed to his misdeed. **Moral**: never annoy a nerd larger than yourself.

Exercises

1. Extend the example mail program above so that it prompts for user input and generally provides a friendly front-end to sending mail.

2. Write a socket server program that simply returns the time on the current system. Write a client that calls the server, and sends you mail reporting on how far apart the time on the local system is, versus the time on the current system.

3. In the previous exercise, the server can only state what time it is at the instant the request reaches it, but that answer will take a certain amount of time to travel back to the client. Devise a strategy to minimize or correct for errors due to transmission time. (Hard—just use a heuristic to make a good guess.)

Further Reading

"More Legends of Caltech"

William A. Dodge, Jr.
published by the California Institute of Technology, Pasadena, Calif., 1989.
(This book has no ISBN).

TCP/IP Network Administration

Craig Hunt
O'Reilly & Associates, Sebastopol CA, 1994
ISBN 0-937175-82-X
The modest title hides the fact that this book will be useful to a wider audience than just network administrators. It is a very good practical guide to TCP/IP, written as a tutorial introduction.

Teach Yourself TCP/IP in 14 Days

Timothy Parker
Sams Publishing, Indianapolis, 1994
ISBN 0-672-30549-6
When a book starts off with an apology for the dullness of the subject material, you just know that the author has some unusual ways about him.

Unix Network Programming

W. Richard Stevens
Prentice Hall, NJ 1990
The canonical guide to network programming.

The file "animals.txt" contains
queenbee raven
swan terrier
urchin vixen
wallaby xoachi
yellowjacket zebra

Running the program results in
aardvark butterfly
that finishes input line 1

carp dalmatian
that finishes input line 2

eagle fish
that finishes input line 3

gopher hippo
that finishes input line 4

inyala jackal
that finishes input line 5

kyloe lamb
that finishes input line 6

moose nanny-goat
that finishes input line 7

opossum pandora
that finishes input line 8

queenbee raven
that finishes input line 9

swan terrier
that finishes input line 10

urchin vixen
that finishes input line 11

wallaby xoachi[1]
that finishes input line 12

yellowjacket zebra
that finishes input line 13

---

1.   An "xoachi" is a little-known animal whose name I made up.

CHAPTER
14

- Getting Internet access

- Downloading software

- Future Java developments

- Further Java resources

Future
Developments

"Lord Hippo suffered fearful loss.
By putting money on a horse
Which he believed, if it were pressed,
Would run far faster than the rest."

—*Hilaire Belloc, Selected Cautionary Verses.*

This chapter gives you the information you need to move forward from here. It is in two sections. First, how to get Internet access. Second, what lies ahead in terms of Java products and services.

As everyone knows, the only real way to learn a programming language is to write some programs in it. For that you need the Java system, and a Java-capable Web browser. This book comes with a CD that contains the Java compiler system for Windows NT, Windows 95, Macintosh, and Solaris 2.x. However, you may want to download a Web browser, or later releases of Java. We assume elementary familiarity with utilities like anonymous FTP for retrieving files from Internet hosts.[1]

---

1. If you do not have this knowledge, the Krol book referenced at the end of the chapter will provide it.

In theory, you could forego the Web browser and Internet access, and just learn Java application programming on your local system. In practice, however, this would be a mistake. You would be missing a key part—seamless client-server programming on the network—which is responsible for the vast interest in Java.

Getting Internet Access

As a preliminary to obtaining the software, you should get an Internet connection. Many readers of this book will already have Internet access through their employer or educational institution. If neither of these sources is available to you, perhaps your town has a library service that offers an online connection, or perhaps you can sign up for a computer class that comes with a student account at a local college. Or you may just prefer the convenience of Internet access in your own home, just as most people have a phone connection and some people have a cable TV connection. An Internet connection at home is readily obtained in most parts of the developed world with a commercial Internet Service Provider (ISP). You connect to the ISP via a phone call, and the ISP is directly connected to the Internet.

Choosing your ISP

In many cases, you will have a choice of Internet Service Provider (ISP), so these two checklists indicate the ways to evaluate them. The first checklist is mostly about the way you connect to the ISP. The second checklist covers the services the ISP offers.

You will need some kind of personal computer at home: a Macintosh, a "Wintel" (MS Windows/Intel) box, a workstation running Unix or one of its variants like Linux. Your system must support a graphical user interface. A VT100 compatible ASCII terminal is no longer good enough.

ISP connections are invariably provided by dialling in from your home, so a large part of the first check list has to do with the telephone service. You may well find that the other members of your household make you get a second phone line instead of tying up your family's main number.

Checklist—ISP connectivity

[   ] **Local calling area** (not a toll call)

So that you don't bankrupt yourself with long distance phone charges you need an ISP to have a Point of Presence (POP) local to your home. An acceptable alternative is a dial-back system where you call in, and they immediately call you back so that the call is billed to them (their size gives them bulk discount with the Telco). A toll-free call-in number is also acceptable.

[   ] **Free communications software**

You will likely need some communications software for your system. This software is needed to make the connection and keep it going. The ISP should know what is needed for the different Operating Systems, and supply it without charge.

[   ] **28.8kbps lines (V34) or better**

The phone line between your home and the ISP is going to be the slowest link in the system. The ISP needs to use the fastest commercially-available modems. At the time of writing (10:17pm, Saturday December 2 1995) these are 28.8kbps modems. These will adapt to slower speeds automatically, so even if your modem is not rated that high, it can still communicate. You will get frustrated with a slow modem before very long, and when you finally upgrade no change is needed at the ISP end. If you need to buy a modem, don't fall for the false economy of a slow one.

[   ] **An adequate modem pool**

It's frustrating to get a busy signal when you dial in to your ISP. They need to keep adding modems as their business grows, and preferably have a policy such as "at least one SS20 class machine per 100 users" or "no new clients if the modem pool is maxed out more than 3 hours/day."

[   ] **SLIP/PPP**

To run a Web browser on the Internet, your computer system will need an IP connection. This can be provided over a phone line by one of two alternatives:

- SLIP   Serial Line Internet Protocol
- PPP   Point-to-Point Protocol

Either is adequate, but PPP provides more features (none of which you will be using if you only ever connect to your ISP from home).

[   ] **No or low hourly connect fee**

The Internet can be an interesting place, and you might spend more than a few hours there. Ideally, there will not be a "per-hour" connection time fee. Some ISPs offer no fee access outside normal business hours. It's also OK if there is a large monthly allowance of free connect time, with a low hourly charge when that is used up.

[   ] Base monthly charge

You'd like the monthly charge to be as low as possible. Expect to pay about the same as basic cable tv service costs. In my area (Silicon Valley, California) that's about $25–30 per month.

[   ] System support

This is where most ISPs fall down. Support is expensive to provide, but usually generates no revenue. As a result, you may find almost no help is available if you have an unusual connection or set up problem. Ask questions to gauge how much system support is offered. What happens if you delete a file by accident? Will they recover it from backup for you?

Sometimes a lively user community can partly compensate for lack of support, by answering common questions.

[   ] Amount of disk space provided

You are going to be downloading files, and perhaps saving them temporarily in your ISP account. How much disk space is bundled in with your account, and how much do they charge for extra use? Some ISPs will provide bulk storage for short periods of time so that large file transfers will complete, but you must dispose of the file shortly thereafter.

There are certain items that the ISP may boast, which you don't actually care about. These include:

- **56K, T-3, or T-1 service**
  You don't care about the bandwidth of the ISP's pipe to the Internet. As long as it's big enough, that's all that matters.

- **Internic registration**
  Most people don't need their own domain name.

- **Static vs. dynamic IP addressing**
  Either is fine for you.

- **Co-location (where you have your machine at their site)**
  This is really for business and commercial users. For you, half the fun is frobbing the hardware personally.

That covers the connection between your home and the ISP. Now you need to consider the range of Internet services that you will get.

Internet Connectivity

There are different levels of Internet connectivity, each providing different services and applications. Although the terminology is not yet in general use, Internet document RFC1775 describes the hierarchy of services.
You can retrieve the description via anonymous FTP from "ftp.internic.net" in file /pub/rfc1775.txt

The levels of service available through most ISPs are:

Client Access

The user runs applications that employ Internet application protocols directly on their own computer platform, but might not be running underlying Internet protocols (TCP/IP), might not have full-time access, such as through dial-up, or might have constrained access, such as through a firewall. When active, Client users might be visible to the general Internet, but such visibility cannot be predicted. "Visibility" means "able to chat on-line."

Mediated Access

The user runs no Internet applications on their own platform. An Internet service provider runs applications that use Internet protocols on the provider's platform, for the user. User has simplified access to the provider, such as dial-up terminal connectivity. For Mediated access, the user is on the Internet, but their computer platform is not. Instead, it is the computer of the mediating service (provider) which is on the Internet.

Messaging Access

The user has no Internet access, except through electronic mail and through netnews, such as Usenet or a bulletin board service. Since messaging services can be used as a high-latency (i.e., slow) transport service, the use of this level of access for mail-enabled services can be quite powerful, though not interactive.

Your ISP needs to offer "client access" in the above sense. Mediated access or messaging access are not good enough for the WWW.

Checklist—ISP Services

[   ] **Web access and a Java-capable Web browser**

You absolutely need access to the World Wide Web, through a browser with a graphical user interface (not text-only). This is why you need a computer system at home, rather than just an ASCII terminal. The browser must be Java capable.

You will want to put up a Web home page announcing your existence to Cybernauts. The ISP should provide you the disk space and connectivity to create your own home page.

[   ] FTP access

The File Transfer Protocol allows you to retrieve files from remotes sites. Eventually this will all be done with WWW access, but until the entire world has converted, you still need the lower-level functionality that FTP provides.

[   ] WAIS, gopher, and archie

These are all ways to search the Internet, to locate sites and files of interest. The ISP must provide easy access to these utility programs.

[   ] No censorship

Some ISP's (notably AOL) impose censorship on their customers. This behavior is often a misguided response to pressure from political or watchdog groups flexing their muscle. Censorship occasionally makes ISP's look ridiculous, as in 1993 when Prodigy was using an automated screening program. One contributor to a musical discussion had a posting returned on the grounds that he was using language "inappropriate to the Prodigy service." He was discussing Bach's B Minor Mass—the movement titled "Cum Sancto Spiritu." America Online committed the same faux pas in November 1995, when they declared the word "breast" taboo—thereby making it impossible for breast cancer patients to contact one another for information and support. The major use of the keyword was allowing these patients to find each other. Check the censorship policies of your ISP, and give your business to companies that provide unrestricted access.

[   ] Usenet news and other services

If the ISP provides Web access (which is essential), they are almost certain to provide Usenet news access, telnet, and e-mail services too. These are not essential, but they are very nice to have and there is no reason to exclude them. Usenet news should include the alt or alternative newsgroups, not just the mainstream collection. Check whether these services are bundled in with your Internet access.

It is no exaggeration to say that Java is being ported to more platforms, with more urgency than any other piece of software in the history of the computer industry. People want this software and they want it now.

The market share among high-volume desktop platforms looks roughly like this:

IBM PC and PC compatibles	90%
Macintosh	9%
Unix (all versions)	1%

ISDN: Integrated Services Digital Network

For now, the most common dial-up connection is via a modem. Even the fastest modems are several orders of magnitude slower than dedicated network connections. People use modems because there has been nothing better.

The better alternative will not be long in coming. In fact it has been waiting in the wings for at least a decade. ISDN or "Integrated Services Digital Network" is a digital service (in contrast to the existing analog phone wiring) providing an effective 128Kbit/sec channel across a phone line. Compare that to the best modems that are only one quarter the rate. Faster throughput speeds can be achieved by installing higher rated lines with multiple ISDN channels. The key fact about ISDN is that it brings the speed and reliability of digital transmission to the desktop, rather than relying on analog technology for the last leg.

Your ISP should have an ISDN plan. ISDN is currently only available in urban areas.

Engineers used to joke that ISDN meant "It Still Does Nothing" because the service is taking so long to catch on. In truth, it was a solution in search of a problem. That will change when ISDN finally solves the "vicious circle" that has bedeviled it:

> ISDN is not popular because it is costly.

> ISDN is costly because it is not popular.

The Web is the problem that ISDN has been waiting to solve.

However a different picture emerges if you tabulate only desktop platforms that are connected to the Internet. When Java was launched, the breakdown was roughly:

Unix (all versions)	90%
IBM PC and PC compatibles	9%
Macintosh	1%

For this reason, the first 3 ports were done in this order. Coming from Sun, Java was naturally developed on Sun workstations under the Solaris 2.x (Unix) Operating System. A port to Windows 95 and Windows NT rapidly followed, and was released at the same time as the Solaris version. Sun staff have completed the first Mac port and now Apple has stepped up to do it themselves.

Ports are also underway or nearing completion to most other platforms of significance. Details can be obtained from these sites:

Other Platforms

IBM: Windows 3.1, AIX and OS/2 ports are underway by IBM, they have announced products under the code name of "Cyberparts." See the IBM Web page at   http://ncc.hursley.ibm.com/javainfo/

DEC: a port to Alpha OSF/1 is being done by the Open Software Foundation. For information, see   http://www.gr.osf.org:8001/projects/web/java/

SGI: See http://www.sgi.com/fun/free/web-tools.html

Hewlett-Packard: The Open Software Foundation (OSF) is working on a port to HP/UX on the Precision Architecture. For information, see http://www.gr.osf.org/java/

linux: Several independent ports to linux have been made. See   http://www.blackdown.org

NeXT: A port to the NeXTstep environment is underway. See   http://www.next.com

AT&T: The Open Software Foundation (OSF) is working on a port to AT&T Unix. For information, see   http://www.gr.osf.org:8001/projects/web/java/

Amiga: http://www.yahoo.com/Computers/PCs/Amiga http://www.lls.se/~matjo/PJAmi/PJAmi.html

The system is referred to as the JDK—Java Development Kit. It includes a java compiler (javac), a java bytecode interpreter (java), a debugger (jdb), and an applet viewer ("appletviewer") that lets you run an applet in the absence of a Web browser.

Getting a Browser

The next piece of software you need is a Java-capable Web browser. The majority of users prefer a Netscape browser, or Sun's own HotJava browser. These were the first two Java-capable browsers available, but all other browser suppliers are racing fast to catch up. Simply put, if a Web browser is not Java-capable from this point on, it will not be used by anyone knowledgeable. You need a Java-capable browser so you can:

- Experiment with www browsing

- Run applets (little Java applications) that are embedded in Web pages.

In these early days of the Web and Java, companies are eager to meet the pent-up demand for products. They are releasing early so-called Beta versions of their software. They are even making the Beta versions available without charge. The Beta versions are not supported products, and often are very buggy. It can be a frustrating experience trying to work with Beta software. Avoid it if possible.

Software is often available on a choice of media, commonly CD and diskettes. If your system has a CD ROM reader, look for the software on CD ROM, because it avoids swapping 11 diskettes in and out (e.g. to install Win-95). 🍒

The Birth of a Software Product

The classic model for software product releases follows three phases:

Alpha release. The alpha software is the first version that has the major functionality in place. The software will still be very buggy, but enough of it works well enough to release to other departments in the company for test and use. As the inevitable defect reports come back, the problems will be tracked and fixed, so it can move to the next phase of the cycle.

Beta release. You enter the Beta cycle immediately after the alpha cycle is complete. As many as possible of the bugs have been found and fixed, and a new release is generated. This Beta software is made available to outside testers. It may be made widely available to anyone who asks for it (like Windows NT Beta) or it may be given only to a small group of highly qualified partner companies.

The point of Beta test is to locate bugs that can only be found with use and misuse in typical customer environments. The big problem with Beta testing is that you are now so far advanced in the development cycle that it may not be possible to fix any but the most heinous bugs that are uncovered, and perhaps not all of them.

FCS release. FCS stands for "First Customer Shipment." As the Beta period (typically some multiple of months) winds up, the bug-fixing criteria get stricter and stricter. This is because unrestricted bug fixing will destablize the product, at a time when you are aiming for maximum reliability. Typically no new functionality is allowed in the Beta period, and towards the end, only really serious bugs can be fixed: bugs that eat data (data corruption) or bugs that cause core dumps. Finally 6-8 weeks before the end of Beta the software is built for the final time, and put through in-house regression testing. Any last minute problems are noted and either reported in the release notes, or fixed on a case-by-case basis. The CDs are duplicated, sent out to the distribution channels and become available for purchase on the FCS date.

> **Microsoft Trojan Horse?**
>
> In a news report headlined "Microsoft Trojan Horse stymies net use" Interactive Week reported in September 1995, that the use of Microsoft Network removed a file that was essential for network software (like Netscape Navigator) from competitors.
>
> The news story went on to explain if you upgrade from Windows 3.x to Windows 95, it automatically replaces the windows socket library Winsock.dll with a new version that only works with Microsoft's Internet access software. Not only is Microsoft Network given the most prominent place of display on the window interface, it also disables all its competitors.
>
> Only the most knowledgeable of users will be able to track down the problem, and reconfigure the compatible version of the library. Suppliers of competing software only had two options: rewrite their software to use the new Microsoft library—except that Microsoft was very reluctant to release information on the Application Program Interface (API) of the new Winsock environment. The only other choice, which Netcom and many others took, was to immediately abandon use of the new winsock.dll, move the old compatible winsock code elsewhere and hide it from the Microsoft upgrade program that overwrites it.
>
> In December 1995, the United States Department of Justice (the arm of the Federal Government that enforces anti-monopoly laws) announced it was investigating the incident.

What's in the JDK

When you unpack the Java Development Kit and install it, you'll find that you have these components:

filename	what it is
javac	compiler, java source to byte code
java	interpreter, runs byte code
jdb	debugger
appletviewer	Allows java programs in Web pages to be run without using a Web browser.

These are the tools you will use most frequently. There are also a few special purpose utilities.

javadoc	Creates html documentation files from clues embedded in Java source.

javah	Creates C header files that correspond to Java objects. This is useful when creating programs that mix languages.
javap	A tool to print out byte codes and class information
javaprof	A profiling tool to tell you which statements in your program were executed the most often.
javakey	A tool to manage security utilities
jar	A tool to help pack and unpack archives

Java Developments

The development of Java-related products can be classified under six primary headings: performance, development tools, library enhancements, networking, security, and hardware. Here are the high points of those we have not covered earlier in the book.

Performance

This is the number one request from users, and probably the single highest priority item. Java, being an interpreted system, is currently an order of magnitude slower than C. But C was designed to be close to the hardware and only has built-in datatypes that are directly supported in hardware.

You have to pay something for the abstractions that Java provides and for the built-in structured types like String. On the positive side, modern workstations have MIPS to burn compared with earlier hardware, and are only going to improve. But there are a number of improvements that can be made in the software too.

Performance-oriented implementations of the Java virtual machine are on the way. We can expect optimizing runtimes that detect the frequently traveled paths in a program, and compile down to native code as the program is being executed. More performance improvements can come from a "Just-In-Time" compiler that does an additional step of compiling the byte code to native code on the client, as well as interpreting it. Thus the first pass through a block is interpreted, then you pay the cost of compilation, then passes are done at compiled code speed.

Development Tools

Just as C is ubiquitous on hardware now, there will be Java ports to many more platforms—everything from a Cray to your TV remote control to your smart cards. At that point the consumer electronics goal of the original project will have been met, proving that if you wait long enough the world will eventually pass by your front door. But for some of the world it's only because they're lost.

We've already mentioned the just-in-time compilers, and we can expect the full range of conventional development tools too. I, for one, would like "indent" to properly format programs, and "java lint" to warn about questionable code constructs. Tip: the Unix C version of indent works fine on Java source and does 95 percent of what you want.

Java is a perfect match for the kind of integrated development environment which is commonplace in the PC space, but which has yet to become established among Unix professionals. If such an environment is written in Java (and it's hard to believe that anyone would be dumb enough to use a different language), then of course it is instantly portable to Unix, Windows, Macs, etc.

> Here's an amazing fact about Java portability. One large company developed a Java IDE completely written in Java. It was targeted to Windows and Solaris platforms, and never tested on anything else. Customers lliked it so much they started to run it on their Macs, SGIs, and other systems, *and it just worked!* Some very low level stuff to do with debugging wasn't functional but 95% of the system developed for Windows and Solaris just worked on other platforms right out of the box. A tremendous testament to the portability of Java and the skills of the programming team.

Some of the first IDEs on the market are quick adaptions of C++ IDEs, with time-to-market as a major goal. Hence these are not written in Java, and not available for all platforms yet.

The Javascript language will get some practical use. Javascript is completely unrelated to Java. It is a simple scripting language which can be embedded in an HTML file. It offers loops, and conditional tests. The idea is to put some of the power of a programming language in the hands of non-programmers who want to create Web pages with applets, without needing to become Java-heads. Javascript was briefly named "Livescript" before Netscape saw which way the wind was blowing. The intersection of Java and Javascript is the empty set. Microsoft have a knock-off of Javascript, known as JScript.

Networking and Distributed Processing

In its brief life, Java has already become the de facto WWW programming API, and may soon become the Internet programming API. There are more innovations possible, including client/server windowing. At present, the Java AWT and its native peer window component have to be on the same system. There is no technical reason why they cannot be separated, so that users can run a window system down a PPP connection.[2] In practical terms this would allow you (well, alright, me) to dial into the office and run Java applets on a powerful office work-station, displaying the results on a PC at home. One of the design achievements of NeWS (Sun's Network-extensible Window System) was the decoupling of dis-plays. A NeWS program could send its results to any workstation on the same net. This can soon become true for Java.

Java will consolidate its distributed processing and windowing capabilities, and move to provide a common windowing front end to databases, in particular. Sev-eral companies announced that they are developing tools in this area.

- Oracle is making its corporate "PowerBrowser" Java capable. Oracle recently stunned the computer industry by demonstrating a prototype $500 "Internet terminal."

- Sybase announced it is licensing the Java system for use with its data-base products.

- WebLogic offers a portfolio of DBMS tools and services based on Java connectivity and portability. These are further described at: http://weblogic.com/

Tools like these are placing Java squarely in the enterprise computing sector.

Adobe has licensed Java and announced that it will integrate Java into both its PageMill authoring tools, and Adobe Acrobat. Adobe Acrobat is a software prod-uct aimed at interactive browsing. Just as Postscript is a language that describes how a document should look, allowing different output devices to do the best they can to render it, Acrobat is a language that describes in a device-independent manner how a screen should look. If it's written in Java, it can also be platform independent. Acrobat is really just a sophisticated version of HTML. A publisher can put text on a CD in Acrobat format, and anyone with an Acrobat browser can view the text in a nice formatted and font-rich form, regardless of whether they are on a Unix system, a Mac or a PC.

Security

The restrictions imposed on applets for security reasons are a little onerous with good reason. Everyone wants Java to be free from the kinds of viruses that per-vade the MS Windows environment. No one wants to see the return of the 1988

---

2. Think of PPP ("Point to Point Protocol") as carrying TCP/IP services to a system without a dedicated IP address. PPP is often run down a telephone line, e.g. between your workstation and your home PC, so you can work from home.

Internet worm.[3] More work remains to be done to ease the restrictions without compromising system integrity.

Hardware and Firmware

A recurring idea in computer science is designing an architecture that is particularly convenient or efficient at executing a specific language. Past attempts include:

Algol-60:	early Burroughs processors
Lisp:	the Symbolics Lisp Machine
COBOL:	many processors optimized for BCD arithmetic.
Ada:	Rational Computers

None of the examples to date have been conspicuously successful. The Lisp Machine was driven out of business by general purpose Unix workstations. The end of the Cold War spelled the end of massive budgets for defense contractors to blow on "cost-plus" contracts, taking the Ada machine down with it. Burroughs was swallowed by Unisys which in turn isn't exactly breaking any new ground in computing these days. Will the Java machine fare any better?

A lot of companies think so, and are betting on it. It costs upwards of $1 billion to design and build a completely new computer architecture these days. If you can leverage existing facilities and technology, you can possibly do it on a shoestring of just $100 million, so anyone betting on a Java-specific chip is making a pretty significant investment.

Oracle has already demonstrated their Network Computer, and you don't exactly have to be Nostradamus to predict that the lights are burning late in their handsome Redwood Shores, CA offices as they try to figure out exactly how best to bundle Java with it. Silicon Valley is a pretty small community when you get right down to it, and one hears all kinds of talk about Java chips, Java workstations, Java PCs, Java terminals, Java supercomputers and Java microcomputers.

Sun Microsystems has announced a family of Network Computers and Java chips, Pico Java, Micro Java, and Ultra Java, covering a range of price/performance points.

3. See "With Microscope and Tweezers: An Analysis of the Internet Virus of November 1988" by Mark W. Eichin and Jon A. Rochlis, Mass. Institute of Technology, February 1989. This paper starts off describing the Internet as "a collection of networks linking 60,000 host computers" which seems hilariously insignificant in contrast to today's Internet. We've come a long way.

Companies can license picoJAVA today, and chips based on the picoJAVA design will generally available in 1998.

picoJAVA is not a chip, but rather a core design around which a variety of chips for different target markets can be implemented. Some information was released at Hot Chips in August about the picoJAVA architecture and more information was disclosed at the Microprocessor Forum in October.

From this, it is public knowledge that several large semiconductor companies intend to license picoJAVA, including LG Semicon, Mitubishi, NEC, and Samsung). In addition, Sun will produce a chip based on picoJAVA known as microJAVA.

Some points that came out at Hot Chips were:

- The picoJava core directly executes the Java bytecodes

- It maintains an on-chip stack

- Can "fold" many common, simple stack/local variable movement byte-codes into the following instruction and execute both in a single cycle.

- It has a modern, pipelined, RISC-style of design. "This isn't your father's Burroughs B5000." It has one cycle execution of simple ALU operations and the like.

- Provides hardware support to facilitate GC, thread management, and object creation (what exactly that support may be is still under wraps. It speeds up all phases of Java program execution, not only the instruction execution time.

Two big characteristics working in favor of Java-on-a-chip are: (1) the performance speed-up; and (2) the well-defined virtual machine which makes the task easier than trying to "siliconify" other high-level languages. Java is built on a well-defined stack-based virtual machine with the byte code instruction set, supported by a runtime library. It's also possible that tighter integration into the operating system could provide some of the benefits of a Java chip at a fraction of the cost.

The virtual machine was defined with the Java language in mind, but people were quick to realize that other compilers could be targeted to it. This would provide them with instant ports to any platform that supported Java. Not all languages are good candidates for meeting the requirements of the Java VM. C++ is a little too lax in its use of pointer arithmetic to be a good fit. However, the language experts at compiler company Intermetrics have already targeted their Ada 95 compiler to the Java VM, and created quite a stir by demonstrating it working at a 1995 Ada convention. Their Web site is at http://www.inmet.com.

What Will Microsoft Do?

One of the big wildcard questions was "what does Microsoft intend to do?"

People questioned whether Microsoft sincerely plans to embrace the technology, or will somehow try to act as a spoiler. Certainly it is very hard to find examples of companies that have succeeded in a collaborative venture with Microsoft. The mighty IBM was humbled, burned even, by its abortive attempt at joint development on OS/2 with the Redmond giant.

Stac Electronics tried to make a deal with Microsoft for Stac's data compression software. According to court documents, the deal fell apart on Microsoft's unwillingness to pay per copy royalties. But Microsoft just went ahead and put Stac's software technology into MS-DOS 6 anyway[a]. Stac won a court judgement for $120 million against Microsoft in February 1994, later settling for $90M to avoid a lengthy appeal. In the book "Start-Up", Jerry Kaplan claims that Microsoft pinched his idea for pen computing when he showed them the concept to ask for applications porting. Instead Microsoft started a project to produce their own pen computing OS.

The whole concept of platform independence strikes at Microsoft's lock on desktop software. Microsoft must be furious about this, to say the least. It was faced with choosing between embracing the technology or ignoring it. If Microsoft embraced Java, Microsoft risked appearing to endorse a competing technology. If Microsoft ignored Java, Microsoft risked being left behind.

Before Java, Microsoft owned the desktop absolutely. Now they have already lost the browser desktop to Netscape, and are fast losing control on interesting desktop APIs to Java and Sun. Microsoft's answer is to try to embed Java in a honey pot of proprietary ActiveX code. Developers who want to push the limits of Windows will use these ActiveX controls, and their code will only ever run on Microsoft platforms. Developers who are interested in portability will carefully avoid these lock-ins and their code will run everywhere.

[a] One journalist asked "Just what kind of game does Microsoft think it's playing here?" and immediately provided his own answer: "Monopoly." Monopoly is a trademark of Parker Brothers.

We can also expect to see a lot more demand for graphics designers, illustrators, and artists. Java can animate your Web page, true, but you still need something to say, and an interesting way in which to say it. Consider the "Neon sign" applet that used to be at

http://java.sun.com/JDK-prebeta1/applets/contest/NeonSign/index.html.

This is an impressive looking applet that shows a flickering neon sign, spelling out the name of the applet author. The more you look at this, the less there is to it. The applet just consists of two images, one with the neon sign dark, and one with it lit up. The applet randomly switches back and forth between them, so it appears that the sign is flashing. But all the cleverness of this applet is in the glossy artwork—and *that* is precisely the part that most programmers cannot supply for you.

Other Java Resources

Half the point of Java is accessing the resources of the WWW. Here is a collection of favorite sites. If you check in with the Java ones periodically, you will always be well-informed about new developments.

http://www.javasoft.com (also reachable as http://java.sun.com)   The Sun Java site. Download software, look at applets, read the most up-to-date documentation and user guides.

http://www.gamelan.com   The Gamelan site. Named after an Indonesian musical ensemble, the Gamelan (pronounced to rhyme (approximately) with "come along") site is a rich resource for Java code, Java applets, hints, libraries and all kinds of information.

Gamelan is sponsored by the EarthWeb organization, an Internet consulting and services company. The Gamelan site is a treasure house that should be your second port of call after the Sun site.

http://www-net.com/java/faq   The mother of all FAQ lists. This site contains pointers to the various and several Java FAQ lists that public-spirited programmers are maintaining to help spread the information.

You can also access some of these individual FAQ sites directly at:

http://www.best.com/~pvdl
http://www-net.com/java/faq/faq-java.txt
http://www.city-net.com/~krom/java-faq.html
http://java.sun.com/faqIndex.html
http://www.digitalfocus.com/digitalfocus/faq/index.html

http://www.io.org/~mentor1/jnIndex.html   This is the URL for Digital Espresso—a weekly summary of traffic on the comp.lang.java newsgroup. The volume of traffic there is enormous (several thousand messages per week), so a weekly summary really helps those who want to keep up without getting mired in the detail.

http://www.javaworld.com   The best online Java magazine. Has back issues at http://www.javaworld.com/common/jw=backissues.html

http://java.sun.com/doc/language_specification   The Java language specification. Also available as a 700 page book.

http://www.yahoo.com   Yahoo started life as a part-time project by a couple of Stanford students. It has rapidly blossomed into one of the premier Web searching and indexing sites. You are not a Web aficionado until you have a "connection timed out" while trying to reach yahoo.

http://www.dimensionx.com or http://www.dnx.com   Another early adopter of Java. This site is rich with applets, ideas and general Java know-how. Well worth a visit.

http://www.fbi.gov/topten.htm   The FBI "Top Ten most wanted" list. Check this every month to see if any of your co-workers have made it onto the list. If so, make history and be the first to turn them in by e-mail.

http://www.ccil.org/jargon/jargon.html   The Jargon File. Everything you don't need to know about programmer slang, and less. Also available as a book, lord help us. Version 3.0 came out in August 1993 as The New Hacker's Dictionary second edition (ISBN 0-262-68079-3), published by MIT Press. They finally re-edited that bizarre and confusing saga of Guy Steele's about the Palo Alto ice cream store. It's still not a very funny story, but at least now you can understand what the point would be, if it had one. Guy Steele is currently responsible for writing the Java Language Specification.

ftp://ftp.ora.com/pub/examples/windows/win95.update/regwiz.html   Find out the truth about the Microsoft Registration Wizard snooping your hard disk for competitors' products! Learn how expert programmers use debugging and file monitoring tools to see what is really happening in a system. A detective story with a moral at the end.

Don't forget to read the Java newsgroups, starting at comp.lang.java.programmer. There are about half-a-dozen Java newsgroups, and they are very high volume. Maybe I'll see you there. I wrote the FAQ guide for comp.lang.java.programmer, and you can read it in the newsgroup. Once you are practiced in your skills as a java programmer, you might like to take the Sun Java certification test. Details are available on Sun's website http://www.sun.com.

Conclusion

Programmers get interested in Java for many different reasons. Perhaps you started out by hearing that Java made possible executable content in Web pages. Perhaps your initial reaction, like mine, was "So what?" Maybe your boss asked you to investigate Java after reading something in "The Economist" magazine, or the Wall Street Journal, or Time, or Newsweek, or the New York Times. It's highly unusual for a programming language to receive so much attention from the main-stream media, especially before the product has even reached the First Customer Shipment milestone.

The amount of media coverage of Java naturally raises some questions in the minds of programmers. It begins to look like the kind of exaggeration more usu-ally associated with the entertainment industry. But that is not what is happening here at all. Sun was completely taken by surprise by the Java phenomenon, just as much as everyone else. As the significance of the language grew and grew, a series of increasingly senior managers were brought in to lead the program. Investment in the language—inside Sun and outside—grew too.

Scott McNealy, the CEO of Sun, has occasionally remarked that Sun made a mistake by not whole-heartedly backing the NeWS window system when it was first devel-oped in 1987. As a result, it has taken nearly a decade for the Unix world to resolve the conflicting windowing system alternatives. Scott has commented in the past that he will personally ensure that superior Sun software technology is never again stifled through wavering commitment, and he is certainly delivering on his prom-ise. The chief architect of NeWS was James Gosling—the chief architect of Java.

Sometimes tremendous interest in a product is not the result of overselling or col-lective trend-following. Sometimes it really does happen because the world recog-nizes the right product, in the right place, at the right time. Java is a better mousetrap, and the world is beating a path to Sun's door. There has been a con-vergence of mighty trends that Java is well placed to address.

Not much in Java is completely new. What is new is the combination of all the things, put together in a simple package, and made available on highly-generous terms from computer industry technology leader, Sun Microsystems. While executable content in Web pages is novel, it isn't such a big deal in itself. Java is an enabling technology for what will follow.

Java is producing a "paradigm shift"—a fundamental rethinking of the established ways of software development. Paradigm shifts lead to tremendous upsets, but also tremendous opportunities. The development of the internal combustion engine was a paradigm shift, and there were undoubtedly people in 1876 who were asking "But Herr Otto, so what if you can spin that big flywheel with a petrol motor?" What implications does it have for software distribution channels if you can pull applets to your system with a Web browser?

Past computer industry paradigm shifts have included the trend to minicomputers, which DEC rode to great prosperity throughout the 1970s. That was followed by the "migration to the desktop" spearheaded by the Apple II PC and reinforced (tardily) by the IBM PC. The "migration to the desktop" paradigm shift almost bankrupted DEC as they failed to anticipate it and then came up with a succession of failing strategies to cope with it. It did bankrupt other, even less well-prepared companies like Wang.

Convergence of Mighty Trends

As the computer industry closes out the last five years of the Millennium, the times are characterized by the following mighty trends:

- Popularization of the Internet
- Computer industry blending into telecom industry
- Consumer electronics merging with PC technologies
- Computer industry drive to multimedia everything
- Rejection of the complexity of C++
- Desire for independence from Intel and Microsoft desktop monopolies
- Resurgence of threads and object-oriented programming.

and, as always,

- More and more computing power for less and less investment.

Partly by accident, partly by design, Java is located at the point where all these paths come together.

This time around we are just at the beginning of the cycle, but already it is clear—there are fortunes to be made and lost out there. This is an exciting time to be in the computer business, and an especially exciting time to be a computer programmer. As the turbo-talk goes, "Java is a simple, object-oriented, distributed, interpreted, robust, secure, architecture-neutral, portable, high performance, multithreaded, and dynamic language." The importance is not really in any one of these but in the combination of all of them. How will the computer industry be changed by the client/server metaphor extending across the Internet? Sun was the first to offer a computer system with a Web browser as its primary interface to everything but Microsoft is working hard to put this into Windows 98. What happens next is up to you.

Important! Above all, remember: have fun!

Some Light Relief

The Origami Kamikaze water bomber

Sometimes people criticize the work done by programmers as "paper pushing." That's not really accurate, what we do is more "electron pushing," but there is one way we can make the label "paper pusher" come true. Do you want learn how to create little paper airplanes loaded with annoying cargo, and launch them at your work colleagues? Yes, of course you do. Here's how.

Origami is an ancient and honorable technique of delicate paper folding. It takes finesse, skill, and subtlety. So we certainly won't be considering *that* any further. Instead, this section explains how to make a paper airplane that takes a payload. Not only can you impress your co-workers with paper airplanes, but you can also bombard them with an air delivery of confetti, glue, or shaving cream from the far side of the room. People will be talking about you for days to come, and your manager will certainly remember your achievements when the review period comes around.

One warning here, at the age of 14 I dropped a paper waterbomb on the head of schoolfriend "Piffer" Tully from an upstairs classroom. He didn't see who did it, and I felt it better not to burden him by claiming responsibility. Now 25 years later it is probably safe to own up (Ha, ha, ha, Piffer!), and also alert you to the fact that not everyone appreciates the drollness of saturation bombing by paper airplane.

So pick your targets carefully, or stick to launching blanks. As always, observe the three cardinal safety rules when working around electronic equipment: (1) make sure you know where the main circuit breaker is located; (2) keep a grounding strap around your wrist, and most important; (3) wait till your boss goes on a lunch break before starting this project. Figure 13-1 shows how you make the Kamikaze water bomber.

First, take an ordinary sheet of 8.5" by 11" paper, and make it narrower by cutting off 1.5" or so, to make 7" by 11". Then follow these instructions:

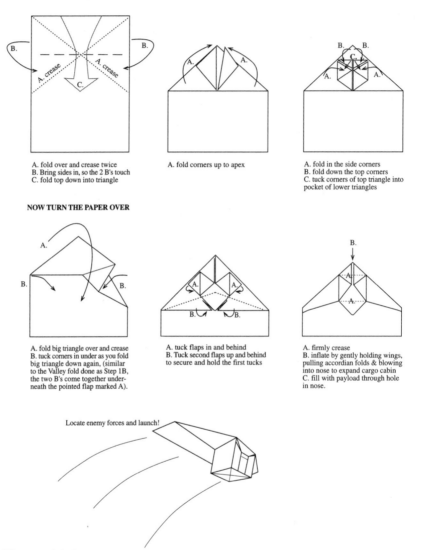

A. fold over and crease twice
B. Bring sides in, so the 2 B's touch
C. fold top down into triangle

A. fold corners up to apex

A. fold in the side corners
B. fold down the top corners
C. tuck corners of top triangle into pocket of lower triangles

NOW TURN THE PAPER OVER

A. fold big triangle over and crease
B. tuck corners in under as you fold big triangle down again, (similar to the Valley fold done as Step 1B, the two B's come together underneath the pointed flap marked A).

A. tuck flaps in and behind
B. Tuck second flaps up and behind to secure and hold the first tucks

A. firmly crease
B. inflate by gently holding wings, pulling accordian folds & blowing into nose to expand cargo cabin
C. fill with payload through hole in nose.

Locate enemy forces and launch!

Figure 14-1: The Kamikaze water bomber

Fold up wings, and fill with payload through hole in nose. Umm, the hole in the *plane's* nose, that is. Launch and enjoy.

Origami is relaxing and fun. Just the thing for unwinding after a busy day chasing electrons. If you've really got a lot of spare time, check the origami models at http://www.cs.ubc.ca/spider/jwu/origami.html

There's a praying mantis there that takes 100 steps to complete!

P.S. My Origami Java chip will be released soon.

By The Way. . .

Some companies are so desperate for Java programmers, that they are stating their requirements in terms of "hours of experience" in the same way that flying experience is measured.

Seen recently on comp.lang.java

```
From: (name removed to protect the guilty)
Newsgroups: comp.lang.java
Subject: Freelance job for C++/Java Programmer
Date: 27 Jan 1996 23:26:28 -0800
Distribution: world
We are now looking for: an experienced C/C++, Java programmer.
Around 4 years experience on Windows & Mac preferred,
minimum of 100 hours with Java required.
```

Personally, I never hire programmers based on how long they have been in the workforce. It's much more relevant to find out what programs they have written and what they're interested in. But this posting is an interesting insight into market economics.

Further Reading

LAN Times Encyclopedia of Networking

by Tom Sheldon
publ by Osborne McGraw-Hill, 1994
ISBN 0-07-881965-2

The back cover describes this as "covering A (Appletalk) through X (X Windows)" and it is absolutely right: the sections on Y and Z were completely missing from my copy. Har har. Just funning you. This is an excellent and easily-understood encyclopedia of anything and everything to do with networks. If you can only afford one book on data communications, this is absolutely the one to buy.

The Whole Internet

by Ed Krol,
publ. O'Reilly & Associates, Sebastapol CA, 1994, (second edition).
ISBN 1-56592-063-5

An excellent and exceptionally able description of all key aspects of the Internet for the intelligent lay-reader. Also contains detailed descriptions of the applications that you can run on Internet.

APPENDIX A

The obsolete JDK 1.0 Event Model

We describe the old JDK 1.0 event model here because you might see it in old code, or have to maintain programs that use it. The 1.0 event model was based on inheritance. The class Component is the percent of most screen controls (scrollbar, button, etc.). Component has a method handleEvent() that the runtime system calls whenever the user does something with a control. handleEvent() looks at the incoming event and splits it off into a call to various mouse methods like mouse-Drag(), or action().

Your code can override `handleEvent()` and get a first look at all incoming events, or it can override the specific lower-level event handler (such as `action()` or `mouseDrag()`) that is called by `handleEvent()`. The most common case for handling control input is just to override `action()`. Inside `action`, you examine the event parameter to decode exactly what kind of event has occurred.

The event handling routines return a boolean value: `true` if it consumed the event, and, not `false` but an explicit call to the parent handler if the event was not handled. This complication arises because there are two kinds of hierarchy: physical nesting (`Canvas` is in a `Panel` that is in a `Frame`) and inheritance (`myOtherCanvas` is a subclass of `MyCanvas` which is a subclass of `Canvas`). An event needs to be propagated up both the hierarchies to find the right handler. People found this confusing (it *is* confusing) and few Java books explained it well.

Here is the simplest example: the event handling code for a button press. In the old JDK 1.0 inheritance-based model, in an applet this was:

```
public class myClass extends Applet {

    Button apple = new Button("press me");

    public boolean action(Event e, Object o) {
        if (e.target instanceof Button)
            if ("press me".equals((String) o)) {
                // do button handling stuff...
                return true;
            }
}
```

Adding `action()` to an applet was just like adding `init()` or `start()`: it overrode the preexisting method of that name in the `Component` parent class several parent classes up from `Applet`.

A Few Words on Getting a GUI Event

Just as adding widgets to a panel or frame is easy, so getting back user input is also straightforward. Everything hinges on the method with this signature:

```
public boolean action( Event e, Object o)
```

The method is part of every Component, so all of the buttons, choices lists, etc., inherit it and can override it.

Whenever a user operates a Component (presses a button, clicks on a choice), the action method is called. The "Event e" argument contains much information about the coordinates of the event, the time it occurred, and the kind of event that it was. If the event was a keypress, it has the value of the key. The other argument is a generalized object that contains extra information in some cases.

The event contains a field called "id" that indicates the type of event it is (e.g. KEY_PRESS, MOUSE_DOWN, LIST_SELECT, etc), and hence which other Event variables are relevant for the event. For keyboard events, the field called "key" will contain a value indicating the key that was pressed/released and the modifiers field will contain the modifiers (whether the shift key was down, etc).

For KEY_PRESS and KEY_RELEASE event ids, the value of key will be the unicode character code for the key; for KEY_ACTION and KEY_ACTION_RELEASE, the value of key will be one of the defined action-key identifiers in the Event class (PGUP, PGDN, F1, F2, etc).

The class Event can be seen in full in directory $JAVAHOME/src/java/awt/Event.java.

A summary of the event class is:

```
public class Event {
    public static final int SHIFT_MASK;
    public static final int CTRL_MASK;
    public static final int META_MASK;
    public static final int ALT_MASK;

    public static final int F1; // the F1 function key
    public static final int F2;
      // ...
    public static final int F12; // the F12 function key

    public static final int KEY_PRESS;
    public static final int KEY_RELEASE;
    public static final int KEY_ACTION;
    public static final int KEY_ACTION_RELEASE;

    public static final int MOUSE_DOWN;
    public static final int MOUSE_UP;
    public static final int MOUSE_MOVE;
    public static final int MOUSE_ENTER;
    public static final int MOUSE_EXIT;
    public static final int MOUSE_DRAG;

    public static final int ACTION_EVENT;
    public static final int GOT_FOCUS;
    public static final int LOST_FOCUS;

    public int id; // what the event was (uses the constants above)

    public Object target;  // the component generating the event.
    public long when;     // the timestamp

    public int x;
    public int y;     // x and y are where the event happened.

    public int key;  // the key that was pressed

    public int modifiers;   // the state of the modifiers

    public int clickCount; // number of clicks from the mouse

    public Object arg;    // an arbitrary argument, not always used

    public boolean shiftDown();   // true if shift key down
    public boolean controlDown(); // true if ctrl key down
    public boolean metaDown();    // true if meta key down

}
```

You get an object of this class sent to the action routine for each GUI event.

So for example, if the "Q" key is pressed, these fields (others will be set too) will have the values shown in the event object sent to the container of the key:

```
id=KEY_PRESS, key=81, modifiers=SHIFT_MASK
```

For some events (like key presses, and mouse movements), the target is the container. For others (like buttons, scrollbars, and text fields), the target is the widget itself. Don't be fooled by the implication that the "target" is where the Event is going to. Sometimes it is where it has come from.

If the mouse is dragged, this event object will be sent to the container of the key:

```
id=MOUSE_DRAG, x=x_coord, y=y_coord,  modifiers=0
```

When you drag a mouse or a scrollbar, many, many events are sent. It doesn't wait until you have stopped moving the object, it generates an event for each slight movement (not necessarily each pixel of movement).

If the center button of a 3-button mouse is pressed, these are some of the fields of the Event object:

```
id=MOUSE_DOWN, modifiers=ALT_MASK
```

If the right button of a 3-button mouse is pressed, these are some of the fields of the Event object:

```
id=MOUSE_DOWN, modifiers=META_MASK
```

The modifiers field in the event is how Java portably handles the different number of mouse buttons Mac: one, Windows: two, and Unix: three. You should be able to hold down the ALT or META (shift or control) key and click the left mouse button to make it appear as a center or right mouse button event. This is totally broken in JDK 1.0.2.

The object o in the action routine is not always used. When the event is a button, it holds a string that is the label of the button. When the event is a menu item being selected, it holds a string that is the menu item's name.

For each container that a widget is added to, the programmer has the opportunity to provide an overriding version of:

```
public boolean action(Event e, Object o)
```

and to use that to determine exactly what the event was, and from that take action to deal with it. The action method must return true to indicate it has consumed (dealt with) the event.

Obtaining Mouse and Keyboard Input

The previous section described how various widgets interact with the user. This section describes how mouse and keyboard events are passed to your program. It is done in a very similar way to what we have already seen for widgets.

Events go to the Component that is the immediate Container of the place where the event happened. The class Component has a method `handleEvent()` with this signature:

```
public boolean handleEvent(Event evt)
```

If you look at handleEvent in file $JAVAHOME/src/java/awt/Component.java, you'll see that it contains a switch statement based on what the event was, and it really factors out all the keyboard and mouse events calling individual methods to handle all the possibilities for those.

A list of some of the specific Event handlers that `handleEvent()` factors out is:

```
public boolean mouseDown(Event evt, int x, int y)
public boolean mouseDrag(Event evt, int x, int y)
public boolean mouseUp(Event evt, int x, int y)
public boolean mouseMove(Event evt, int x, int y)
public boolean mouseEnter(Event evt, int x, int y)
public boolean mouseExit(Event evt, int x, int y)

public boolean keyDown(Event evt, int key)
public boolean keyUp(Event evt, int key)

public boolean action(Event evt, Object what) //when a widget is
touched
```

The programmer can override these to provide the callback routines that window systems use for event handling.

To see what's really going on with events, insert this line at the start of your version of handleEvent.

```
System.err.println("Event: " + e.toString() );
```

You'll be amazed at the number of events that are generated by the simplest mouse motions. This method converts each to a string and prints it. 🐝

Use inheritance to create your own version of the Button and Choice classes in an example Applet. Override "action()" within each of these two classes. Now it is much easier to decode which event has come in. If the "myButton.action()" has been invoked, it must have been an instance of myButton that was operated. (Easy). 🐝

Capturing Individual KeyPresses

Write an action() method that will handle all of the widgets in the previous section, and for each print out what the event is. (Medium).

FAQ

Here is an example of how a game program might capture individual key presses as they are made. Note that only certain events are available from certain widgets. This can be even more annoying than those smirking kids in the Mentos commercials.

```java
import java.awt.*;
import java.applet.*;
public class game  extends Applet {

    public void init() {
        resize(450,200);
    }

    public boolean keyDown(Event evt, int key) {
        System.out.println("Got: " + (char)key );
        return true;
    }

}
```

What could be simpler?

Handling the Quit Event

You will usually want to put the three or four lines of code that deal with a window being quit or destroyed (when the user has finished with it—this is usually a standard choice on the frame menu bar). The code looks like:

```java
public boolean handleEvent(Event e) {
    if (e.id == Event.WINDOW_DESTROY) {
        System.exit(0);
    }
    return false;
}
```

You don't have to exit the program. That would be appropriate when the user quits from the top-level window. For a lower-level window, the right thing to do may be to hide the window, and release the resource for garbage collection by removing any pointers to it.

All the Event handling methods have a boolean return type. This is used to answer the question "Did this method fully handle the event?" If it did, return true. If it did not, (Whoa! Trick answer coming!) return the result of calling the superclass's event handler to propagate the event up the containment hierarchy. To understand why, let's look at a partial solution to the previous Programming Challenge.

```java
import java.awt.*;
import java.applet.Applet;

public class mb extends Applet {
    myButton mb;

    public void init() {
        add(new myButton("press me") );
    }
}

class myButton extends Button {

    public myButton(String s) {
        super(s);
    }

    public boolean action(Event e, Object arg) {
        System.out.println("myButton pressed!");
        return true;
    }
}
```

Here we see a very common form of inheritance: subclassing an AWT widget to provide some slight refinement of behavior. Normally, our "action()" method is a common method that might handle a dozen kinds of event. In this case, when the button is pressed, control is transferred to the myButton.action() method and no decoding of "what Event was this?" is needed. We know it must have been a myButton that was pressed. 🐛

Now, we may have created several levels of subclass of Button, myOtherButton extends... extends myButton extends Button. Each adds some slight twist, and each has its own overriding action() routine. Our intent will be to first try handling the special button event in the lowest subclass. If that doesn't want it, then we almost certainly want to pass the event up the inheritance hierarchy. (If that isn't what we want then why did we bother creating the inheritance hierarchy?) However, what will actually happen is that the runtime system will propagate the unconsumed event up the containment hierarchy.

For Advanced Students Only

The fact that you return "true" from the Event handler leads the normal programmer to assume that one should return "false" if more processing is required by the containing class.

Bzzzt! The idiom is that you "return super.handleEvent(e)" to pass the event up the inheritance chain if your method doesn't consume the event.

This is because there are two possible chains to follow to look for the event handler:

1. Up the chain of containers: (Event is in a Panel which is in a Frame which is in a Window...)

2. Up the chain of subclasses: (Event is from myOtherButton which is a subclass of myButton, which is...)

What you usually want to happen is for the runtime to try both hierarchies. The runtime system should make the event go up the chain of superclasses for a given widget, and then go to the enclosing container, exhaust all its superclasses, and so on.

This will occur if your Event handler, instead of returning false, does:

```
return super.handleEvent(e);
```

None of this is necessary if you do not have a chain of subclassed widgets. On the other hand, it doesn't hurt to write the statement this way regardless. If you don't have a big inheritance hierarchy myButton.action() will call Button.action() which simply returns false anyway. 🐛

APPENDIX B

Powers of 2 and ISO 8859

Refer to Table B-1 for Powers of 2

With n bits in integer two's complement format, you can count:

unsigned from 0 to (one less than 2^n)
signed from -2^{n-1} to (one less than 2^{n-1})

Refer to Table B-2 for ISO 8859

Characters 0x0 to 0x1F are the C0 (control) characters, defined in ISO/IEC 6429:1992

Characters 0x20 to 0x7E are the G0 graphics characters of the 7-bit code set defined in
ISO/IEC 646-1991(E) — essentially the 7-bit ASCII characters.

Characters 0x80 to 0x9F are the C1 (control) characters, defined in ISO/IEC 6429:1992

The unshaded characters comprise the Latin-1 code set defined in ISO/IEC 8859-1:1987 though the symbols "Þ" and "þ" (0xDE and 0xFE) are approximations to the capital and small Icelandic letter "thorn." The actual letters are too weird to be in character sets anywhere outside a 12-mile radius of Reykjavík.

631

Table B-1: Powers-of-two from 2^1 to 2^{64}

2^1	2	2^{17}	131,072	2^{33}	8,589,934,592	2^{49}	562,949,953,421,312
2^2	4	2^{18}	262,144	2^{34}	17,179,869,184	2^{50}	1,125,899,906,842,624
2^3	8	**megabyte** 2^{19}	524,288	2^{35}	34,359,738,368	2^{51}	2,251,799,813,685,248
2^4	16	2^{20}	1,048,576	2^{36}	68,719,476,736	2^{52}	4,503,599,627,370,496
2^5	32	2^{21}	2,097,152	2^{37}	137,438,953,472	2^{53}	9,007,199,254,740,992
2^6	64	2^{22}	4,194,304	2^{38}	274,877,906,944	2^{54}	18,014,398,509,481,984
2^7	128	2^{23}	8,388,608	**terabyte** 2^{39}	549,755,813,888	2^{55}	36,028,797,018,963,968
kilobyte 2^8	256	2^{24}	16,777,216	2^{40}	1,099,511,627,776	2^{56}	72,057,594,037,927,936
2^9	512	2^{25}	33,554,432	2^{41}	2,199,023,255,552	2^{57}	144,115,188,075,855,872
2^{10}	1,024	2^{26}	67,108,864	2^{42}	4,398,046,511,104	2^{58}	288,230,376,151,711,744
2^{11}	2,048	2^{27}	134,217,728	2^{43}	8,796,093,022,208	2^{59}	576,460,752,303,423,488
2^{12}	4,096	**gigabyte** 2^{28}	268,435,456	2^{44}	17,592,186,044,416	2^{60}	1,152,921,504,606,846,976
2^{13}	8,192	2^{29}	536,870,912	2^{45}	35,184,372,088,832	2^{61}	2,305,843,009,213,693,952
2^{14}	16,384	2^{30}	1,073,741,824	2^{46}	70,368,744,177,664	2^{62}	4,611,686,018,427,387,904
2^{15}	32,768	2^{31}	2,147,483,648	2^{47}	140,737,488,355,328	**bubbabyte** 2^{63}	9,223,372,036,854,775,808
2^{16}	65,536	2^{32}	4,294,967,296	2^{48}	281,474,976,710,656	2^{64}	18,446,744,073,709,551,616

Table B-2: ISO 8859 8-bit Latin-1 character set and control characters

Least significant 4 bits of the byte

	0	1	2	3	4	5	6	7	8	9	A	B	C	D	E	F
0	nul	soh	stx	etx	eot	enq	ack	bel	bs	ht	lf\n	vt	ff	cr\r	so	si
1	dle	dc1	dc2	dc3	dc4	nak	syn	etb	can	em	sub	esc	is_4	is_3	is_2	is_1
2	space	!	"	#	$	%	&	'	(	)	*	+	,	-	.	/
3	0	1	2	3	4	5	6	7	8	9	:	;	<	=	>	?
4	@	A	B	C	D	E	F	G	H	I	J	K	L	M	N	O
5	P	Q	R	S	T	U	V	W	X	Y	Z	[	\	]	^	_
6	`	a	b	c	d	e	f	g	h	i	j	k	l	m	n	o
7	p	q	r	s	t	u	v	w	x	y	z	{	|	}	~	del
8	*n/a*	*n/a*	bph	nbh	*n/a*	nel	ssa	esa	hts	htj	vts	pld	plu	ri	ss2	ss3
9	dcs	pu1	pu2	sts	cch	mw	spa	epa	sos	*n/a*	sci	csi	st	osc	pm	apc
A	nbsp	¡	¢	£	¤	¥	¦	§	¨	©	ª	«	¬	shy	®	¯
B	°	±	²	³	´	µ	¶	•	¸	¹	º	»	$^1/_4$	$^1/_2$	$^3/_4$	¿
C	À	Á	Â	Ã	Ä	Å	Æ	Ç	È	É	Ê	Ë	Ì	Í	Î	Ï
D	Ð	Ñ	Ò	Ó	Ô	Õ	Ö	×	Ø	Ù	Ú	Û	Ü	Y	Φ	β
E	à	á	â	ã	ä	å	æ	ç	è	é	ê	ë	ì	í	î	ï
F	∂	ñ	ò	ó	ô	õ	ö	÷	ø	ù	ú	û	ü	y	Φ	ÿ

Index

Java™ Development Kit
Version 1.1.x
Binary Code License

This binary code license ("License") contains rights and restrictions associated with use of the accompanying software and documentation ("Software"). Read the License carefully before installing the Software. By installing the Software you agree to the terms and conditions of this License.

1. Limited License Grant. Sun grants to you ("Licensee") a non-exclusive, non-transferable limited license to use the Software without fee for evaluation of the Software and for development of Java™ compatible applets and applications. Licensee may make one archival copy of the Software. Licensee may not re-distribute the Software in whole or in part, either separately or included with a product. Refer to the Java Runtime Environment Version 1.1 binary code license (http://www.javasoft.com/products/JDK/1.1/index.html) for the availability of runtime code which may be distributed with Java compatible applets and applications.

2. Java Platform Interface. Licensee may not modify the Java Platform Interface ("JPI", identified as classes contained within the "java" package or any subpackages of the "java" package), by creating additional classes within the JPI or otherwise causing the addition to or modification of the classes in the JPI. In the event that Licensee creates any Java-related API and distributes such API to others for applet or application development, Licensee must promptly publish an accurate specification for such API for free use by all developers of Java-based software.

3. Restrictions. Software is confidential copyrighted information of Sun and title to all copies is retained by Sun and/or its licensors. Licensee shall not modify, decompile, disassemble, decrypt, extract, or otherwise reverse engineer Software. Software may not be leased, assigned, or sublicensed, in whole or in part. **Software is not designed or intended for use in on-line control of aircraft, air traffic, aircraft navigation or aircraft communications; or in the design, construction, operation or maintenance of any nuclear facility. Licensee warrants that it will not use or redistribute the Software for such purposes.**

4. Trademarks and Logos. This License does not authorize Licensee to use any Sun name, trademark or logo. Licensee acknowledges that Sun owns the Java trademark and all Java-related trademarks, logos and icons including the Coffee Cup and Duke ("Java Marks") and agrees to: (i) to comply with the Java Trademark Guidelines at http://java.com/trademarks.html; (ii) not do anything harmful to or inconsistent with Sun's rights in the Java Marks; and (iii) assist Sun in protecting those rights, including assigning to Sun any rights acquired by Licensee in any Java Mark.

5. Disclaimer of Warranty. Software is provided "AS IS," without a warranty of any kind. ALL EXPRESS OR IMPLIED REPRESENTATIONS AND WARRANTIES,

INCLUDING ANY IMPLIED WARRANTY OF MERCHANTABILITY, FITNESS FOR A PARTICULAR PURPOSE OR NON-INFRINGEMENT, ARE HEREBY EXCLUDED.

6. Limitation of Liability. SUN AND ITS LICENSORS SHALL NOT BE LIABLE FOR ANY DAMAGES SUFFERED BY LICENSEE OR ANY THIRD PARTY AS A RESULT OF USING OR DISTRIBUTING SOFTWARE. IN NO EVENT WILL SUN OR ITS LICENSORS BE LIABLE FOR ANY LOST REVENUE, PROFIT OR DATA, OR FOR DIRECT, INDIRECT, SPECIAL, CONSEQUENTIAL, INCIDENTAL OR PUNITIVE DAMAGES, HOWEVER CAUSED AND REGARDLESS OF THE THEORY OF LIABILITY, ARISING OUT OF THE USE OF OR INABILITY TO USE SOFTWARE, EVEN IF SUN HAS BEEN ADVISED OF THE POSSIBILITY OF SUCH DAMAGES.

7. Termination. Licensee may terminate this License at any time by destroying all copies of Software. This License will terminate immediately without notice from Sun if Licensee fails to comply with any provision of this License. Upon such termination, Licensee must destroy all copies of Software.

8. Export Regulations. Software, including technical data, is subject to U.S. export control laws, including the U.S. Export Administration Act and its associated regulations, and may be subject to export or import regulations in other countries. Licensee agrees to comply strictly with all such regulations and acknowledges that it has the responsibility to obtain licenses to export, re-export, or import Software. Software may not be downloaded, or otherwise exported or re-exported (i) into, or to a national or resident of, Cuba, Iraq, Iran, North Korea, Libya, Sudan, Syria or any country to which the U.S. has embargoed goods; or (ii) to anyone on the U.S. Treasury Department's list of Specially Designated Nations or the U.S. Commerce Department's Table of Denial Orders.

9. Restricted Rights. Use, duplication or disclosure by the United States government is subject to the restrictions as set forth in the Rights in Technical Data and Computer Software Clauses in DFARS 252.227-7013(c) (1) (ii) and FAR 52.227-19(c) (2) as applicable.

10. Governing Law. Any action related to this License will be governed by California law and controlling U.S. federal law. No choice of law rules of any jurisdiction will apply.

11. Severability. If any of the above provisions are held to be in violation of applicable law, void, or unenforceable in any jurisdiction, then such provisions are herewith waived to the extent necessary for the License to be otherwise enforceable in such jurisdiction. However, if in Sun's opinion deletion of any provisions of the License by operation of this paragraph unreasonably compromises the rights or increase the liabilities of Sun or its licensors, Sun reserves the right to terminate the License and refund the fee paid by Licensee, if any, as Licensee's sole and exclusive remedy.

GRAPHIC JAVA 1.1
Mastering the AWT, Second Edition
DAVID M. GEARY

900 pages; (includes CD-ROM)
ISBN 0-13-863077-1

- Revised and expanded to cover 1.1 AWT features: the new event model, lightweight components, clipboard and data transfer, etc.
- Includes more than 40 custom components—convenience dialogs, rubber-banding, image filters, etc.
- A comprehensive guide to the Abstract Window Toolkit for JDK 1.1

GRAPHIC JAVA 1.1 (Second Edition) has been completely revised to cover all of the AWT features provided by the 1.1 JDK. It provides detailed descriptions of every aspect of the AWT, including:

- Lightweight components
- Graphics Colors and Fonts
- Event Handling
- Image Manipulation
- Clipboard and data transfer
- Menus
- Printing
- Dialogs
- AWT Layout Managers

In addition, GRAPHIC JAVA 1.1 comes with the Graphic Java Toolkit (GJT)—a set of freely reusable Java packages that extend the functionality of the AWT. The GJT provides over 45 high-level components, ranging from image buttons and scrollers to toolbars and convenience dialogs.

The accompanying CD-ROM includes all of the example code from the book, ready to run on Solaris, Windows 95 and Windows NT along with the JDK1.1 for those platforms. The complete source code for the GJT for Solaris, Windows 95/NT, and Macintosh is also included for JDK 1.0.2 and JDK 1.1.

JUST JAVA 1.1,
Third Edition
PETER van der LINDEN

700 pages; (includes CD-ROM)
ISBN 0-13-784174-4

In JUST JAVA 1.1, the author of the classic Expert C Programming: Deep C Secrets brings his trademark enthusiasm, straight talk, and expertise to the challenge of learning Java and object-oriented programming.

In this updated Third Edition, you'll find all the fundamentals of Java programming, including Java object-oriented techniques, types, statements, string processing, as well as more sophisticated techniques like networking, threads, and using the Abstract Window Toolkit. You'll also discover more examples than ever, along with updated coverage of future Java APIs—including the Java Database Connectivity (JDBC) API completely updated to include coverage of JDK 1.1.

TOPICS INCLUDE:

- The Story of O—object-oriented programming
- Applications versus applets
- Identifiers, comments, keywords, and operators
- Arrays, exceptions, and threads
- GIGO—Garbage In, Gospel Out
- On the Internet No One Knows You're a Dog

The CD-ROM includes all source code for examples presented in the book along with the latest JDK for Solaris, Windows 95, Windows NT, and Macintosh.

INSIDE JAVA WORKSHOP
LYNN WEAVER and BOB JERVIS

ISBN 0-13-858234-3 (includes CD-ROM)

INSIDE JAVA™ WORKSHOP™ takes you on a working tour of the Java development environment from Sun Microsystems. You'll learn everything you need to create, test, debug, and publish portable Java applications. Starting with an insider's view of how to think about your development problem before you begin, the book gives you an understanding of and experience with every tool in Java WorkShop, plus developer tips and tricks from the team who created Java WorkShop. CD-ROM contains Java WorkShop 30-day free trial, plus all the examples from the book. Second Edition coming Fall 1997.

JUMPING JAVASCRIPT
JANICE WINSOR and BRIAN FREEMAN

1200 pages; (includes CD-ROM)
ISBN 0-13-841941-8

JUMPING JAVASCRIPT™ is a hands-on tutorial with loads of examples that will show both programmers and non-programmers how to use JavaScript to easily incorporate the interactivity of Java into their Web sites. It covers both basics such as scripting concepts, embedded Java applets, image maps, and buttons as well as advanced topics such as creating Java-Script objects and the cookies property. CD-ROM contains all the scripts discussed in the book.

WEB PAGE DESIGN
A Different Multimedia
MARY E. S. MORRIS and RANDY J. HINRICHS

200 pages; ISBN 0-13-239880-X

Everything you always wanted to know about practical Web page design! Anyone can design a web page, but it takes more than basic HTML skill to build a world-class Web site. Written for Web page authors, this hands-on guide covers the key aspects of designing a successful Web site and shows how to integrate traditional design techniques into Web sites. Contains sixteen full color examples of successful Web pages, and techniques for:

- Cognitive and content design
- Audience consideration
- Interactivity, organization, and navigational pathways
- Designing with VRML and Java
- Working with templates, style sheets, and Netscape™ Frames
- Evolving your design

HTML FOR FUN AND PROFIT
Gold Signature Edition
MARY E. S. MORRIS

306 pages; (includes CD-ROM)
ISBN 0-13-242488-6

A special edition of the best-seller, with a new chapter and HTML examples specifically about working with the Netscape browser. If you are interested in writing HTML pages for the World Wide Web, HTML FOR FUN AND PROFIT is for you. Step-by-step instructions present all the information you need to get started with Web page authoring. Although the examples are based on working with the UNIX® system, authoring on PC and Macintosh platforms is also discussed.

EXPERT C PROGRAMMING:
Deep C Secrets
PETER van der LINDEN

352 pages; ISBN 0-13-177429-8

EXPERT C PROGRAMMING is a very different book on the C language! In an easy, conversational style, the author reveals coding techniques used by the best C programmers. EXPERT C PROGRAMMING explains the difficult areas of ANSI C, from arrays to runtime structures, and all the quirks in between. Covering both IBM PC and UNIX systems, this book is a must read for anyone who wants to learn more about the implementation, practical use, and folklore of C!

CHAPTER TITLES INCLUDE:

- It's not a bug, it's a language feature!
- Thinking of linking
- You know C, so C++ is easy!
- Secrets of programmer job interviews

THREADS PRIMER
A Guide to Multithreaded Programming
BIL LEWIS and DANIEL J. BERG

319 pages; ISBN 0-13-443698-9

Written for developers and technical managers, this book provides a solid, basic understanding of threads—what they are, how they work, and why they are useful. It covers the design and implementation of multithreaded programs as well as the business and technical benefits of writing threaded applications.

The THREADS PRIMER discusses four different threading libraries (POSIX, Solaris, OS/2, and Windows NT) and presents in-depth implementation details and examples for the Solaris and POSIX APIs.

PROGRAMMING WITH THREADS
STEVE KLEIMAN, DEVANG SHAH, and BART SMAALDERS

534 pages; ISBN 0-13-172389-8

Multithreaded programming can improve the performance and structure of your applications, allowing you to utilize all the power of today's high performance computer hardware. PROGRAMMING WITH THREADS is the definitive guide to multithreaded programming. It is intended for both novice and experienced threads programmers, with special attention given to the problems of multithreading existing programs. The book provides structured techniques for mastering the complexity of threads programming with an emphasis on performance issues.

TOPICS INCLUDE:

- Synchronization and threading strategies
- Using threads for graphical user interfaces and client-server computing
- Multiprocessors and parallel programming
- Threads implementation and performance issues

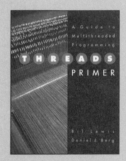

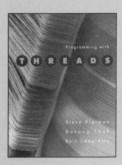

"[Expert C Programming] is essential, instructive, light-relief for C programmers... Five stars for Peter van der Linden."
— STAN KELLY-BOOTLE, Contributing Editor, *UNIX Review*

"[The authors] explain clearly the concepts of multithreaded programming as well as the useful little tricks of the trade."
—GUY L. STEELE JR. Distinguished Engineer, Sun Microsystems Laboratories

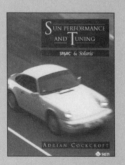

AUTOMATING SOLARIS INSTALLATIONS
A Custom Jumpstart Guide

**PAUL ANTHONY KASPER
and ALAN L. McCLELLAN**

282 pages; (includes a diskette)
ISBN 0-13-312505-X

AUTOMATING SOLARIS INSTALLATIONS describes how to set up "hands-off" Solaris installations for hundreds of SPARC™ and x86 systems. It explains in detail how to configure your site so that when you install Solaris, you simply boot a system and walk away—the software installs automatically! The book also includes a diskette with working shell scripts to automate pre- and post-installation tasks, such as:

- Updating systems with patch releases
- Installing third-party or unbundled software on users' systems
- Saving and restoring system data
- Setting up access to local and remote printers
- Transitioning a system from SunOS™ 4.x to Solaris 2

SOLARIS IMPLEMENTATION
A Guide for System Administrators

GEORGE BECKER, MARY E. S. MORRIS, and KATHY SLATTERY

345 pages; ISBN 0-13-353350-6

Written by expert Sun™ system administrators, this book discusses real world, day-to-day Solaris 2 system administration for both new installations and for migration from an installed Solaris 1 base. It presents tested procedures to help system administrators improve and customize their networks and includes advice on managing heterogeneous Solaris environments. Provides actual sample auto install scripts and disk partitioning schemes used at Sun.

TOPICS COVERED INCLUDE:

- Local and network methods for installing Solaris 2 systems
- Configuring with admintool versus command-line processes
- Building and managing the network, including setting up security
- Managing software packages and patches
- Handling disk utilities and archiving procedures

SOLARIS PORTING GUIDE,
Second Edition
SUNSOFT DEVELOPER ENGINEERING

695 pages; ISBN 0-13-443672-5

Ideal for application programmers and software developers, the SOLARIS PORTING GUIDE provides a comprehensive technical overview of the Solaris 2 operating environment and its related migration strategy.

The Second Edition is current through Solaris 2.4 (for both SPARC and x86 platforms) and provides all the information necessary to migrate from Solaris 1 (SunOS 4.x) to Solaris 2 (SunOS 5.x). Other additions include a discussion of emerging technologies such as the Common Desktop Environment from Sun, hints for application performance tuning, and extensive pointers to further information, including Internet sources.

TOPICS COVERED INCLUDE:

- SPARC and x86 architectural differences
- Migrating from common C to ANSI C
- Building device drivers for SPARC and x86 using DDI/DKI
- Multithreading, real-time processing, and the Sun Common Desktop Environment

"This book is a must for all Solaris 2 system administrators."
— TOM JOLLANDS,
Sun Enterprise Network Systems

"[This book] deals with daily tasks and should be beneficial to anyone administering Solaris 2.x, whether a veteran or new Solaris user."
— SYS ADMIN,
May/June 1995

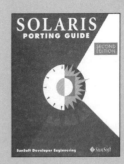

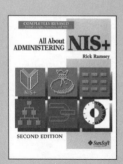

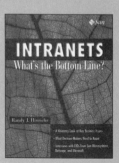

INTRANET SECURITY:
Stories From the Trenches
LINDA McCARTHY

300 pages; ISBN 0-13-894759-7

Do you have response procedures for systems break-ins? Is your e-mail encrypted? Is your firewall protecting your company? Is your security staff properly trained? These are just a few of the security issues that are covered in INTRANET SECURITY: STORIES FROM THE TRENCHES. Author Linda McCarthy, who in her job as a worldwide security team leader at Sun has broken into thousands of corporate intranets, presents detailed case studies of real-life break-ins that will help you make your systems safer. She explains how each breach occurred, describes what steps were taken to fix it, and then provides a practical and systematic solution for preventing similar problems from occurring on your network!

CREATING WORLDWIDE SOFTWARE
Solaris International Developer's Guide, Second Edition
BILL TUTHILL and DAVID SMALLBERG

ISBN 0-13-494493-3

A new edition of the essential reference text for creating global applications, with updated information on international markets, standards organizations, and writing international documents. This expanded edition of the Solaris International Developer's Guide includes new chapters on CDE/Motif, NEO/OpenStep, Universal codesets, global internet applications, code examples, and studies of successfully internationalized software.

INTRANETS:
What's the Bottom Line?
RANDY J. HINRICHS

420 pages; ISBN 0-13-841198-0

INTRANETS: WHAT'S THE BOTTOM LINE? is for decisions makers, who want bottom line information in order to figure out what an Intranet is and how it will help their organizations. It's a compelling case for the corporate Intranet. This book will give you a high-level perspective on Intranets and will answer your questions: What is an Intranet? What is it made of? What does it buy me? How much does it cost? How do I make it work? How do I know it's working?

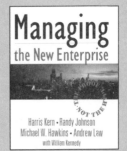

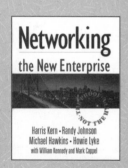

The *Just Java 1.1 and Beyond* CD-ROM requires Windows 95, Windows NT, Solaris 2, or Macintosh (System 7.5). NOTE: Because this is a cross-platform CD-ROM, Solaris users may encounter a warning message when loading the CD indicating the presence of files that do not conform to the ISO-9660 specification. These warning messages should be ignored.

Windows 3.1 IS NOT SUPPORTED